A Life-Centered Approach to Bioethics

Biocentric Ethics

This book approaches bioethics on the basis of a conception of life and what is needed for the affirmation of its quality in the most encompassing sense. Lawrence E. Johnson applies this conception to discussions of controversial issues in bioethics, including euthanasia, abortion, cloning, and genetic engineering. His emphasis is not on providing definitive solutions to all bioethical issues but rather on developing an approach to coping with them that can also help us deal with new issues as they emerge. The foundation of this discussion is an extensive examination of the nature of the self and its good and of various approaches to ethics. His system of bioethics is integrally related to his well-known work on environmental philosophy. The book also applies these principles on an individual level, offering a user-friendly discussion of how to deal with ethical "slippery slopes" and how and where to draw the line when dealing with difficult questions of bioethics.

Lawrence E. Johnson is an Affiliate Research Fellow in the humanities at the University of Adelaide in South Australia. He has also taught at West Virginia University and Flinders University. His articles have appeared in numerous scholarly journals, including *International Logic Review*, the *Review of Metaphysics*, *Environmental Ethics*, the *Monash Bioethics Review*, and the *Journal of Natural History*. He has also contributed to several literary journals.

A Life-Centered Approach to Bioethics

Biocentric Ethics

LAWRENCE E. JOHNSON
University of Adelaide

CAMBRIDGE
UNIVERSITY PRESS

CAMBRIDGE UNIVERSITY PRESS
Cambridge, New York, Melbourne, Madrid, Cape Town, Singapore,
São Paulo, Delhi, Dubai, Tokyo, Mexico City

Cambridge University Press
32 Avenue of the Americas, New York, NY 10013-2473, USA

www.cambridge.org
Information on this title: www.cambridge.org/9780521154208

First published 2011

Printed in the United States of America

A catalog record for this publication is available from the British Library.

Library of Congress Cataloging in Publication data

Johnson, Lawrence E.
A life-centered approach to bioethics : biocentric ethics / Lawrence E. Johnson.
  p. cm.
Includes bibliographical references and index.
ISBN 978-0-521-76626-5 (hardback) – ISBN 978-0-521-15420-8 (pbk.)
1. Bioethics.   I. Title.
QH332.J64   2010
174'.957 – dc22   2010027351

ISBN 978-0-521-76626-5 Hardback
ISBN 978-0-521-15420-8 Paperback

Research for this book was facilitated by a grant from Australia's National Health and Medical
Research Council.

For Marion, who did not have a good death

Contents

1

Introduction

It is no more than to state the obvious to remark that life is a matter of absorbing interest to all of us. It is, literally, of vital importance to us, a matter of life and death. Experiences of illness, health, reproduction, and death are normal and central features of our human existence. So too are decisions, practical or moral, that have to be made concerning such matters. Even when they do not directly concern us – as inevitably they shall – such matters are yet of human interest. With changes in our own lives, we as individuals face issues and problems that are new to us. Those close to us have their own problems with which they, or we, must cope. For these reasons alone, issues concerning death, dying, chronic illness, maintenance of health, euthanasia, abortion, and a patient's rights and autonomy all receive considerable attention. The moral dimension of such issues is the subject matter of *bioethics*. One cannot well summarize the central concerns of bioethics. They are too diverse for that. Moreover, bioethics is in constant change. The issues are continually undergoing metamorphosis because of our increasing knowledge and technical capabilities and the ever-widening range of their application. Genetic engineering, cloning, and other aspects of reproductive technology, to cite only one range of examples, raise increasingly complex and insistent problems. From time to time we find ourselves trying to answer questions that could not even have been asked a few years ago. Meanwhile, old questions linger on or mutate into modified form. Not only is there no one central set of bioethical issues, there is no uniquely correct way of resolving bioethical issues. The best we can do is to go on trying to find the best fit possible with the continually mutating demands of moral practice.

As explained by Warren T. Reich, editor of *The Encyclopedia of Bioethics* (1978, p. xix),[1]

Bioethics . . . can be defined as the systematic study of human conduct in the area of the life sciences and health care, insofar as this conduct is examined in the light of moral values and principles.

[1] Warren T. Reich, ed., *Encyclopedia of Bioethics* (New York: Simon and Schuster Macmillan, 1953, new ed. 1983, p. xix).

Bioethics is an area of interdisciplinary studies whose focus depends on the kinds of issues it examines and the nature of ethical theory.

This will do as a working approximation but by no means as a final and definitive statement. Nor shall I attempt to provide a final and definitive statement. I doubt that there can be one because what affects life and health (or departures therefrom) go beyond even the ever-changing boundaries of both science and health care. Rather, I intend to show how conceptions of a sort that I term *biocentric* can give us increased insight into the diverse issues of bioethics.

In discussing bioethics I believe that it is best not to begin by discussing bioethics. That would be to begin in the middle. Indeed, more generally, I would say that in discussing ethics in any form it is best not to begin by discussing ethics. Any meaningful discussion of ethics – as of so many other important subjects – depends on concepts and presumptions of one sort or another. Without them we can go nowhere. If we are not clear on what our concepts and presumptions are, how they work, and why we hold them, then our thinking will be unclear and our conclusions unreliable. Certainly in our concepts and presumptions concerning ourselves, there is a great lack of clarity. In our disagreements with one another we are likely to achieve little more than frustration and an exchange of ignorance and prejudice, and perhaps of unkind invective. For such reasons the character of public debate on bioethical issues has sometimes been quite disappointing.

In this book I intend to throw some light on some of the concepts and issues important to bioethics: What is human life? When does it begin? End? What is it to be a person? What is good for a person? As well as discussing these concepts and issues (and various others), and perhaps even more important, I shall try to indicate how we can better go about thinking of living beings and their problems, doing so on the basis of biocentric conceptions. I thereby try to further our understanding of bioethics conceptually and to make it easier for us to deal with bioethical issues in practice. In due course I shall go on to explore some of the practical implications.

To whom is this book addressed? Before I try to answer that question, I shall pose and try to answer another one: What is philosophy? Notoriously, it is hard to specify just what the subject matter of philosophy is. We may perhaps proclaim that it is the critical discussion of the broadest and most fundamental questions of human existence. It deals with questions such as these: What is reality? What is real? What is good? How do we know? How should we live?

Another sort of explanation proceeds by example, pointing to past figures and saying that philosophy is the sort of thing with which Socrates and Plato, and people like that, were concerned. As far as it goes, such approaches usually work fairly well in practice. Socrates and the usual others really were doing philosophy, and questions such as those concerning the nature of reality are certainly philosophical questions. Nonetheless, there must be more to it than that. Philosophy encompasses a wide range of issues, including such areas as computational theory, aesthetics, philosophical linguistics, philosophical biology, and much else. We can philosophize about issues the classical Greek philosophers, for chronological reasons, could never have addressed – for example, cloning. Indeed, one can philosophize about anything whatsoever. What can all of these diverse areas of inquiry possibly have in common?

I believe we do not do well to ask what the subject matter of philosophy is. Philosophy, I believe, is not a subject matter at all, is not about anything in particular. I understand philosophy to be an *activity*. Philosophy begins in wonder. We wonder about something and we try to figure out how to understand it. We try to answer questions but we also do more than that. The key point is that in philosophizing we try to work out what the appropriate questions are, what we require of an adequate answer, and how we are to go about trying to obtain good answers. We may replace one question by another that, on reflection, we find more productive of understanding. Some approaches are more illuminating than others, and some questions lead to better answers than do others. It is much like trying to bring into better focus something that is not sufficiently well focused. What is the method for getting our understanding into better focus? There are many and diverse methods, no one of which works for all philosophical inquiries, though they may be very useful for a great many inquiries. One may use logic, or linguistic analysis, or a search for inner intuition – or one may adopt some other approach (all of which have innumerable different versions). One who is philosophizing tries various approaches until one finds or invents a way of getting a better focus on what one was wondering about. In the course of doing that one develops a better understanding of what would be required of better answers.

This is not to say that every question is a philosophical question, nor that every act of wondering is philosophical wondering. (I wonder if it will rain on Saturday.) Characteristically, to philosophize is to form, or reform, the fundamental ideas on the basis of which we inquire into what we are wondering about. One need not be a professor or student of philosophy to philosophize. We philosophize whenever we engage in this activity of trying to get some object of wonder, and our thinking about it, into better focus. As well as being a scientist, Galileo was philosophizing when he rethought how we are to go about obtaining knowledge of the physical world. As it is commonly expressed, he shifted the emphasis from *why* questions to *how* questions in explaining the way the world works. Experimentation, measurement, and precise description were the better keys to understanding rather than speculation about divine intentions. Einstein philosophized about the fundamental concepts of physics, rethinking notions that others had taken for granted, such as notions of space, time, and simultaneity. Freud helped us rethink some of our fundamental ideas about our minds. If his answers did not prove to be correct ones, his questions yet proved to be very useful. Darwin reshaped our thinking about life and species (once thought, as the term *species* suggests, as being a specific and immutable category) and led us to do much rethinking about ourselves and our place in the world. Examples may be multiplied at length. Then again, some who did the philosophizing were generally known as philosophers and greatly influenced our thinking about a great variety of things. We find Aristotle with an important role in the history of biology, physics, and much else. Psychology owes much to John Locke and William James. Pythagoras, Descartes, and Leibniz contributed greatly to mathematics as well as to philosophy. Again, examples may be multiplied.

When we already have settled on what we regard as the right sorts of questions and on our means of answering them (for whatever the purpose is at hand, that being much or most of the time), then we are no longer doing philosophy. We may be doing skilled, insightful, and brilliant work answering important questions in an important field of inquiry, but the philosophizing was when we were formulating, criticizing, or reformulating the fundamental questions, or the accepted means of addressing them. At some stage in every science, and in every other worthwhile field of inquiry, the activity of philosophizing had to go on. From time to time we have to return to philosophizing. To put it in terms that Thomas Kuhn made famous, during periods of "normal science," when our *paradigm* – our fundamental system of assumptions, concepts, questions, criteria, and methodology – is in place, we then systematically engage in doing that science. When the paradigm finally breaks down in the face of applications to which it is not equal, we then have to rethink our inquiry and to criticize our concepts, assumptions, methods, criteria, and questions. That is a different activity. That is philosophy, though those who do it may not be known as philosophers. To be sure, putting it this way is more than a bit simplistic, as if science were either a matter of following a strict recipe or else tearing one up and searching about for another strict recipe. Whether to technical procedures or to cognitive frames of reference and their interpretation, we make adjustments from time to time, small ones as well as large. In small degree or in large, philosophizing goes on.

Not only does philosophy begin in wonder, but we can philosophize about anything we can wonder about. That is anything at all, which is one of the reasons why I personally love philosophy. Philosophy begins in wonder, and good philosophy stays in contact with wonder. We do not have to be on a par with Plato or Galileo to wonder and to philosophize. To some degree, virtually everyone philosophizes. We can philosophize about little things as well as big ones, and sometimes the little ones get big. Archimedes wondered why his bathwater ran over the way it did. A small child may wonder whether she, like the rest of the world, can (apparently) no longer be seen when she closes her eyes. She is trying to figure out how it all works, and in doing so she is doing some worthwhile philosophizing and gaining a better purchase on the world. There is no telling where and to what that might lead her.

Matters of bioethics, life and death, are well worth wondering about just because of the wonder of it. They are fascinating in themselves, if sometimes a little scary. All the more are they worth wondering about because of their impact on human life. This book is addressed to all – whether they consider themselves to be philosophers or not – who would care to accept my invitation and join me in wondering about bioethics, and in trying to adjust the focus in our thinking about such matters. For all of us, such matters impact on our own lives. My intended audience is not restricted to professional philosophers focusing on bioethics as an academic discipline – though I do hope to offer them some useful material. My intended audience is composed of those who care about these matters of life and death and who wish to join me in exploring them from the perspectives that I offer.

I shall offer some ideas (and ways of dealing with ideas) as being helpful for us in understanding bioethical issues more clearly and in dealing with them more satisfactorily. I shall not offer a complete theory of bioethics, much less deal with *all* bioethical issues. There are very good reasons for that: One is that bioethics spans a huge and diverse range of issues, sometimes related to one another only distantly, if at all. Any theory that was sufficient in general would likely be too vague in many applications. Moreover, new issues are constantly emerging. A complete theory could well become incomplete by next weekend. For example, with respect to stem cells and cloning, the landscape of both the possible and the problematic changes with great frequency. I do hope to offer a perspective from which we can better focus on and deal with the issues as they emerge.

Another reason I do not try to offer a complete account of bioethics is my conviction that ethics – and not just bioethics but all of ethics – can never be finalized. This is not because it is relative, arbitrary, or subjective. Rather, it is because ethics has to do with the real world, the depth and complexity of which can never fully be exhausted. Most emphatically, ethics is not just a matter of some list of moral rules. Rather, ethics is about a complex reality that systems of rules can deal with only imperfectly. We must continually find better ways to adjust to the demands of that complex and transforming reality.

A Note on Moral Nihilism

It is often said – sometimes seriously and sometimes in taking a posture – that there are no moral values save those, if any, that we make up ourselves for whatever our purposes might be. No set of moral rules has any genuine authority. After all, who is to say what is moral? (Note, though, that this is a rhetorical question; it is generally meant not as a question but as an irrefutable argument.) Therefore, you should or ought to leave me (us) alone to do just as I (we) please. You follow your inclinations and I will follow mine. To be sure, there is a real moral value in a code of live and let live (within certain limits), but it does not really work to found an ethical code on ethical nihilism. A no less valid conclusion would be that I have no reason other than practical consequences for not being as nasty as I please with a moral nihilist. Who is to say I shouldn't just blast your rotten head off? That, however, is a bit of an ad hominem argument. Perhaps it is also an ad hominem argument to proclaim that I, if not the moral nihilist, want to say more than just that I and Hitler have different personal inclinations about interethnic relationships. How are we to respond to the moral nihilist?

We must grant that it is logically possible that all self-consistent value systems are purely arbitrary. Nevertheless, it is not possible to live without values of some sort. Just using language or even thinking thoughts requires some values, if only arbitrary ones, and so does doing anything rather than something else. Furthermore, doing things may entail consequences that we might find more or less agreeable or disagreeable. Accordingly, it would be in our broader self-interest to investigate the nature and implications of our own values (as even moral nihilists must have) and those of others. We can then better understand the values of others and better understand and implement our own more effectively.

A Note on Moral Progress

Moral philosophy is not a science, yet in one important way it proceeds like science. There is a constant interplay between theory and practice. As Kuhn famously explained,[2] science proceeds by applying paradigmatic theories to applications, periodically developing better paradigms that can handle cases the old ones could not. Moral philosophy also proceeds by trying to develop progressively more satisfactory fits between ethical theory and moral practice. In moral philosophy as in science, there is no one precise and encompassing formula by means of which we can generate progress. There is no general theory, unless we make one up afterward, by means of which we can determine that from Newtonian Physics the next step is Relativity Theory and after that Theory X – and, for that matter, that Darwin's theory of evolution by natural selection has to come along when it did. This would be absurd. Yet scientific progress does happen. This is clearly so even though no scientific theory is ever totally conclusive.

Progress is also made in ethics. Moral progress was made when it was first thought that maybe there was right or wrong to how we treated those outside

---

[2] Thomas Kuhn, *The Structure of Scientific Revolutions*, 3rd ed. (Chicago: University of Chicago Press, 1996; originally published 1962).

of the family or tribe. Moral progress was made when various thinkers proposed some form of the Golden Rule.[3] Moral progress was made when it was thought that cruelty to animals might have a moral dimension. To varying degrees, moral progress is made when we think out the nature and implications of the values we recognize and is made when we adjust them to make a more acceptable fit with reality. In part this is a matter of rethinking our values, and in part it is a matter of rethinking how we apply them and to what we apply them. I attempt to contribute here to progress of this sort.

* * * * *

I begin, in background chapters, by exploring and criticizing some of the concepts and presumptions that have figured prominently in recent discussions of bioethical issues. These we have largely inherited from the past. My aim is to throw some light on their nature and implications and on their inadequacies. In particular, unclear ideas about what we are and what is good for us have often muddled our thinking about bioethical issues. Indeed, they continue to muddle our thinking about much else. Our dubious concepts and presumptions stem from the past but they persist now, and they influence our current understanding and handling of bioethical matters. In connection with forming concepts I shall consider problems of line drawing, slippery slopes, and varying cultural perspectives.

In later chapters, I present some alternative biocentric conceptions as offering a clearer and more useful understanding of bioethical issues. When they are relevant, I also bring in additional conceptions that may shed additional light on our topic. I try to present the material in a sensible order, but I cannot proceed in linear order. Bioethics, like so much of life, does not have a linear order. Because I wish to keep the various aspects of the inquiry in touch with one another, and moral theory with moral practice, I shall do some zigzagging back and forth. My intent is that this will be conducive to greater overall clarity.

I approach bioethics from the perspectives of the biocentric conceptions that I espouse. I am one whose ethics and related conceptions are life centered. I believe in the moral importance of all life (including, not just incidentally, all nonhuman life). In what follows *I am concerned only with human life*, and I argue that the perspectives of a biocentric ethic – with its attendant conceptions of the nature and significance of life, and its ways of going about thinking about life – have important implications for bioethics in purely human applications. One comes to different perspectives and conclusions concerning human applications than one would come to were one to start out with an anthropocentric (human-centered) understanding or

---

[3] It was not just Jesus who did this. Various thinkers of other times and places did this, such as Confucius in the sixth to fifth century B.C.

even one that centered on sentient beings. Most discussions of bioethical issues, as it happens, are either anthropocentric or sentientist in their orientation. I hope, therefore, to indicate an alternative approach to bioethics, an approach that is not just different but that offers us useful insights based on a truer and more adequate understanding of human life and interests. To restrict the current discussion to human bioethical issues, with only an occasional glance beyond, is a quite arbitrary limitation – but one cannot do everything at once. Even in purely anthropocentric applications, starting from biocentric rather than anthropocentric considerations can often lead to better results on a stronger rationale.

But why am I concerned with only *human* bioethics? It seems like trying to isolate just one part of a spectrum, which can only be done artificially. Human interests are not the only living interests nor the only ones with moral significance. The interests of animals count and so, too, I believe, do those of plants, species, and the biosphere as a whole. These things are interrelated. Even the best of bioethics and the best of medicine need the support of a good public health system, a decent society in which to function and flourish, and a healthily functioning environment in which to live. The optimum is a healthy life in a healthy world. I have a few things to say about some of those things elsewhere.[4] Here I am dealing with another part of the whole spectrum not because it is a separate part, which it obviously is not, but because it is an important center of wide interest and because it seems like a more or less manageable portion.

For now, I only sketch the principal features of the biocentric approach that I advocate. Subsequently, I shall explicate and argue for them in more detail. From there I shall go on to discuss how they apply to such problem areas as euthanasia, abortion, genetic engineering, and diverse others, and how they offer us insights that go beyond those that can be derived from conceptions that are not biocentric. I shall attempt to establish that a biocentric approach is both conceptually valid and practically useful.

As I develop it, a biocentric foundation for ethics requires, in outline, the following principal features:

1. A living being is best thought of not as a *thing* of some sort but as a living system, an ongoing life process. A life process has a character significantly different from that of nonliving processes.
2. The interests of a living being spring from its own particular character and lie in whatever contributes to its coherent effective functioning as an ongoing life process. That which tends to the contrary is against

---

4 Lawrence E. Johnson, *A Morally Deep World: An Essay on Moral Significance and Environmental Ethics* (New York: Cambridge University Press, 1991). As the title suggests, the book is principally concerned with environmental ethics.

its interests. Physical illnesses and mental distress, such as pain, frustration, and neurosis, are all instances of breakdown in our coherent effective functioning, of breakdown in our ability to maintain ourselves within a range of favorable states.

3. I maintain further that the interests of *all* living beings are morally significant, in proportion to the interest. Here, though, I shall be concerned only with human beings.

4. As a separate and optional extra, I accept the biological idea that some living systems other than individual organisms are living entities with morally considerable interests. Species, such as *Homo sapiens*, are such entities. (The interests of *Homo sapiens* may perhaps be affected by the results of our decisions, as in certain hypothetical cases of genetic engineering.) This controversial possibility is peripheral to my main discussion and is offered only as a possible extension once the major structure is in place.

I developed these ideas, in certain directions, in *A Morally Deep World*. In the current book I draw on the biocentric principles developed there at some length, further developing them and applying them to issues of human bioethics. A biocentric ethic has applications to our thinking about autonomy, abortion, voluntary and nonvoluntary euthanasia, and genetic engineering, and to other matters that confront us both in theory and in practice. Not only can a biocentric approach help us to address and cope with bioethical problems that confront us now, it can, as I argue in subsequent text, provide a coherent rationale with which to engage further problems as they emerge. This is important because new bioethical issues frequently do emerge. We can never give all the answers because we never have all the questions before us.

I contend that biocentric conceptions can throw useful light on important issues of ethical concern, be they issues of bioethics or issues from other areas. Just as the facts of physics, though they cannot solve all scientific questions, have to be presupposed in all scientific matters, so does our living character have to be presupposed in all human matters. *Whether or not ethics in its full scope can be derived from biocentric conceptions, certainly all ethics must do justice to our nature and interests as living beings of the kind that we are.*

These biocentric conceptions offer us a richer understanding of our self than is generally presupposed in ethical theory. This may at first seem paradoxical. Does not a biocentric approach stress our nature as *biological* beings, when actually we are rational and cultured beings as well? Seemingly, a biocentric ethic would offer us not a richer conception of the human self but only an impoverished one. However, it is a principle of a biocentric ethic that we must consider each life on its own terms, for the sort of being that it is. Be it predator, prey, or plant, each being has its own nature, its own interests, and its own place in the scheme of things. We humans are very different beings, and we too have to be considered for the kind of living beings we are with the kind of lives we live as humans and as individuals. The interests of a human being are complex, reflecting our complex makeup physically, mentally, and socially. Among other things, we are rational and cultural beings – and we are social beings. There is far more to our lives than our metabolic processes or our role in an ecosystem. That the rational and cultural elements are centrally important in our lives a biocentric approach not only accepts but insists on. That is part of our makeup as living beings of the particular sort we are.

However, much of ethical theory as it has been developed, including much of bioethical theory, presupposes a view of us human beings as sentient and rational decision-making consciousnesses, seemingly divorced from the nonconscious aspects of our being, our biological character, and our evolutionary background. Moreover, it is widely but incorrectly taken for granted that we are radically discrete individuals. Our nature and well-being interests span *all* of the aspects of our being, in our individuality and in our connectedness. Our ethics, to be adequate, must do likewise.

I would add that whether we are *only* living beings, and whether our welfare can fully and adequately be characterized in biological terms, are further questions – both of which might or might not be answered in the negative. I shall not attempt to answer those questions, though I have my own thoughts on these matters. Biocentric conceptions can accommodate views according to which we are both living beings and spiritual beings. Any alleged incompatibility between the two is the result of some misconception. Whatever else might be said about us, though, we *are* living beings and our nature as living beings is vitally relevant to the issues of bioethics.

I shall not be offering any system of bioethics as providing us with one comprehensive formula for finding *the* valid ethical answer for every bioethical problem. No ethical system can do that. All claims to the contrary are at best mistaken. I sometimes have the impression that some of my fellow professional philosophers are so fond of comprehensive systems that they overlook the complexities of the living world. I shall be offering biocentric conceptions as being, first and importantly, true and, in consequence, frequently useful considerations in approaching bioethical issues. In the following discussion I offer a form of *virtue ethics* (to be elaborated on in due course) as a natural partner of biocentric conceptions. Together they form a combination that is a powerful tool in addressing bioethical issues. The principal virtue to be advocated is that of *life affirmation*. Of course any system of bioethics (at least any worthy of serious consideration) is life affirming in some form or another. What I am advocating, which is somewhat beyond the usual, is a system of bioethics that is based on life affirmation on the basis of these biocentric conceptions and as a virtue rather than as a principle. But these are things that must be explained more slowly.

In the following chapters I also shall be considering some important logical issues that do not spring from biocentric ethics or even particularly from bioethics. Nor are they resolved by such ethics. However, these are issues of importance to bioethics and if we are to address bioethical issues adequately, we must do so on the basis of thinking clearly about them. In particular I shall address the particularly vexing swarm of issues that arise from that hoary old poser, "Where do you draw the line?" It is easy to become lost and misled in such issues, and I try to offer useful guidance. As well I shall argue against the well-established myth, invoked by biologists and philosophers alike, that DNA is some sort of a *language* for encoding instructions, or something of the sort, for building an organism. Although of some use as an explanatory myth, it is indeed a myth and ultimately becomes misleading and creates problems. On any approach to bioethics, be it biocentric or any other, we do well to avoid being misled.

PART I

BACKGROUNDS

2

Some Background

Self and Reason

Like all forms of life, we develop from our past. That is true of us as individuals, and it is true of us collectively. Even as we engage in our current thinking about one thing or another, we largely do so by means of the concepts and presuppositions we have at hand. Some we may have developed ourselves, but many we have gathered from our ambient culture and inherited from its past. We may not be conscious of our ideological inheritance. We may be no more directly aware of it than we are of the language we use, though like our language, it infuses our words and thoughts. Indeed, many concepts and presuppositions have become embedded in the very structure of our language. For that matter, we who speak the language Shakespeare spake may not be conscious that we so often invoke the master wordwright, that we can scarcely avoid doing so in using the language he did so much to shape. Our Shakespearian inheritance is a glorious cultural treasure and, more broadly, there is much hard-won wisdom in our inherited ways of thinking with its concepts, presuppositions, and associations. Still, our inherited ways of thinking are not the ultimate in conceptual resources any more than Shakespeare is the last and only word in literature. These inherited conceptual resources are the most readily available to us and inevitably bear on our thinking. We would do well to be aware of them and to critically assess them as well as we can. This is very much true in bioethics as well, and in this chapter I am particularly concerned with our inherited conceptual resources in application to bioethics and our thinking about ourselves.

To give a full analysis of our inherited ideas and ways of thinking in Western thought, or even of those that influence our bioethical thinking (which is a considerable proportion of them), would be an encyclopedic project far beyond the scope of this current undertaking. Even if I could fully complete such a project – and I know that I could not and doubt whether anyone else could – such an endeavor would obscure the aims of *this* project. In this chapter I try to highlight certain central inherited ideas about what we are and that continue to influence our thinking about bioethical issues, to indicate the general nature of their implications, and, as relevant, to indicate something of their shortcomings. This is to lay the foundation for my subsequently presenting alternative ideas and ways of thinking as being more adequate. In Chapter 4, I further discuss problems in our use of language, with particular reference to the difficulties in making distinctions, drawing lines, and avoiding slippery slopes.

What Are We?

What do we believe ourselves to be? We are, of course, living beings and human beings. We evidently are able to agree on that, if on little or nothing else. Even that much agreement is nebulous as there is not yet full agreement on what it is to be alive or on what it is to be human. Rarely do we have any clear idea what *we* mean by these things ourselves. Nevertheless, we can usually recognize another living being, or another living human being, when we encounter one, using some criterion or other. We may have trouble with some difficult cases, perhaps borderline cases, but usually we can distinguish well enough for our immediate purposes. Even so, we need to look more closely at this matter of what we are or think ourselves to be. My purpose here is not just to resolve difficult or borderline cases, though doing so can be quite important in certain bioethical applications. Our ideas about what we humans are, and our operational criteria for deciding such matters in particular cases, lead us not only to decide what is or is not human but also, on a daily basis, to make decisions that affect the course and quality of our own lives and those of others. Misconceptions concerning who and what we are, I suggest, can lead to misguided life decisions and adversely affected lives.

Historically and currently, two frequent and important elements of our self-conception are that we are rational beings and that we are spiritual beings. *Homo sapiens,* we call ourselves, "[hu]man the knower" (or " . . . the wise"). We often define ourselves as "the rational animal." This begs a few questions: Are we really all that rational or wise? Are we the only beings with such capacities? Is rationality definitive of what we *are?* (For that matter, what sort of thinking is rational?) Perhaps we should not try to put so much weight on rationality alone. Maybe there is more to us than that. One suggestion, and this certainly is not an incompatible idea, is that we are more than merely material beings – that we have, or are, souls, our true nature being spiritual. Many people think both of these things to be true, that we are mind–souls, and this is a thought that has an ancient and venerable lineage. In the West such ideas go back to the Jews and Greeks of antiquity.

A major current of Greek thought identified our soul with our rationality, our mind, that divine spark within us that separates us from the mere brutes and makes us what we are. Socrates, shortly before he was required to drink hemlock and die, was asked by one of his followers what he and the others should do with him after he was dead. As recorded by his disciple Plato in the *Phaedo* (115b), he replied that they might do whatever they liked – if they could catch him. His point was that he, his real self, was not his body and would not die with it. What they were left with would not be Socrates. During this last dialog between Socrates and his followers, he explained that our true self, or soul, has the capability of knowing truth and being – real truth and real being, not their confused and transient shadows that make up the material world. Real truth and being, the Forms or Ideas, are eternal and not subject to the vicissitudes of the material world. Being able (with effort) to know the Forms, our mind–soul must be of a similar nature. Mere matter could never attain knowledge. Being of a similar nature as the Forms, our mind–soul must also be immortal, not subject to what befalls our body. In *Phaedo*, Socrates says this:

On the one hand we have that which is divine, immortal, indestructible, of a single form, accessible to thought, ever constant and abiding true to itself; and the soul is very like it: on the other hand we have that which is human, mortal, destructible, of many forms, inaccessible to thought, never constant nor abiding true to itself; and the body is very like that.

. . . that being so, isn't it right and proper for the soul to be altogether indestructible, or nearly so? (Plato, *Phaedo* 80b)

Note that not only is Socrates explaining his concept of the soul and its immortal nature, he is also expressing a disdainful attitude toward the body. We might question that and we might also question whether the body is really "never constant nor abiding true to itself."

A few days earlier, when he was on trial for his life, Socrates had reassured his friends that "[n]o evil can come to a good man" (Plato, *Apology*, 41). That was not to deny that all manner of unpleasant things can happen to a person, good persons being no exception. They can suffer poverty, illness, physical injury, and social disapproval. They can be put to death. Socrates was acutely aware of that. His point was that the only true harm and the only true benefit happen to the soul, which is our true self. What happens to our body, one way or another, is superficial and of only trivial or illusory importance. Moral corruption is the one true harm, whereas tending and perfecting our soul is what is truly good for us. So long as we remain good, no harm can come to us. Plato developed these points further in his own writings. According to Plato, our highest good lies in contemplating and being in communion with the highest reality. The highest reality, according to Plato's *The Republic* (XXIII: 502b–508b, and XXVIII: 539b–540b), is that unity that is the source of Truth, Beauty, and Goodness. It is in communion with the highest Good that our divine rational soul finds its own good. Any good in the material world is only a shadow of the Good.

Philosophers of the Stoic school, though they differed widely from Plato in several matters, also claimed their philosophical descent from Socrates.

They wholeheartedly adopted the doctrine that the only injury that may befall us is moral. If anything, they put even more emphasis on the rational than did Plato. The Stoics held that there is a divine rationality that organizes and guides the universe that is inherent in all things. They found an order and purpose in the world that indicated to them that there was reason (God) behind it all, and that the world was organized for the benefit of rational beings. The nonrational part of the world, such as sticks and stones, animals, and our own bodies, are there for the benefit of those beings that are rational. Our purpose in life, our good, is to live in accordance with the law of nature, that is, the divine reason and will, and it is that which our own true nature is. To be truly human is to be truly rational, to be truly good, and to be truly divine. Animals, not being rational, have no part in the good, save only as a means to the ends of rational beings. That goes for our own body as well. It is our inner life that matters. The good life is the one of reason, good intention, and resignation to the divinely good law of nature. External events are only partially and haphazardly within our control. What we can learn to control properly is our responses to things and our own intentions. Pleasure and pain are, in themselves, morally indifferent. They are morally relevant only insofar as they might tempt us to alter our thinking or attitudes: hence the famous Stoic indifference to pain. Hence, too, the saying of Marcus Aurelius that life can be lived well even in a palace (see his *Meditations* V:16). As Emperor of Rome, he was in a position to know well the distractions of power and privilege, and in his own virtuous life he demonstrated that the distractions can be successfully overcome.

As we shall see, views such as those of Plato and the Stoics, that decisions affecting the body are of moral importance only insofar as they might affect our spiritual career, are bound to have profound effects in bioethics. These views have had a lasting and deep-seated influence in the Western tradition. Not only have they had an impact on our secular thinking, they also have greatly influenced Western religious thought. One might say that Platonists and Stoics worshipped reason, identified as God, whereas the ancient Jews worshipped God, identified as the source of all reason, all truth, all life, all being, and all goodness. The only good life, the only life that is not entirely wretched, is one of total dedication and obedience to that God. Platonist, Stoic, and Jew alike held that the most important thing for us is our spiritual condition and career, our relation to the divine. The body is dismissed as having only subservient value, and as being a source of moral danger. Christianity developed from both Jewish and Greek thought.

Christianity, at least as it came to be understood, held that God took human form for our edification and salvation. What this God is, though, is not easy to understand, to say the least. God is evidently a person, one who is rational. A perfect God must be perfectly rational. As Christianity spread beyond its Judaic roots, seeking and gathering converts from the pagans of classical antiquity, it was natural that it be interpreted in terms of the concepts readily available and (at least apparently) applicable. The Christian God came to be understood on the model of the divine reason that the Stoics revered, the source of value and being, and the inexpressible ultimate reality of Platonism, the source of all being, all truth, beauty, and goodness.

As we are told in the Gospel of John, which was written in Greek,

In the beginning was the Logos [Λογοσ], and the Logos was with God, and the Logos was God.

. . .

And the Logos was made flesh, and dwelt among us, full of grace and truth. (John I: 1, 14 KJV)

The term Λογοσ, sometimes inadequately translated as *Word*, and having no fully adequate translation into English, may roughly be approximated as *rational essence*. It is the rationale; it is that which makes anything that is anything at all whatever it is. In the Logos we have the rational itself, the rational essence of the whole universe. God, insofar as God is understood at all, is understood to be Truth itself, the fundamental essence of all being and all value.

We, male and female, were made in the image and likeness of God (Gen. I:26, 27 KJV). We too have Logos; we are rational–spiritual beings. Unlike God we have limitations, particularly since our fall from grace and expulsion from Eden. We are the lowest part of the spiritual realm, but we are the highest part of material creation, the only part of it that does have soul. All of this fits in pretty well with Stoicism and Platonism. Saint Augustine (A.D. 354–430) developed the line of thought even further in a Platonistic direction. God, and that which is like God or of God, is all that is of value. Moreover, such is all that is real. The things of this material world have no more reality than the flickering shadows Plato tells of in his Allegory of the Cave (*The Republic*, XXV: 514a–521b). They have reality only to the extent that they partake of the Godly. Evil does not exist. Evil is, precisely, that which lacks reality, which lacks the Godly. To the extent that we lack Godliness, that we do not value Godly things, to that extent we become less real. We suffer accordingly. The torments of Hell are the torments of lessened existence, the erosion of our very being. However, no evil can come to a good Christian. What we must do is to resist and avoid the snares and temptations of this material world of shadows. Instead of the City of Man, with its vanities and falsity, we must focus on the City of God and make that our home. A system of bioethics based on such a foundation will attribute only minor and derivative value to bodily matters.

In passing, though I will make some further mention of this later, I note that much of the information just given will seem strange to the Hindu and Buddhist thinkers of South and East Asia. They too tend to downplay worldly things, agreeing that the important thing is our spiritual condition. From there, however, they differ widely from Western thinkers. The equation of the soul, our true self, with mind or ego seems quite bizarre to them. In their view, our conscious self, which reasons, feels, desires, and says "I," is part of the illusion we must come to transcend. Our true self is something more real and more fundamental than that. Moreover, a soul may be associated with a nonhuman material body, one with a nonrational and nonhuman mind. This may well have happened to us in past lives. Not only that, a god can take an incarnation as an animal. Vishnu, the Hindus tell us, not only took human form as Krishna but also had previous lives as a boar and as a fish. It was the same self, that of Vishnu, on each occasion, yet that self also assumed the consciousness of a boar or a fish. Other gods took other forms. For his part, the Buddha was said to have had a previous life as a rabbit. In this point of view, it was no more absurd for a god to take animal form than it was for one to take a human form.[1] Either way it is an instance of a godly self taking a limited form, but in this Asian conception what takes the limited form is something more real than consciousness or rationality, and different in kind. It is the god's self taking on the animal's consciousness. In contrast, the Greek god Zeus might take the outward appearance of a swan or something else, but always one with the god's consciousness, not a swan's. To the classical Western mind it was absurd that God, Logos itself, should take any form less than human. Paul thought it unthinkable that animals should have any part in spiritual things (1 Cor. 9:9–10). To South and East Asians, soul is not the same thing as consciousness, and tending our soul properly goes far beyond tending our thoughts and consciousness. It is a matter of the well-being of our whole being. A Hindu or Buddhist system of bioethics will accordingly take a somewhat different approach to issues than would one based on classical Western conceptions.

Are there any strands in Western thinking that see us as being more or other than intellects? There is a long tradition that considers us primarily as sentient beings, with our intellect being only part of the story and perhaps in a subservient role. For one, Epicurus, in the fourth to third century B.C., held that pleasure is our one fundamental good. He was therefore a *hedonist* (from the Greek term for pleasure, *hedone*). Terms such as *epicure* and *epicurean*, not to mention *hedonist*, have come to suggest a dedication to self-indulgence and dissipation. That is quite unfair to Epicurus, who actually advocated a life of moderation, serenity, contemplation, and morality. Life is more pleasant, he held, when we have modest desires, for then we are less vulnerable to frustration and disappointment. As did Gautama Buddha, his near contemporary who also sought an end to suffering, he held that much of our suffering stems from inappropriate desires doomed to

---

[1] The Buddha was not held to be a god, to be sure, but he was certainly a great and very advanced soul.

disappointment. Realizing this, we wisely use our rationality to serve our best interests as sentient beings. That we are *only* sentient beings will be hotly denied by many, and hotly denied will be the claim that serving our sentience is our highest good. Yet whatever else we might be, sentience is part of what we are, with our pleasures, pains, and all of our feelings being important to us. Seemingly, an adequate system of bioethics would have to take this into account in some way.

Archrationalist though he was, Plato himself came to recognize the importance of our feelings or passions in our makeup. In the beginning of the *Phaedrus*, Socrates (as presented by Plato) expresses the view that our rational soul is the only part of us that has any value, and that our emotive and appetitive aspects lack all worth. Then, as Plato dramatically presents it, Socrates is stopped by his familiar spirit (his *daimonion*), who intervenes from time to time to tell him when he is going wrong. Socrates then develops a view according to which our emotive and appetitive elements are valuable parts of our soul. All three parts of the soul, of course, must be properly directed by reason. The emotive and appetitive elements provide power to the soul and so can be used to carry it upward. In his Simile of the Chariot, Plato tells us that the soul is to

be likened to the union of powers in a team of winged steeds and their winged charioteer.... a pair of steeds... one of them is noble and good, and of good stock, while the other has the opposite character, and its stock is opposite. Hence the task of our charioteer is difficult and troublesome... All soul has the care of all that is inanimate, and traverses the whole universe, though in ever-changing forms. Thus when it is perfect and winged it journeys on high and controls the whole world; but one that has shed its wings sinks down... what we must understand is the reason why the soul's wings fall from it, and are lost. It is on this wise... by reason of the heaviness of the steed of wickedness, which pulls down his driver with his weight, except that driver have schooled him well. (Plato, *Phaedrus* 246a–247b)

The horse of inferior breeding, our bodily appetites, is the one that draws our soul down through its attachments to worldly and therefore inferior objects of desire. The way to prevent the fall of our soul is not to try to get rid of the unruly horse (which could not possibly be done even were it desirable to do so) but to guide it in the right direction. This is a matter of getting our desires properly in order. The charioteer, our mind, does this with the aid of the well-bred horse, the emotive or spirited element. Properly directed, the spirited element of the soul is a powerful agent for controlling our appetites and redirecting them upward. Improperly directed, it is a powerful agent in helping them destroy us.

Although our reason has the leading role in guiding us, guidance is not solely a matter for reason. That is because *we* are not solely a matter of reason. All three aspects of the soul are aspects of our whole self. All three must work together, each modifying the action of the others. In isolation the rational mind becomes stale and arid from lack of nourishment. We must not lose contact with our broader and more complete self. Given input and power from our whole being, our rational mind can then fulfill its role at the reins. Even so, it is the charioteer, our rational and immortal soul, that is to provide the fundamental direction, and it is that part of us that is carried up on high to communion with the Forms. It seems strange to me – and here I believe there is an unresolved internal tension in Plato's account – that these other aspects of us should be so important to our wholeness and functioning, yet not share in our good.

In contrast, the *Katha Upanishad*, of the classical Vedic tradition of India, offers us a very different simile, also comparing the self with a chariot.[2] For the *Katha* (1, 3, 3–11), the soul is the lord riding in the chariot. The charioteer, the mind, is a servant of the soul. The intellect, as well as the passions, is part of the nonsoul. Neither our intellect nor our passions take part in our truest good. Our good is a matter for our soul, which transcends our mind and all the rest of our lower part. We, for our part, are left to ponder for ourselves what our soul has to do with our intellect and our sentience. Is it a matter of either, neither, or both?[3]

Aristotle presented a more integrated view of us as complex living and thinking beings than did either Plato or the *Katha*, and to him we owe much of our contemporary presumptions about our sense of self. He held that there is a hierarchical scale of being that ranges from high to low in particular things, according to how much a thing's rationale or form predominates over matter in its makeup. Form is one thing, matter is something else. Mere material body is down at the very bottom of being. Sometimes a body has life, but a body itself is not life. What makes matter alive is soul, which is the form or rationale of that living being. Inherent in the soul is its end or purpose. To be alive is to have a purpose. To live well is to follow our inherent purpose and fulfill our proper potential. Even plants have natural purposes of their own: They act so as to take in sunlight, water, carbon dioxide, and so on, and produce seeds. These are not conscious purposes, but they are purposes nonetheless. Like plants we have bodies and metabolize. Like plants, and like all other living beings, we therefore have a nutritive (or vegetative) soul. But there is more form in our soul than in plant souls. Unlike plants, though in common with (most) other animals, we have movement and sensation. Only beings that can move have, or have a use for, sensation. Animals have a soul that is nutritive and sensitive, being capable of sensation, desire (again, not necessarily conscious), and movement. Some souls go higher

---

[2] I explore this further in my "From the Chariot: The *Phaedrus* and the *Katha*," *Darshana International* 126 (1992): 42–57. This paragraph, and the previous two, partially stem from that article.

[3] For a further discussion of the contrasting conceptions of true self, East and West, see Johnson, "Profiles in Princeliness: Hal and Arjuna," *Soundings* 58 (1980): 94–111; and "On the Self: The Chandogya," *Darshana International* 99 (1987): 69–83.

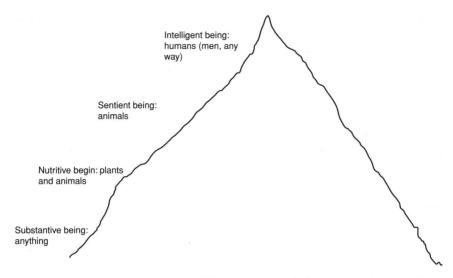

Figure 1.

than that, having consciousness as well as sensation. Here the passions or emotions start to come in and play a role – and so on up. We might think of this as being like a pyramid. The base of the pyramid is material body. Only some bodies have life, even fewer of them have animate life, and fewer yet have consciousness. As one would inevitably expect, we humans (and whatever gods and spirits there might be) are up at the apex of the pyramid. Unlike lower and lesser beings, we have rational souls. Rational mind, *nous* [vouσ], is the highest and best part of us (Figure 1).

In Aristotle's conception, the world is a purposeful and well-ordered hierarchy. Plants serve the purposes of animals, and animals are here to be of benefit to us rational humans. Within ourselves we are a hierarchical complex of functions, actualities, and potentialities. Our *nous* depends on the lower parts of the soul. Only through those lower parts is it able to exercise its rationality. Our well-being, our *eudaimonia*, consists of the overall effective functioning of that complex on all levels, with the healthy development of our potentialities. Our highest good is in the development and exercise of our rationality. One part of the function of our rationality is to control and guide the lower part of ourselves. The purpose of the lower part of our nature is to serve the good of our rational nature, and its best and highest good is to serve it adequately. According to Aristotle, we live so that we may think well. Ideally, our rational mind ought to be free to pursue intellectual interests of our own rational choosing, without being encumbered by the pursuit of material needs. He tells us that

[I]t is clear that the rule of the soul over the body, and of the mind and the rational element over the passionate, is natural and expedient; whereas the equality of the two or the rule of the inferior is always hurtful. The same holds good of animals in relation to men. . . . Where there is such a difference as that between soul and body, or between men and animals . . . the lower sort are by nature slaves, and it is better for them as it is for all inferiors that they should be under the rule of a master. (Aristotle, *Politics* 1254b)

Some humans, not being capable of rationally guiding and controlling their own lives, are slaves by nature. This includes most barbarians and even a few Greeks. It is better for those unfortunate beings, as well as for us, that they be controlled and guided by rational men. Similarly,

. . . the male is by nature superior, and the female inferior; and the one rules, and the other is ruled; this principle, of necessity, extends to all mankind. (Aristotle, *Politics* 1254b)

Women are, of course, less rational than men and are more emotional and subjective. After all, women are only incomplete men. Women are more closely tied with material nature, men with transcendent rationality. In reproduction, women merely contribute matter, whereas the male contributes the form; and so on. (I remind you that this stuff is Aristotle's and not mine!)

I find some things to worry about here – things currently more insidious than his views about slavery and women that I need not waste time refuting. To be sure, there are also strong points. We are whole beings, not just rational beings, and our well-being is a matter of our whole being. It also seems right that our good as a living being is a matter of our own particular character as the particular living being each of us is. Why, however, should the exercise of reason be our *highest* good? Granted that rationality is part of our character as human beings, and that exercising it is part of our human good, it does not follow from this that the exercising of it is our highest and most central good. Nor does that follow from our being the only rational beings. If we are the unique rational beings, then it follows that, uniquely, rationality is part of our good, not that it is the highest part. Nonetheless, using our mind well *is* part of our good.

For Aristotle, the higher importance of rationality was one of those things that are so clearly true that they do not really need to be argued for. *Obviously* that which is rational is superior to what is not rational. Indeed, one must grant that the rational is superior to the *irrational*. That $2 + 2 = 7$ is not useful arithmetic. For one who desires to continue to live, it is irrational to drive on bald tires.[4] In addition to the rational and the irrational, there is the *arational*, that to which the concepts of rationality and irrationality

---

4 To be sure, those who wish to dissemble may find that it is very productive, that is, rational, to speak or act in ways that are deceptively irrational. One can make rational use of the irrational.

do not apply. Some things just are. For instance, if I feel a sensation of pleasure, it might be possible to explain it rationally or irrationally and to draw rational or irrational conclusions, but the pleasure itself is neither rational nor irrational. It just is. The law of gravity just is. Much of the world, including much of what I personally regard as the best part, is arational. Epicurus suggested that our rationality is good for us because it serves our sentience. For my part, I think it is a mistake to look for *the* highest aspect of our being, that which it is the function of the rest of our being to serve. Instead, I will propose that our highest good lies in our overall effective functioning as whole beings, encompassing our rationality and all the rest of us. Of that, I shall offer more later. For Aristotle, it was self-evident and in no real need of argument that rationality was the highest being and our highest good.

Aristotle may mislead us into thinking that the various aspects of our selves can be understood as *distinct* features, as if each higher layer were just an add-on, and he does us a further disservice by proclaiming that one aspect of us is higher than another. He went so far as to maintain that although the lower parts of our soul arise from the body and perish with it, our rational soul (form, *nous*) preexists the body and survives it. This immortal soul is our true self. Still, although he analyzed us into distinct modules, Aristotle did well to remind us that we are complex beings and not simply rational beings. We are each of us an interconnected and purposeful whole. This is likewise true of the entire world. It is like an organism, or perhaps we could even say that it *is* an organism. Each part has its role in the whole and certain purposes to fulfill. That life has to do with interconnection, role, and purpose was an assumption widely shared for centuries after the coming of Christianity.

Christianity, for centuries the dominant force in European thought, found much to its liking in Aristotle's conclusions, as well as in those of Plato and the Stoics. Aristotle held that the very highest being, and the greatest and most fundamental value, is an unmoved mover. This unmoved mover is pure reason and is the moving force and the final purpose of the whole universe. The Christians naturally identified this entity as their God. They also found congenial Aristotle's belief that we have a rational soul that is intrinsically different from our lower nature. Having been created with this *nous*–soul, we were made in the image and likeness of God. It was as this soul that the medieval Christian looked for admission to the Kingdom of Heaven.

In the Christianized Aristotelian conception, the world as a whole is much like an organic living being, moving toward the fulfillment of God's rational purposes. Much as our living bodies are made and organized for our benefit, we and all things else have our interconnected and ordered places in God's plan. In the material world, of course, we are at the center of the plan. This is because we are the only part of the material world that does have soul. Everything else in the material world, from the stars in the sky to the grass and pebbles under our feet, serve to give us material sustenance or spiritual edification. They declare the glory of God or, when wisely understood, illustrate moral and spiritual truths. God does nothing in vain. This was the view that prevailed until the Renaissance, when we came to rethink so many of our ideas about ourselves and the world.

Toward More Modern Ways of Thinking

During the Renaissance we came to have greater confidence in our ability to understand the world on the basis of reason and factual investigation. New scientific methods were being developed, and old certainties were being called into question. We had lost our presumed place at the physical center of the universe and our moral place also seemed less certain. The startling claim made by Galileo (1564–1642) that the material heavens did not revolve around the earth provoked indignation because it appeared to threaten our place in God's scheme of things. At the same time, it was becoming more and more clear that not everything was created for our own special benefit. Galileo was again annoying when he claimed that the planet Jupiter had four moons, previously unknown. This seemed suspicious, as presumably Aristotle would have mentioned them had they existed. More-over, that they could not even be seen (except through this newfangled and suspect gadget, the telescope) and that they had no earthly use would suggest – if they really were there – that God had created something that was not directed toward humans.

Even worse for our self-conception was the mechanistic conception of nature that was coming into vogue. (In this also, Galileo was a key player. Perhaps the remarkable thing is not that he was persecuted but that he did manage to escape with his life.) As time went on, our prevailing image of the world came to be that of its being like a gigantic piece of clockwork. The world is much grander than any human contrivance and perfectly engineered, but it follows the same fundamental mechanical laws. The stars and planets moved mechanically, as did their representations in a mechanical orrery. And on Earth as it is in the heavens. If we could but fully understand it, we would realize that all the phenomena of the physical world are subject to mechanical explanation. *All?* Yes, in a world of matter in motion, life too was coming to be seen as a complex mechanical interaction in matter. Mechanical representatives of animals and humans could be crafted and made to perform various actions. What we could contrive was limited only by the shortcomings of human craftsmanship, not by any evident limitations to mechanical possibility. From the stars in the sky to the tides of the sea, to the fall of an apple, it all apparently followed the laws of mechanics. This seems to include living bodies as well. Bones, muscles, and ligaments, the course of various bodily fluids through bodily channels – everything that we can observe seems to be susceptible to mechanical explanation. There was no evident reason why plants and animals could not also be machines, though of a construction far superior to that of any current human contrivance. That was certainly the implication of the mechanistic conception. That also suggests the possibility that we humans are merely mechanisms.

This was quite a remarkable and exciting time in our history. As Western civilization emerged into the Renaissance and the Enlightenment, we had expanding hopes and we had new worries that we had never had before. On the one hand, there was growing confidence that we were making progress on a number of fronts: in our knowledge of the world, in the secular arts and sciences, and in our ways of living. Socioeconomic conditions were changing as well, and we were developing new ways of thinking and doing in human affairs. On the other hand, we had worries about whom and what we are. We also had worries about how we could find reliable knowledge in the face of uncertainty. There was a growing skepticism about tradition and authority, religious or secular. It was becoming clear that Aristotle did not have all the right answers. It was also becoming strongly suspected – though you had better lower your voice if you said this out loud – that the Church did not always have the right answers either. Just what the right answers were was hard to say. New alternatives as well as old certainties were subject to doubt and often to refutation. Seemingly, there were some possible grounds for doubting any belief, new or old, that one might have. What, then, are we to believe?

Descartes

René Descartes (1596–1650), one of the most brilliant and influential thinkers of his or any age, tried to meet the skeptical challenge by putting our knowledge and our means of attaining it on a firm foundation. He wanted to base it on reason, that on which we humans pride ourselves. He was concerned to discover and validate truths about our world, and about ourselves. One of the things he wanted to ascertain was whether we humans really were radically distinct from the material world, as we liked to believe – or were we only machines, complicated assemblies of matter in motion, as many feared? Our first problem was to find a way in which to obtain reliable knowledge in the face of doubt and uncertainty. In point of fact, Descartes had a demonstrated capacity for finding truth. He made worthwhile discoveries in physics and astronomy, and in mathematics he was one of the all-time greats. His analytic geometry revolutionized the field, paved the way for calculus, and helped open the way for modern science. Without it, much of science would be literally unthinkable. For that matter, we are all indebted to Descartes whenever we use a graph, correlating one quantity (e.g., stock prices or temperature) with another (e.g., time).

Descartes proposed that we apply mathematical reasoning in our search for truth. That was not to suggest that we are to try to find all truth in mathematics, but that in our search for truth we are to use the style of reasoning characteristic of mathematics. If we can reason on the basis of assumptions that we *know* are true, and if we reason carefully and rationally (à la mathematics), then we can be sure of our conclusions. In his *Rules for the Direction of the Mind*, he offers us guidelines for thinking accurately and productively about whatever we desire to inquire into. These have become so widely accepted that to state them now seems to be to state the obvious:

Method consists entirely in the order and disposition of the objects toward which our mental vision must be directed if we would find out any truth. We shall comply with it exactly if we reduce involved and obscure propositions step by step to those that are simpler, and then starting with the intuitive apprehension of all those that are absolutely simple, attempt to ascend to the knowledge of all others by precisely similar steps. (Descartes, Rule V)

If we wish our science to be complete, those matters which promote the end we have in view must ... be included in an enumeration which is both adequate and methodical. ... (Descartes, Rule VII)

If in the matters to be examined we come to a step in the series of which our understanding is not sufficiently well able to have cognition, we must stop there. (Descartes, Rule VII)

If, after we have recognized ... a number of simple truths, we wish to draw any inference from them, it is useful to run them over in a continuous and uninterrupted act of thought, to reflect upon their relations to one another, and to grasp together distinctly a number of these propositions so far as it is possible at the same time. (Descartes, Rule IX)

Finally we ought to employ all the aids of understanding, imagination, sense, and memory. ... (Descartes, Rule XII)

Once a "question" is perfectly understood we must free it of every conception superfluous to its meaning, state it in its simplest terms, and, having recourse to an enumeration, split it up into the various sections beyond which analysis cannot go in minuteness. (Descartes, Rule XIII)

Fundamentally, Descartes' method involved breaking a question or problem down into is component parts and then employing cool and detached reason to move systematically, one step at a time, from true premises to true conclusions. If we get to a step of which we cannot be certain, we are to stop there, instead of inserting guesses in place of certainty. We proceed only when certain. In this way we build a structure of rational thought on the firm foundation of true assumptions and valid method. If we have built well, the structure of our thought will match the structure of the world, and what we believe will be true.

To the extent that this seems as obvious and self-evident as scarcely to be worth mentioning, to that extent we are intellectually heirs to Descartes, for his method was groundbreaking in his day. Moreover, at that time it was revolutionary to suggest that we humans, flawed as we are, could, through our own means, attain certain knowledge about the nature of the world or about ourselves. It was widely thought that the ancient Greeks had discovered everything of value that the human mind on its own could discover, and that any further knowledge had to be on the basis of divine revelation. For that reason, Descartes is often described as being the father of modern philosophy. He offered us a way of conducting philosophy as a means by which human beings using human reason can arrive at truth. Philosophy need no longer be the handmaiden of theology. This is easier said than done, and Descartes himself failed more than once. As an ideal, though, it has inspired Western thought from that day to this. Reason can lead us to truth, and deficiencies of reasoning can be made good only by better reasoning. This is sound common sense, evidently, and frequently practical. We have gained many truths through following such methods. As we shall see, however, there are some quite problematic elements buried in Descartes' method and conclusions. These continue to have repercussions for us, not least in bioethics.

Let us look now at some of the conclusions he drew in his attempts to apply the method.[5] If we are to start with assumptions that it is impossible to doubt, that does not seem to leave us with much leverage. What can we not doubt? Descartes pointed out that we might doubt whether the world around us, other people, or our own bodies exist. We might be dreaming all of this. Or rather, Descartes might be dreaming it. He did not yet know that anyone else existed. This, of course, brings us to what Descartes found as his indubitable starting point. Though he was determined to set aside everything that he could possibly doubt, he could not doubt the fact of his own existence. There is sound reason for that. If he were wrong in thinking that he existed, he had to exist in order to be wrong. If he doubted, he had to exist to doubt. If he were being deceived by an evil demon who created a nonexistent fantasy world in order to trick him, though the demon might fool him about all else, he had to be to be deceived. *Cogito ergo sum*, Descartes confidently reasoned, I think therefore I am. At this point, his knowledge about himself is still very limited. All he knows for sure is that he is a thinking being. He does not actually know that there is a material world out there, or that he has a body, or that anyone else exists.[6]

---

[5] For the particulars of Descartes' reasons and conclusions, see his *Meditations on First Philosophy*.

[6] I once had the experience of dreaming that I was conducting a class on Descartes. One of the students in the class was using Descartes' argument to proclaim his certainty of his own existence. Yet neither that class nor that particular student actually existed. The proof is airtight only for the thinking being using it (if there is one).

Descartes goes on to argue for the existence of a perfect being, God. (It is illogical to think that a perfect being might suffer the imperfection of nonexistence.) On that basis he argues for the existence of the material world, including his own body, and for the existence of other people and their bodies. (A perfect and therefore good God would not allow us to be deceived about such things.) His arguments on these points need not detain us. I will mention, though, that critics have found those arguments to be far less rationally conclusive than did Descartes – however much one may be convinced of the truth of the conclusion that the world and other people do in fact exist. Nevertheless, it is almost universally agreed that we can be rationally certain of our own existence as thinking beings.

As thinking beings we perform mental actions and have mental qualities. Descartes went on to elaborate a whole theory concerning mind and body. He proposed a *dualism*: There are two kinds of stuff in the world – or, more formally, two kinds of *substance*. There is mental substance and there is material substance, and each kind of substance has its own sort of qualities. Material substance, of which our own bodies are composed, is characterized by extension and has such features as weight, velocity, temperature, spatial location, and so on. Mental substance is characterized by consciousness: We think, feel, doubt, believe, wonder, love, hate, and all that sort of thing. Material events cause material events, and mental events cause mental events. However, these substances are so radically different in character that material events cannot cause mental events, or vice versa. For mental substance to affect material substance, it would itself need to have some sort of material property. For material body to cause a mental event, it would have to have some sort of mental property. Its fundamental character would then have to be a state of consciousness rather than any state of matter. We need not worry that we thinking beings are merely complex bits of physical matter acting according to mechanical laws. Whatever our bodies might be, we are thinking beings. We are mind–souls.

Descartes gives us a conception of ourselves as conscious, thinking, rational choice-making beings. The body is there only as a mind-support system. Our feelings as well as our rational thoughts take place in the mind as aspects of our thinking. But is there nothing beneath the mental surface? Indeed, in Descartes' conception there is a great deal beneath our conscious surface, but what is beneath the surface is more mind and the sort of things that inhabit them: ideas. In addition to ideas that we generate and often store, we have a stock of valuable ideas implanted in us by God for our benefit. We implicitly know, for instance, the fundamental laws of logic. We understand that a statement cannot be both fully true and fully false at the same time and in the *same* sense – though we might not be able to explicitly express that truism that we know implicitly. Moreover, God gives us certain important conceptions, such as that of *perfection*, to name one of many. We can imagine a perfect being (God) or a perfect triangle, yet we have never had any experience at all of perfection. Some things come closer than others, but nothing in our experience is absolutely perfect (e.g., that exact-looking triangle printed in a geometry book will look somewhat the worse under a high-powered microscope). We must have been born with the idea as we could not have derived it from experience, and the only thing capable of giving it to us is the perfect being. Being benevolent, God gave us this store of *innate ideas* – actual presuppositions, or schema, for forming our thoughts. The intricacies of this scheme, which has since been developed in far greater detail, need not detain us. What is important is that Descartes is recognizing that our human makeup gives shape and direction to our thinking. We are not *just* rational beings. Nor could anything be that alone.

Because we are creatures of the mental realm, we are more than mere animals. Animals, Descartes tells us, are *only* bodies. They have no consciousness. If they did, they would be able to use language to some degree, as even the least intelligent person is able to do. (Remember, this was a long time before hand-signing chimpanzees or the systematic study of cetaceans.) Having no consciousness, animals have no thoughts at all, rational or otherwise; they have no desires or intentions; and they can feel no pain, for pain is a condition of a consciousness. An animal is merely a complex machine that, in various ways, affects and is affected by its environment. The yelping of a kicked dog is only a physiological reaction. It is no more indicative of pain than is the squeaking of a wagon wheel in need of grease. Lacking a mind, it lacks anything with which to experience pain. There is therefore no point in trying to minimize an animal's experience of pain. I am by no means unique in finding that sort of thing hard to accept. Indeed, the biological sciences have long since concluded that animals do have experiences of some sort, including painful ones. For that reason, the treatment of animals in research is an important bioethical issue. However, as we are concerned here only with humans, I shall not pursue these points.

For our purposes here there is worse to come. Descartes had to accept and find some way to account for the palpable fact that we, as minds, do have some sort of contact and causal interaction with bodies. If we perceive the world in any way at all, that is the world bringing about some change in our consciousness. You and I may perceive the sunset differently but something has to be getting through to us if we can know that the sunset is there at all. Caffeine, alcohol, or hot and humid days affect our thinking. Our thinking affects the physical world, as when we decide to move our hand. If things mental and physical *can* affect one another, then the independence of mind from body that Descartes was keen to defend was endangered. Sensibly, he argued that the affects of alcohol and the like occur on the physical side of the gap between the physical and the mental. Instead of the mind being affected, what is affected by the alcohol (or other substance) is that portion of the physical with which the mind communicates.

Obviously, that does not solve the problem. It only pushes the difficulty one step further back. If mind and body are radically different things that cannot interact with each other, then how can the mind have even a distorted communication with the physical world? How could it ever even come to suspect that the latter exists? Notoriously, Descartes proposed that there was just a *tiny* bit of interaction through the pineal gland. That gland is located right at the center of the brain, neither on one side nor the other, in what looks like a good spot for minimal interaction to have extensive consequences. This is renowned as being one of the worst theories in the history of philosophy. If interaction between different substances is a logical impossibility, then just a *little* interaction is as impossible as a lot. Descartes was able to convince himself of things that I consider extremely implausible, but I doubt whether even he gave full credit to the pineal-gland theory. Perhaps we should interpret it as meaning something like this: "Well, whatever! It must be possible in *some* way, because it does happen."

Here Descartes is faced by what has been a perennial problem for mind–body dualisms. Wanting to preserve mind from being reduced to matter and following the laws of matter, he assigns it a different form of reality out of the reach of the laws of matter. However, if mind and matter really are separate from each other, then they cannot have even the most benign form of interaction (such as your seeing your own hand in front of you, or wiggling a finger). Nevertheless, if we do bring mind and matter back together in some way, we again run the risk of mind being taken over by matter. If influence from matter can come in via the pineal gland (or in any other way), it might then be a controlling influence on our mind. Descartes has a further problem here. He concedes that animals, purely material beings, can do a great deal in the way of sensing and responding to the world. So too do we, with our eyes, ears, autonomic (reflex) nervous system, and the like, all being on the body side of the pineal gland. Evidently, there is a lot on that side. Moreover, he has to concede that alcohol, caffeine, and other substances can in some way influence our thinking, again presumably on the body side of the pineal gland. If so much is going on in the body, might it be that *everything* we had thought mental is occurring in the body? Maybe what we really need at this point is a different way of looking at things.

Our Heritage from Descartes

There is much for which we owe thanks to Descartes and his philosophy, quite apart from his contributions in physics and mathematics. Although we might smile at his pineal gland, or feel outraged by his view of animals, Descartes played a major role in (re)establishing philosophy as a secular and rational undertaking. Not only did he give us confidence that we could carry on the enterprise, he gave us a useful method for doing so. The method – that of breaking a problem down into its simplest parts and starting from the most fundamental truths, then working toward a solution one rational step at a time – has served us well in countless things, from organizing dinner parties to establishing a national electricity grid. Science still finds guidance from his method as well as use from his mathematics. Nonetheless, may we sometimes still be led astray by his methods and assumptions?

In our heritage from Descartes we have, together with the useful elements, inherited some serious difficulties. His conception of the human self, together with the assumptions built into his method, continue to plague us in many respects. This is not least true in connection with bioethics. Let us start, as did Descartes, with our self. As he presents it, our very essence is to be a conscious, thinking, rational choice-making being. In the form of innate ideas we are given some shape and direction for our thinking. Nonetheless, our thinking requires more shape and direction than can be provided by innate presumptions and schema for forming ideas. To see how this is so, we need to look beyond his particular conclusions concerning the self and take a more critical look at the method that Descartes bequeathed us.

The faults of Descartes' method continue to lead us astray in several important respects. These are fundamental systematic flaws, not just a matter of making particular logical errors or jumping to unwarranted conclusions. Perhaps the most problematic is the atomistic assumption that the world, and our thoughts about it, divide into simple separate facts. It is rather as if the world were composed of individual facts and their compounds. So too our thoughts are held to come in simple units and their compounds. When we think clearly, our thoughts fit their respective facts. This view of things can be an adequate and useful approximation for particular purposes. The more mechanical the subject matter, the better it works. However, it is a view that is mistaken in more ways than one, and it is particularly misleading in application to living beings.

In the first place, note that we take an active role in generating distinctions of many sorts and, as it were, drawing dotted lines across the face of reality. Reality, however, is under no necessity to divide according to our superimposed lines. The features we note and the distinctions we draw tend to reflect our interests, values, and motivations (as individuals or as a culture). We distinguish qualities, things, mental states, actions, and so on according to what we find the most useful for us. Famously, the Inuit (Eskimos) have a large number of words for snow. Other people in other places draw their own distinctions as suits them. Where they draw their lines may be inconsistent with where we find it convenient to draw ours. Any thoughts we have, any concepts we have, and any language we use depend on the distinctions we draw. There is no uniquely right way of describing the world, and all ways reflect our interests and values. Moreover, if we were purely rational beings – without desires, attitudes, preferences, aversions, or any other of those arational and therefore nonrational things – in what terms could we think rationally? Why would we think at all? We would need an *arational* desire for something or other to be moved to think about anything. Even an impulse toward self-preservation serves arational ends. An indifference to life is apathetic, certainly, and not characteristically human, but it is not illogical. Again, if we had a desire to pursue knowledge for its own sake – which Aristotle held we did – that in itself would still be an arational desire. Furthermore, any terms in which knowledge could be pursued would reflect some arational set of concepts and desires. In a later century, the seventeenth, David Hume declared that "Reason is, and ought only to be, the slave of the passions, and can never pretend to any other office than to serve and obey them" (*A Treatise of Human Nature*, Book 2, Part 3, Section 3). We have motivations of many sorts upon which we may act, rationally or irrationally, but what moves us to act in even the most rational manner is arational. We may use reason to control or alter passions, as when we try to control anger or become more compassionate, but even here we are using one arational motivation to limit another.

To put it in more modern terms, even the most powerful and infallible of computers would not actually *do* anything until some instructions were programmed into it. Otherwise it would just sit there useless. *Purely* rational considerations can never motivate us to act. Thus, not only do our passions give our reason its very shape, they also remain in mastery over it. Descartes' conception of the self is therefore too thin. There is more to us than just the conscious rational surface. Part of us is a powerful arational engine driving the whole.

Descartes also misleads us by presuming that our thoughts can be divided into distinct and separate units. Can we take them one at a time or in abstraction from the thinker? Only to an approximation. Our thoughts are part of an encompassing system. It is not just that each thought must be in the context of other thoughts. Our thoughts are in the context of our sensations, perceptions, emotions, expectations, and every other aspect of our entire being, conscious or unconscious. What we are is part of what we think. Each person is unique, and each person's thoughts are unique in character. My belief that tomorrow is Friday will differ somewhat in character from your belief that tomorrow is Friday (e.g., "Then I can go party!" or "Another lonely weekend coming up"). In communication we can never convey exactly an identical idea from one person to another. Nor need we do so. To communicate adequately we need to bring about an understanding adequate to the purposes at hand. The problem is not to eliminate fuzziness around the edges but to keep it from interfering. I need not grasp everything *Friday* means to you to get the message that it is not Thursday. We communicate far more effectively if we realize that meaning does not reside solely in words but in the intentions of the language user in a particular circumstance at a particular time.[7] That is true whether we are speaking or writing or whether we are listening or reading. In bioethical situations in particular, we have to allow for the fact that we are dealing with whole people, with their beliefs, doubts, fears, ignorances, and aspirations. Common sense, when we have paused to heed it, has long since told us that. It has also told us that there is more to medical matters than specific symptoms and conditions, specific responses, precise answers to precise questions, and particular choices. I am offering no radically new conclusion here. I shall offer biocentric conceptions, with their more holistic conception of the self, as meeting a need that has long been recognized.

Relatedly, Descartes' scheme also leads us astray in our thinking about the natural world by assuming that facts can exist and be understood in isolation from one another. Not only do we import our interests and values into what we take as being independent and objective, we also err by assuming that facts can really be separate from one another. Again, that is one of those things that can be approximately true and a workable presumption for certain purposes. Even so, everything is to some degree connected with everything else, and often in surprising ways. That being so, it is impossible to do only one thing at a time. Consequences continue to radiate through the system, perhaps snowballing as they go, sometimes rebounding unexpectedly to our inconvenience. This is particularly a consideration in connection with living systems. We are learning that the living world is like a web such that when one strand is plucked, the whole web vibrates.

One sad example of the consequences of not knowing this is provided by the early European settlers of Australia. Good Enlightenment people that they were, they tried to improve the country a bit at a time. It seemed obvious: A land with rabbits is more valuable than a land without them, the difference being exactly the useable value of the rabbits (for food, fur, or sport). That was elementary logic. Unfortunately, it did not work out that way. The rabbits altered the character of the whole system, much for the worse. The more we learn, the more we learn how intricately things are interconnected. It is no longer surprising to the thoughtful that hair spray in New York can cause skin cancer in Australia.

So too with a living human being. What affects us in any aspect of our being may well affect us in some other. We have learned that any drug or treatment affects the whole system, and that every drug has side affects – though we may lose sight of that in our quest for particular pills for particular ills. We have also learned that supposedly purely subjective states of mind may concretely affect one's physical condition – as well as vice versa. Possibly, any aspect of the physical or the mental – not that we can fully distinguish the two – can affect any aspect of either. Again, these are things we already know

---

[7] I go into these matters in far more detail in my *Focusing on Truth* (New York and London: Routledge, 1992). The topic need not detain us here.

but often forget. Mechanical thinking is not an adequate tool in thinking about humans in bioethical situations. There is a lack here to be rectified. In later text, I propose biocentric conceptions as helping to meet that need. First, however, there are further problematic aspects of our cultural heritage to be noted.

Further Questionable Heritage

From our cultural past, from Aristotle and Descartes particularly, but with many other inputs, we have inherited a broad conceptual scheme. This cultural heritage continues as part of our thinking about the world we live in and about ourselves. In many ways it has served us well. We have made much practical progress by using atomistic methods of analytical reasoning. We are also able to point to moral progress in some areas. Respect for the individual person, and his or her ability to think sensibly and choose his or her own values, is central to our modern consciousness – even when it is honored in the breach. This is certainly superior to approaches that neglect the individual's moral status in favor of some supposedly greater good. Nevertheless, our cultural heritage also leads to problems. Central to the difficulties are some inherited concepts that can be expressed in terms of an array of ordered contrasts:

Form	Matter
Mind–Soul	Matter
Universal	Particular
Rational	Nonrational–Emotional
Morality	Sentiment
Objective	Subjective
[Hu]man	Nature
Male	Female

(Such a list of contrasting pairs could be extended to considerable length.) There is thought to be a sharp contrast between the left- and right-hand members of each pair. In each case, the one listed on the left is the more real, the more rational, and the more valuable. It is the standard by which the other is judged. Accordingly, it is appropriate that it should dominate over the one on the right.

I find much about which to be suspicious in this scheme. I question the sharp distinction between the left and right columns, and I question the presumption that the one side is inherently superior to the other. Take form and matter, for instance. Form, to be in the world, must be in matter (or at least in something). Granted that matter, to be of value (to us), must be shaped appropriately, there is also the correlative point that whatever rational form we might have in mind, we cannot make any practical use of it unless there is something to which to apply it. Even on the most abstract level, our reasoning about the world, if it is to be of value (to us), must conform to fact. For its part, all matter, even a wispy cloud, has some form, even if it is not form that we find apparent or interesting. If form and matter are so mutually dependent, how can it make sense to say that one is superior to the other? Again, as we have previously noted in consideration of Descartes, the objective cannot be separated from the subjective, or the rational from the nonrational. Ideas and values are implicit in our facts. The supposed contrasts break down, as does the supposed value differential between them. We should also carefully note that the arational is very, and very importantly, different from the irrational. This point is obscured if we lump them both together under *nonrational.*

Perhaps the worst feature in this heritage in its effect on our thinking, and most in need of exorcism, is the limited and mistaken conception it gives us of ourselves. There is more to the difficulty than objective–subjective and rational–nonrational. There is also more to it than the supposed dichotomy in characteristics and value between male and female that also breaks down, for reasons that have been well canvassed elsewhere in recent years. Still, these conceptions and contrasts linger on to haunt the recesses of our thinking. We often distort reality, including the reality of our own being, by trying to fit things into separate and preformed categories. Among the worst in its effect on us is our culturally inherited conception of the mind-self and the contrast between [hu]man and nature. Thereby we become alienated from the world around us and from our own selves. We are our complex beings with immense depth. We are not even in essence purely mental beings. Our mentality is only the surface of our in-depth being. These faults are in addition to the faults of mechanistic thinking in terms of atomistic facts, truths, inferences, and knowledge.

We are complex living systems in a complex world, much of which is itself a complex living system. Although we are indubitably individuals, we are also part of the world, without definite or absolute boundaries physically, biologically, morally, or socially. Our lives are bounded by our bodies only to a poor approximation. We need a better understanding of our lives, our selves, and our good to cope effectively with the demands of human life. Not least we need a better understanding to help us cope with the pressing and increasing demands of bioethical problems. These are points that I develop in subsequent chapters.[8]

* * * * *

Thus far I have largely been presenting matters in the light of secular conceptions. We certainly are living beings and, as part of our living, we

---

[8] In passing, I point out that unless we can think of our environment in terms that are less atomistic and more holistic, we will continue to have problems coping with or even comprehending our environmental problems. That, however, is not the subject of this book.

are intelligent beings, cultured beings, and much more. Perhaps, though, we humans are far more than that. Perhaps we are spiritual beings, beings with souls. Indeed, it may be that on the most fundamental level, each of us *is* a soul. Certainly such beliefs are widely held, with a history going back well beyond our ability to trace. If we are spiritual beings, then it may well be that our spiritual well-being is far more important to us than any mental or physical aspect of our biological well-being. This would raise important issues and have important implications in bioethics. Implications would extend not only to the morality of abortion and euthanasia, which are the topics that most immediately spring to mind, but also well beyond.

It is not easy to specify what a soul is or what is good for one. Being of a different order of reality, souls, we are told, cannot be materially harmed. The most that might happen is that material events might help or impede a soul's spiritual career, perhaps by obstructing its doing whatever it is in this world to do – such as by killing its body and so depriving it of the means. Or material events might lead it in spiritually right or wrong directions. We might perhaps be led to disobey one of God's commands, with seriously adverse consequences for our spiritual welfare. If, for instance, as the Jehovah's Witnesses believe, God has forbidden blood transfusions, then one (particularly one aware of the prohibition) might prudently avoid them, even at the cost of biological ill health or certain death. We may disagree with Witnesses about whether theirs is the correct interpretation of Scripture or about whether any writings actually are truly Scripture, but the belief itself cannot be refuted. What God does or does not forbid, and what implications this might have for the well-being of our souls, are not matters that can be resolved through secular reasoning.

As it happens, I do feel a considerable interest in matters spiritual. I mention them in connection with bioethics not least because people in life-and-death situations often do develop a keen interest in such matters. However, my primary concern here is to approach bioethics on the basis of secular reasoning in the light of our character as living beings. Our spiritual beliefs, however high might be their divine authority, apply to us, if at all, as what we are, which includes our being alive. Somewhat later, I shall offer some further thoughts on souls (though certainly not a comprehensive discussion of their nature) and on what their significance might be for bioethics. In the next two chapters, however, we look at some of the traditional systems of ethics and traditional conceptions of our good – and at their difficulties, particularly in application to bioethics. In no small part these difficulties spring from inadequate conceptions of our nature and needs as living human beings. I offer biocentric conceptions as helping us to alleviate these difficulties.

3

Some Background

Approaches to Ethics

Ethics is concerned with the evaluation of our actions and their motivations as they regard others (and perhaps ourselves) for good or for ill. We ask how we ought best to act. What effects on others and us are good or bad? What actions are right or wrong? What are the considerations by means of which we may decide? Many ethical discussions focus on questions of what moral rules we ought to follow, how we are to validate them, and how we ought to apply them in particular sorts of difficult situations. In this chapter I begin by discussing what, in recent times, have been the two most influential approaches to ethics. One approach has been primarily concerned with getting good results; the other has been primarily concerned with the rightness and wrongness of actions, and with our inviolable moral status as persons. Both of those approaches, in their many manifestations, have their flaws. Some, though not all, of these flaws have been significantly compounded by incorrect and inadequate conceptions of ourselves and our good – and, more generally, compounded by other dubious elements in our intellectual heritage. It is generally taken for granted that what we are and what is good for us is sufficiently well understood, and that the important issues concern what we ought to do about it. Ethical discussion on such a basis can still be very fruitful and valuable. Nevertheless, as I argue in subsequent text, traditional styles of ethics must be augmented, and transformed, by more adequate conceptions of ourselves and our interests. With more adequate conceptions we might hope to retain and reconcile the better features of each approach. Subsequently I attempt to do that. I also hope to offer some justice to some of the less influential approaches to ethics. I then try to show how better conceptions, particularly better conceptions of self and our good, together with a better understanding of the nature of ethics and moral action, can help us to cope with difficulties and complexities of bioethics.

Utilitarianism

The fundamental inspiration of utilitarianism is the commonsense conviction that we ought to act so as to bring about the best consequences. That conviction has always been popular, but utilitarianism became articulated as a social and philosophical force at what seemed just the appropriate historical moment for it: during the Enlightenment Era, at the time of England's Industrial Revolution. There was then great and growing faith in our capacities as rational beings to understand the world in which we live, to rationally improve our ways and conditions of living, and thereby to produce the best outcomes.

Jeremy Bentham (1748–1832), reformer and philosopher, famously proposed that we approach ethics and politics as a rational applied science, using carefully engineered means to bring about beneficial ends. Instead of living according to the precepts of ancient authority, worn-out tradition, or historical accident, we should plan our lives with the same rational care that a manufacturer puts into planning a factory for producing some desired product. Much as the manufacturer tries to operate so as to produce the greatest value of some commodity for the least expense, we ought to act so as to bring about the greatest surplus of benefit over cost. Individually we ought to act so as to bring about the greatest benefit. As a society we ought to determine what will probably bring about, as it is usually put, "the greatest good for the greatest number," and then act accordingly. He makes this claim:

[The greatest happiness principle] states the greatest happiness of all those whose interest is in question, as being the right and proper, and the only right and proper and universally desirable end of human life. (Bentham, *Introduction to the Principles of Morals and Legislation,* Chapter 1, Section 1, note 1)

We are to try to amass as great an amount of utility as possible, much like building up a healthy bank account or gross domestic product.

When we are faced with a choice of actions, we calculate the probable results of each alternative. We are to take into account the intensity of the good and its duration, its certainty, its purity (the degree to which it is unpolluted by bad), its fecundity (how productive it is of further good over the long term), and the extent to which the good is shared by others. What it all comes to is that we are to act so as to bring about the maximum probable good overall and in the long run, taking into account the probabilities and whatever possibilities there may be of adverse consequences. We are to consider as many possible consequences as we can trace, then act in the way that *probably* has the greatest overall balance of utility over disutility. (This may lead us to accept disutility, such as the pain of some dental or medical treatment, for the sake of greater overall benefit.) Of course we can never be entirely sure what will have the best consequences as these cannot be matters of certainty or exact calculation. As a practical man, Bentham was well aware of that. Still, as a practical matter, we must take some course of action, even if it is to do nothing (usually a poor choice), so we are to do whatever, on the evidence, seems to offer the best probable results. In the face of fact and uncertainty, we are to proceed much as might a prudent investor calculating how to get the maximum probable return on an investment, taking into account risks as well as potential benefits.

Bentham himself was a hedonistic utilitarian. He followed in the footsteps of Epicurus, holding that *the* good is pleasure. Pleasure is the one thing everyone values in and of itself, and so it is the one *intrinsic* good. Any other good, when it is good, is so as an *instrumental* good, an instrumentality toward pleasure. Money, health, social position, food, poetry, and everything else is good only insofar as it brings about pleasure. The hedonistic conception of our good is severely inadequate, as I have already argued. An important thing to note, though, is that utilitarianism is not necessarily linked to hedonism. We tend to link them because of Bentham's influence. Utilitarianism calls on us to maximize the good, whatever the good happens to be. We may decide that it is some form of well-being more encompassing than pleasure, or that it is the satisfaction of prudent desires, or that it is some intuited but indefinable property, or that it is anything else. Possibilities, though not plausibilities, are unlimited. Facetiously, one might even imagine a sadomasochistic utilitarian trying to maximize pain. Whatever the good is, utilitarianism calls on us to bring about as much of that as possible.

Utilitarianism has some very strong points in its favor. In insisting that ethics has to do with the impact of our actions on others, and on ourselves, and that good ethics have good results, utilitarians have a valid point that must be incorporated, in some form or other, by any plausible system of ethics. Moreover, utilitarianism gives us a rationale for reform, for us – individually and collectively – to improve our ways of doing things or to abandon them in favor of something better. The English utilitarian reformers of the nineteenth century had a very commendable record in bringing about needed improvement. They made strides in penal, legal, and political reform, as well as improvements in public education, health, and sanitation.

Still, there is a down side to utilitarianism. In fact, there is more than one down side. Of course any form of utilitarianism will have a challenge in determining *the* intrinsic good we are to maximize. If there are more than one such good, how are we to weigh them in a common scale? (There is, moreover, a line of thought that holds that there is nothing whatsoever that is of intrinsic value, morally, except right or wrong actions and the intentions with which we perform them.) Even were we able to reach agreement about what our good is, there would remain substantial disagreement about the claim that the thing to do is to try to bring about the maximum probable amount of it. Is perhaps there more to morality than just trying to maximize something? For example, we may ask whether we are distributing the utility fairly. We may question whether anyone's rights are being violated. An associated complaint against utilitarianism is the claim that it uses people as mere instrumentalities for maximizing some other intrinsic good.

Various examples might be urged that make a pure utilitarianism look implausible or downright immoral. In *Hard Times*, Charles Dickens satirizes a rigid, supposedly rational utilitarianism through the character of Mr. Gradgrind, a "man of facts and calculations," and the schoolmaster McChoakumchild, who teaches these ideas in the classroom. A girl, Sissy Jupe, laments to her friend, Louisa, that she (Sissy) is just too stupid to understand what is being taught:

"Mr. McChoakumchild . . . said, Now, this schoolroom is a Nation. And in this nation, there are fifty millions of money. Isn't this a prosperous nation? Girl number twenty, isn't this a prosperous nation, and an't you in a thriving state?"

"What did you say?" asked Louisa.

"Miss Louisa, I said I didn't know. I thought I couldn't know whether it was a prosperous nation or not, and whether I was in a thriving state or not, unless I knew who had got the money, and whether any of it was mine. But that had nothing to with it. It was not in the figures at all," said Sissy, wiping her eyes.

"That was a great mistake of yours," observed Louisa.

"Yes, Miss Louisa, I know it was, now. Then Mr. McChoakumchild said he would try me again. And he said, This schoolroom is an immense town, and in it there are a million of inhabitants, and only five-and-twenty are starved to death in the streets in the course of a year. What is your remark on that proportion? And my remark was – for I couldn't think of a better one – that I thought it must be just as hard upon those who were starved, whether the others were a million, or a million million. And that was wrong, too."

"Of course it was." (*Hard Times*, Chapter ix)

Dickens, through Sissy, was hammering home the point that there is more to getting good results than just maximizing utility. There are issues of how widely and fairly distributed are the costs and benefits. Even one individual is morally important. Dickens is using heavy satire to make these points. McChoakumchild is even more of a caricature than Gradgrind usually is. Nonetheless, during this era of Enlightenment Rationalism and Industrial Revolution, there were many who had great difficulty grasping the points being made. Society at large accepted some conditions as necessary, and it could conceive of no way to give people a bigger slice of the pie than that of making the pie bigger.

Unlike McChoakumchild, philosophical utilitarians were concerned for the public benefit, often passionately. The reforms for which they worked did produce many good results – yet how could fairness and justice be brought into the utilitarian equation? Can these things be quantified on some scale, as utility is claimed to be? One doubts it. Even if one could find a measuring scale, there is still the problem that maximizing more than one independent variable is not something that it is logically possible to do on any systematic basis. If it comes to a choice between greater utility or greater equity of distribution, how are we to trade one off against the other? How are we to set the moral rate of exchange? Without some workable rate of exchange, things get badly out of kilter. We can, to be sure, work out trade-offs between different goods in terms of how much of one we might prefer to how much of another. We may prefer some degree of equality of distribution to some greater degree of utility. This really has the effect of reducing all goods to one fundamental good, that of preference satisfaction. As we shall see in the next chapter, such an account has its own serious problems.

Consider a further problem: Suppose we could maximize utility through an act that (seemingly) victimizes someone in a way that is most unjust. Perhaps we might lynch some unpopular person to please the angry multitude. Again, we might conceivably have to conclude that the pain of one person murdered to make a "snuff movie" is outweighed by the pleasure of viewing sadists (who prevent the film from becoming known to the general public). Or let us take a hypothetical example from bioethics. It often happens that people die who might have lived, had suitable organs or tissues been available for transplant. In other instances, although it is not a matter of life or death, the quality of lives might be greatly improved. Transplanted corneas would be a great boon for some people. There just are not enough organs or tissues available. Some day we may solve the problem, perhaps through cloning and tissue culturing, but what do we do right now? Perhaps we could select one patient in the hospital, through a selection procedure that was as fair and random as possible, and sacrifice that person for the greater good. Heart, kidneys, liver, lungs, blood vessels, bone, corneas – there are all sorts of bits that might be utilized. The net score would be one person dead who would otherwise be alive, several other people who would be alive when otherwise they would be dead, and the added bonus of there being yet others whose lives were improved. This seems ghoulish, to say the least – in an almost literal sense – and no one proposes it seriously. However, can such a suggestion be faulted on utilitarian grounds alone?

Utilitarians are quick to point out that there are disutilities to this sort of thing as well. For one thing people are likely to worry about going into the hospital, for fear that they might be carved up for spare parts. That is an irrational fear, of course. This utilitarian procedure would (by our hypothesis) actually improve our chance of survival. Still, people being what they are, they would worry. They might even be worried about walking alone near a hospital, particularly after dark. Such a procedure would certainly offend the sensibilities of those who think it to be an infringement of rights and an immoral outrage. Even if they are not utilitarians, their utility must also be taken into consideration. Other disutilities might be found. As for Sissy Jupe's concerns about breadth and equity of distribution, there too the concerns of even nonutilitarians such as Sissy must be taken into consideration. The envy and resentment of those who get a smaller share of the benefits are disutilities that also must be accounted for. In addition, there are further disutilities caused if those with smaller shares get annoyed enough to upset the entire system – and so on.

Utilitarians are keen to argue that if all relevant considerations are taken into account, the consequences of utilitarianism will not really be repugnant. Certainly they are correct in pointing out that there are likely to be disutilities to these unattractive things – though I often suspect that sometimes the books are being juggled in order to get the desired bottom line. Occasionally, useful acts of injustice can be gotten away with. In any case, critics of utilitarianism – and there are a goodly number of them – consider that appealing, accurately or otherwise, to contingent side effects is fundamentally misguided. They take the point of view that some ways of acting toward people are wrong, and other ways are right, quite apart from any validation by calculation of consequences.

Critics of utilitarianism often suggest that its seemingly unfair and unjust aspects are merely symptoms of a flaw that runs deeper and is quite basic to utilitarianism: that it regards only utility, rather than people, as being of fundamental value. Whatever happens to people is irrelevant except insofar as, and to the extent that, it affects the balance of utility. We, and any other consideration, may be sacrificed on the altar of utility. Things that are nasty and unfair are undesirable *only* as they lead to disutility. Let us now consider the principal approach alternative to utilitarianism, an approach that attempts to put the emphasis back on those beings whose welfare is at issue.

Deontological Ethics

Instead of morally evaluating actions solely by weight of their anticipated consequences, deontological ethics puts the emphasis on the nature of the action itself. Whereas utilitarian ethics is concerned with rightness and wrongness in terms of the *goodness* or *badness* of the intended results, deontological ethics revolves around *right* or *wrong* actions. Deontological ethics does not dismiss results as irrelevant. What we do to others is very relevant. Murder, for example, is wrong because of what it does to people. However, it is not wrong because the balance of pros and cons comes out that way, it is wrong because one ought not to treat people that way. Deontological ethics (from the Greek word *deon*, meaning "that which is binding, necessary") emphasizes rights, duties, and principles. We must respect others appropriately. But what validates rights, duties, and principles? Answers vary, and many rationales have been offered. Perhaps God or God's delegates give us a divinely sanctioned set of shalts and shalt nots. Perhaps we are able to learn, through intuition or some other means, that some actions have the quality of rightness or wrongness to them. (For example, double-crossing a friend is a rotten thing to do.) Perhaps we can somehow establish moral principles on the basis of rational principles and mutual respect. All of these ideas have been tried.

Person of the Enlightenment era that he was, Immanuel Kant tried to establish morality on a sound rational foundation. Like the laws of mathematics, chemistry, or physics, a minimum condition for moral law to be valid must be that it is universally true. It should hold unequivocally that it is right to do X in circumstance, and not just that it is right to do X in Y *if* the contingent consequences of doing so happen to turn out in a favorable way. Kant called, that is, for categorical imperatives rather than merely hypothetical ones. There were to be no *if*s about it. Valid moral principles are those that could be rules applied universally. We must ask, "What if everyone followed that rule all the time?" (A proposed moral rule that failed this test would be defective. That we should always be truthful is an acceptable rule, for instance, whereas that we should always tell lies or commit mass murder are not.[1]) This is a minimal logical requirement, but there is more to it than that. Matters do not just center on our own actions and outcomes. We are never to try to assume some privileged position for ourselves, in exemption to the universal moral rules. There seems to be something quite profoundly right within this approach.

What Kant has given is a rationalistic analogue of the Golden Rule of Jesus: *Do unto others as you would have others do unto you.* Like Jesus, he points to an understanding of *why* certain ways of treating others are wrong. Jesus, however, was not the first or the only person to teach this. This is an idea that has appealed to people around the world as going to the very heart of morality. Previously, the Jewish rabbi, Rabbi Hillel, had offered such a teaching. Independently, and considerably earlier, in China, Confucius (K'ung Fu Tse, 551–479 B.C.) had offered a more elaborate version. His fundamental insight is that moral rules are validated with reference to our own heart and our own standing as beings worthy of moral respect, with equal consideration to be extended to all. This came to be known in China as the Principle of the Measuring Square: using oneself as a standard to assess our treatment of others. Confucius gave this explanation[2]:

The man of *jen* [goodness or human-heartedness] is one who, desiring to sustain himself, sustains others, and desiring to develop himself, develops others. To be able from one's own self to draw a parallel for the treatment of others – that may be called the way to practice *jen*. (Confucius, *Analects* VI:28)

---

[1] If we all followed the lying rule, that would just attach a *not* to every sentence. We would all learn to understand that so the truth would always be understood and no lies accepted. Liars depend on the truth commonly being told. The murder rule could not be followed because the human race would be exterminated before we all complied.

[2] For further and very readable discussion, see Fung (1948). I rely on Fung for the Confucian quotations.

Here the great Chinese sage offers us what is clearly a version of the Golden Rule. He goes on to usefully augment it with a negative version:

Do not do to others what you do not wish yourself. (Confucius, *Analects* XII:2)

Thus, from within us, a true moral standard is always available:

Is *jen* [human-heartedness] indeed far off? I crave for *jen* and lo, *jen* is at hand. (Confucius, *Analects* VII:29)

We are to treat all others (that is, all other persons) as beings who, equally with ourselves, are worthy of moral respect; they are not to be treated just as means to our own ends or as a cog in some great machine. Kant expressed that idea, explicitly equating other persons with rational beings, in a further-elaborated version of his fundamental doctrine of acting on universal principle:

Rational nature is . . . an end in itself. . . . The principle: Act with reference to every rational being (whether yourself or another) so that it is an end in itself in your maxim, is thus basically identical with the principle: Act by a maxim which involves its own universal validity for every rational being. (Kant, *Groundwork of the Metaphysics of Morals*, AK 437–438)

As social beings we derive benefits from other people, finding them useful for many of our purposes. We cannot get along without them. What is wrong is to use them only as means to some end, to the exclusion of treating them as being ends in their own right. Following Kant's principle would, for instance, rule out any scheme for sacrificing living people as a source of spare parts, quite apart from any utilitarian computation of consequences. Indeed, there would be a considerable number of human rights that could not be overridden.

* * * * *

Before we continue with deontological ethics, I offer some brief thoughts about putting the Golden Rule into operation. That we ought to act toward others as we would have them act toward us in like circumstances is a moral insight of the first magnitude, and employing it appropriately can be of considerable practical importance in bioethical applications. Nevertheless, there are better and worse ways of interpreting and applying this insight. We do well to ask what we would want and how we would feel were we in the other person's shoes. It is too easy, though, to make that an issue of how *we* would feel in the other person's shoes – we with our particular wants, needs, attitudes, and prejudices. That characteristically leads to insufficient insight and empathy. Laws against sleeping in city parks would not inconvenience me in the slightest, but what about those who have nowhere else to sleep? Perhaps this seems too obvious. How about the physician in California who put a blanket DNR (do not resuscitate) order on all the occupants of a rest home, without bothering to go through particular cases? If they were there, what did they have to live for? That was to impose his own priorities, not recognizing that some people there might have things that, for them, were worth living for. What is good for *them* in their shoes? A better approach is to try, so far as we are able, to imagine ourselves as that other person in those circumstances, with his or her own particular wants, needs, attitudes, prejudices, and life values. This can require some effort and may require developing a skill. As I develop it, the ideal toward which we must strive is to give due weight to the interests of each, in proportion to the interest (regardless of how different or similar an interest is to our own).

More Deontological Ethics

John Rawls, in his *A Theory of Justice*, offers an alternative formulation of deontological ethics that, like Kant's, centers on the conception that we must treat everyone with equal fairness and have general principles that do not admit of self-interested exception and that do not allow anyone to be victimized for the sake of anyone else.[3] This is a *contractarian* ethic, based on a hypothetical mutual agreement – what we *would* agree to, were we wise and totally impartial. In an explanatory myth, Rawls calls on us to imagine that we are disembodied beings in some celestial waiting room, prior to our taking our place on earth. We know the laws of science and the general principles of economics and other social sciences, but we are behind a "veil of ignorance" that keeps us from knowing anything about the life we are to take on earth. We do not know whether we are to be male or female, intelligent or dull, black, white, or any other hue; we do not know if we will be robust or sickly, or prone to mental disorder, and certainly we do not know what position we are to have in society. Before we go into the world we, from this "original position" behind our veil of ignorance, are to draw up rules for how the world is to be governed. The point of this imaginative scenario is that rules drawn up in such a way would not be subject to distortions based on selfish personal interests; they would be fair to all. Such rules are fit for us to adopt in this world. At what sort of rules would we arrive from this detached position? Prudence dictates that we would draw up rules that ruled out any form of bias, self-interested exception, or unfairness. We would not allow society to be sexist because we do not even know if we are to be male or female. Similarly, slavery and any form of racism would be ruled out, as would be any great disparities of wealth, power, or privilege, as we would not know ahead of time what our own circumstances might be. We would want to rule out any possibility that we would get the rough end of things. Moreover, any inequalities would have to benefit the least favored. We would also want a good range of social services, medical and other, as

3 John Rawls, *A Theory of Justice*, rev. ed. (Cambridge, MA: Harvard University Press, 1999; originally published by Harvard University Press, 1971).

we might be the ones to need them. Rawls then is pointing toward a way by means of which we could work out how fairly and justly to treat others as, to put it in Kant's way, ends in themselves. Just what the final set of rules would come to is a big question that would require an extended answer (and has received more than one). I cannot pursue that here, but clearly the result would be a set of rights and guarantees, and duties on the part of individuals and society as a whole to respect them. Many of our obligations and entitlements would be relevant to bioethical issues. The intention of Rawlsian ethics is to provide fairness and justice, and those living in a society that did function according to such rules presumably would have fairly good lives. Such a system would therefore have considerable utility. This, however, is by no means a utilitarian ethic as our entitlements may never be sacrificed to utility against our will.

There are problems about Rawls's contractarian approach. As with any system of firm rules, there is doubt that they can do justice to all (including extreme) cases. I shall offer more on that shortly. Specifically relevant to Rawlsian ethics is the question of who is to be behind the veil of ignorance; who is to be legislating from that original position? That is a myth, of course; the fundamental issue is that of whose interests are to be taken into account and provided for with rigorous and scrupulous fairness. Is it all humans and only humans behind the veil? If it is just a blind lottery whether we are to be born male or female, black or white, intelligent or dull, and all the rest of it, why is it not a lottery whether we are born human or animal? Why should the interests of even the most limited and undeveloped human have precedence over those of a chimpanzee who might be far more intelligent and socially skilled? The chimp did not ask to be born a chimp any more than the human asked to be born with brain damage. The issue here, that of the moral status of nonhumans, is highly important in its own right, but it need not detain us in our inquiry into human bioethics.[4] Of central importance for our purposes here is the question of what *humans* are to be behind the veil.[5] What about one who is to become a neonate with only a brainstem, having neither capacity for consciousness nor prospect of a long life? Does that entity have a right to life? Or does it have a right not to continue with such a life? Or are we to hold that it is not a person at all and so with no moral standing at all? Then there is the matter of those who *might* become

---

[4] Whether animals, and possibly other living entities, even species or ecosystems, are entitled to moral consideration is a question of great moment. It not only concerns our relations with the world around us but an investigation of the issues also sheds light on why we humans are entitled to moral consideration.

[5] There are technical problems about how we are to provide for future generations – as if they already preexist, when in fact how we live affects which possible people will go on to make up future generations. Issues here also go well beyond bioethics, but certainly there are bioethical issues in connection with genetic engineering, where we might make momentous decisions about how future generations are to be constituted.

persons in the fullest sense. Do their rights commence when they are born – or at some previous time? We can frame the myth of the veil in different ways to get different answers. The nonmythical issue here is that of whose (or what's) interests are to count, and on what rationale. Rawlsian ethics only cuts in when we have decided (or presupposed) that issue and go on to ask how we are to treat with fairness all beings with moral standing. How we settle the question of who counts will affect what conclusions we come to about abortion, for instance, and about individuals with diminished capacities. Once we have settled on who has moral standing, contractarian ethics is a complex matter of determining what our interests are and how they are best to be protected. Always it is a matter of our just entitlements.

A Tension between Utilitarian and Deontological Ethics

It has long been an observation of mine that however inclined people might be toward utilitarianism in other instances, people veer quite sharply in a deontological direction when they are in need of medical care. They want their *rights*. They are to be treated for their own utility, not any other. Patients demand it and society as a whole demands it, and the healing professions – in principle, if not always in practice – proceed on the basis of firm rules, rights, and duties. No harm is to be done to the patient, that is the first thing, and steps are to be taken for the patient's benefit and with the patient's concurrence. Confidentiality and other rights are to be respected. Deontological ethics, be it Kantian, Rawlsian, or any other plausible version, lends itself to this approach.

It is not just a matter of ruling out treating people contrary to their interests or against their will (let alone chopping them up for useful parts). There are many experimental research projects that would most probably produce extremely valuable results – valuable not only for knowledge for its own sake but also valuable in terms of providing the knowledge to save other lives. Perhaps it would be many other lives. These projects, however, are quite risky for the experimental subjects. Institutional Ethics Committees (and the one I am on is no different) are *very* careful about such proposals. It is not just a matter of getting people to sign an agreement. Nor is it just a matter of obtaining free and informed consent, though there is a great deal that has to go into those things. Any risk must be proportional to the potential benefits. Cancer patients might be offered a risky experimental drug if it offers a corresponding and reasonably possible benefit, and if they are informed of the alternatives and freely consent to the risk. We do not ask, nor do we allow, people who do not stand to benefit to take such substantial risks as that. They might be asked to take slight risks, perhaps, but not substantial ones. (There are *slight* risks to anything, even taking a tiny blood sample.) This is based on the principle that allowing them to take such risks would be unfairly exploitative of them. Boundary lines here are vague and debatable, obviously, but the principle is that any person who is an experimental subject, or potential subject, must *always* be protected even in the face of great social or medical utility to the contrary.

Nevertheless, there remains an unresolved problem in ethics, or at least a problem that has not been resolved to general satisfaction. This is the problem of reconciling or adjudicating between the conflicting (or apparently conflicting) demands of utilitarian and deontological ethics. The utilitarian or deontological ethicist can, with high degrees of plausibility, point out the mote in the other's eye. The motes are there. An exclusive reliance on utilitarian considerations can lead to results that are, at least apparently, unjust, unfair, a violation of rights, and just plain *wrong*. Nonetheless, an insistence on absolute rights or inviolable principles can lead to consequences in which, at least apparently, it would be grossly immoral to acquiesce. Rules can be too rigid, even to the point of being a serious infringement on the legitimate moral claims of others.[6] These weaknesses in our leading approaches to ethics have had serious and practical implications for bioethical applications. A major but, I believe, ultimately unsuccessful attempt has been made to resolve the difficulty, an attempt that I discuss in the next section. Here I try to elucidate what the difficulty is and why it raises immense practical difficulties in bioethics.

We have already shuddered at the gruesome hypothetical situation of killing people to quarry their body parts for the use of other living people. The situation is not entirely hypothetical because it has sometimes been done illegally, though there is no controversy about it being grossly immoral. Other cases, both actual and hypothetical, are more controversial. Consider the case of Robert McFall, who was dying from aplastic anemia, a rare form of bone-marrow disease. He needed a marrow transplant to fend off what would otherwise be almost-certain death. Only one suitable potential donor could be found, a cousin, David Shimp. Marrow donation involves having a needle inserted into the hip bone, with a small amount of a viscous fluid being drawn off from the marrow. A person undergoing this procedure would have a somewhat sore hip for a short while but would not need hospitalization. Furthermore, it would not take this person's body long to recover from the slight loss. After some hesitation, Shimp refused to make the donation. (This seems to have been due to pressure from Shimp's wife, acting from unclear motivation.) In the legal case of *McFall v. Shimp*,[7] McFall sought a court injunction forcing Shimp to submit to further tests and, in due course, to the donation.

---

[6] A notorious poser concerns whether we should lie to the homicidal maniac about the whereabouts of an innocent person whose hiding place we know. We shall see other examples in the following text.

[7] *McFall v. Shimp*, 10 Pa. D. & C.3d 90, Court of Common Pleas of Pennsylvania [United States], Allegheny County, July 26, 1978.

When I have discussed this case in classes or seminars, there has been nearly universal agreement that it was morally wrong of the potential donor not to make the donation, *but* that it would also be morally wrong of society to legally compel or otherwise force people to give up portions of their own body against their will. Human rights must triumph in the face of utility. The court decided likewise. The plaintiff lost the case and, three weeks later, his life.

The presiding judge, Judge J. Flaherty, explained the decision he found himself forced to make:

The common law has consistently held to a rule which provides that one human being is under no compulsion to give aid or to rescue.... Our society, contrary to many others, has as its first principle, the respect for the individual, and that society and government exist to protect the individual from being invaded and hurt by another. Many societies adopt a contrary view which has the individual existing to serve the society as a whole.... For a society which respects the rights of one individual, to sink its teeth into the jugular vein or neck of one of its members and suck from it sustenance for another member, is revolting to our hard-wrought concepts of jurisprudence. Forcible extraction of living body tissue ... would raise the specter of the swastika and the Inquisition, reminiscent of the horrors this portends.

... it is ordered, adjudged, and decreed that the request for a preliminary injunction is herewith denied.

The tension between deontological rights and utilitarian considerations is here seen as tension between individual rights and utility, social as well as individual – with reference to the bad consequences of allowing utility to triumph over individual rights. The law then takes a strongly deontological stance. Although this case occurred in the United States, it is relevant to any legal system drawing on English Common Law. More broadly, it is relevant to any system of government that claims to be based on individual rights.

There are also real-life moral and legal problems about postmortem donations of organs or tissues, involving apparent conflicts between utilitarian considerations and rights or duties. People frequently do die who might have lived had they received organs or tissue from other people who had already died. There is general, though not universal, agreement that matter should not be taken from the deceased contrary to their known prior wishes. Some utilitarians might disagree (though we would have to take into account disutilities from the outrage of next of kin, or of others who might be offended). Does the living person have a right to the organ that would save his or her life, or do the rights of the deceased or (the latter's) next of kin prevail? What if the deceased potential donor has not expressed a prior preference? Deontologists may differ among themselves. Should there be a law that holds that people are *presumed* to consent, unless they make a prior statement to the contrary? If we enforce that law, we run the risk of inadvertently violating the deceased's actual prior preferences. If we go the other way we risk violating a presumed right to life. On my own driver's license is a notation that I am willing to be a donor of anything that might be useful. Even that does not settle the issue, as it is policy where I live to seek consent from the surviving next of kin. This is said to be for ethical reasons. Sometimes consent is withheld, and the potential recipient dies. Does this violate the rights of the late would-be donor and those of the suffering patient, or does it respect the rights of the living kin? (Or is it selfish avoidance of responsibility on the part of a medical fraternity that has more to fear from living kin than from dead donors or dead potential recipients?) This does not appear to be something that can be settled entirely by considerations of utility – saving lives versus offending some people. Yet how are we to temper utilitarian with deontological considerations? I am not going to offer a solution here. I do point out that utilitarian and deontological ethics alike can look morally suspect when overly insisted on.

Consider a further range of cases: Instead of bone marrow, suppose I were requested to give a donation of blood. Let us imagine there is something special about my blood: Once I was bushwalking in the Northern Territory and was bitten by a poisonous snake. I just barely survived, and now my blood has an antivenin for that kind of snake. That is not true, nor is it biologically very plausible, but let us imagine it. Perhaps two liters of my blood are required to save the life of one person bitten by that species of snake. The donation would not kill me, but it would weaken me, and I might have to spend a day or two in the hospital to recover. Again, when I have asked people, there has been general agreement that I ought to make the donation but that I ought not be compelled to. Suppose now that the amount of needed blood were only one liter, which would bring about less discomfort for me. Or suppose it were only a half-liter, which is the standard amount for a blood donation. I have given dozens of such donations without ill effect (that is true), but this time I refuse. Should I be compelled? No? What about one-fourth of a liter (and so on down to a half-teaspoon of blood)? Now let us imagine that instead of saving one life, my blood would save two lives – or it might save those of a whole troop of Boy Scouts. As we keep going in this direction, utilitarian considerations become more persuasive in the face of rights that appear increasingly petty. Can utilitarian considerations *ever* override my right to bodily integrity? Legally, the answer remains no. Morally, is there a point where one has an obligation to override a trivial instance of someone else's right if it would prevent some far greater harm? The question itself is a utilitarian question, but considerations of utility become harder to deny. Let us use the philosopher's prerogative and keep imagining even more extreme cases.

Suppose that at some critical juncture a single strand of hair from my head could be used to prevent the total destruction of the human race and all life on earth. (Imagine some story about my special DNA.) Would it be morally justified to take a strand of my hair contrary to my wishes? My refusal to cooperate would arguably be a matter of my using others as a means to my own meanspiritedness. According to law, though, unless we have entered into a special relationship with the other, we have no obligation to save or to rescue, whatever the consequences. Must deontological moral principle follow civil law all the way to such an extreme?[8] Is there no point at which the increasingly important needs of others take moral priority over my increasingly trivial rights?

At one extreme, utilitarianism condones consequences that seem morally repulsive and in need of being ruled out by deontological restraints. At the other extreme, deontological rigidity of principle can lead to consequences that seem no less morally repulsive and in need of being overridden by a commonsense insistence on avoiding catastrophically bad consequences and bringing about good ones. It is not just the problem of where do we draw the line. To be sure, drawing lines can be very important in practice. As well as problems in practical line drawing, though, there are fundamental conceptual difficulties here. There seems to be something fundamentally wrong with both utilitarian and deontological ethics that could lead to such quandaries. Actually, there is more than one thing wrong. I believe that part of the difficulty is our misconception of what we are, as bearers of rights or beneficiaries of utility. Another part of the difficulty is our misconception of our own good. Biocentric conceptions can contribute to the resolution of each of these difficulties. There are also important issues about the nature of morality and moral action. Of these matters, I offer more in later text. First let us look at what has become the leading and best-known attempt to reconcile utilitarian and deontological ethics.

Rule-Utilitarianism

In general, we want to bring about the best results possible. Even so, it can be very comforting to have some firm and solid "no-ifs" rules and principles in place, ones we can get along with and rely on. Several moral philosophers have proposed that we combine these features, doing so on what is fundamentally a utilitarian foundation. However, instead of calling on us to do that particular act that is most likely to maximize the good, such philosophers call on us to follow that set of moral *rules* that, if we follow them, is most likely to bring about the best results. This is *rule-utilitarianism*, as distinguished from *act-utilitarianism*. Following a rule may, in a particular instance, give poorer results than doing that act called for by act-utilitarianism. Nevertheless, proponents of rule-utilitarianism maintain that overall and in the

---

[8] Here our concern is to explore the issues of differing ethical systems. In a later chapter, I offer a discussion of "slippery slope arguments," according to which if we allow one course of action we will inevitably permit other, highly objectionable, courses of action.

long run, it will bring about greater good than will act-utilitarianism. To continue our lugubrious examples, following the rule that medical patients (or other people) are not to be killed for utilitarian purposes, are not to be subjected to any form of treatment contrary to their will, and are not to have research experiments performed on them without their informed consent will bring about better results. There is utility in security, and in a sense of security, and rule-utilitarianism has the advantage there. More generally, rule-utilitarianism can rule out at least the most blatant or identifiable forms of unfairness or injustice. It offers a very attractive combination of utility together with a welcome recognition that we also need rules and a recognition that we *do* need to give people the security of being recognized as ends in themselves, as having rights.

There are difficulties with rule-utilitarianism. One difficulty is that it tends to collapse into act-utilitarianism. Suppose there were some individual case wherein doing a particular act, as recommended by act-utilitarianism, would give a probable result of greater utility than that given by following the rule recommended by rule-utilitarianism. Perhaps we could add an *additional* rule, to the effect that rules should be followed or else overridden, according to which would lead to the better probable results. Following this proposed rule would lead to better probable results in some instances, and, by definition of the rule, could never lead to results that were probably worse. Accordingly, by definition of rule-utilitarianism, we must accept the rule as one of our set of morally optimal rules. However, having this rule puts us right back into act-utilitarianism: We are to do whatever act probably leads to the best results. That leaves us with all the problems of act-utilitarianism – and this problem gets worse.

Suppose that you, being an upstanding rule-utilitarian, with like-minded people around you, are in charge of a major hospital. Naturally you would indignantly repudiate any suggestion that any of the rules protecting patients' rights might be overridden for any reason. Making such statements would have the better consequences. At the same time, as a rule-utilitarian, you want to bring about the best consequences for your patients (and whosoever else might be affected). You follow the rule that a rule is to be broken when breaking it leads to better consequences. (You take into account, with all the other aspects, the possibility that the rule breaking might be detected – in which case you would plead ignorance, inadvertence, a computer error, or whatever.) Following that rule, you take good care not to take any chances when there is an appreciable chance that you will be detected. Being a hypocrite does not worry you because being a hypocrite – while scornfully repudiating hypocrisy – is morally justified when validated by good consequences. Once in a while you see a chance to get away with breaking a rule for good effect. It might even be a matter of carefully bringing about a well-assessed death in order to replenish the organ bank, though it would usually be something far less drastic. If we really are dedicated utilitarians, this is okay with us. However, if we found act-utilitarianism repugnant, we again find ourselves confronted with those features we found repugnant. We have some protection from the repugnant features in the form of rules, but these rules may be dissolved at any time by a rising tide of hypocrisy sanctioned by utility. With rule-utilitarianism, as before, I have a strong suspicion that we are trying to exclude on the strength of rubbery appeals to contingent utility that which ought to be excluded for noncontingent moral reasons.

In spite of its difficulties, rule-utilitarianism, as it has been developed by various moral philosophers, does offer a potentially useful means of balancing two rival approaches to ethics. So long as we do not push it to the point of collapse, such an approach can be of great practical value. If utilitarianism can accommodate, or partially accommodate, the idea that there ought to be some firm no-ifs guarantees that we can rely on – and if it can do this while giving us an assurance that things will probably turn out for the best – then so much the better. Certainly there is considerable utility in sound rules, particularly in the difficult and often urgent practical applications of bioethics. There have been various other attempts to have things the best of both ways, but this is not the place to canvass them in detail. What I have tried to illustrate is how both of these general approaches to ethics tend to go off the rails on one side of the track or the other. None of the attempted articulations of rule-utilitarianisms seems fully able to mix or reconcile utilitarian and deontological ethics while retaining what is of value in each – and avoiding what is worst in each. I believe that we need to take a very different approach to ethics, with several matters requiring reconsideration. One among them is the role of moral principle.[9]

Utilitarian and deontological approaches to ethics, at least as they have been predominantly developed in the past, both seem to me to be crippled by an inadequate conception of what a person is. Each approach takes a person as being some sort of an individual unit-thing. Each takes us as individual unit-things *having* something. Utilitarianism considers us to be unit-entities capable of having utility – pleasure, preference satisfaction, or whatever else it might be. The objective for us, individually or collectively, is to get as much utility as we can. Deontological ethics sees us as being ends in ourselves, entities with inviolable moral status and our own ends to be respected, and it elaborates some surrounding network of rights, duties, and principles regarding those entities. I believe that there are *two* fundamental mistakes being made here concerning our self and our good. These

---

9 There is, of course, more to be said for or about rule-utilitarianism than I have covered here. Indeed, this concept has roots going back to John Stuart Mill's *Utilitarianism.* Those who wish to consider rule-utilitarianism further may consult Richard Brandt's *A Theory of the Good and the Right* (Amherst, NY: Prometheus Books, 1998) or R. M. Hare, *Essays on Bioethics* (New York: Oxford University Press, 1996).

mistakes, jointly and severally, cause unnecessary confusion and misdirection. There is the mistake of taking ourselves to be things of some sort, rather than as the dynamic ongoing life processes we are. Compounding that is the mistake of taking our interests and ends as being something else, something *had* by us, rather than as being features of what we are. Having an interest in something *is* being a certain sort of life process, with whatever we have an interest in tending to maintain that life process healthily. Being that sort of a life process is to have that interest, and having that set of interests is to be a life process of that sort. Ethics has to do with respecting the lives of others appropriately. I attempt to do justice to these points in subsequent chapters, where we shall take a closer look at life and our good. Now, though, there are some further points to be considered concerning our approaches to ethics.

Morals and Principles (and God)

It is commonplace that a moral person is one who acts on principle. Instead of following perceived self-interest or personal inclination, the moral person follows the moral law. In bioethical applications, with so much at stake, it is especially and often urgently true that we need the guidance of clear and sound principles, with clear and sound rationales for applying them. A feeling that there are no proper and determinate rules in place can cause considerable discomfort and sense of insecurity. (Moreover, there is an ever-present fear that a poor principle or an inappropriate scheme of interpretation might send us careening down a slippery slope to some moral calamity. Slippery slopes are the subject of a later chapter.) At this point, I would pose the important – but often neglected – question of the relationship between sound moral principle and right and wrong. Are acts right when they are called for by sound moral principle and wrong when they are in violation of such a principle? Or are sound moral principles sound because they do distinguish accurately between right and wrong? If the former is true, that is, if right and wrong are determined by sound moral principle, then the primary task of ethics is the very difficult one of identifying the correct moral principles. A necessary step is to ask what makes sound moral principles sound. It would be going in a circle to claim that sound moral principles are those that distinguish right from wrong, because right and wrong are here held to be defined by moral principle. But perhaps things properly are the other way around. If sound moral principles are determined by what is right and wrong, then the problem is to shape the moral principle to fit the moral terrain that it is intended to be about. Then the important first step, also very difficult, is to identify that rightness and wrongness that makes sound moral principles sound. For my own part, I hold that moral principles are to moral reality as maps are to terrain. The former, when good, represent the latter well. If this is so, then, as virtue ethics suggests (see the subsequent text), a moral person is not so much one who acts on good moral principle as one who is inclined to act in accordance with what makes good moral principles good.

Let us return to the first alternative, that right and wrong are determined by moral principle. What features do sound moral principles have that make them sound, and actions in accordance with them right? Kant, as we will recall, held that sound moral principles are those that we could take as universal law, binding in all instances. That does rule out many things that ought to be ruled out (e.g., armed robbery) and rules in many things that ought to be ruled in (e.g., kindness). However, some things can be taken as general principles that nevertheless seem morally neutral (e.g., some rule about stepping on cracks in the sidewalk). Even worse, some principles (e.g., one enjoining us to torture people to death on their fiftieth birthday) seem quite immoral in spite of its being logically possible to take them as universal principles. Only a perverse will could will such a principle to be a universal law. As well as being universal in form, a sound moral principle must also have an acceptable moral content. That is, it must be something a rational person could actually *will* to be a universally applied law, and that is presumed to exclude such things as the torture rule. Kant, accordingly, came to the principle of treating others as ends in themselves, with all of us having equal standing before the moral law and none of us to be made victim. But that moral principle, worthy as it is, is not validated by its logical form alone. Similarly, the rules that Rawls would advocate from behind the veil of ignorance are to be validated in terms of their absolute fairness and respect for the individual.

If moral principles cannot be validated by their logical form alone, is there any other way in which they could be validated – except in terms of the rightness or wrongness of what they are about? Here we are asking whether there is some *other* alternative, so that rightness and wrongness can be defined in terms of principle without our going in a circle. If the logical form of the principle is not enough, and if it is not the moral content of the rule that validates it (because we are making the assumption that things are the other way around), then the only other possibility seems to be that what validates a moral principle is its *source*. Perhaps right and wrong are determined by the laws and customs of our society or the dictates of its rulers. Right and wrong then are whatever they say is right and wrong – be it mutual cooperation, slavery, sexism, child abuse, kindness, the law of blood feud, or anything else. As well as possibly good features, history (not to mention current reality) provides far too many examples of societies with seemingly very bad features. If morality is no more than compliance with whatever code is current, then no moral code, no matter how vile it might seem to be, could ever morally be in need of improvement. The moral lines it draws would be just the right ones, drawn in just the right places, as the code is definitive of rightness. Do we say then that slavery, or whatever else, is morally good for *those* people? Perhaps we should look for a better source of morality.

A widely shared view, both past and present, is that *the* moral rules come from a source that creates rightness (and thereby determines what wrongness is) as well as stipulates what the rules are. God creates the world and brings rightness and wrongness into being. God's law, therefore, is the moral law, and the moral law is God's law. In bioethical matters of life and death, we very often look to (our conception of) God's law for guidance. However, the comfort we take in the thought that rightness is created by divine fiat might perhaps ebb somewhat if we ask whether torture and general nastiness would be good if God so decreed. The conclusion that they would be good, if God so decreed, would follow repulsively but logically, if God's will arbitrarily established what was good and what was not. God's being good would mean no more than that God wills what God wills. One likes to think that God is better than that, and that to believe that God is good is to believe something positive about God that amounts to more than just believing that God is God.

Many years ago Socrates (again as reported by Plato, this time in the *Euthyphro*) asked a notably pious young Athenian about that. Are actions right or wrong according to whether they are in accordance with God's will? Or does God approve of them or not according to whether they are right or wrong? Socrates' respondent, Euthyphro, foundered on the question. One might sympathize, and not merely because Socrates was well known for being a difficult person to answer. However convinced we might be of the centrality of God to morality, it seems rather disappointing that morality and God's goodness should be so arbitrary. It does not seem right that there should be as little to goodness as that. It is possible to sidestep the difficulty, while maintaining the stature of God and of goodness, if we hold that God and God's goodness are all expressions of one fundamental reality, something that by its nature has to be and has to be what it is. One might equate God, goodness, and ultimate reality, or we might think of it some other way, but the fundamental point is that such a being must be inherently good. What noun we used would be of only minor importance.[10] What is important for our purposes is that goodness and rightness are not, except metaphorically, made, or made what they are, by edict. Nor are they made by being part of some codification. Rather – if God's goodness is to mean anything of actual significance – valid moral rules and principles are validated by their

---

[10] In orthodox Indian Brahmanism (or Hinduism), it is held that the highest and infallible truth (including the moral law) is contained in the Holy Word, the *Vedas*. Being absolutely true, and therefore absolutely real, the Vedas are necessarily existent and self-creating. In each world-cycle – every few billion years or so – people transcribe them anew, yet the only authors of the Vedas are the Vedas themselves. The Hindu gods themselves are thought to be derivative from that higher reality of which the Vedas are an expression.

content in terms of rightness and goodness. Accordingly, here I set aside theological speculation, however interesting or uninteresting that might be. Given that we can locate no plausible rationale for validating moral rules and principles in terms of their form or source, then, whether God is part of the story or not, the indication is that we must look to their moral content.

There are more than rules and principles with which we must be concerned in morality. Not only must our moral principles in some way be validated in terms of their moral content, we also must not allow our concern with the principles to eclipse our concern for that moral content which the principles are about. For example, as we have already noted, an excessive dedication to the principle of maximizing utility can lead to results that are clearly and grossly unjust to individuals. Similarly, an excessive dedication to deontological principles protective of individual rights can lead to results that are no less morally repugnant. Further, we would do well to bear in mind that morality is not fundamentally a matter of acting in accordance with principle but of acting in accordance with what valid principles are about. This has often been a particular problem for deontological ethics. For instance, the Kantian view calls on us to follow principles and, more generally, to treat others as ends in themselves. We are to do so because it is a matter of moral principle. If we show kindness and consideration to another because we care and sympathize, but not because of any dedication to principle, then in Kantian terms our act is morally neutral. Kindness and consideration are desirable, but they are only incidental to morality. Indeed, the morally good act must be done not just from dedication to what is a moral principle but from dedication to it *because* it is a moral principle. Merely following the rules is no more enough on its own than is compassion.

An implication of tying morality to principle is that animals, children, and, one suspects, most people most of the time are not capable of acting morally. This seems to me to be a very impoverished conception of morality, for reasons that are illustrated by the following instance. Experiments have been contrived wherein rhesus monkeys, alone in a cage, may obtain food only by pressing a lever.[11] They rapidly learn how to do that. Suppose now that things are contrived so that another monkey, in a nearby cage, receives an electric shock when the food lever is pressed. The monkey receiving the shock cries out in pain. The monkey with the lever still gets the food but soon realizes that the other monkey gets hurt in the process. What then does the monkey with the lever, and therefore the choice, do in that situation? The truth is that some monkeys do not seem to give a damn, obtaining

[11] The experiment is described by the experimenters, Stanley Wechkin, Jules H. Masserman, and William Terris, Jr., in their "Shock to a Conspecific as an Aversive Stimulus," *Psychonomic Science* 1 (1964): 47–48. James Rachels discusses some of the ethical implications in his "Do Animals Have a Right to Liberty?" in *Animal Rights and Human Obligations*, ed. Tom Regan and Peter Singer (Englewood Cliffs, NJ: Prentice-Hall, 1976), pp. 205–223.

food as frequently as before. Some people, undoubtedly, would be like that, too. However, the majority of the monkeys show reluctance to cause pain to the other monkey. Some will suffer hunger for a considerable period rather than injure their fellow monkey. That this is not blind instinct is indicated by the fact that the monkeys do vary so widely in their responses. Also experimentally ruled out as influencing factors are sexual differences, relative position in the monkey dominance hierarchy, noise levels from the afflicted monkey, and acquired aversion to the experimental apparatus. In contrast, some factors have been shown to be relevant. Monkeys are less likely to shock former cage mates. Moreover, monkeys that have been on the receiving end of the shocks are less likely to be willing to cause them. These findings suggest that those monkeys reluctant to cause shock are being compassionate. In the case of monkeys previously shocked, painful memory evidently sharpens their "do unto others" inclinations. Is the compassionate monkey's reluctance to cause hurt moral in character? We can make the answer *no* by definition if we define morality to require acting from respect for moral principle. The monkey does not use language and has no awareness of moral principle. Still, although it knows neither Golden Rule nor any principle about utility or ends in themselves, the monkey acts in accordance with what gives such principles content. It seems to me to miss much of the point of morality to dismiss a compassionate aversion to the suffering of others as morally neutral. As I see it, following even the best of rules is not the object of morality, or its essence, but is only a means to it. Once we allow ourselves to be open to the thought, other instances may suggest that the behavior of animals can have elements of moral significance. Dogs, notoriously, often seem to have a sense of justice or duty. Our concern, however, remains with human beings.

Rules and rationality do contribute greatly to human morality. Without careful and rational thought, even the best of motivations can go astray. Roads to many disasters have been paved with good intentions. Nonetheless, rationality cannot be enough. David Hume famously remarked that we cannot reason our way from *is* to *ought*:

> In every system of morality which I have hither to met with . . . the author proceeds for some in the ordinary way of reasoning, . . . when of a sudden I am surprised to find, that instead of the usual copulations of propositions, *is* and *is not*, I meet with no proposition that is not connected with an *ought* or an *ought not*. . . . as this *ought* or *ought not*, expresses some new relation or affirmation, it is necessary . . . that a reason should be given, for what seems altogether inconceivable, how this new relation can be a deduction from others, which are entirely different from it. (Hume, *A Treatise of Human Nature*, Book 3, Part 1, Section 1)

Yet no reason can be given. Elsewhere, Hume makes this remark:

> Where a passion is neither founded on false suppositions, nor chooses means insufficient for the end, the understanding can neither justify nor condemn it. It is not

against reason to prefer the destruction of the whole world to the scratching of my finger. It is not contrary to reason for me to choose my total ruin, to prevent the least uneasiness of an Indian or person wholly unknown to me. It is as little contrary to reason to prefer even my own acknowledged lesser good to my greater, and have a more ardent affection for the former than the latter. A trivial good may, from certain circumstances, produce a desire superior to what arises from the greatest. (Hume, *Treatise*, Book 2, Part 3, Section 3)

Even if rationality were a necessity for morality, it must be conceded that it cannot be sufficient. Some psychopaths are all the worse (more dangerous) for being highly rational. We need some appropriate attitude and inner motivation for acting morally, some commitment to some value calling on us to shape our lives and actions accordingly. Alternative approaches to ethics seek to overcome these difficulties. Instead of just asking what the rules should be like, perhaps we need to ask what *we* should be like. For a start, perhaps we need to *care*. We need to care not just about our own goals and outcomes; we need to care about others for their own sakes. The rhesus monkey, unlike the psychopath, was able to rise to that level.

Ethics of Care

In *Caring: A Feminine Approach to Ethics and Moral Education*, Nel Noddings suggests that the patriarchal voice of rules and principles should be balanced by the maternal voice of caring.[12] This is not to exclude men, but it is to call for an ethic that "is feminine in the classical sense – rooted in receptivity, relatedness, and responsiveness" (*Caring*, p. 2). As she explains (p. 83),

I am claiming that the impulse to act in behalf of the present other is itself innate. It lies latent in each of us, awaiting gradual development in a succession of caring relationships. I am suggesting that our inclination toward and interest in morality derives from caring. In caring, we accept the natural impulse to act on behalf of the present other. We are engrossed in the other. We have received him and feel his pain or happiness, but we are not compelled by this impulse. We have a choice; . . . If we have a strong desire to be moral, we will not reject it, and this strong desire to be moral is derived, reflectively, from the more fundamental and natural desire to be and to remain related.

This ethic of caring centers on concern and motivation. The one who cares "is wary of rules and principles. She formulates and holds them loosely, tentatively, as economies of a sort, but she insists upon holding closely to the concrete. She wants to maintain and exercise her receptivity"(p. 55). We must never allow regard for principle to lead us to lose contact with that caring that is the very reason for, and essence of, morality. Noddings

---

[12] Nel Noddings, *Caring: A Feminine Approach to Ethics and Moral Education* (Berkeley: University of California Press, 1984).

cites the biblical case of Abraham, who is commanded by God to sacrifice (kill) his son, Isaac. Abraham reluctantly prepares to do so, in obedience to higher principle, though God lets him off the hook at the last moment. She makes this statement (p. 44):

> The Mother-as-God would not use a parent and child so fearfully and painfully.... Mother-God must respond caringly to Abraham as cared for and to Isaac as cared-for, and she must preserve Abraham as one caring in respect to Isaac.
>
> Everything that is built on this sacrificial impulse is anathema to woman. Here, says woman, is my child. I will not sacrifice him for God, or for the greatest good, or for these ten others. Let us find some other way.

Certainly there is something grotesque about an ethic that requires us to turn our back on our loved and innocent child, to harden our heart, to stifle our impulse to care for those close to us. In Noddings's view it would be characteristically masculine rather than feminine for a god to ask such a horrible thing as child sacrifice, and characteristically it would be only men who would seek to comply and only men would write it up into Scripture. What we, men and women, need in our ethics is caring. Certainly Hume and Noddings are right in thinking that even the most well-constructed system of rules and principles would be of no moral use without some appropriate impulse or motivation, without caring. To use a post-Humean simile, it would be as uselessly inert as a fine computer without a supply of electricity. Still, we might be able to use such an object as a doorstop or as a paperweight. For their part, rules, when followed, may be of some use – but without caring they are not morality.

But is caring enough? In Noddings' scheme, those who lack empathy are not moral agents. They may learn and coldly follow a set of moral rules, possibly a very good set, because they find it convenient to do so. If they follow them without caring, though, then they are not acting as moral agents. I quite agree with Noddings that some form of regard and concern for others is morally requisite. Nevertheless, I must believe that there is more to morality than caring on its own. We may care about too few, or in the wrong way, and caring may give us little or no guidance in coping with moral dilemmas. It is a sad but persistent fact of human history that we often tend to distinguish between *us* and *them*, with our caring and sense of mutual obligation concentrated on us. The others are of reduced concern to us, if any at all, particularly when their interests conflict with the interests of those about whom we care more. The others may be outside of the family, or the tribe, or the nation, or the religion, or the race, or the language group, or on the far side of some other demarcation between us and them. In some locales in some times past, most white people would have found themselves unable and unwilling to care about black people as they did about other whites. They might have had some benevolent care, as they did for dogs and horses, but that would be a lesser concern.

Reasons might be advanced why we should develop an attitude of caring about people of other groups – but, then, they would be *reasons*, and the caring that resulted would be shaped by rationale. Without moral rationale, caring can become blind partisanship wherein we condone or condemn, support or oppose, according to the perceived interests of our own group. Most of the great atrocities of the twentieth century (and starting the twenty-first) have been done in the name of caring for particular others. Furthermore, caring alone is not always able to solve a moral dilemma. A woman may worry about whether to abort or to carry to term a pregnancy that would result in a child with a severe birth defect. She may care about the life within her, and about her family, and it may perhaps be that however she decides, her decision is justified as well as motivated by her caring. Yet in her caring she may desire intensely to make the morally right decision, to adjust her caring so as to do what is right. That requires more than just a reality check to confirm what in point of fact she does most care about. What she needs and strives for is a morally sound rationale for her caring. Because of considerations such as these, I draw the conclusion that at least sometimes there is more than caring required. Whereas rationale without caring is morally empty, caring without rationale is morally blind. Let us now consider a related approach to ethics, one that also emphasizes the importance of caring yet that seeks to incorporate it within a wider moral framework.

Virtue Ethics

Virtue ethics places the moral emphasis on the overall character and motivation of the person acting, and therewith on the overall character of the person's ways of behaving. Fundamentally, it is a matter of the person's way of *being*. It is claimed that it is preferable for us to have (be) a good character. Caring, as appropriate, is a very important feature of good character, but there is held to be more to having a morally good character than that. Unfortunately, the term *virtue* has come over many years to have quite negative connotations, suggesting that which is petty, prissy, or sanctimonious. Its opposite, *vice*, has come to have similarly petty connotations. Playing cards and drinking beer are said to be vices. Good (virtuous) little girls do so and so . . . ad nauseam. This is merely a degenerative trivialization of the basic idea. The fundamental conception, which must be elaborated, is that right actions are the sort of thing that people with sound character do. More properly, and certainly more relevantly to ethical conduct, *virtue* (from the Latin word *virtus*, meaning "worth") is strength, wholeness, and integrity of character, being the way a person's character is best to be. *Vice* (from the Latin word *vitium*, meaning "fault" or "defect") is defect of character, which tends to vitiate it. (Being vicious is to have a vice, a defect of character.) There has been a spirited revival of virtue ethics in recent times, and it certainly has applications to many contemporary ethical issues, including not least those of bioethics.

The immediate challenge is that of how we are to determine what it is to have a good character. Who is to say? One may doubt whether there is any one way in which it is best for a person to be, for, as we all know, one person's meat is another person's poison. Is there anything that is good for everyone? Which ways around do things go? Is a virtuous character fundamentally to be defined as one expressing itself through virtuous acts? Or can a virtuous character be defined independently, with virtuous acts being those expressing a virtuous character? For that matter, why should I *want* to have a good character? Broadly, the answer of virtue ethics (according to my interpretation, anyway) is that there are some ways of being that are preferable for us to have, by reason of what we fundamentally are, though this will be within broad limits and will vary between individuals. Virtuous acts are those expressive of a virtuous character. This is another one of those ideas that has roots going back to thinkers of classical times, prominent among whom was Aristotle. Before I pursue the topic of virtue ethics further, or further explore its roots, I intend to canvass some of the leading conceptions of our good and to explore the nature of life and health. On that basis I offer some further thoughts on virtue ethics. This will also allow me to defend virtue ethics, as I develop it, from major criticisms commonly directed against virtue ethics.

4

Some Background

Our Good

Many of our quandaries and difficulties in bioethics, as well as in other connections, are due to our having inherited inadequate or mistaken views about our good. Any ethical system must in some way take into account what is good or bad for us, harmful or beneficial. Bad assumptions lend themselves to bad ethics. Many ethical systems fail us by presupposing inadequate conceptions, or offering us none at all, leaving us to grope in a vacuum. Bad assumptions about what is good or bad for us have been as harmful as bad assumptions about what we are, and often enough they have been systematically related. Here I look at some of the leading conceptions of our good, and I attempt to show that they are wrong or inadequate because of flaws in the presumptions about our character and needs as living human beings.

We ought not to wrongfully harm others, an ethical system will tell us, and it will go on to draw conclusions about what sort of thing is or is not wrongful. However, that is only a part of "wrongfully harm others." What about *harm* and *others*? These shortcomings create difficulties for us in deciding how to act rightfully rather than wrongfully. For instance, is euthanasia or abortion harmful to the living being whose life comes to an end? Is life always good for a person? Can death ever be good for a person? Can it be neither good nor bad? We also need to ask what it is to be a person. Is a brain-dead human a person? Is a person in a genuinely irreversible coma still a person? Was an anencephalic neonate ever a person? Is an embryo in the early stages of development a person? If not, does harm or benefit to such a being carry any moral weight? Can anything be harmful or beneficial to such a being even if it were deemed to be a person? To be able to do ethics properly and apply it in practical applications, we would do well to have adequate conceptions of what harm or benefit to people consists of, and why. Whatever our answer, we need to ask why that particular answer rather than another one is the correct answer. If it all depends, on just what does what depend?

Later I discuss bioethical issues on the strength of more developed ideas about the nature of our good and how it has to do with our character as living human beings. First it would be useful to inquire into our good, or those things that have been proposed as our good. The results of such inquiry will give some shape, though not final shape, to the matter of what ethical approach it would be appropriate for us to adopt. If ethical behavior concerns how we are to respect one another's good, then it would be useful to know what we are respecting.

What is good for us? Many things can be good for us: food, shelter, winning the lottery, having people be pleasant to us, taking a nice walk, and much else. Nonetheless, these things are good for us, when they actually are good for us, only insofar as they are *instrumental* goods. They are useful toward more fundamental goods. Money or food is no value to us unless we can use it beneficially. What, however, is good for us in its own right and not as a means to something else? That would be an *intrinsic good* for us.[1] Historically, various things have been proposed as being our intrinsic good, and it may even be that more than one of them is good for us. Pleasure has been proposed as being our intrinsic good, as has the exercise of rationality, spiritual growth, and various other things – and there is the liberal-minded proposal that identifies each individual's good with the satisfaction of that individual's desires or preferences, whatever they might happen to be. Whatever it is that is proposed as being our good, we would do well to ask whether it is good for us because we value it, or whether we value it because it is good for us.

Pleasure and Other Mental States

I start by arguing against the view that our good is pleasure. I then go on to argue that our good is not to be identified with any mental state. In so doing, I intend not just to indicate that such views are incorrect but also to give some indication of what conception of ourselves is presupposed and why such views might be found attractive. Pleasure and other mental states may be very good for us, perhaps intrinsically so, but there is more to us than our consciousness. I maintain that we need an understanding of our good that goes deeper than our conscious surface. I intend through all this to lay the groundwork for a biocentric conception of our good.

That pleasure is, in itself, nice to experience, few would dispute. Inappropriate pleasures may lead to bad consequences, but pleasure itself is,

---

[1] Terms used, and the use of terms, vary considerably here. Some writers use the term *inherent* value. Some use the term *intrinsic* value for that the existence of which is of value in its own right. A thing of beauty, for example, may be said to be of intrinsic value – even though it be in the eye of no beholder. Here I am concerned with what is intrinsically good *for us*. Later I venture a few remarks about other sorts of value.

tautologically, pleasant. Many philosophers, from the ancient days of Epicurus to the twentieth century, have held that our intrinsic good is pleasure, with our mind and every other aspect of us being there to serve us in obtaining pleasure. From the earliest days a great many people have acted as if they thought that were true. Can we accept that pleasure is our intrinsic good? Pleasure and other mental states evidently do have a lot to do with our good. However, are mental states in and of themselves intrinsically good – or is that so only under some circumstances? Do we perhaps have more than one intrinsic good?

One of the traditional arguments against hedonism concerns the nature and source of pleasure. Suppose one could gain great pleasure from gross self-indulgence rather than from the moderation and contemplation advocated by Epicurus. Worse, we might imagine various *extremely* tacky forms of pleasure seeking, involving doing horrible and disgusting things to other people, though I will leave the details to the reader's imagination. Would pleasure obtained in such a way be as good for the person pursuing it as would be the same amount of pleasure from an untainted source? There is a strong whiff of ad hominem thinking about this line of argument. It puts hedonists in the position of seeming to condone loathsome practices, ones from which they as well as we would resile. A true hedonist, though, would have to say that, in itself, pleasure is pleasure whatever its source, and that equal amounts of it are of equal intrinsic goodness. What contributes to such pleasure will not be good for others adversely impacted, and it may lead to adverse consequences for the pleasure seeker. A life of gross self-indulgence, not to mention criminality, is riskier, and more in danger of disappointment and displeasure. Nonetheless, one might be lucky and have a pleasant life that way. It has happened more than once. If pleasure is *the* good, then such pleasure, and such a life, must be good for that person, however bad his or her living it might be for the rest of us. We may accept that, or we may look for another alternative.

John Stuart Mill, a nineteenth-century hedonist – at least he thought he was a hedonist – resisted such conclusions. To take the stock example, he found it difficult to accept that the pleasure derived from playing push pin was as good as the same amount of pleasure derived from reading fine poetry. (Push pin was a popular and seemingly harmless pub sport of the era. It was nothing nasty but nothing evidently uplifting either.) We must consider side effects, asking whether one or the other is the more productive of pleasure in the long run. Will one source of pleasure lead to frustrations? Will it lead to virtually nothing? However it adds up, a strict hedonist has to say that what is equally pleasurable is equally good. Mill broke with strict hedonism, holding that some pleasures are *better* than others. For those who can attain it, the pleasures of fine poetry are the better pleasures. Instead of our having some amount or another of one intrinsic good, this seems to indicate that there is an intrinsic good other than simple pleasure (or that some pleasures are better than an equal amount of some other pleasures). Perhaps that pleasure is not good in itself but good to the extent that it has some further quality. No matter how we figure it, if we accept Mill's thinking, we no longer have a strict hedonism.

For anyone who does accept strict hedonism – and none of the afore-mentioned considerations have logically refuted it – I have some *very* good news for them. It is possible to obtain lives with very high levels of pleasure, scientifically guaranteed. Our brains have pleasure centers (more properly, pleasure systems) that, when given suitable electronic stimulation, produce sensations of immense pleasure.[2] Laboratory rats that were fitted with plea-sure buttons that they could push themselves constantly self-stimulated, to the exclusion of all else. The buttoned rats would ignore food, water, and sexually receptive rats of the opposite sex until they blissfully died of hunger or thirst. When these buttons were tested on prisoners – they did things like that in those days – the prisoners were very pleased with it. (It is now thought unethical to experiment on people who cannot give free and informed consent.) Though they said that they could not adequately describe the pleasure, they reported that it was "even better than sex" – praise indeed from prisoners. If pleasure were the intrinsic good, then hav-ing a functional pleasure button would be the ideal condition. Many people have taken such considerations to indicate that although pleasure might be part of the story, there are other aspects to our good as well (possibly even including those things that Epicurus himself advocated as being conducive to our good).

In *Brave New World*, Aldous Huxley portrayed a society wherein people experienced very high levels of pleasure.[3] By means of social engineering, psychological conditioning, biophysical intervention, and genetic engineer-ing, there is created a society of people with very pleasurable lives. They have what they like, like what they have, and feel minimal levels of frustration or disappointment. I have even known one or two people who would have liked to move into that Brave New World. Most who have read the book have felt repelled by the empty pointlessness of the life depicted there and the

---

[2] Anecdotal material is available at considerable length (see James Olds' "Pleasure Centers in the Brain," *Scientific American*, 1956). A pleasure button is sometimes called a *Delgado button* because Yale University's Dr. Jose Delgado demonstrated (in the bull ring in Cordoba, Spain) how he could stop a charging enraged bull dead in its tracks through the use of a remotely operated device fitted to the bull's brain. Such devices affect the medial forebrain bundle in the amygdala, a part of the brain's limbic system. See *New York Times Magazine*, December 15, 2002, Section 6, p. 116. It is now considered to be very questionable whether we should perform experiments on people who are in highly dependent situations, as prisoners gen-erally are. Only people who give free and informed consent can properly be experimented on. I discuss this in Chapter 15, Ethics and Biomedical Research.

[3] Aldous Huxley, *Brave New World* (New York: HarperCollins, 1998; originally published 1932 by Harper & Brothers).

superficiality of the human relationships. Although the residents of Brave New World were conditioned to like their pleasurable lives, were they still missing something important? Or, in thinking that something is missing, are we perhaps reflecting our own conditioning? Again, there is something of the ad hominem argument here. Would we care to *admit* that we would prefer pleasure buttons or life in the Brave New World? If we do have such a preference, we cannot be refuted. The claim that pleasure is the good is not one that can be disproved. Nor can it be proved. Neither is it possible to prove or disprove a claim that the good is the color yellow, or pain, or anything else that one might name. What we can ask is how well hedonism, or any other theory, fits with the facts of human experience.

We may take or leave the hedonist's claim that pleasure is *the* good we ought to pursue. Some hedonists have gone further and tried to claim that, in point of fact, pleasure is the one thing we all *do* pursue. Every other goal we might have, they claim, is of value to us because ultimately it produces pleasure (or because we intend that it will). We are told that we seek our goals, whatever they are, for the pleasurable feeling of gratification their achievement gives us. Otherwise, they ask, why would we be bothered to pursue them at all? This is a claim that can satisfactorily be refuted. Although it is true that all or nearly all people pursue pleasure some of the time, and that some people pursue it exclusively, the plain fact is that many people *do* find some things sometimes to be preferable to pleasure. Perhaps they value artistic creativity or other forms of achievement, or love, or perhaps developing (or avoiding) a certain type of character. Many people are willing to suffer great pains, or at least some pains, for the sake of loved ones, or for the sake of some other value they hold dear. Pleasurable gratifications, if they arise at all, are usually valued but not exclusively. If Beethoven and Mozart were in pursuit of pleasure as the one good, then they were two of the most incompetent boneheads in history. The claim that pleasure is the one and only good is unprovable and implausible, but the claim that it is the only thing people do recognize as being good in itself is just plain false.

It is difficult to find any current thinker who maintains that pleasure is our one intrinsic good. Theoretical hedonists are very scarce these days. Could it be that our intrinsic good is a matter of one or more mental states *other* than (or in addition to) pleasure? Suppose that we could expand the range of available experience beyond the narrow pleasure offered by *Brave New World.* Suppose we could experience love, knowledge, achievement, or anything else of those things that people have desired in addition to pleasure and often in preference to it. There is a catch, of course: What I am proposing is the *experience* of those things. Following a suggestion by Robert Nozick (pp. 42–45),[4] let us imagine we had a virtual reality device that could be

---

4 Robert Nozick, *Anarchy, State, and Utopia* (Oxford: Blackwell, 2001; originally published 1974).

plugged into a person's central nervous system, giving that person not only experiences of great pleasure but also experiences of love, aesthetic contemplation, marvellous adventure, immense achievement, spiritual ecstasy, or anything else one might desire. The experiences would be qualitatively indistinguishable from the real thing. Moreover, the experience machine could be programmed so as to provide experiences appropriate to us and our responses as individuals. Within the experience field thereby generated we might act autonomously, and we might even act with moral agency and reciprocity in our dealings with those virtual people we experience, with no indication from our experiences that we are dealing with unreal people and unreal events. Beyond doubt, such a device would be very popular, could it be perfected, and such experiences would be of considerable value to us. Unlike the pleasure button, an experience machine is not yet technically feasible, but we can still perform our thought experiment. Already many people greatly value their experiences of virtual reality.

But could the experience machine give us the good life? Would we be willing to be attached to it on a permanent basis? Being attached would assure us a lifetime of just the sort of experiences we desire, yet we would be in a cubicle in some institution with wires and tubes inserted into us. It would be very safe there, and the vitamin-enriched, low-cholesterol nutrient solution, together with the attendant highly skilled medical staff, would keep us going for a very long time. We would be quite unaware of all that, once we were plugged in. Meanwhile we would be having a wonderful life with rich rewards and accomplishments, having a superb love relationship with a delightful but unreal person, taking pride in our wonderful but also unreal children . . . and all that. This is starting to seem like a sick joke – but is that reaction a decisive objection? If we do agree that it would not be preferable to have our real life shrivel up into almost nothing, then we commit ourselves to the view that there is more to our good than experiences or mental states, however valuable they might be. *If* our reactions are to be trusted, then perhaps our good must be connected with reality in some more robust way. How are we to decide?

While we are thinking about that, let us now consider another sort of example that suggests that our good is not necessarily tied to what we experience. This time let us approach it from the angle of what is *not* experienced rather than what is. Unlike the example of the experience machine, cases of this sort have, regrettably, occurred. Suppose that a woman is unconscious in a hospital. A male staff member slips into her room and, knowing that he will be undisturbed for a sufficient amount of time, proceeds to have sexual intercourse with the woman's unconscious body. She never learns of this, and it never makes any difference to her consciousness. There is no pregnancy, no infection or injury, not even a tiny bit of soreness. The man never tells anyone, not surprisingly, and no difference to any of the woman's mental states ever occurs. The man did not obtain her consent, but does this mean that the woman has been wronged, that her interests have been infringed? What difference, he rationalizes to himself, does it make to her?[5]

We can protest that what happened is contrary to what she desired, or to what she would have desired had she considered the question. We can also protest that the man *used* her, that he used her as a mere means to his own ends. There is no reason, however, why we cannot use another person as a means to our own ends – so long as the person is not negated as a morally significant being in his or her own right. I use the barber to get a haircut. He uses me to get money. I have, moreover, used a distant stranger in a public park as an object by means of which I might focus a pair of binoculars. I used her body as a means to my own ends. I doubt whether that distant stranger would have objected – but had it been contrary to what she would have preferred, that would have been of little moral significance, or none at all. It was, after all, a public park. What makes the difference moral? Both women were being used. Let us further assume that this was contrary to their would-be preferences, even those of the woman in the park. In neither case did it make a difference to the woman's mental states. Was the woman in the hospital really wronged?

I do wholeheartedly agree that the woman in the hospital was raped, that she was wronged. She was, I believe, used in violation of her best interests. But we can maintain that her good was violated only if there is more to her good, or harm, than her mental states. It cannot just be the experience of her desires being honored or violated, for that would be a mental state she never had. If it makes no difference to her mental states, why should her desires matter? Why should they matter more than a distant woman's wish not to be sighted in a public park through binoculars, or perhaps her preference not to be thought of at all? We may conclude that the raped woman's desires about such things count in any case, or that the wrongness has something to do with her integrity as a person (which is what I believe), or we may give some other account – but if her interests have been infringed, then there is more to her good than mental states.

I have asked people, students and nonstudents, about these cases. There was near unanimity that the woman in the hospital had been wronged. There was more difference of opinion about the experience machine. By far the greatest number said they would not be willing to settle for life on the experience machine in the wired cubicle, exchanging their real life for the artificial one. Perhaps sincerely or perhaps for the sake of argument, some people opted for the experience machine. For unfortunate individuals who live lives of very poor quality, it might actually be preferable. Usually, the people I questioned have rejected the idea. Still, perhaps our rejection of accounts that define our good in terms of mental states might be dismissed

---

[5] In contrast, the woman who wakes up after the spiked drink characteristically does have consequences with which to cope.

as being entirely a matter of emotive prejudice. For that matter, we could dismiss as mere emotive prejudice the rejection of *any* account of the good that was not internally inconsistent or contrary to material fact. Even so, some accounts are better than others, more plausible in terms of human life. Accounts that would define our good exclusively in terms of our mental states owe us an explanation of why it is sensible to neglect the rest of life except when it affects our mental states, and with it, they owe us an explanation as to why our reaction of distaste at the prospect of having the other aspects of our life compromised is ill founded.

Let me now pose a further question: Which would be better, having those wonderful experiences on the experience machine, or having the same wonderful experiences in reality with all those nice things actually happening and for real? Remember, those experiences are qualitatively indistinguishable. One cannot tell them apart from the inside. Everyone I have asked has agreed that it would be better to have those things for real and not just have them in experience. To agree to that is to agree that there is more to our good than mental states. The *difference* between these cases is, by hypothesis, not a difference of experience. Therefore any difference in value between them, any difference at all, would presuppose that there is some value that is not entirely a matter of mental states.

Would it be possible to do justice to the presumed truth that our human good does have a great amount to do with our mental states, pleasurable and otherwise, while yet recognizing that there is more to us and to our good than the conscious surface? What I intend to develop in due course is a biocentric conception of our good that would do just that, finding our good not only in our mental states but also in our life a whole. Mental states are only part of us, though they constitute a major portion, and good mental states are only part of our good. Such an account might provide an attractive alternative, though it would still have to be subjected to critical scrutiny. Next, however, I prepare the ground further by considering a leading alternative account of our good.

Preferences and Prudent Desires

One alternative approach to characterizing our good has become fairly widespread. It stems from the recognition that people are different and value different things. There is no one thing we all value, certainly not pleasure or any other mental state. It may be that what is good *for us* is a matter of individual cases, varying from one person to the next. Accordingly, whatsoever we prefer is *our* good. This is very much in the liberal tradition of recognizing each person's autonomy and respecting people individually as the supreme judge of their own best interests. (Who do we think we are to tell other people what is good or bad for them?) In this tradition, it is held that the satisfaction of a person's preferences is what is good for him or her, and that whatever contributes to the satisfaction of our preferences is in our interests.[6] One may like the game of push pin, another may like poetry, and a third something else. Nor are they necessarily pursuing these various things as sources of pleasure. People may considerately prefer some things to pleasure: love, artistic expression, achievement of some sort, social approval, self-approval, some form of spirituality, and so on. People may be willing to suffer a great deal of displeasure to achieve these ends. Michelangelo certainly did not have a very pleasant life, nor did he seem to pursue pleasure with any diligence, but on this account we need not deny that he had a good life. Most important, this account puts *us* in charge, as the supreme judge and arbiter of what is good for us. However, our liberal impulse to accept people's choices as definitive of their good should not lead us to ignore the question of whether their choosing is what *makes* what they choose their good. As we shall see, the issue of the relationship between our good and our autonomy will be a persistent one.

It should be noted that this approach, like many other approaches to ethics, presupposes that we are conscious, self-aware, choice-making rational beings. In practice, however, including a great deal of bioethical practice, we have to bear in mind those who are exceptions to that presupposition or are only marginal. We may lose some of our capacities, temporarily or permanently. Infants and people with mental incapacities of one sort or another may never be able to form much, if anything at all, in the way of considered preferences. Or they may have preferences for what is clearly – at least in a prima facie sense – bad for them. They may entirely lack preferences against death or what is likely to lead to it. Does that mean that death is never bad for a person who lacks preferences to the contrary? Again, such people might have various desires, compulsions, obsessions, or ill-founded fears that disrupt their thinking. Might we increase their overall amount of good done by appointing some wise guardian to edit, augment, or overrule whatever preferences they might have? That seems like common sense for extreme cases, but it presupposes the centrality of some factor more fundamental to their good than their preferences.

If our good is constituted ex nihilo by our preferences, which are absolute and not contingent on some thing's happening to be good for us, then there

---

[6] Although this approach tends in a somewhat subjective direction, we must be careful not to interpret our terms in an overly subjective way. *Satisfaction* does not here refer to a cozy feeling of contentment. Something satisfies a preference if it is the fulfillment of that preference. This may or may not result in a feeling of satisfaction. This is the same sense in which it might be said that the number 3 satisfies the equation $(x^2 - x) - 6 = 0$. That is, setting x equal to 3 makes the equation come out right. Similarly, *interest* does not necessarily refer to something in which we happen to feel interested. In the sense used here, something is in our interests if it contributes toward our good. I have an interest in having an adequate intake of Vitamin C, and this would still be the case even if I did not care about vitamins or had never even heard of them. Taking enough Vitamin C in some form would satisfy that interest.

could be no way of inferring what would result in the greatest amount of preference satisfaction for a being who has expressed no preference. We could redeem the lack only if we could know what people would prefer, were they in a position to have a preference. On what basis could we do that? We could avoid the problem altogether by taking our good to be a function of our inherent well-being interests as living beings of the sort we are. Fulfilling those interests would in fact tend toward the satisfaction of our desires, but in this approach our good would not be constituted by our desires. I advocate this latter approach. Before I go into that, though, let us look at the other approach, the option that defines our good in terms of what we *would* prefer.

It is not just infants and the intellectually challenged who might have difficulties forming the right preferences. Quite typical people might be ignorant of some important fact. You may desire to drink a cup of coffee, not knowing that someone has put cyanide in it. Again, a person intellectually capable of forming high-level preferences may make a poor choice because of some mental aberration, anything from the brief lapses of attention to which we are all subject, on to full-blown psychosis. People with fetishes may desire to do very strange things to themselves. Some have desired to chop off perfectly good (and very useful) bits of their own body. A way around this difficulty of missing or inappropriate preferences is to formulate the principle so that our good is defined in terms of our *prudent desires*: what we would desire were we well informed and thinking clearly about things. As Peter Singer puts it (p. 80),[7]

... we make the plausible move of taking a person's interests to be what, on balance and after reflection on all the relevant facts, a person prefers.

In this account, ethics becomes not only subjective but subjunctive. What is decisive is not necessarily what we actually do happen to prefer. Our preferences may or may not coincide with our prudent desires. Strictly speaking, for his grammar to follow his logic, Singer should have explained his conception of the good in terms of "what . . . a person *would* prefer."

As a criterion of our good, this approach has much to be said for it. For practical purposes, it is generally better by far to accept people, at least minimally competent ones, as being the best judges of what is good for them. Attempts to impose society's wisdom on people may indeed make a few gains, but only at the risk of the severely negative effects of authoritarianism. Another advantage to this prudent-desire conception can be utilized to provide a very practical and effective instrument for adjusting social policy to the public good, via a process of cost–benefit analysis. How do we expend the public purse or otherwise set priorities to achieve the greatest amount of good for people? In essence, what we do is to determine, as best we

[7] Peter Singer, *Practical Ethics* (New York: Cambridge University Press, 1979).

can, everyone's preferences, from most to least preferred, set everyone's package of preferences at equal value, and then set our priorities and make our expenditures in such a way as to bring about the greatest probable amount of preference satisfaction. Accordingly, we fund hospitals, roads, sports, education, law enforcement, arts, and the like in such a way as to maximize the satisfaction of the public's diverse preferences. Within the health budget, we fund neonatal care, cancer or cardiac therapy, and so on, according to how we can obtain the best cost–benefit ratio in terms of the public's preferences. In this conception, the public good is an aggregation of individual goods, and it changes with it. Fortuitous events or successful campaigning (on the part of, say, the Anti-Cancer Foundation or advocates of women's health issues) can therefore result in changes not only in what the public interest is perceived to be but in what the public interest *is*.

As an account of our good, there may seem to be something excessively political about this conception. In its favor is the consideration that it may well provide a useful practical criterion for determining people's good, and it has the virtue of recognizing people's autonomy. It offers a means of reconciling radically different views. Still, we might ask whether it has things the right way around. Are things good for us, individually or as a society, because of our preferences? Does our good spring into shape only when we form a preference? Or do we prefer things because we hold them to be good for us? If the latter, then we may ask what the good is that we try to track with our preferences. A preference account in its way tries to take a middle ground here. What is valuable is valuable not directly because we value it, but because we *would* value it under appropriate circumstances. (Or because following that account of our good would in fact lead to more preference satisfaction in the long run.) Even so, the key determinate to being valuable is being valued. For my part, I shall argue that our well-being interests, in turn determined by our character as living beings, determine our good.

Before I argue that, though, it would be well to note an important aspect of how our desires are closely coordinated with our good. Though I deny that our good is to be *defined* as the object of any sort of desire, it is true that our desires shape our good and in some part actually do create it. This is true in both a trivial and a nontrivial sense. If I choose between two indifferent alternatives, then my choosing one makes its attainment a project of mine. If I flip a coin to decide between two different styles of coffee at a coffee shop, then there is some small bit of frustration if the option favored by the coin turns out not to be available. That is *very* trivial. However, the more we invest in our choices and in the further consequences of our choices, the less trivial things become.

We often have to make choices, and we make them even though we never know the full consequences of what we choose. Choice, chance, and circumstance, with much of the unpredictability of a kaleidoscope, combine to reshape our good. They reshape what we *are*. At some point in our lives we might take up an active interest in one thing rather than another. With some degree of arbitrariness we might choose between amusements, hobbies, career paths, or marital partners. A childhood hobby selected because of something seen at random on TV might shape an entire career path and way of life. Perhaps a student might choose between going to law school and entering a doctoral program in English literature. She finds both alternatives attractive and has the talent and aptitude for either. In choosing one of the options she moves into a different set of circumstances and develops different aspects of her personality and aptitudes. (Or she may develop the same aspects differently, but I think there is more to it than that.) As she lives, and therefore changes, some things become less important to her and some things matter more. Progressively she comes to have needs, desires, aversions, and potential satisfactions different from those she would have had if she had taken the other alternative. To some degree she develops into a different person. It is not just that, for whatever reasons, internal or external, she develops different means to her ends. She comes to have differing ends, with differing relative priorities among her ends.

Our good may be shaped by our choices to a relatively high degree, or to a relatively low one, but it is only shaped, never entirely determined, by our choices. Sartre proclaimed that "existence precedes essence" (*Existentialism is a Humanism,* p. 26).[8] First, we are. Then we make ourselves what we are (and our good what it is). This is one of those things that are importantly true but only partially true. We cannot create ourselves ex nihilo through our choices. If our student lacked the ability to pursue the career she chose, or if it led to a life of misery or frustration, then that would have been the wrong choice for her. If she is equal to her choice and the results are satisfactory for her, then, whichever choice it is, it becomes the right one for the person she becomes. What one becomes flows, healthily or otherwise, out of what one is. In opting for a particular career path she adopts that path as a means of pursuing her well-being in terms of such things as self-development and self-expression, self-esteem and social esteem, aesthetic satisfaction, and perhaps the income by means of which to pursue other benefits. The student might, by either option, rationally pursue ends that are good for her. However, she cannot choose her way into any future she desires. Our starting makeup, our choices, and the world around us *all* play a role in shaping our good.

Even though choice is by no means omnipotent in selecting and shaping our good, it can play a surprisingly robust role in the face of objectivity. Consider a person who is a dedicated heavy drinker and smoker. His smoking and drinking constitute a severe threat to his physical health. There is

[8] Jean-Paul Sartre, *Existentialism Is a Humanism* (New Haven, CT: Yale University Press, 2007).

the strongest evidence, we are convinced, that his activities are bad for him. As an adult he has the right to make his own mistakes – a right with which it would be dangerous to interfere – but evidently he is making one. The smoking drinker may well disagree. He may be aware of the risks and agree that the threat to his health is severe, yet believe that the fulfillment he gets smoking and drinking among his friends in the pleasant and comforting atmosphere of his favourite pub outweighs those risks. It may also be that he lacks the will power to make the break, in which case making himself miserable trying would only make matters worse. Suppose, though, that he does decide to quit and is able to do so successfully, finding some alternative values and sources of fulfillment, and living a longer life equally satisfactory to him. Seemingly he made the right decision for the person he became in consequence of his choice.

In contrast, suppose he weighs his probable personal costs and benefits and decides to keep on smoking and drinking, which he does mostly happily until his somewhat premature death. A shorter life is not necessarily a worse one. Seemingly he made the right decision for the different values of this somewhat different person. Or, things could go the other way. He might blunder into the wrong decision, judged from whatever perspective he adopted. In making his choice, he may overestimate or underestimate the cost or benefits – the pains and frustrations of trying to quit, the upset to his social life, or the pains of physical illness. Hindsight might or might not give him cause to regret his decision. Here too the values he chooses will significantly affect the assessment of the consequences. Similarly, a cancer patient might choose between a harrowing and probably ineffective program of chemotherapy or letting nature take its course, either way committing to certain values. A person may struggle for artistic or spiritual achievement, doing so at the price of physical health. A cliché example is that of the malnourished artist struggling long, hard hours in a dingy garret to achieve great art. People do in fact self-sacrifice for what they regard as worthwhile ends – but that is because a commitment to such ends is often developed as part of our nature as living, thinking, human beings. Doing this, the person develops certain interests as part of his or her well-being; not doing it, the person develops others. A choice can be made to be the right choice by the very making of it. Even so, for this to be true, the choice must be consistent with what we are and with what our overall good is and can become.

Here we have been assessing decisions and outcomes with reference to the values of the person as that person *becomes* through modification by the values adopted or declined. Let us now ask whether, as he makes the choice, one of the alternatives is better for him *at that time*. In the case of the smoking drinker, is it better for him to develop into the nonindulger (or minimal indulger) with new values and priorities or to proceed into the future with fewer changes, largely as the person he was? What is the best outcome for that life at the point of choice? In retrospect he might approve or disapprove either choice. In prospect, his decision in favor of one course of action shapes his good (whether or not that good is achieved) and so is, to a significant extent, self-validating. Are there any grounds, then, on which we might fault his choice? We have already noted that it might perhaps be faulted in practical terms – if, for instance, he underestimates the probability or the pains of cancer. Could we, however, fairly claim that he elected to adopt the wrong values? This we could do only if one set of values were, in independent fact, worse for him to adopt. I do argue that some choices and values – we might say some alternative persons into whom we might shape ourselves – are better for us than others in terms of the well-being interests of what we are now. My claim is that although our good is shaped by our choices, better choices are true to ourselves and to our good. There is a self that shapes our ends, rough hew them how we will.

I maintain that it is incorrect to take our good as inherently being determined by our prudent desires or preferences. Our choices, at least our properly thought-out ones, *normally* coincide with our good, and as we have noted, our choices play an active role in *shaping* what our good is. Just as obviously, our desires tend to be shaped by our good. Still, we can get muddled and fail to make prudent choices. Attempts to define our good in terms of prudent desires have an inherent flaw. To define our good in terms of what we would desire were we to be *well informed* and *thinking clearly* will work only if we have an adequate purchase on those terms. I argue that both of those terms are problematic, presupposing some more fundamental conception of our good. I argue further that the only way to avoid this circularity of defining our good in terms of good would be to rest *well informed* and *thinking clearly* on our well-being interests, which then (on pain of circularity) cannot be defined in terms of our preferences or desires. To start with, what is it to be well informed? To know every fact in the universe would be out of the question, but perhaps, as Singer suggests, it is a matter of what we would choose if we knew the "relevant" ones. Which facts are relevant? The answer has to be that any fact is relevant that might influence our desires. Nevertheless, if our good is just a matter of what we would arbitrarily decide, then *any* fact might influence our decision in some direction. Sometimes it is only a matter of arbitrary decision, but in the generality of cases it is not. Most of the time our decisions do or would reflect how things might affect us, for better or for worse. This is to say that we desire our perceived good because we perceive it to be good for us. Being well informed is knowing what makes a difference to our good.

The prudent-desire account of our good faces a hurdle with *well informed*, and it faces an even higher one with *thinking clearly*. We have already noted that not all prudent desires are desires. Could it be that some prudent desires are not prudent? Might a person be well informed, think clearly, and yet have a perverse desire for something very contrary to her or his self-interest? The prudent-desire theorist, holding that prudent desires constitute our interests, would wish to deny that. Could we perhaps dismiss such a possibility on logical grounds, maintaining that if a person knew the facts (unless the person were self-sacrificing for some further good, such as the welfare of another person), then a perverse desire would constitute proof that the person was not thinking clearly? This is a bad tactic for the prudent-desire theorist, as it tacitly presupposes that some choices are incompatible with clear thinking. For my own part, I am quite happy to make that assumption, as it implies that well-being considerations determine our prudent desires. Therefore, directly or by means of prudent desires, they determine our good. That is not something prudent-desire theorists can allow, as they wish to define in the opposite direction. They wish to define our good in terms of prudent desires and therefore in terms of clear thinking – and therefore in a circle – as clear thinking, as a workable concept, presupposes an adequate regard for one's own good.[9] Because both *well informed* and *thinking clearly* presuppose an independent conception of our good, I suggest that we bypass prudent desires and define our good directly in terms of our well-being interests.

For illustration, consider a person suffering from apotemnophilia, a neurological disorder that afflicts approximately 200 people around the world. Possibly as a result of damage to the right parietal lobe, such people, who are otherwise considered sane and rational, have a fetish about amputation. A man might believe that his left leg is not "really" part of him and want to have it amputated. Apart from the fact that he arrived at what is obviously the wrong answer, how can we fault his reasoning? It makes sense given his premises and values. He knows about the material effects and yet wants to have a part of his body removed – and so does a person who goes to the dentist for an extraction. Why is the extraction presumed to be a sensible choice that it is the right of the person to make although the desire for amputation is considered evidence of insanity? It is indeed insane – but it is not illogical. There is more to clear thinking than being logical. Faults in our thinking may be conative as well as cognitive. Perverse desires are no more impossible physiologically or psychologically than they are logically, yet they are not clear thinking. The proof that the apotemnophilic is not thinking clearly, at least in this regard, is that his thinking is so very severely out of touch with the whole of his well-being interests. No other proof can be required or given. One might sacrifice a healthy leg for one's life, or for some greater cause – an instance of moral heroism – but it is not a sensible choice for one's own personal good. To be sure, it must be granted that in extremis a person's mental states can become so twisted that losing a leg would be less damaging than the personal trauma of continuing with it.

9 It is tempting but unworkable to define clear thinking only in terms of thinking in regard to the accepted cannons of logic. People with serious mental health problems may think logically but on the basis of bizarre premises or without any adequate sense of proportion.

However, that could only be if the person's thinking has become so distorted as to be highly prejudicial to that person's overall best interests.

There is another respect in which prudent desires track our good imperfectly. Remember, prudent desires need not be actual desires. We might have a prudent desire for something that we do not actually desire. If we are deprived of that it will be a loss to us only insofar as it has an impact on our well-being, but not otherwise. Suppose that I have found myself in charge of a group of young children happily playing in some suburban backyard. Should I tell them if I see the ice-cream truck passing by out in front? It is foreseeable that if I so informed them, they, thinking quite clearly, will conceive a desire to go get some ice cream. However, their play is so happy that I cannot believe that the ice cream would make them any happier. If that is so, then do I deprive them of a good if I do not mention the ice-cream truck?[10] If they do find out about the truck, then the frustration of their desires would be a relevant (though not necessarily decisive) consideration. If they do not actually find out about it, then there is no impact on their well-being. They may be deprived of something they *would* have desired, but they have not been deprived of a good. Again, the conclusion is that prudent desires do not necessarily determine, or even track, our good.

Where and how do you draw the line? Questions inevitably arise in connection with any claim that a person's conclusions about his or her own good are not always accurate or the product of clear thinking. People who desire healthy limbs amputated are clearly not well, and doctors who do that are properly found guilty of malpractice. Nevertheless, there are middle cases that are harder to determine because again they are a matter of degrees and gray areas. (We could find a whole range of cases from cosmetic surgery alone.) It is not that what we think, or what we would think under certain conditions, tracks our good unless – up until the point that, suddenly – we are insane. It is quite implausible that up until a particular point we are sane and our good is what we would think it to be, and after that we are not able to think clearly. Rather, how well our thinking tracks our good is a matter of degree. It is also a matter of kind. Our thinking has many different aspects, many of them arational and many of them nonconscious. We may be quite skilled in some sorts of thinking and little skilled in others. We may track our good poorly in some ways, yet very well in others. We may do so very badly at it that society must intervene to protect itself, or our self. (Yet there is also a danger to both society and the individual if intervention is too freely undertaken.) There can be no exact formula for determining whether people are thinking clearly enough about their own good. Nonetheless, coping with grayness will be easier if we bear in mind that clear thinking is not one

---

[10] For the sake of focusing on the issues, let us rule out possible side issues that might make a difference one way or another. If one of the children had diabetes, for instance, it would be a different matter.

thing but many, and a matter of degree, and that what is good for us is at some level presupposed in any attempt to give an account of clear thinking or prudent desires. This calls for us to ask ourselves more closely what our well-being interests are, as the kinds of being we are. First, though, I note a few of the other things suggested as constituting our good.

Good as a Way of Being

If our good is not pleasure, nor any other mental state or experience, and if it is only contingently related to our prudent desires – much less to gold or glory – what is left? Instead of something we might have or experience, perhaps our good is some condition of what we *are* – or of what we might become. Along these lines is my suggestion that our good is constituted by *our well-being as whole living beings.* So too are various other suggestions that have been made about what our good is and where it lies. Spiritual conceptions have always been leading candidates, finding our good in our having a good relationship with God or with something else divine, or in our spiritual health and development. Perhaps our good lies in communion with Truth or Beauty or something else of transcendent value. Perhaps it is some state of character or personal development we might achieve. Clearly, these alternatives may well overlap.

We live in an age that tends tacitly to avoid ideas that suggest that our good is a state of being to be attained or maintained. Rather, our Enlightenment heritage accustoms us to think of goods, or our good, as something we have or might have, rather than something we might be or become. It is presupposed to be something we can possess or compile. Our cultural heritage also suggests that in the event that the treasures we ought to obtain are not, or not all of them, earthly goods, then perhaps we ought to be compiling riches in Heaven and making sure that our bottom line there is not in the red. The rewards of a Godly life and the hazards of an ungodly one have been graphically depicted, and the hope of Heaven or the fear of Hell can be an effective curb on bad behavior. On that level it seems that our good has much to do with mental states, particularly pleasure and pain.

However, higher level religions tell us that the end of religion is far beyond pleasure and pain and that it lies in spiritual integrity, wholeness, some sort of union with the divine or transcendent. Some people think that way about Beauty, holding the pleasure of something beautiful to be trivial in comparison to the higher value of beauty itself and our communion with it. It may be that Truth is the highest thing. It may be that these are really the same suggestion differently conceived. Such is the view of the poet who wrote that "Euclid alone has looked on beauty bare."[11]

---

[11] Edna St. Vincent Millay, "Eight Sonnets," in *American Poetry: A Miscellany*, ed. Louis Untermeyer (New York: Harcourt Brace, 1922), p. 198.

A common element in these suggestions is the idea that our good is some condition of our being that we might aspire to attain. It is not something that we might have, but something we might become. What that might be has been variously described, with various means recommended for its achievement. In one way or another, all of these conceptions of our good presuppose some sort of a conception of what we are and how what we are might be brought to fulfillment. Whatever we might be, though, we are living beings of a human sort. I suggest that it might repay our efforts now to inquire more closely into what it is to be alive, and what we might be able to learn about our good as living beings. It would seem likely that this might have some important bearing on our good as human beings. Eventually, I will offer the conclusion that our good is not anything we have or experience, nor any static state of being to be attained. Rather, our good is a *way* of living. Our good, I suggest, lies in our living well. Subsequently, I shall go on to ethical applications, applying the material developed about our good as living human beings in addressing some of the key issues of bioethics.

Although I am specifically concerned with human bioethics, I am strongly aware that this is nonetheless a very artificial distinction. Ultimately, as I suggest later, our life, our well-being and good, and the moral character of our lives all have dimensions that go well beyond the specifically human sphere, let alone the bounds of human bioethics. There are some matters that must be attended to before we proceed much further. There are some issues of logic and language that we will explore in the next chapter – and we will need to take a far closer look at the nature of life.

5

Elusive Lines, Slippery Slopes, and Moral Principles

Why is his nature so ever hard to teach
That though there is no fixed line between wrong and right,
There are roughly zones whose laws must be obeyed?
(Robert Frost, *A Further Range*) [1]

Already in discussing biological and ethical issues I have offered some
remarks, explicitly or implicitly, that were critical of some of our ways of
thinking about life and ethics. Now I continue on to discuss some important aspects of how our *language* and our use of it can affect the quality of
our thinking about biological, bioethical, and other matters, sometimes for
the worse. I will not explore this topic in full depth. That language affects
our thinking is not news. Many volumes can and have been written on this
topic, and I have contributed to their number. My purpose here is to highlight important ways in which our language and our use of it can influence
and often muddle our thinking about bioethical issues. More broadly, it is
not just a matter of language but of the broader conceptual schemes within
which we use language. In the discussion I pay particular attention to issues
about where lines are to be drawn, and about what have become known as
slippery slope arguments. Such matters are of immense moment wherever
we are trying to make important decisions about what to do, but our particular concern in this chapter is with their immense moment in the practice
of bioethics. We shall see this importance not least in connection with questions of euthanasia and abortion, which I introduce by way of example. In
this chapter, though, I will not draw moral conclusions about these very
important moral subjects. My endeavor here is to shed some light on issues
of lines and slopes. This will be useful when we do consider these and many
other topics.

* * * * *

[1] Robert Frost, *A Further Range* (New York: Henry Holt, 1936).

There is some irony in the thought that our thinking may be subject to being misled by the character of the languages we use and by our way of using them. Our use of language is central to our human rationality, and seemingly to our human moral status. In reason and the use of language we humans take our superiority for granted. These things are part of our being human and essential to our ways of coping with the world. We think about things, noting what we regard as their principal characteristics; we reason about them, and we take action accordingly. Language serves us not only to communicate ideas from mind to mind; it also serves us as a tool in organizing our thoughts within our own mind. In their development, human languages drew on the experience and wisdom of the ages, and they offer structures on which we are able to flesh out our own particular thoughts, being rich with resources for describing, categorizing, drawing distinctions, and making inferences. We see the world around us in terms of various things, actions, and properties thereof, with our diverse words being correlated with them in various ways. We like to think that our thoughts about reality *do* match reality, at least closely enough for our own purposes. On the clarity of our conceptions and their applicability to what they are supposed to be about depends the efficacy of our thinking. Our confidence in our ability to learn how to understand the world and to think about it to our advantage has been encouraged by our day-to-day life and further fed collectively by our innumerable advances in science, technology, and (despite numerous setbacks) civilization. Inevitably, though, there must be a downside. Sometimes we are misled by our language, or by our use of it. Sometimes we impute to the world features that actually are projections of our own mind.

The language we speak, as we speak it, is most assuredly not just a collection of words taken together with a set of grammatical rules. It requires a broader framework. For us to acquire a language and apply it to the world around us and make it work, we need to have a framework of presumptions and skills, driven by our needs and concerns. We also need the sort of brain that can deal with it. Without those things, no language could take root within us. We employ a vast complex of conceptual schemes, most of which is not apparent on the surface, not even to ourselves. In this regard our conceptual schemes are similar to our very lives, and they are also similar in being subject to continuous change as we live. It is a matter of continuous interaction with our world. From the cradle (and even before) onward we are deluged with sensory input from both within and without, and we must cope with it some way. We learn to identify patterns of things and events by our own experiences, and we are given further input from people around us. They guide us and give us information, and we observe and otherwise interact with them.

It also may be, as some have suggested, that our thoughts are first given shape or content by the innate structure of the human mind. In one way and another, we come to perceive and understand the world according to some conceptual scheme we have come to adopt and to adapt in response to our own encounters with our world. It is not just that we develop some particular way of thinking about or describing what we perceive. It runs much deeper than that. Our very ways of perceiving are shaped by our experiences and expectations and perhaps by our makeup as *Homo sapiens.* For illustration, recall some lecture or other presentation when you saw an image projected wrong-way up. Before it was turned over you may have had difficulty working out what was what, yet when it was shown right-way up you could easily see what it was. What did you see the second time but not the first? Each time there were the same shapes and colors in the same internal relationships with one another. What was different was that the second time you were able to see the image *as* something. Even before they get so far as our consciousness and language, our perceptions are shaped by our conceptual schemes.

We come, then, to make some distinctions and not others, and to acquire various ways of perceiving and habits of mind. Our conceptual scheme includes the distinctions we make (or do not make) and our beliefs, including those we presuppose and may not know we have. Often our thinking rests on tacit presuppositions about the way the world is, assuming that certain things or sorts of things have particular features, boundaries, and their interrelations. Often our thinking rests on ways we have of responding to the world. Very often, indeed invariably, it incorporates or presupposes some scheme of values. It incorporates skills, practices, attitudes, desires, and aversions. Again like life, it is more a matter of what we *do* than it is of some concrete entity. Furthermore, we are always doing many things at one time. More frequently than we might care to admit, a crucial factor in our decision making is what for us goes without saying and goes without thinking. Our use of language and the distinctions we make have a great deal to do with the logic, and sometimes the illogic, of many arguments that arise concerning bioethics.

As linguistic or cultural groups, and as individuals, from one to another we think with differing conceptual schemes. Those who study another language rapidly learn that different languages draw distinctions, and recognize relationships, along different lines. We incorporate differing presumptions into our thinking. Even as individuals using what is said to be the same language, it is noticeable that other people use words in somewhat different ways and have differing concepts. No two people share quite the same conceptual scheme, nor can any of us stand back and refuse to think in terms of some conceptual scheme. None of us can be so skeptical as to make no presumptions whatsoever. As thinkers and language users, we must already be using *some* sort of a conceptual scheme and, of course, we at least start from what we absorb from the people and world around us. In our conceptual schemes as well as in our language, we adopt and adapt from what is around us – though inevitably we will go on to personalize it some-what. As I previously noted, we also tend to presume that our conceptual schemes work as well as they do because they and reality actually do make a fit, that reality is (sufficiently) accurately mapped by the conceptual scheme we have developed in response to our own interests and experiences. More-over, we can easily come to think of some differentiations in reality, once we have marked them, as being sharper than they actually are. Accordingly, for instance, a person from one culture might come to see a particular shade of color as being *clearly* more similar to its fellow blues than to any green – not because the physical difference really is that sharp but because the person is habituated to distinguish in just *that* way. Another person from another culture might be culturally conditioned to see that same shade as being clearly more similar to its fellow greens than to any shade of blue.

How well do our conceptual schemes actually fit reality? That is a ques-tion that is too easy to ask and too broad to answer. How might we even think about it except from *within* the confines of some conceptual scheme, however tentatively we might employ it? The fact that we hold them suggests that our conceptual schemes work well enough for most of our purposes most of the time. Still, however satisfactory we might find our own concep-tual schemes, one may well doubt whether any conceptual scheme could fit the whole world with absolute accuracy and adequacy. To be sure, just where we happen to distinguish between blue and green is arbitrary and unimportant, so long as it does not detract from our communications with others. In point of fact, though, our conceptual schemes sometimes do let us down badly in matters of importance. This is particularly likely to happen if we take them too rigidly, or if we try to apply them beyond their home range of appropriate application. This can well happen in bioethics when we are confronted with new problem areas that we have to think our way through. The old tools of thought may not be enough.

To continue, though first without examples so emotionally charged as those in bioethics are likely to be, let us consider the supposed difference between frogs and toads. That the former are smooth and green whereas the latter are brown and warty is a distinction that works very well for many people in many places nearly all of the time. There is no reason that they should drop the terminology. Nonetheless, the distinction is of very little use biologically. Some "frogs" are more closely related to some "toads" than they are to other "frogs" – and conversely, as well. The terms do not accurately follow biological distinctions. Good enough in its place, the distinction is best left behind by a herpetologist trying to sort out the fauna in the back blocks of New Guinea. Similarly, the distinction between mushrooms (good to eat) and toadstools (potentially lethal) can be highly useful in local application. However, the distinction does not follow the lines of biological distinction, and being one or the other cannot be universally correlated with evident characteristics. Shape, color, gill pattern, and whether the plant turns silver black – each one of these criteria can be applied usefully in regional application. Nevertheless, their being applied outside of their home range can and has killed people.

Often in bioethical practice we are confronted with novel situations and novel areas of application. Our natural inclination is to reach for the old familiar terms and distinctions, plus the conceptual scheme in which they are embedded. Sometimes they can help us, but sometimes they let us down badly. We do well to note that the terms *human being, human life,* and *person* are among those that can get us into trouble. Most of the time we can use these terms interchangeably without difficulty. Normally, anything we see that is any of those things is all of them. However, what do we do if someone (e.g., Peter Singer) makes the claim that an anencephalic child is not truly a person whereas some intelligent animals (such as a sign-language–using chimpanzee) are persons and are morally entitled to be treated as such? One might dismiss the claim out of hand as being biologically absurd. The anencephalic child is a living being, one that can be demonstrated to be an instance of *Homo sapiens.* DNA tests would resolve any possible doubt. The chimpanzee is not a *Homo sapiens.* Therefore, the former is a person whereas the latter is not. Nonetheless, taking this line begs the moral question and ignores important conceptual issues. This is not to say that the conclusion is necessarily wrong. My point here is that the issues of what, morally, constitutes personhood require being faced and dealt with, at least if we are going to arrive at worthwhile conclusions. We cannot just ward off these issues with a dictionary. It would be just as absurd to claim that the chimp is a person because it walks on two legs and reminds us of people we know. To try to deal with such questions on the grounds of unexamined linguistic habit is to fall short in our aspirations to be thinking and morally aware people. *Life, death, person, mother* – such terms and concepts (and many others) are thrust into novel situations in bioethics, and they require cautious handling as we try to cope thoughtfully with contemporary and emerging bioethical issues.

Consistently with past usage, there can be more than one way to extend old distinctions into new territory. The distinction between *east* and *west,* for instance, does not really apply out in interplanetary space. Still, there are innumerable ways in which the term could be extended to apply there. We obviously would want to make the use of our terms as practically convenient as possible, and so we would want it to approximate to our terrestrial use of them. (East must still be opposite to west, and perpendicular to north and south.) Yet we cannot determine *the* meaning of *east* in such an application just by trying to discover it in our past usage. There is no one-and-only true meaning to be found there. Bioethical decision making often requires us to make similarly underdetermined distinctions, while yet making decisions that are more urgent, with much riding on what we decide. The concept of *death* is one that is being pressed into active service in previously unfamiliar territory. At one time, people were either dead or alive. If one could not tell which, one could in a very short while. With modern life-support systems and their increasing capabilities, though, it can be difficult or impossible to decide, even when the medical facts are available. People may be kept alive, if alive it is, for months or even years on a life-support system, beyond all hope that they will ever recover consciousness. It is well known that this is so, but there is certainly no consensus about whether they are alive or about what their moral status might be. Numerous life processes may continue, and we might agree that the heart and kidneys, for example, of such a person are still alive. However, in such cases, is Fred Bloggs (or Karen Ann Quinlan), the person, still alive? It may be that a large proportion of their body is alive, but that does not answer the question of whether *they* are alive. What does answer it? *We* have to answer it. Instead of looking for an answer under the microscope or in some particular interpretation of past usage, we have to decide what way of drawing distinctions is most responsive to important differences and bests serves the needs and purposes we have in drawing them. Just when death occurs and what it occurs to is a topic for us to explore elsewhere. My point here is that the conclusions we come to about death are in some part contingent on our *ways* of thinking.

Though there are many and various ways of projecting our dotted lines across the face of reality, some of which are better than others, reality does not come with dotted lines already in place. No more does the earth's surface carry ready-made lines, be they lines of longitude or boundaries between legal jurisdictions. Yet some maps are better than others by far. With maps or with concepts, some distinctions are easier to demark than others. The distinction between ice and water, for instance, is usually fairly sharp – but how many bands are there in a rainbow, how many colors? Answers vary from one individual to another and from one cultural or linguistic group to another, with some placing the band transitions in a different way or location than others do. Nevertheless, certainly there are different colors. Just as certainly, there is a difference between the planet Jupiter (the largest planet in our solar system) and the rest of the universe that is no less real for Jupiter's lacking any exact boundary. I am told by astronomers that it does not have any real surface. From the outer atmosphere in, it just gets thicker toward the center – becoming very thick indeed.

It is a matter of cases how well the distinctions we make, and the conceptual schemes in which we employ them, work out in practice. It is a matter of what we are talking about and of our purposes and objectives in talking about it. As we develop them, our conceptual schemes may work well or poorly in serving our needs. Nonetheless, there will always be a touch of artificiality to them – and because of the sort of beings we are, and because of how we interact with the world, it is never entirely possible to avoid imputing to the world features that are projections of our own conceptual schemes. Some of what we project, such as lines of latitude or the bands in a rainbow, may serve very useful functions. Some of what we project, such as the many superstitions of gamblers, may serve to mislead us.

In Praise of Imprecision

It is not just *where* we draw our distinctions that is important. Important also is the degree of narrowness and rigidity with which our distinctions are interpreted. There are positives and negatives in the vagueness and indeterminacy that are such frequent features of our conceptual schemes. To be sure, everything else being equal, precision (when accurate) communicates more information than does imprecision. Moreover, imprecision and vagueness have come to have a very bad moral reputation – and one must grant that they are by no means entirely innocent of the charges that have been laid against them. We all know to our cost how insufficiently scrupulous people may take advantage of imprecise language to mislead people or to make shabby excuses for bad behavior. But then again, we all know how language, very precise and narrowly interpreted, can be used to mislead people. Be sure to read the fine print. Hairsplitting also can be used for bad excuses. The fault is not with the degrees of precision afforded by language but with our human use of and response to it. Those who deceive intentionally, or who intentionally leave open the possibility of so doing, are morally remiss. Furthermore, we are imprudent if we do not take care to adequately understand what we accept from others.

To condemn rigidity in our conceptual schemes would be absurd. Our conceptual schemes would fall into a useless heap without the appropriate rigidity. Still, our conceptual schemes can never do our thinking for us, and sometimes we allow our use of them to distort our thinking. That can happen if we insist on interpreting and employing them *too* rigidly. Employing some flexibility is vital to much of our human communication. In contrast, an overly loose structure can lead us into sloppy thinking. We can be thankful that rigidity and flexibility can coexist within the same system. Without bones your arm would be as useless as it would be with no degree of flexibility at all.

Precision, however, is not always possible and appropriate for human purposes in the world we humans face. Some things about which we might be concerned, perhaps such as moral rightness or life and death, have considerably more vagueness and indeterminacy at their boundaries than do many other things. Sometimes we want to say something when there is no need for precision. ("John is quite tall." "Exactly what do you mean by *tall*?" Who cares? He is over two meters.) Sometimes we want to stretch a term to make a point. "Aye, there's the rub," said Shakespeare's Hamlet. Not that *rub* can literally mean what it is made to mean there, but it was made to mean that most effectively. For that matter, *stretch* also springs from metaphor.

What I am saying here goes against a great deal of what we have been taught explicitly or by implication. It is widely presumed to be more rational, more useful, *better* if our thoughts can be shaped in terms that are defined with rigor and absolute precision. As intellectual heirs of the Enlightenment we are heirs of Descartes and his method of rational inquiry. This called upon us to think one step at a time, going logically from one clearly and distinctly perceived truth to the next, each shaped in precise terms. As it happens, Descartes' method works better in some applications than it does in others. It works quite well in mathematics. A principal feature of mathematics, comforting to some and infuriating to others, is that within its framework, questions that *meaningfully* can be asked have definite and demonstrable answers.[2] Within that framework there are no gray areas or room for legitimate differences of opinion. Descartes, who was one of the finest mathematicians of all time, was seemingly trying to generalize to apply to all of reality that method that succeeded so well for him in mathematics.

The method of Descartes works very well for dealing with those things that do (at least for relevant purposes) come in units with well-defined properties and precise boundaries. It works well, for instance, for account keeping and for things of a mechanical nature, from Lego blocks to highly complex forms of structural engineering. It works well for quite a lot more than that. This is despite the fact that just about every thing in the real world, including Lego blocks, has boundaries that are at least *somewhat* indeterminate. If we examine physical objects at the atomic or subatomic level, their boundaries appear much less definite than they do from here. Nor are their properties entirely self-contained, as things are always being influenced in little ways by their surroundings. (Just by my being where I am, I produce slight – infinitesimal – thermal and gravitational distortions in my next-door neighbor's saltshaker.) Still, for almost all purposes almost all of the time, such differences are unnoticed, unnoticeable, and totally irrelevant. For a huge range of purposes we can safely proceed by using Descartes' method. However, for some things, a method like that of Descartes will not fare as well. The difference is *not* that some things, unlike others, have somewhat indeterminate properties and boundaries. It goes well beyond that. In part, what makes the difference is that for some things, including some very important things, the fuzziness at the edges is substantially and crucially relevant on a practical level. Black-and-white thinking is frequently a too-crude tool for moral or biological thinking.

Another related shortcoming with Descartes' approach is that some things do not have an entirely self-contained identity. Rather, they have

---

[2] However, there is Gödel's Theorem, which establishes that within some complex systems there are truths that cannot be demonstrated within that system. Even so, those extra truths can be demonstrated with full mathematical rigor from outside of the system, and Gödel's Theorem can itself be demonstrated with full mathematical rigor.

their identity in terms of a wider system. The plant is part of what it is to be a leaf. A discussion of life, or of most matters concerning it, is very much an enterprise in which the application of Descartes' method of thinking – in terms of discrete well-defined properties and units – is quite problematic. Life tends not to come in that sort of unit, nor to be restricted to properties of that sort. A living entity, an ongoing process, or rather a complex of ongoing processes, occurs and maintains itself only in relation to its surroundings. Its surroundings and its interrelations with what is in its surroundings are part of its identity. Nor is it possible to draw any precisely determinate boundary where the living entity's processes leave off and other processes occur. Not only are our life processes and those around us fluctuating and without determinate boundaries, the processes intermingle and sometimes coincide. Where, for instance, do our digestive processes leave off and those of our intestinal flora start? How can we sharply distinguish between the metabolic processes of mother and fetus? Again, as our life is a complex of innumerable processes, no percentage score nor any other one- or few-dimensional assessment could specify the state or degree of our health except very loosely and under-informatively. Any number of highly precise and specific facts may be involved, but health goes beyond any precise or rigid categories. There are many forms of workable balance and many forms and degrees of departure therefrom. This imprecision, however, is not because health is just a matter of choice, opinion, definition, or subjectivity. Certainly it is not because there is no truth to the matter. On the contrary, it is just because our health is a real feature of our living being that the framework of a conceptual scheme cannot so easily capture it.

It is one of the most wonderful and beautiful aspects of language, and one of its indispensable features, that for most purposes most of the time, we are able to *adaptively* use language to convey our intended meaning. We are able to discuss colors, for instance, or health, quite sensibly and effectively. In a particular context of use, for the purposes we then have, we are able as a matter of course to adapt our use of words to convey our meaning. Multiple description, analogy, tone of voice, body language, and many other devices serve our ends in communication. Think of the innumerable ways in which *Hamlet* might be interpreted and presented. A language that was incapable of imprecision would be a poor thing indeed, quite incapable of many of the vital tasks we require of language. We are not always doing the sort of thinking or communicating that Descartes commended. Nor should we be. Imprecision is an indispensable virtue by means of which we are able to stretch old concepts to convey new sorts and shades of meaning from one person to another (or to help us think it through for ourselves). Often we say things we have never said before, doing so in new situations for purposes peculiar to those situations – and we often do so about things of a sort not catered to by traditional methods. In the rapidly changing world of biology, biotechnology, and bioethics (as well as much else in this emerging twenty-first century), we very much need the element of flexibility that the imprecision of language allows for us to shape our use of language so as to more precisely express our meaning.[3] Very strongly, then, I support the claim that it is not a defect but a desirable feature of our language that it has an element of looseness, fuzziness, and indeterminacy. Instead of being a limitation on language, it is the very feature that helps us to constructively transcend limitations.

Sometimes we can combine precision with novelty by expressing our meanings through well-constructed combinations of meanings that are precise and preexisting. Advances in technology depend on this. But, then, such things as novel tastes and smells are difficult or impossible to describe to those not familiar with them. Wine tasters are notorious for the colorful sorts of expedient they resort to in order to convey their intended meaning. Unfamiliar moral situations also may put great strain on our conceptual schemes. We have come to a time when a child can have more than one biological mother, when *life* and *death* are no longer as clear-cut as once they were, and neither are *person* and *human life*. We may be able to exactly specify what we are referring to in purely biophysical terms, but that does little to tell us where the moral boundaries are to be drawn. Much less does it tell us what moral conclusions are to be drawn. The aforementioned terms and many others must be reinterpreted to meet emerging possibilities, and new terms and concepts must be developed to help us deal with new realities. Important distinctions must be recognized, even when they strain language, whereas false or misleading distinctions must be resisted. All the while we must avoid wandering into linguistic morasses or falling down treacherously slippery slopes. In developing our distinctions one notorious difficulty – an

---

[3] I go into these matters more extensively and thoroughly in my *Focusing on Truth* (New York: Routledge, 1992). A full discussion here would detract from current purposes. To be brief, in that book I reject the outmoded conception of truth as being a matter of a particular proposition corresponding to its own particular fact. The conception of a world composed of unit facts, to which we refer precise units of meaning, is unsustainable. (There are traces of some of the more unfortunate features of Descartes' scheme to be found in this conception.) However, it is true that statements are the saying (by someone) of something about some subject of discussion (not necessarily a particular thing), and true statements are those such that what one is talking about is as described. Present purposes in the particular circumstances determine the criteria for whether the description is met, and they determine, though only as precisely as need be, the boundaries of what we are talking about. We can meaningfully and truly (or falsely) say "The eastern sky is red" without having precise criteria for just what sector of the sky is eastern or just what is to count as red. Furthermore, others can normally understand us. It depends on our communicational purposes in that instance. Are we artists discussing a proposed subject for a painting? Are we discussing the weather ("sailors take warning")? A critical time in the Chinese Communist revolution? Just what is being said and whether it is true depends accordingly. In general, then, neither in our words nor in the world will there be precise lines. Normally, though, they will be sufficiently precise and so placed as to fit our purposes on that occasion. Their very flexibility can be a vital aid in serving those purposes.

important one, though not the only one – is that of drawing and defending the conceptual lines we draw. Going with it is the practical problems of drawing and defending our distinctions in practical application. Let us now take a further look at this matter of drawing the line.

Where Do We Draw the Line?

Part I: Precision, Determinability, and Accuracy

> Before I built a wall I'd ask to know
> What I was walling in or walling out,
> And to whom I was like to give offense.
> (Robert Frost, "Mending Wall")[4]

As well as posing conceptual difficulties, this business of drawing lines often involves us in practical difficulties of great magnitude and considerable urgency. In bioethics it is especially and often confrontingly true that moral principles and their practical applications require specified limitations on our actions. We must decide what may or may not, shall or shall not, be done. This inevitably and quite appropriately leads to controversies about where boundaries can best be drawn and what might be the consequences of drawing them in one way rather than another, and about whether they can properly be drawn at all. Where ought we to, and where can we, draw the line? Some ways of making distinctions and drawing up the rules just do not work out well in practice. Nor is that the worst of it. Widely employed are arguments to the effect that were we to accept some rule or principle, or condone a certain course of action, then, by a series of necessary extensions, we would be forced to incur outcomes that are highly repugnant. For instance, researchers might ask a Research Ethics Committee to approve a project allowing them to contact hospital patients identified as being smokers. They want to ask them to agree to be interviewed about their attitudes and experiences concerning quitting smoking. Though it would be potentially useful and minimally invasive, this would still involve giving information about patients (i.e., that they smoke) to some who are not part of their clinical care team. While the Committee is pondering that, another researcher asks to be allowed to go through case notes for patients in a number of different categories, checking how well administered drug doses and responses correlate with theoretical guidelines. Again, this might gather important knowledge, but it would be even more invasive of patients' privacy. The researchers, inevitably, maintain that the former consideration far outweighs the latter. The Ethics Committee wonders where this sort of thing will lead. Are we to have researchers rummaging through people's medical files for any purpose deemed expedient? Researchers meanwhile

---

4 Robert Frost, "Mending Wall," *North of Boston* (London: David Nutt, 1914).

complain bitterly about where restrictions on their activities appear to them to be likely to lead.[5] Obviously, this leads us straight into the closely related problem of slippery slopes. For now, though, let us stay with lines. Not only is this topic an essential part of dealing with the topic of slippery slopes, it also is one of immense importance in its own right, theoretically as well as practically.

Frequently, in all manner of discussions, we are challenged to draw a line between some A and B. One commonly suggested inference is that if we cannot draw an adequate line between A and B, then causing or allowing A will have the effect, either logically or by some chain of human response, of bringing about B. Looking at it the other way, we might say that ruling out A may lead us to rule out B. Where do you draw the line? Posers are especially frequently put forward in connection with bioethical issues – euthanasia and abortion being obvious examples. When one is challenged to draw a line between A and B, there characteristically will be at least some apparent difference between them. It is precisely because there is an apparent difference between the murder of a postnatal person, for example, and the abortion of an early embryo that line arguments are used to argue that there is no morally relevant difference, or at least that causing or allowing abortion would inevitably lead to postnatal murder. There are obviously differences, but it is argued that they are not morally relevant ones, or that they are otherwise not suitable for stopping a slide. Without some apparent difference, a line argument would only be a pointless inquiry into whether A was A. As well as an at-least-apparent difference between A and B, there also must be an at-least-apparent gradation of cases between the two, challenging us to find a relevant and defensible way of distinguishing between them. To challenge someone to draw a line between cats and comets would be not only pointless but also downright silly.

Unless the evident difference between A and B in a poser concerning where one draws the line is entirely illusory (which it can be), it is always possible to draw *some* sort of a line. We can draw the line between people who are tall and those who are not tall at 180 cm. We can draw it at 140 cm. Nonetheless, we want more than just any old line. We can draw lines good, bad, or mediocre – but what makes a good line good is not an easy matter to specify. Clearly, a good distinction (line) is one that is useful for us with respect to whatever purpose we have in trying to draw the distinction in the first place. For distinctions to be useful for us, they must not create difficulties by putting things into unworkable categories or, more broadly, by being unfaithful to reality. Beyond that, our distinctions are better as they better help us to think or communicate about some matter of concern to us, and help us to achieve our goals in doing so. Insofar as we are concerned

---

[5] These examples are abstracted from actual research proposals made at major research centers. Details must obviously be suppressed.

to draw distinctions for moral or procedural rules, it is important that we have well-chosen distinctions and coherent purposes.

A very important factor that is often involved in discussions involving whether suitable lines can be drawn is a call for *precision*. Arguments based on the supposed difficulty or impossibility of drawing a suitable line are at their best – most plausible and most useful – when, as well as an apparent difference between *A* and *B*, and a gradation between them, there is also some reasonable presumption that any acceptable distinction must be precise. Legal and other regulatory matters are commonly thought to require precision. After all, laws and rules have to be interpreted, followed, and enforced. So too, often, are moral principles held to require precision. It is very much preferable for us legally if we can have a clear and sharp distinction between legal and illegal, and it is useful for us morally to have clear and sharp distinctions between right and wrong. Our distinctions are supposed, by we who make them, to be about something – about apprehended dangers to the public welfare, or about the moral character of certain acts. Our distinctions are supposed not to be merely arbitrary, though it remains true that the exact location of the boundary might well be. Such distinctions as we can draw are able to track what they are about only to an approximation and somewhat arbitrarily.

To illustrate some central points I will again start with a less controversial example from outside the field of bioethics. Common sense tells us that car headlights ought to be on when it is too dark to drive safely without them, and that traffic laws ought to require it. Public safety demands it. But, of course, just where do we draw the line? With no specific line, the defense would commonly be that "it wasn't *really* dark, not as *I* understand the term." We might draw a quite precise line in terms of *lumens*, a scientific measure of light intensity. There would be a degree of arbitrariness to any particular number of lumens we settled on, and no particular number of lumens would exactly correlate with any particular and measurable degree of road safety. The greatest problem in practice, though, is that precise lumen levels at particular times and places would be difficult to establish in retrospect, when trying to enforce the law, or in prospect when trying to obey it. A more workable way to draw the legal line would be to legislate that lights must be turned on when we are driving between certain times that are set with reference to sunset and sunrise. That would give us precise and mostly workable lines, ones that would vary sensibly with the changing daylight hours of the changing seasons. Even so, that would not take into account such factors as rain or cloud cover, or speed limits on particular roads.

As a general matter of utility (and of equal justice before the law), we do want our laws and other binding rules to be fairly precise and drawn in such a way that their application in practice can be determined with workable ease. Of course *fairly precise* and *sufficient ease* are themselves rubbery terms – and where does one draw the line in applying them? It is better for us not to draw lines for them. Rather, for each rule, we should find the best fit we can between *precision, determinability,* and *accuracy* (fidelity to reality).[6] In general, it will not be possible to maximize all of these desirable qualities simultaneously. To specify conditions for the mandatory use of headlights in terms of time of day would be about as precise as specifying in terms of lumens, but it would be far more determinable. Lumens more accurately, but less determinably, correspond with the requirements of road safety. To require that headlights be on when that would nonnegligibly contribute to road safety would most accurately reflect what the law is there to do. Obviously, however, such a requirement, without further stipulation, would be hopelessly imprecise and difficult to determine. At best, a statement relating lighting to road safety might serve to clarify the intention of some more manageable rule.

Let us now return to bioethical applications. Issues of precision, determinability, and accuracy loom large here. Suppose the proposal is to permit abortion, let us say early-term abortion. How then do we keep from sliding on to middle- and late-term abortion, infanticide, or the murder of competent adults? There is a continuous progression of possibilities from *A* on to (and far beyond) whatever *B* we can mutually agree is objectionable. So where do we draw the line? Any number of lines can be drawn along the way – but are there any that are not arbitrary? Wherever we draw the line, holding that abortion is permitted (at least in specified circumstances) up until time *t*, the challenge is to justify *that* specific point in time in preference to all others.

Is the living entity whose termination is in prospect significantly different from what it was one second before or one second after time *t*? Neither the time of birth nor any other time after conception seems to be so distinguished. (If seconds seem excessively large units at any stage, we can go by microseconds.) All the way to birth and beyond, there seems to be no exact point in time, nor any exact point in development, at which we can draw an entirely nonarbitrary line marking a morally significant difference in the characteristics of the embryonic life. Therefore, antiabortionists proclaim, the only appropriate place to draw the line is at the moment of conception.[7]

---

[6] It is important to remain alert to the difference between *precision* and *accuracy*. These are not the same thing and they do not always go together. To say that I am 214.637 cm tall would be quite precise. However, to say that I am approximately 177–178 cm, although less precise, would be far more accurate.

[7] Actually, there is no such moment. Conception is a process that lasts approximately twenty-four hours and that has no exact start or finish. (In consequence, neither has pregnancy an exact starting point. Birth too is a process that does not occur at one exact moment.) The contrast between conception and pregnancy is one between two continuous and inexactly bounded processes, one lasting about twenty-four hours and the other lasting about nine months. However, for the sake of following this argument, let us not take advantage here of these inconvenient facts.

Let us take stock of some key issues at stake here – asking not so much about abortion as about line drawing. Given that we cannot draw an entirely nonarbitrary line between *A* and *B*, what is that presumed to indicate? It might be any of the following:

1. There is no difference between *A* and *B*.
2. There is no morally significant difference between *A* and *B*.
3. Although there might be a morally significant difference between *A* and *B*, there is no way to locate just where a transition takes place.
4. People being as they are, if we allow *A*, there is an unacceptably high risk that *B* will happen.

A person might make none, one, or more than one of these inferences. In connection with abortion, one might hold that it is murder. Conversely, one might hold that if abortion and murder are somehow to be distinguished, they are nonetheless morally equivalent. Again, one might agree that although very-early-term abortion is (probably) not murder, there is no way to determine at just what time it does become murder. Or, it might be that early-term abortion, although morally acceptable in its own right, is too risky because its acceptance would lead to an unacceptably high risk of objectionable outcomes. One might perhaps draw more than one of those inferences, and one might not clearly distinguish between them.

Let us again detour by means of the less contentious topic of the Motor Vehicle Code, before returning to apply the points developed to bioethics. I assume that we can all agree that in the interests of public safety, we need speed limits of some sort on public roads. We may agree that 200 kph (approximately 124 mph) is too fast, but once we go beyond o kph, where do we draw the line? If 200 kph is too fast, how can we deny that 199.999 kph is too fast? Starting at the other end, if o kph is not too fast, then surely neither is 0.001 kph – and so on. We are not entitled to draw from that the absurd conclusion that o kph = 200 kph. Nor can we conclude that there is no difference in public safety, nor that there is no moral difference between driving a suburban street at 40 kph and driving it at 180 kph. Nor would it be sensible to conclude that as no definitive and nonarbitrary line can be drawn, we must remain at zero. If adhered to, that policy would certainly ensure that no innocent person were ever killed in a traffic accident – yet even so, it would still have an adverse impact on the rights and interests of many people. Obviously, there is a gray area between safe enough and too unsafe, one that, moreover, will vary with particular circumstances. There is no way in which we could determine just where *too unsafe* starts, even if (contrary to fact) it did start at some exact point. Just as obviously, some sort of line must be drawn and enforced – and some lines are better than others even though all will be somewhat arbitrary.

It is also true that some people will speed, whatever the limit is. If we allow people into cars at all, some will drive them too fast. Even were there some *exact* point at which speed becomes unsafe, a point at which an infallible something on the dashboard lit up and went "beep," some people would still speed, and a few would try to see how many beeps they could register. The fact that there is no exact point at which speed becomes too unsafe undoubtedly does create (or at least serve) a temptation inclining some people, though not all, to speed. Many who wish to go a bit faster will see no good reason to restrain themselves at just exactly the legal speed limit. It is widely believed and often true that it is only with imperfect accuracy that laws fit the reality of what they are supposed to be about. It is, for example, hard to specify just what murder is, as it gradates into manslaughter, which gradates into other things. Looseness of fit with intended effect is particularly notorious in laws that set quantitative limits, as witness not only speed limits and minimum drinking age but stages (if any) in pregnancy when abortion is to be permitted.

Continuing for the moment with speed limits, there is no clear reason why a nice round 60 kph (approximately 37 mph) is inherently a better speed limit than 59 kph or 61 kph. Moreover, because everything up to that point is considered acceptable, we feel that the next tiny bit must be okay also – particularly when it suits our purposes, and so too for the next little bit after that. We are inclined to think that if the speed limit is 60 kph, *surely* there is nothing really wrong with doing 61. We would feel quite hard done by were we to get a traffic citation for that. Normally, law and enforcement, each making allowances for human nature, the police set their radar for something a bit higher, maybe 65 kph. Knowing that to be so, we may feel quite aggrieved were we to get cited for doing (only) 66. We may well feel that 70 and a bit more is okay when the road looks clear and the police are not looking. I must admit to sometimes having such tendencies. Nevertheless, I and most of my fellow miscreants realize that it cannot really work that way, that if we really were to accept each marginal increment as being *fully* as good as what went just before, then we would have to accept speeds that any sane person would deem absurd and almost certainly fatal. The danger of speed continuously increases, even if it is a continuum. There will always be people inclined to speed, but a reasonable person knows that we must impose some limit, albeit with some arbitrariness to it, in the gray zone between safe enough and too unsafe. We must often draw the line somewhere, be it at a good somewhere or at a bad or a mediocre somewhere, so we try to get the best fit we can. However, if no line can be drawn that works better than having no line at all, we may be better off not trying to enact laws, even though we might well be convinced (and rightly) that there are important differences from one side to the other. Where no workable line is possible, wise legislators prefer to legislate as little as possible. Accordingly, the law generally prefers to have as little to do as possible with personal morality, social interactions, and domestic relationships.

People usually prefer their moral principles, as they do their statutory laws, to be as clear as possible about where they do and do not apply, with clearly drawn lines. That is, they usually do unless they wish to get away with something. Rightly, with moral principles as with laws, we tend to be suspicious of those who try to bend the rules so as to exempt their own actions. Ethicists, though, I note with some chagrin, are rarely allowed the indulgence of nonspecification commonly extended to lawmakers. Although we do not expect statutory law to guide us in all things – and we would deeply resent it if it did – it is often demanded of a set of moral principles that they resolve all matters that might be brought before them. Lines must be drawn through the grayness, resolving it into zones of determinate moral black and white. If a proposed moral principle does not draw the line, or does not draw it with comforting sharpness, a desire for moral clarity may lead us to want to replace it with one that does. However, an insistence on precision can be counterproductive. As we have noted, the most precise lines, and those that make it easiest to determine which side of the line one is on, are not necessarily the most accurate. A moral principle that draws precise lines and gives us definite answers may thereby give us easy or convenient answers with perhaps a comforting sense of knowing just where we are. However, it may not give us the morally best answers, nor even give us answers that are adequately close to being the morally best answers.

Another indulgence rarely allowed to ethicists, though often to lawmakers, is that of employing a degree of arbitrariness. If we need a speed limit, then the speed limit has to be *something*, so legislators enact one, even though we all know that a different one arguably as good could replace any specific limit. Legislators make legality. Ethicists, however, do not *make* morality. They give an account of it, but the difference between right and wrong is supposed to be neither arbitrary nor at their discretion. Fair is fair, and wrong is wrong. If we make laws on bioethical matters, or are members of an ethics committee that draws up rules and approves or rejects courses of action, arbitrariness in our decisions is frequently not well tolerated. Nonetheless, it is just as true that there are some moral gray areas as there are legal ones, and that sometimes we must cope with them and work around them. We may hope nonetheless that some line can be drawn through that grayness that at least has the virtue of ensuring that nongray matters, one way or another, are put on their appropriate side of the boundary.

In sum, a challenge of where to draw the line only has as much force as the presumption that a definitive line is requisite. For some purposes, an inability to adequately draw such a line between *A* and *B does* mean that we must take them to be equivalent (even if we know they are not). If some people of legal age are banned from drinking alcoholic beverages on the beach, all are. If the hoodlums and slobs cannot drink there, neither can we. If we can, they can. That is how the law works. However, not everything works that way – not everything can. We should not allow the asking of the question automatically to create a presumption that any acceptable line must necessarily have all three virtues of being precise, being accurate, and being fully determinable. In many situations in the real world, particularly in bioethics, there are very important differences that cannot be delimited by such lines but with which we must cope nonetheless. We cannot leave them alone because, like life and death, they certainly will not leave us alone.

Where Do We Draw the Line?

Part II: Some Parlor Games that can become Serious Indeed
For serious purposes I here offer some seemingly innocent pastimes for consideration. As games they are neither likely nor intended to take the world by storm, though some of my associates and I have pleasantly filled some idle moments with them. I offer them as exemplars of principles that have some serious applications. In one of the games, one person names two very different things and the other players try to state some features they have in common. For example, a gold brick and a mountain lake: Neither is a living being, both are made of material heavier than wood, and both are usually attractive. A half-eaten orange and the action of flying a kite: Each may feature in a pleasant spring outing. It will become clear that *any* two things will have something in common. The game soon becomes one of trying to add some humor to the description. Recently, I heard an astronomer's joke to the effect that comets are like cats in that they have tails and do what they like.

Of course, one can go on to more elaborate forms of the game. Finding differences is just too easy, so I propose a somewhat more complex game. In this game, one person names *three* different things, and the challenge is to find something that each pair of them have in common to the exclusion of the third. No matter how similar A and B might be, and how different C is, there will always be something that B and C have in common, but not A. Tweedledum, Tweedledee, and the Andromeda Galaxy: Tweedledee and the Andromeda Galaxy are the two further to the right. There will always be something. The point of all this, of course, is that *any two things can be united by one description and separated by another.*[8] These are truths that can be put to use for many purposes – many of which are, to say the least, problematic (and possibly nefarious).

It is a consequence of these principles that any proposed course of action A can be described as being unprecedented, or as being only another

---

[8] These things can be proven by formal logic, though the proof would be only a tedious distraction from our current inquiry. We assume the Principle of the Identity of Indiscernibles: That if there is no difference at all between two things, then they are not two things; they are the same thing.

instance of what has long been known and accepted. So too can any possible outcome B. Even a moral enormity on the scale of Auschwitz could be described as a social welfare initiative intended to alleviate unemployment. But do I dare to eat a peach? The time, the place, the circumstances, and the specific qualities of that particular peach unite to form a novel occurrence with unknown consequences. Our descriptions can be made to fit our inclinations. For example, if we are opposed to course of action A, we can always find some heinous course of action B that has some features in common with A. We then argue that we must never allow any course of action that comes under the common description, lest we slide down the slippery slope to B. How persuasive the argument is will depend on our rhetorical skills of presentation and the plausibility of the assumption that the common description captures the essential features of A and B, with differences being too minor to arrest a likely progression from one to the other. This may indeed be the case – or it may not. If we are opposed to active voluntary euthanasia, we can point out that euthanasia is an instance of the intentional killing of innocent human life. This description also applies to many of the things that happened at Auschwitz. We do not want to slide down the slope to that, so we had best not permit any form of euthanasia.

In contrast, if we were in favor of legalized active voluntary euthanasia, we would probably stress its compassionate element and argue that it gives people an important measure of control over their life. There are countless precedents in favor of compassion and respect for autonomy. Moreover, we can find features in common between the prohibition of active voluntary euthanasia and odious practices. We might even find the very same disgusting destination at the foot of the slope. To prohibit active voluntary euthanasia is to override people's autonomy over their own life and its continuation, and to prevent the relief of suffering that could otherwise be alleviated. If we are to override people's autonomy over their own life and its continuation and to acquiesce in their suffering, where will it all end? Such indifference to personal autonomy and to human suffering was an odious feature of Auschwitz . . . and so on. It will not be possible in every case to counterpropose a plausible slippery slope to just the same appalling destination as that proposed by one's opponent. Still, with a bit of ingenuity, one can propose a slippery slope from *anything* one wishes to oppose down to *some* bad consequence. There will always be something we can contrive to use. ("What, you think I should help my infirm grandmother cross the street!? I would totally lose my independence were I to give in to all of my family's demands. I would become a mere means instead of an end in myself!" Obviously, this sort of argument would be unconvincing to any but the most narrowly self-interested.) The challenge then is to propose the most (seemingly) plausible slope to (seemingly) plausible bad consequences. Setting and undertaking such challenges would serve as the basis for yet another parlor game. More to the point for present purposes, the

possibility of contriving a slope from anywhere at all to somewhere undesirable does serve as a basis for good and bad argumentation designed to
persuade. Certainly we must never conclude that as one can contrive some
slippery slope from anywhere to anywhere, any argument is as good as any
other and any conclusion is as good as any other. We do better to refine our
reasoning than to abandon reason.

We must be wary of those who make the worse appear the better cause, as
Socrates was accused of doing. Nonetheless, the decisions we make, about
the rules we make or about other things, do have consequences, and we
should be thankful to those who, like Socrates, point out unthought-of
implications of our ideas. In practice, often in bioethical practice, our problem is to evaluate such arguments and their practical implications. Because
of the importance of slippery slope arguments, particularly to bioethics,
I discuss them now more closely. In doing so, I draw particularly on the
material of the last two sections. From our discussion of line drawing and
description, I offer these as points of reference in the face of speculation
and partisan advocacy:

1. Things – in particular, courses of action – can be meaningfully different and successfully distinguished even when
   (a) no precise and nonarbitrary line can be drawn between them,
       and even when
   (b) they can both be subsumed under some description.
2. Lines that are the most precise, or the easiest to draw, may not be
   accurate.
3. Things can be meaningfully and importantly or relevantly similar
   even when
   (a) a precise line can nonarbitrarily be drawn between them, and
       even when
   (b) they can be subsumed under different descriptions.
4. Moreover, that things can be put under a common description does
   not necessarily mean that they are relevantly similar with respect to
   the particular issues under consideration. Most especially, it does not
   mean that causing or allowing one course of action will mean that we
   will, or must, or ought to, or cannot avoid allowing to happen some
   other course of action with which it has something in common.

Slippery Slopes

Recall the example previously noted of a Research Ethics Committee faced
with proposals by researchers asking for access to patients' records. The
committee must decide what it will or will not allow, where it will draw the
line. As well as wanting to allow what is morally acceptable and to disallow
what is not, the committee and interested others worry where it will all lead.

Do we fall onto some slippery slope? Slippery slope arguments suggest an image of a person high on an icy mountain slope. If that person takes a misstep there, she or he will slide down the slope. Having nothing solid to grab onto on the way down, the person must crash to destruction on the rocks below. The best thing, obviously, would be to not take that fatal misstep in the first place. Arguments like that, when well presented, can be very persuasive.[9] Sometimes they actually are sound arguments. Sometimes they most assuredly are not. I shall not be so bold as to propose a general algorithm for assessing slippery slope arguments, determining which are sound and which are not. There can be no such algorithm that is valid. What I shall do is offer some observations and propose some principles as offering us useful means for keeping our footing as we traverse slippery slopes.

In generic form, slippery slope arguments maintain that if A is caused or allowed to happen, then, by means of a series of (at least apparently) intermediate cases, B will necessarily, or at least quite possibly, occur. As B is presumed to be very undesirable, A ought not to be caused or allowed. We must not do A, lest B happen. In particular instances, of course, slippery slope arguments vary widely among themselves. Commonly, a distinction is made between slippery slope arguments in the *logical* form and those that occur in what is often called the *psychological* form, though I prefer to think of the latter more broadly as the *human-response* form. Arguments of the latter sort have to do with how human beings (or human institutions) are likely, as a matter of fact, to respond to A being caused or allowed – whether the response is due to psychological factors or any other human factor. A slippery slope argument in the logical form claims that if we cause or allow A, doing so has the logical effect of causing or allowing B.[10] One complicating factor is that these forms of slippery slope argument often blend into one another.

Slippery slope arguments of whatever form come in endless variety, particularly those concerned with human responses. As a result of that variety and

---

9 It is significant that conveying the point seems to call for the use of a metaphor of some sort: *thin end of the wedge, primrose path, domino effect, opening the door, toe in the door, opening the floodgates, camel's nose in the tent,* and *widening the net* are others among the many graphic images that, though they vary in nuance, are used to convey the same general point. Such arguments ask us to make a mental leap from the thought of our doing or allowing one thing to the thought that some further thing would follow in consequence. By their very nature, therefore, such arguments invite our imagination and invite imaginative names.

10 By slippery slope argument of the logical form, I mean a slippery slope argument dealing with issues of supposed logical implication. B is a logical implication of A if it is universally and necessarily impossible for B to be false when A is true. That Tabby is a cat logically implies that Tabby is a feline. That Tabby likes catnip may be very probable, and a practical conclusion to draw, but it is not a *logical* implication of Tabby's being a cat. It is important to note that though a slippery slope argument might be in the logical form, dealing with supposedly logical implication, the argument itself might be illogical.

the endless variation and arationality (and irrationality) of possible human responses, there can be no single formula capable of handling them all adequately. However, I do offer some suggestions for dealing with them. To start with, we should keep well in mind that in actual practice in particular circumstances, it can be unclear what the nature of the supposed slope from A to B is thought to be. Opinion presenters often wax indignant about the horrors of B, and therefore of A, without clearly indicating just how we are likely to fall from one to the other. So, trivially obvious as it appears on paper, and as treacherously easy as it is in practice to handle negligently, the first thing to do is to ascertain as best we can how A is alleged to lead to bad consequences. This can be quite difficult to pin down.

Is it perhaps a logical version of a slope argument? If we are legislators, members of ethics committees, or otherwise concerned with reaching conclusions about what is or is not to be done or allowed, we may well be working within the framework of specific rules and definitions, or we may be drawing up such a framework. It could be that within that framework, B is a logical instance of A. We must first ask whether A, in all of its logical implications, is itself worth doing or allowing. If it is, then in our considering whether and how to proceed we must take care to be as clear as possible about how we are to draw our lines and implement such safeguards as might be appropriate, so as to avoid there being slippery slopes down to where we do not want to go. We do not want to set a logical precedent for that which we do not want to condone or have happen. Returning to our initial example, the Ethics Committee might wish to agree to allow researchers to obtain information about which patients are or are not smokers, so that they may request interviews. If the committee establishes as a rule that researchers may have access to information about who has what condition if they would be using the information for significant research, that would give leave to those researching smoking to proceed. Nevertheless, that same rule would also give the go ahead for researchers to obtain information about which patients have schizophrenia, HIV–AIDS, or other conditions about which they might be highly sensitive. The committee might recoil from that logical implication and seek some other way of doing things.

Sometimes the (supposed) logical implication is less direct. It may be claimed that though B is not formally an instance of A, there is yet no *relevant* (to what?) or *essential* difference between them. Therefore, it is argued (or perhaps only asserted), if either of them is permitted or prohibited, then so ought the other to be. If the Ethics Committee disapproved a simple breach of privacy for one specific project (such as AIDS), so the argument goes, then it ought to disapprove any breach of privacy for another specific project (such as smokers). More to the point, if it approved a breach for the latter project, it would be acting wrongly (arbitrarily, inconsistently, or immorally) if it did not approve one for the former – or so eager researchers would argue. (Looking ahead, the committee might take care to avoid setting a new, or apparently new, precedent.) Those who equate abortion and euthanasia with murder sometimes argue that if murder is illegal, then abortion and euthanasia ought likewise to be illegal and that if these were to be made legal, the lack of an essential difference between them and other forms of murder would eventually lead us to condone murder in its other forms. Often, as here, slippery slope arguments of a logical form shade into slippery slope arguments of the human-response sort. In effect, the argument here is that *A* logically implies *B* *if* we set aside irrelevant details in their definition or characterization. But *are* they irrelevant? Irrelevant to *what*, and for *whose* purposes? Very important questions might easily get begged here. Slippery slope arguments in the logical form can be sound ones. We certainly do have to be alert to undesirable implications, particularly when we are drawing up formal rules. Nevertheless, some slippery slope arguments in the logical form are not sound. There may be differences that are relevant and important, and we may be able to specify them so as to rule out undesired implications.

Similarly, slippery slope arguments in the human-response form may be sound or unsound. Certainly any adult who spends some time in charge of children rapidly learns that one must be careful about what one allows. Every child in the group will likely enter a claim. Moreover, just about anything permitted might conceivably be stretched to serve as a precedent for further concessions. With some people, adults as well as children, it often is a matter of *give them an inch and they will (try to) take a mile* – to invoke yet another metaphorical turn of phrase for a slippery slope argument. Human beings frequently do respond to perceived opportunity in accordance with their particular inclinations.[11] Slippery slope arguments being possibly sound as well as possibly unsound, it will not do just to dismiss slippery slope arguments out of hand and across the board. In proportion to their strength they command our thoughtful attention. How then are we to go about assessing these arguments?

Assessing Slopes

I reiterate the caution that, as I believe, it is impossible to develop some precise formula that is capable of dealing with the complexities of alogical human responses. Nor could we even develop one capable of dealing with the logical implications of causing or allowing all possible practices *A*, as there would be an incalculable infinitude of possible human applications. Certainly I would be foolish were I to attempt to present such a

---

[11] Nor is it always a matter of opportunity, at least not in any positive sense. As a chronic tobacco addict, I am still occasionally tempted to take a puff – but I *know* where that slippery slope is likely to wind up. In my case the slippery slope argument is quite sound. Accordingly, I have not had a smoke for decades.

formula. What I shall do is offer some key points as being useful considerations in dealing with a very considerable proportion of slippery slope arguments. As an opener, I suggest that when confronted with a slippery slope argument we ask whether the argument is in the logical form or in a human-response form. This may not be easy to determine. For my principal bioethical illustrations, I shall draw on arguments concerning abortion. However, my principle concern here is not with abortion but with slopes. Abortion as an issue is addressed in Chapter 12.

If it is argued (as it often is) that *A*, the acceptance of abortion, will lead to *B*, the acceptance of murder, this may be intended and interpreted as arguing that the latter is a logical implication of the former. Yet again, the argument may be that in the absence of a precise demarcation, or in the absence of a difference that can readily be located or agreed upon, any actual differences between the two will not prevent humans from going from the one to the other. Is it that abortion is murder? Or is it that it must eventually lead to murder even were it not murder (nor even immoral) in particular circumstances? These different arguments might not be distinguished even in the mind of the one proposing the argument.

If we are satisfied that a particular slippery slope argument, logical version, is sound, and if we agree that *A* is not worth having at the price of *B*'s occurring, that settles matters for us. (By now, of course, we know not to lose our heads and accept that *B* is *A* just because we cannot draw a precise and accurate line between them. Still, we may have some difficulties in patrolling the boundary.) However, although it settles the matter for us, we should note that it might settle it for us in either or both of two distinct ways. It may be, on one hand, that to allow *A* is to allow *B*, which we have agreed is too high a price to pay. It might, that is, be a sort of reductio ad absurdum: As *B* (murder) is morally unacceptable, *A* (abortion) must therefore be morally unacceptable. On the other hand, it might lead us to rethink and accept *B*. After all, if it is only a matter of *A* (killing insentient life), *B* (early abortion) cannot be too bad. Either way, we must always ask whether there are hidden premises.

In contrast, if the argument under consideration is not a sound logical-version argument, and if we agree that *A* is not worth having at the price of *B*'s occurring, then we would do well to consider whether perhaps the slippery slope argument is instead made on a human-response basis. If *B* is not a logical implication of *A*, it might still ensue from it by means of some chain of human causality. How are we to assess the likelihood of that happening? Predicting how humans are likely to respond to something, particularly something novel, is far from being an exact science (as witness the admissions, or failures, of political pundits, social scientists, and share-market analysts). We can never be *absolutely* certain that bad consequences will not ensue. Even familiar things can have sudden and unexpected consequences. (My pausing to brush my teeth this morning no doubt altered the flow of traffic, conceivably leading to someone's dying or not dying in a traffic accident.) The only way we could certainly rule out bad consequences flowing from the novel would be to rule out the novel entirely. That would be quite agreeable to some people, but it would have extremely bad consequences of its own. We would do better to consider proposals on their individual merits – and, if we decide to go ahead with a proposed course of action, to monitor the consequences and be prepared to clarify or modify our stance accordingly.

One human factor of which we can feel certain is that those with an interest in having course of action *B* allowed will seek to find some approved *A* to serve as a precedent. (For them, of course, unless they are dishonest, it would not be a slippery slope from *A* to *B*, but a progressive development.) If we disapprove of *B*, then we do well to check whether it is a logical consequence of any *A* that we do approve. If it actually is such a consequence, then we do well to ask which is more important to us (and why), *A* or the nonoccurrence of *B*. If *B* is not a logical consequence of *A*, then our next question is whether *B* has, or will be seen to have, enough – whatever *enough* is – of those features that provide the rationale for accepting *A*. We might yet come to see *B* in a more appreciative light. Or we might note relevant differences and perhaps persuade others of them. A related human factor of which we can feel equally certain is that those opposed to the acceptance of course of action *A* will seek to find an obnoxious *B* to serve as an example of that to which *A* will (allegedly) lead. Similarly, we must ask whether *A* has, or will be seen to have, enough of those features that provide the rationale for repudiating *B*. When rival camps are concerned with the same *A* and *B*, we may find *both* camps stressing the similarities between *A* and *B* as they try to recruit, in opposite directions, those who are inclined to favor *A* but oppose *B*.

A remarkable example of strange bedfellows is that of Peter Singer and many of those opposed to his views. Singer notoriously maintains (Kuhse and Singer, 1985)[12] that early postnatal infanticide, as well as late-term abortion, is morally justifiable when (perhaps as the result of a gross birth defect) it would be in the overall best interests of all those concerned. In his view, the early postnatal infant, though human life, is not yet a person (and in some cases might never be, even were it to live on). To the degree that it has interests, it is entitled to some degree of moral consideration, but not to the degree due an actual person. So much could be said for the late- as well as for the early-term embryo. They are not persons and may be killed for utilitarian reasons, perhaps for their own good. Or perhaps one may be killed for the greater good of others, even if the embryo itself would be to some degree the loser. Accordingly, early postnatal infanticide

[12] Helga Kuhse and Peter Singer, *Should the Baby Live? The Problem of Handicapped Infants* (New York: Oxford University Press, 1985).

can equally be justified on the same grounds as early-term abortion. Many of Singer's firmest opponents quite agree with him in putting abortion and early postnatal infanticide in the same basket – though they label that basket *murder*. The feature of early postnatal infanticide that they hold to be morally objectionable, the killing of innocent human life, is present in abortion. They would rule them both out together, whereas Singer would rule them both in. Each side would hope to convince those inclined to accept at least early-term abortion.

Suppose now that we are inclined to favor some *A* and to oppose some *B*, and that we are solicited by those who would convince us to lump *A* and *B* together, either both to be accepted or both to be rejected. We may or may not find, as in the example just given, rival partisans arguing in exactly opposite directions, but there will often be those who agree with us in accepting one thing or rejecting another and who call upon us to draw the conclusions they draw. Being open-minded, we are willing to consider other views and to reconsider our own and to amend them when and as appropriate. We may not be able to give a complete and precise account of what we ourselves do and do not approve but, unless our moral thinking is merely capricious, we should be able to identify significant features of *A* that incline us to approve of it and significant features of *B* that incline us to disapprove. Do *A* and *B* have enough of the same positive or negative features to indicate that we should approve or reject them together? Do we, for example, agree with Singer that abortion ought to be allowed and do we accept his reasons, that of utilitarianism together with the assumption that the embryonic life is not a person? We might accept all of that but not accept his contention that the early postnatal infant is not a person. Our conception of personhood may well differ from that of Singer. Alternatively, our disagreement with Singer's contention that early postnatal infants are not persons would not oblige us to agree with his most vocal opponents about the wrongness of early-term abortion (or about anything else). Although we might not be able to draw a precise moral line between early-term nonpersons and postnatal persons, that would not be necessary for us to noncapriciously oppose infanticide yet favor legalized early-term abortion. We can go part way toward something without going all the way, even though we are unable to draw a clear and entirely nonarbitrary line between the go and the no-go zones. We may well be able to rule some things in and some things out, for sensible reasons, while leaving some things indeterminate.

In considering human responses it is well to bear in mind, always, that the primary force impelling people from *A* to *B* is some inclination to go in that direction. Would legalizing abortion, for instance, force people down hill into condoning murder in the conventional sense (involving the killing of postnatal persons)? Murderers, we might note, do not characteristically seek a moral rationale for their actions, and those who do generally do so in terms of the pressure of circumstances or the objectionable nature of their victim. It is, to say the least, not easy to imagine someone being prompted to commit murder (in the conventional sense) because abortion was considered acceptable. For their part, those who suggest such a slope are rarely if ever primarily motivated by a concern to reduce the incidence of conventional murders. Rather, they typically regard abortion at any stage as being itself murder. The fundamental difficulty, as they would see it, is not so much that abortion leads to evil consequences as that it is evil in itself.[13]

If I am trying to be a morally good person, one who abhors conventional murder, and I am contemplating the issues of abortion, how might I respond to the suggestion of there being a slippery slope to murder?[14] I have no fear that I shall commit conventional murder or that others might be led to do so by the acceptance of abortion. One response might be to accept it not as a slippery slope but rather as a reductio ad absurdum. I might believe that what is wrong with murder is that it is the killing of innocent human life and that, come to think of it, abortion is also an instance of that. I might accept the conclusion that if abortion were morally acceptable, then murder would be also, and that as it is not, abortion also must be wrong. It is often the case that the actual *force* of a slippery slope argument is not so much that we might actually arrive at B as to offer a reduction to absurdity of the supposed truth that *A* is acceptable.

Alternatively, I might reject the claim that what is wrong with murder is that it is the killing of innocent human life. That murder and abortion both come under that particular description I might reject as irrelevant because I might hold that what is wrong with murder is that it is the killing not merely of human life but of a *person* (my conception of which might involve such factors as sentience, self-consciousness, and the like). I might then hold that a postnatal person but not an embryo comes under the morally relevant description. From that I may or not conclude that abortion ought to be legalized. Being aware that there can be real and important

[13] I have not been able to discover one single case of anyone who has committed murder (of a postnatal person) in the conviction that murder must be morally acceptable because abortion is morally acceptable. However, there has been a sprinkling of cases of people who believed that abortion is murder and who, pursuant to that belief, went on to murder postnatal persons associated with abortion clinics. In practice, then, there seems to be a more likely slippery slope to moral disaster from taking abortion to be wrong than from taking it to be morally acceptable. But, of course, this is quite irrelevant. The real question about whether or not abortion is ever morally acceptable is that of whether or not abortion is ever morally acceptable – not whether one conclusion or another leads us on to some projected slippery slope.

[14] I am not concerned here to canvass all possible views on the issues of the morality of abortion. That would be an encyclopedic undertaking and not to the present purpose. My concern here is with slippery slopes where we think that *A* might be acceptable, agree that *B* is not acceptable, and agree that there is a gradation between *A* and *B*.

differences between things that cannot be separated by anything like a clear and definitive line, I might conclude that it would be appropriate to allow abortion up until some stage of pregnancy that is still well short, I am convinced, of where the embryo becomes a person. I do not attempt to determine exactly when the embryo develops into a person; I merely propose a line well short of when it could possibly be a person according to my conception of what a person is. Anything up to that somewhat arbitrary line, and I presume for a way beyond it, is morally acceptable to me. I feel no compulsion to go any further down that slope.

Yet I might also come to conclude that abortion ought always to be prohibited, coming to that conclusion on the basis of similar assumptions. I might agree that an embryo is not a person, at least at suitably early stages, and therefore that it is not morally important. I might agree that killing an innocent person is wrong, and I might also agree that we could draw a line that, if adhered to, would prevent the abortion of any embryonic life that was a person. However, that *if* might have me worried. People being what they are, and unwanted pregnancy being as objectionable to many people as it is, I fear that there will be irresistible pressure to infringe any boundary that might be drawn. No doubt some women will have strong, even heart-rending, reasons for not quite being able to make the deadline. And what is a day, or two, or just a few – especially when we know that the boundary was set very well back from the time when an unborn person might be aborted? We roll down the slope in the familiar way, eventually getting to the point where unborn persons are being murdered. Regarding that as a moral catastrophe of the first magnitude, I draw the conclusion that the only way to prevent such evils from occurring is to prohibit abortion at all stages. I accept this outcome even though I believe that abortion is not morally wrong in itself at a sufficiently early stage and even though I recognize that it might sometimes be much better for individual persons. So, which conclusion is the better? That is not my concern here. *My* conclusion is that a discussion of slippery slope arguments can go only so far. Such discussions can offer some useful points of reference – and I hope I have provided some – but there can be no adequate formula for handling all such arguments. When we are dealing with slippery slope arguments of the human-response variety, we have to assess what the material and moral consequences are in point of human fact. How bad are they morally? How likely are they materially? It is a matter of cases, and it all depends.

Ascending Slopes

Good slippery slope arguments, as we have noted, can help us to decide whether or not it would be prudent to do *A*. We assess the probable costs and benefits in terms of our scheme of values, as our values currently are. From these and from other "what if" arguments we can often derive more benefit than just deciding whether to do *A*. Beyond that, such arguments can help us to critically assess our values, to become clearer about what they are, and to refine and improve them. Then, it is not just a matter of how to seek or avoid outcomes. It becomes a matter of asking which outcomes it would be better to pursue.

Let us here take another look at *McFall v. Shimp*, raised in Chapter 3. In that case, a judge had to rule on the question of whether a person could be compelled to make a donation of bone marrow to save the life of a person who otherwise would surely die. Sorrowfully, the judge had to deny McFall's petition for an injunction and thereby, in effect, to condemn him death. To do otherwise would be to overturn a fundamental rule of common law. This is the

rule which provides that one human being is under no compulsion to give aid or to rescue.... Our society... has as its first principle, the respect for the individual, and that society and government exist to protect the individual from being invaded and hurt by another.

To compel the donation would be to break the law and, beyond that, would be contrary to the very principles on which our system of laws is erected. After that, all manner of horrible things might happen.

To do so would defeat the sanctity of the individual, and would impose a rule which would know no limits, and one could not imagine where the line would be drawn.

There we have what is clearly a slippery slope argument with some scary possibilities lurking down at the foot of the slope. Judge Flaherty invoked the swastika and the Inquisition. This is an argument that has aspects of both the logical form and the human-response form. To grant the injunction would be to negate the law, and to negate the law would be to allow what the law would otherwise forbid. (Unless we contrive some way to replace it with a law we think would work better, which might be a very risky undertaking.) This is a slippery slope in the logical form. In addition, the judge is warning us of the sort of evil that might happen – of what in some societies *has* happened – when the principle of respect for the individual is eroded. We might wonder, even so, whether it might be possible to draw a defensible line allowing McFall to live but ruling out Auschwitz and the Inquisition.

On the face of it, it looks plausible that such a line might be drawn. It is not merely that one can draw some line between any two things. There is clearly a significant moral difference between forcing a person to save life at minimal inconvenience and, in contrast, slaughtering innocent people for no good reason. Still, we would not want to decide things on the basis of simple utility. As we have already noted, accepting the principle that the end justifies the means can lead to some gruesome implications, examples of which are bounded only by our imagination. We might perhaps favor some system of rights that would rule out such atrocities, yet not rule out such a humane thing as saving McFall's life. Could we perhaps have a rule that the rights of society are in some circumstances to prevail over those of the individual? Some societies do take that approach. However, as the judge observed, it was precisely in the name of the good of society that the aforementioned horrors have been perpetrated. Society does have some claim on us certainly, but the law demurs from demanding our life's blood or our bone marrow. (Note, however, that the law can demand a sample of blood from a driver for alcohol testing, and it can draft a person to fight and possibly die in a war.)

Instead of arguing on the basis of the greater good of society, it might possibly be more feasible to shape the law so as to somewhat (but only somewhat) expand the sphere of an individual's right to life. Perhaps after considerable reflection, and thinking our way along a variety of slippery slopes, we might decide that our conception of law, and of a person's inalienable right to sovereignty over his or her own body, must preclude any such thing. Or we might decide that at some point, increasingly trivial personal "rights" may be overridden because of grave personal or social needs. (This could be only in specified circumstances and with appropriate safeguards.) In the United States, for a period of time in the early twentieth century, Mary Mallon – better known as *Typhoid Mary* – was kept in confinement against her will. Though guilty of no crime, she was a carrier of typhoid. Not susceptible to the disease herself, she nevertheless carried the typhoid organism. She thereby infected several others, causing some deaths. However, she would never accept that she was a danger to others. Her rights to personal autonomy, unlike those of Shimp, were overridden – and at considerably more inconvenience to her than Shimp would have incurred.[15] On what rationale could society defend its actions toward Typhoid Mary while defending its inactions with respect to McFall and Shimp? Could it be because Mary's exercising her autonomy as she wanted to was a public danger, whereas Shimp's exercising his was a danger only to McFall? Nevertheless, Shimp was arguably undermining the social fabric of human life. But where, oh where, would such lines of thought carry us? Again, perhaps it is not a matter of autonomy at all but of respect for bodily integrity. That might also lead to some slopes. Or, taking a quite different approach to cases such as McFall and Shimp, perhaps the law could establish that our agreeing to be a donor under specified circumstances is a binding condition of our entry into publicly funded health-care schemes. Should admission to public-health schemes be subject to conditions? Any way of shaping the rules has potential slopes and consequences.

I do not presume to declare how, if at all, the law should be amended to deal with such cases. My concern here is to illustrate how mentally exploring slippery slopes may help us to better and more clearly determine our

[15] For further discussion, see Judith Walzer Leavitt, *Typhoid Mary: Captive to the Public's Health* (Boston: Beacon Press, 1996).

priorities and moral values. Whether as legislators, committee members, or policy makers of some other description, we need to work out the consequences of doing one thing or doing another. Traversing slippery slopes in argument and in our minds, as well as helping us to determine which course of action can best help us bring about optimal results in terms of our scheme of values, can do even more. Just as important, and perhaps even more so, conceptually exploring slopes can carry us forward by helping us to form and refine our values. This is not just a matter of how we are to implement our values but of what values we are to adopt – or to evolve. American society has for years been trying to decide what a person's rights are to his or her own body, as in the two cases just mentioned here. It is also still trying to work out just what is to count as a person. One might mention various instances, from the Dred Scott case (*Dred Scott v. Sandford*) to *Roe v. Wade*, and beyond. It is not just a matter of what the law is but of what the law ought to be. In the Dred Scott case (1857), the U.S. Supreme Court had to rule on whether a Negro slave, having lived for some time in a free state of the union, was still a slave and not a person within the intent of the law. Americans and others are now trying to work out whether an embryonic life is a person within the intent of the law, or whether it ought to be. At the same time, it also must be determined what the moral status of the embryonic life might have to do with the rights a woman has to her own body.

There might be more than one possible accommodation that could be developed between factual reality, our ways of doing things, and our evolving moral and nonmoral values. How we put it all together, which plausible fit we devise between theses factors, may well depend on what direction our thinking starts out on. I am reminded here of a phenomenon sometimes described in works of popular science, having to do with the behavior of certain supersaturated solutions. Being supersaturated, they contain more of a dissolved substance than they can stably retain in solution. Once the process of crystallization gets started, much of the dissolved substance will come out of solution, forming crystals. The process might start as a result of a jolt or to some small impurity, or it might start spontaneously. Some solutions are such that they can produce crystals of more than one form (composed of molecules of the same substance differently arrayed). Which sort of crystal one gets depends on which sort happens to start first. One might even get different sorts in different parts of the same container if crystallization starts in different places independently. One way or another, though, something must eventually crystallize out.

It seems similar when we, so to speak, must crystallize our opinion, adjusting our values in some way. It might be that although we prefer to keep shrugging it off, society as a whole cannot continue to do so. There may be several different forms that our values might take and more than one starting point or route toward settling our values. Much of the art of lawyers, politicians, salespersons, and other persuaders lies in getting us to start our thinking along lines that lead toward our structuring our evaluations in a way favorable to their cause. Much of their art lies in keeping us from thinking along dangerously rival lines. We are to start from the precedents and established principles from which *they* want us to start. Skillful persuaders know to, and know *how* to, get us to accept plausible starting points and then to lead us step by plausible step to their favored conclusions. As we consider their arguments, or our own speculations, we do well to be carefully and critically aware of the distinctions and inferences made and of the principles presupposed. Especially, we need to be critically aware of what general principles are being brought in with particular applications – and what is it that is *not* being said. We all know that what is not overtly said is often of critical importance, though we may easily overlook that in practice.[16]

When someone – even someone we are disposed to trust – presupposes a tacit premise we do well to ask what other lines of thought are possible and to ask what might be their own implications or slippery slopes. To

---

[16] For illustration, and perhaps for fun, let us take one from Shakespeare:

> Antony: You all did see that on the Lupercal
> I thrice presented him a kingly crown,
> Which he did thrice refuse; was this ambition?
>
> . . .
>
> Fourth citizen: Mark'd ye his words? He would not take the crown;
> Therefore 'tis certain he was not ambitious.
> (Shakespeare, *Julius Caesar*, III:ii)

Mark Antony's funeral speech was intended to defend the memory of the assassinated Julius Caesar from the charge of his having been ambitious for power. The speech offers superb pointers for those who aspire to resist (or, less creditably, to be) demagogues. The Fourth Citizen certainly took the bait. We all know that there is *some* connection between ambition and willingness to accept a crown. But what is it?

Caesar did not take the crown	Caesar did not take the crown
All who take the crown are ambitious	All who are ambitious take the crown
Therefore, Caesar was not ambitious	Therefore, Caesar was not ambitious

The syllogism on the right is a structurally good argument. However, it suffers from the important defect that the question-begging second premise is materially false. An ambitious person may refuse a crown for strategic reasons, and many have done so. In contrast, the argument on the left has true premises, but it is not a valid argument as it is structurally flawed. We could equally well argue this: *Caesar did not live in Pompeii; All who lived in Pompeii were Romans; Therefore, Caesar was not a Roman.* Not that Pompeii has anything to do with it, but this ridiculous argument has the same logical form as the one just given on the left, which is equally inadequate. Antony was wise not to go there. Instead, he left the relation between crown taking and ambition to dangle in silence. It was better for him just to hammer the fact that Caesar had refused the crown. His audience should have been more alert for what was not said. As well, the crafty Antony employed another trick worth noting: He did not actually spell out his conclusion that Caesar had not been ambitious. Rather, he left that obvious, though illogical, inference to dangle. The gullible Fourth Citizen, having drawn the inference, felt that it *must* be true. He had figured it out himself.

continue with abortion as our example, perhaps we start out by asking what rights a woman ought to have to her own body and its use. We look back in horror on the institution of black slavery. That one person should be able to *own* another is morally disgusting. The slave is negated as a person, being used as a mere means for the benefit of others. We also may reflect on instances of sexist exploitation and depersonalization. If our thoughts start out along such lines as that, we might come to draw the conclusion that placing restrictions on abortion constitutes an intolerable infringement on a woman's sovereignty over her own body. As Shimp had a right not to have his body utilized for the benefit of McFall, so a woman, it would be concluded, has a right not to suffer a far more invasive utilization by an embryonic life. This is the general conception behind the famous (and controversial) Violinist Argument of Judith Jarvis Thomson (1971).[17] In summation, imagine that you wake up and find out that you have been abducted. Moreover, while you were unconscious, your body was attached to a life-support system maintaining the life of a world-famous violinist who has suffered kidney failure. For medical reasons, your circulatory system is the only one that makes an appropriate match with that of the violinist. It is for that reason that a group of music lovers has plugged him in to your body. You are assured that it is only for nine months, after which time the violinist will have recovered the use of his kidneys and you can go your separate ways. Until then, to unplug him from your body is to condemn him to death. For altruistic reasons you may be willing to endure the massive inconvenience, which is far more inconvenient than anything Shimp was asked to put up with. But what if you are not willing? Do other people or society as a whole have a right to compel you to undergo this prolonged utilization of your body for the benefit of another? Thomson concludes that you do have a right to be unplugged. Though the violinist, like McFall, is undoubtedly a person, we have a right not to have our bodily sovereignty infringed upon for the violinist's sake. Similarly, it is argued, the pregnant woman has a right not to have her bodily sovereignty violated.

However, we might start to structure our thoughts along other lines. We may even start in a different direction from the *same* starting point: detestation of slavery and of other instances of the negation of one person by another, for the latter's benefit. That would include sexism and sexual exploitation. We might conclude that we must never condone anyone's not being respected as an end in himself or herself. Murder, slavery, rape, and all other forms of disrespecting another person as an end in himself or herself must be ruled out decisively. If we believe that the embryonic life is a person, or is otherwise an end in itself, and if we believe that actively killing it is to fail to respect it as an end in itself, then abortion must evidently be ruled out.

---

[17] Judith Jarvis Thomson, "A Defense of Abortion," *Philosophy & Public Affairs* 1 (1971): 47–66.

It is also well to bear in mind that what for one person is a disastrous crash-landing at the foot of a slippery slope may for another be a legitimate inference. As we have seen, a famous, some would say infamous, example is provided by Peter Singer's conditional acceptance of early postnatal infanticide. We may recoil in horror from what is evidently the murder of innocent children. If that is what an acceptance of abortion leads to, then evidently, as its opponents so often proclaim, abortion ought stoutly to be resisted. How could Singer possibly justify such an unpalatable conclusion? It should be noted that he does not maintain that infanticide is justifiable under all or even under most circumstances. Still, an early neonate has not the interests or self-awareness of (most) older people, and some neonates have far fewer interests than do others. If its prospects in life are poor, for instance, as a result of severe birth defects, and if the burdens on parents would be great, perhaps on the whole infanticide would be for the best in such a case. If continuing to live were still in the neonate's own interests, however minimally, then infanticide would not be euthanasia.[18] However, according to this proposed point of view, infanticide might be morally justified nonetheless if the loss to the neonate were small and sufficiently outweighed by overall gains in utility.

If we do not recoil in horror from such a proposal and move toward rejecting abortion, as antiabortion activists would have us do, it might be because our thinking has moved along the same gradient in the opposite direction. We might accept the claim that there is no significant difference in the character of the embryonic life from what it is just before birth to what it is just after. We might also accept the claim that change is gradual and continuous. Nonetheless, we might balk at accepting the conclusion that a woman's autonomy and welfare may be infringed upon for the sake of a mindless blob of insentient biojelly. To accept such a conclusion might seem to us to be a crash-landing at the foot of a slippery slope that we venture onto when we would ban abortion at any stage. We might then ask what qualities an entity need have in order to have a right to life, and we might accordingly advocate permitting or prohibiting abortion with respect to some point in time prior to its having those qualities. Such a point might be before or after birth. Or, we might contend that the living entity gradually and continuously gains in moral significance, with birth itself having no particular importance. Or we might come to some other conclusion.

My concern at this point is not to resolve abortion disputes but to use them to illustrate how we may strive toward finding an optimal fit between moral theory and moral practice in a complexly real world. By hypothetically exploring slopes of varying direction, gradient, and slipperiness, we may achieve either or both of two valuable outcomes: We might substitute

---

[18] As we shall see in Chapter 9, *euthanasia*, properly so called, must be for the benefit of the one killed.

imagined slides down imagined slopes to imagined disasters for real slides to real ones. In addition, as thinking people, we might reshape our values through critical foresight and perhaps some lateral thinking, rather than through reaction to a narrow range of events or in mere acceptance of what we are told by others.

The lines of morality are not like the ideal lines of mathematics. They are broad and deep as well as long. (Edmund Burke, *Reflections on the Revolution in France*)

PART II

LIFE, DEATH, AND BIOETHICS

6

Being Alive

Life, and what is involved in living, has a great deal to do with ethics, even when we are not faced with matters of life and death. As I am proposing a *biocentric* approach to *bioethics*, it is all the more important that I explicate as clearly as possible what I take life to be. I prefer to ask it this way: What is it to be alive? Thus far I have largely postponed discussion of such topics. There is a point of view that holds that avoiding such discussion is wise, inasmuch as it is far easier and less problematic to recognize what is or is not alive than it is to explicate what life is. According to this line of thought, it is unlikely that much of importance should spring from resolving a conceptual issue that is usually so very easy to determine in practice. Distinguishing the living from the nonliving is something we can readily do in most circumstances. Life forms with which we are quite unfamiliar can usually be determined to *be* life forms by a nudge, a microscope, or a casual glance. Even a being as generally untalented as a maggot can quite reliably distinguish dead from living flesh. If we ever find extraterrestrial life, it will most probably be far easier to determine that it is alive than to explain in detail why.

Obviously there are tough cases and there are borderline cases. However, I do not approach the subject of what it is to be alive by concentrating on questions of where to draw the line. To be sure, such questions have their place, and they can be of critical importance in biomedical applications. It can sometimes be quite difficult, yet extremely important, to determine whether life is present. (If brain death occurs but heartbeat and respiration continue, artificially supported, is the person still alive? Is the person dead while the human body lives on? What about anencephalic neonates? There are other such questions that may be asked, and means and criteria must be devised when one is dealing with them.) Our inquiries about life will have some important implications in that regard. Just what, however, are we trying to capture with our criteria for determining when life is present or where lines are to be drawn? My concern is not with drawing lines but with developing an adequate and useful account of what being alive is – of what our lines well or poorly demarcate.

Accordingly, I approach the matter first by exploring what it is to be alive in unambiguous cases. I maintain that mistaken preconceptions about what it is to be alive, and what we are as living beings, have led to consequences that are wrong in practice. This is particularly but not exclusively so in bioethics. I argue that a more biologically informed conception of what it is to be alive, as has been developing in recent years in biology, is preferable because it is true in itself and leads to better consequences for us in practice. A better understanding of what it is to be alive can offer us a better understanding of what we humans are; of where our interests lie and why and to what degree; of how our interests interrelate; and of how we can best respect them. It also can give us matter for far less urgent reflection concerning extraterrestrial or artificial life, as well as nonhuman terrestrial life, all of which too may help us understand ourselves. Throughout, though, my main concern will be with human life. As I attempt to show subsequently, an understanding of what being alive is can give us useful insights into matters of importance for us humans. Of additional importance, it might even help us to decide some of those borderline cases.

Life Is as Life Does

One traditional though old-fashioned answer to the question of what it is to be alive is offered by *vitalism* – the belief that living beings differ from nonliving beings by virtue of having within them a special substance of some sort, one that gives a living being properties not possessed by any nonliving being. It is the life of the living being. This is an idea with a history stretching from Aristotle to the twentieth century. Sometimes this vital substance has been conceived of as being a very subtle fluid, or as an animal heat (the "spark of life"), a life force or *élan vital*, a generative force, or some sort of electricity or magnetism. The principal difficulty with vitalism is that no one has been able to find that special substance. Nor do we know anything at all about it save only that it is whatever it is that causes living beings to be alive. So, we are to understand that living beings are alive because they have something known only for its property of making them alive. As explanations go, that is a flat bust. It is the sort of pseudo-explanation satirized by Molière in his *The Imaginary Invalid*, where the dubious doctor explains that the soporific effect of opium is the result of its having a dormitive quality. It puts people to sleep because it has the quality of putting them asleep. Living beings are alive because they have the quality of being alive.

Let us try again. Instead of trying to start from scratch in defining what life is, perhaps the better approach would be to note which characteristics living beings actually do have. We might then hope to determine that being alive is a matter of having some certain combination of characteristics. That line of approach is certainly worth investigating. Still, such an approach has its dangers. We might wind up with a list of characteristics, but we may have no clear understanding of what they have to do with one another or why they must be on the list. A related danger is that there might be some properties that are shared by all known living beings yet are not necessarily inherent in being alive. All known life lives on Earth (or, in the case of astronauts, originates there). We could make that part of our definition and rule out the possibility of extraterrestrial life. Instead, we would do far better to rule out that definition, as we can imagine some distant planet having beings who behaved in such a way that it would be preposterous to deny that they are alive. They would probably be more alien than E.T. (the famous extraterrestrial being from the film of the same name), but it would be a very anemic definition of life that ruled out on principle their being alive. Could we perhaps rely on some more specific feature, such as having deoxyribonucleic acid, that is, DNA? In the film *E.T.*, the extraterrestrial creature did (improbably) have DNA – that being one of the many ways in which the film gave us a sense of kinship with E.T. Certainly it seems virtually inevitable that any life form would need to utilize *some* system of encoding, maintaining, and replicating information about how it is put together and functions.

That this much is so was known several years before Crick and Watson determined the molecular structure of DNA in 1953. Back in 1944, Erwin Schrödinger, in his pioneering work *What Is Life*,[1] approached his title question as the physicist he was – and he was one of the great ones. What physical constraints or requirements might life entail? At the time when he wrote, the existence of chromosomes was well known, and some minor things were then known about their function and chemical composition. Nevertheless, little as a whole was known on the topic, and very little of what this had to do with life. It *was* known that somehow involved with chromosomes were units of some sort that influences heredity. They were called *genes*, but there was no knowledge of their molecular composition or structure, and there was little knowledge of how they worked. Nothing was then known of their coding, replication, or decoding. A gene was just a something-or-other that somehow does something. Biologically and chemically, this was virtually unknown territory.

Schrödinger asked what would be required for a living system to hold itself together and to replicate its kind. Any living system, even the most simple, is highly complex. It requires the coordination of many things. Large

[1] Erwin Schrödinger, *What Is Life? The Physical Aspect of the Living Cell* (Cambridge: Cambridge University Press, 1944).

amounts of information[2] have to be recorded, maintained, and reproduced. This has to be done reliably, in the face of an environment that is rapidly fluctuating and often disruptive. (It is much like that now, but imagine how much more so it must have been back in the primordial soup from whence life is thought to have evolved.) Clearly, life has to have some means of protecting its order from disruption. Moreover, for it to be life, it must have some means of creating and structuring order in the first place, and it would have to take active steps to do that. Schrödinger reasoned that for life to maintain itself and produce further life, it would require the use of an aperiodic solid. This means of recording, maintaining, and reproducing information would have to be solid to stay together long enough to do the job. It would have to be *aperiodic* because anything periodic could only reiterate the same information. For instance, sodium chloride, or NaCl, forms simple cubical salt crystals. No matter how many times the instructions for a cube are repeated, mere repetition does not allow for further information. By not being regular and predictable, an aperiodic solid could carry much more information. Schrödinger also pointed out that there has to be some system of coding whereby the relevant information can be transcribed and utilized. Complexity must be able to generate further and appropriate complexity if it is to generate or even maintain life. What any of that might have to do with chromosomes was not known. Virtually nothing was known about the physics or chemistry of chromosomes, and virtually nothing about that of the gene. There was similar ignorance about the system for coding and decoding and about the means of replication. Even so, on the basis of the science of his day, Schrödinger was able to compute a reasonable approximation of the molecular size of the gene. Some years later, the discovery of the molecular structure of DNA, and from thence that of chromosomes and genes, evidently vindicated Schrödinger's prior theoretical conclusion. DNA and gene serve as aperiodic solid and unit of code, respectively. Although the human genome project of mapping our human genetic makeup has largely been completed, it will be quite some time before we fully determine

---

[2] Here and in similar instances, I use the term *information* as it is used in Information Theory, as distinguished from its usage in ordinary language, where it has to do with meaning. In the latter sense, the term is used to refer to truths, actual or presumed – statements in some language about some subject matter. For a language to convey information adequately, it must have sufficient complexity. As the term *information* is used in Information Theory, it refers to the complexity of a medium. The complexity of a medium does, incidentally, give it greater or lesser capacity to convey information in the ordinary-language sense, if that is what it is being used for. Or, conveying information can be a matter of conveying complexity into another medium with its own form of complexity. Meaning, or information in the ordinary-language sense of the term, need not be involved. It might be, but it does not have to be. Life is immensely complex, so for it to be maintained and reproduced, obviously there must be some means of maintaining and reproducing complexity, that is, information. Similarly, a genetic *code* does not encrypt or convey meaning. It is a means of conveying complexity.

just what genes do, individually or in combination. This is something I pursue further in a subsequent chapter.

But does the information storage and retrieval system of life require DNA specifically? Perhaps that is the only practical chemical possibility, but that is not something on which it would be appropriate to rule by prior definition. Certainly there is no persuasive scientific reason known why that should have to be the only possibility, or even why that should be probable. We cannot reasonably rule out the possibility that genuine extraterrestrials (if not the movie version) might have some quite different system, springing from some different set of circumstances and available resources, and the differing results of chance. Nor at this stage would it be sensible to rule out some sort of artificial life that might some day spring from biological and computer science, though that too would require some information storage and retrieval system. It may perhaps also be that the information storage and retrieval system of some living being somewhere is not entirely a part of the living being itself, but is somehow implicit (and suitably persistent) in a wider system enveloping that living being. We might possibly be such beings. Perhaps we have been thinking too much in terms of *things* being alive.

Stuart Kauffman brings a refreshingly different perspective to our inquiries concerning the nature and origin of life.[3] Life evolves from other life, but how did the first life start? A traditional approach has been to think in terms of some sort of a primordial soup of diverse molecules, warmed by solar energy and stirred by the occasional lightning bolt. How might this lead to the production, through chemical and physical means, of more and more complex molecules, and eventually to molecules capable of replicating themselves? A major problem is that of getting enough reactions going to produce enough suitable molecules fast enough. If the primordial soup is of oceanic proportions, molecules might find one another much too slowly, or they might get lost before they found one another at all. It would be useful if catalysts could facilitate the reactions. (A *catalyst* is a substance that greatly speeds up some chemical reaction, though it does not actually take part in that reaction.) The more kinds of molecules there are in a system, the greater the chances of there being one that catalyzes some possible reaction. More reactions lead to the production of molecules of even more kinds. Kauffman argues persuasively that when systems are of an appropriate kind and degree of complexity, they can become autocatalytic. A system is *autocatalytic* when it contains a diversity of molecules such that some sort of a molecule in the system catalyzes each kind of reaction in the system. The more the interconnections there are in the system, the more likely that autocatalysis will occur. With enough of the right kind of complexity,

---

[3] Stuart Kauffman, *At Home in the Universe: The Search for the Laws of Self-Organization and Complexity* (New York: Oxford University Press, 1995).

it becomes virtually certain. Even getting near to autocatalysis will greatly increase the speed at which the system produces molecules and develops new varieties. The system itself encodes information and becomes a key factor in the replication of molecules. From replication life develops. In his discussion – which I believe to be a magnificent contribution – Kauffman shifts the emphasis from the development of molecules of particular sorts to the development of *systems* of particular sorts. This evidently gives us a better view of how life originated, and it makes a valuable suggestion, which I take up later, about how life can usefully be thought of as being a system of a sort.

Kauffman also concluded that Schrödinger was not necessarily right in maintaining that life must incorporate a microencoded aperiodic solid to convey and replicate the requisite information. As it happens, life on earth does use such an information system (whether or not exclusively). Life else-where in the universe might have the information, or substantial amounts of it, structured into the ambient system itself. Perhaps some part of the information is in the system and some part of it is in some aperiodic solid (which may not be DNA at all). Even here on earth, some borderline cases replicate themselves without DNA, through the use of biotic resources in their environment. Viruses use living cells of other forms of life to replicate. It is not just that they use the cells as raw material. They utilize the cells' capacity, through each cell's own DNA, to respond to input and replicate molecules. In effect, a virus hacks into a cell's system and tampers with the input, causing the cell to produce multiple copies of the virus. Whether this is enough to qualify viruses as being alive might best be left as a debatable point. Certainly it would be question-begging to rule that they are nonliving entities simply because they lack DNA.[4] Moreover – I get back to this later – there is far more information required for the continuance of human life and for its replication than is contained in our DNA. The presence of DNA is quite a good indicator, here on earth, at any rate, of the presence of life or past life. Nonetheless, it would be too narrow and too question-begging to require it in a general definition of life.

There seems to be no one substance that life *must* have, neither DNA nor anything else. Nor can we look to any *élan vital.* It may be that life requires carbon and water, but even that is not absolutely certain. Perhaps silicon could do the job under some circumstances (on some other planet, if not this one). In any case, we would need some rationale for specifying which combinations of hydrogen, oxygen, carbon, or other substances were the

---

4 I am suggesting that viruses are on the borderline between living and nonliving entities, but this is not to suggest that viruses were intermediate stages in the evolutionary process. Presumably, we must conclude that viruses, as we are acquainted with them, came into exis-tence only *after* the existence of beings with DNA, inasmuch as their means of reproduction requires the existence of beings with DNA.

right ones. Instead of asking of what stuff is life made, it appears much more promising to ask what it is to be alive. Distinguished biologist Lynn Margulis puts it this way:

Life is distinguished not by its chemical constituents but by the behavior of its chemicals. The question "What is life?" is thus a linguistic trap. To answer according to the rules of grammar, we must supply a noun, a thing. But life on Earth is more like a verb. (Lynn Margulis and Dorion Sagan, *What Is Life?*)[5]

Are there any activities by means of which we might recognize even a bizarre or alien life form, whatever its physiochemical composition might be? Moving, breathing, eating, digesting, excreting – such activities as these are widely characteristic of life. Even here we have to be careful not to be too parochial, not to include too little or too much. Not all living things move. Bacteria and many other living things do not breathe in any straightforward sense. Again, some living things absorb rather than eat. We may perhaps lump eating, breathing, and absorbing together as forms of intake of food or fuel, which is then utilized, with the extraction of energy and the emission of waste material. Living things do that – but so too do motor cars, airplanes, and power lawnmowers.

If we are to seek an understanding of life in terms of what living beings do – which still seems like a promising line of approach – we need to develop some more finely grained way of differentiating actions, or some more central conception of what being alive is to do. Is eating, breathing, and the like, as suitably defined, what it is to be alive? In contrast, are such actions *how* living beings (usually) do what being alive is doing? We must find the right level of exactitude and generality. Mae-Wan Ho expressed these questions:

What is life? Can life be defined? Each attempt at definition is bound to melt away, like the beautiful snowflake one tries to look at close up.... I shall offer my own tentative definition... which... at least seems closer to the mark: *life is a process of being an organising whole*... a *process* and not a thing, nor a property of a material thing or structure. As is well known, the material constituents of our body are continually being broken down... yet the whole remains recognizably the same individual.... Life must therefore reside in the patterns of dynamic flows of matter and energy.... From this, one can see that the "whole" does not refer to an isolated, monadic entity.... [I]t refers to a system open to the environment, that

5 Lynn Margulis and Dorion Sagan, *What Is Life?* (New York: Simon and Schuster, 1995; later editions, Berkeley: University of California Press), p. 22. This book is not to be confused with Schrödinger's book of the same title, which it postdates by half a century; indeed, Sagan and Margulis revisit his question. For a further discussion of the scientific history of the topic subsequent to Schrödinger's presentation, with some informed speculation about future progress, see *What Is Life? The Next Fifty Years: Speculations of the Future of Biology*, ed. Michael P. Murphy and Luke A. J. O'Neill (Cambridge: Cambridge University Press, 1995).

enstructures or organizes itself (and its environment) . . . (Mae-Won Ho, *The Rainbow and the Worm*)[6]

This approach puts the emphasis on self-organizing flows of matter and energy rather than on those various activities, such as moving and breathing, by means of which they carry on.

A very striking thing about all living beings is that they have and maintain order, doing so in the face of environmental forces that tend to destroy them and their order. They seem to fly in the face of the Second Law of Thermodynamics, which states that the universe tends over time toward disorder and randomness.[7] Everything that happens somewhat increases the amount of disorder. Ultimately, as projected, this will result in the "heat death" of the universe (in classical thermodynamics, the second law is a basic postulate that applies to any system involving measurable heat energy transfer), wherein no order at all remains. Living beings, however, build and grow and replicate, creating more order in and around themselves rather than less. This is not contrary to the Second Law of Thermodynamics, though, because living beings are not closed systems. A *closed* system is one that does not allow any inflow or outflow of any source of energy, such as heat, light, or matter. It is to closed systems that the second law directly applies. The universe as a whole is necessarily a closed system, and there is no way that it can gain more order. In fact, it must always drift toward less order. However, within a closed system there can be *open* systems, those that do admit a through flow of energy. Although it is not a necessary feature of open systems in general, there are some open systems that are such that within that system the amount of order *increases*. This is not to say that there is some special sort of system that can increase the overall total amount of order there is. Even here the second law applies. Systems that develop increased order *within* themselves can do so only by exporting disorder outside of the system.

These are what have become known since the work of Ilya Prigogine as *dissipative systems*: They maintain themselves by taking in energy and dissipating it in more disorderly form. The total amount of disorder there is in the universe continues to increase, increasing all the more because of the activity of the open system. Thus, although the overall trend in the broader picture is downstream toward disorder, dissipative systems manage, for the

[6] Mae-Won Ho, *The Rainbow and the Worm: The Physics of Organisms* (Singapore: World Scientific, 1998), pp. 6–7.

[7] More formally, the Second Law of Thermodynamics is stated in terms of *entropy*. Entropy is a scientific concept, which has a very precise and technical definition, but which we may take as referring to disorder. The Second Law of Thermodynamics states that the entropy of an isolated system that is not in equilibrium increases any time anything happens in it. Moreover, whenever two systems are combined, the entropy of the resulting system is even greater than the total of the entropies of the separate systems. Inevitably, there is an overall trend toward higher levels of entropy or lower levels of order.

time being, to travel upstream against the current. They utilize energy from some source to increase or maintain their own order, passing on the energy in degraded (less ordered) form. We living beings are dissipative systems. We keep alive by continuously drawing order from our environment and leaving disorder in our wake. Human life, like (nearly) all life on Earth, ultimately feeds on a flow of energy from our sun, using that energy to organize and maintain itself. Moreover, as Prigogine points out, it is characteristic of dissipative systems to arise in systems that are far from equilibrium. He also notes that life exists in systems that are far from equilibrium, and he remarks that

life, far from being outside the natural order, appears as the supreme expression of the self-organizing processes that occur.... [This suggests] the idea that life is the result of spontaneous self-organization that occurs whenever conditions for it permit. (Ilya Prigogine and Isobelle Stengers, *Order Out of Chaos*)[8]

In other words, life springs from disequilibrium situations and must some-how keep its footing in that tumultuous milieu that gave it birth.

What we have here is clearly an important part of the answer. We living beings are dissipative systems. Still, there must be more to it than that. There are other dissipative systems in which a through flow of energy has the effect of creating or maintaining order. A hurricane is one example and a flame is another. Yet another is a refrigerator drawing on a supply of electricity to structure coldness at the price of increased disorder through its heat exhaust. However, none of these things are alive. Living beings and refrigerators are evidently thermodynamically open systems, but what else is required of a living system? Refrigerators do well what they do and flames and hurricanes can be awesome. What, let us ask, does an algal cell have as a living being that those other things lack? It is not the amount of energy or the rate of its flow that makes the difference, obviously. It seems like a step in the right direction to note that algae reproduce themselves, as anyone who has ever kept an aquarium can testify. That is certainly an action in which life is prone to engage. Nevertheless, flames too can reproduce, though flames and algae both require certain minimal conditions in which to do so. In contrast, some living things, such as mules and most members of the worker caste of social insects, cannot reproduce. Again, flames and hurricanes can grow, and crystals can grow too. Therefore, although growth and reproduction are important elements in the story of life, we must look more closely to find what distinguishes life from nonlife.

Let us look at things from a different angle as we ask what distinguishes those dissipative open systems that are living from those that are not. Instead

---

[8] Ilya Prigogine and Isobelle Stengers, *Order Out of Chaos: Man's New Dialogue with Nature* (New York: Bantam Books, 1984), pp. 175–176. His ideas are perhaps most accessible in this book. Prigogine won the Nobel Prize for Chemistry in 1977, for his work on dissipative systems.

of focusing on what they do when things are going well, let us consider what happens when things start to get out of kilter for them. What do living and nonliving beings do then? Wind, rain, lack of fuel, and other things may threaten a fire with extinction, a collapse toward a much lower state of order. What does a fire do when it is in danger of "dying"? Fires go on doing what fires do, burning. A fire may spread to a new source of fuel, or sparks might be carried down wind, thereby starting a new fire, as dictated by external circumstances. What a fire does not do is to respond to a threat by taking action to avoid or minimize it. A hurricane, losing its power when it goes over land, does not then aim for the nearest body of warm saltwater in search of healing. Living beings can do better than that.

All living beings, even humble algal cells, act to maintain themselves. Keeping even one living cell going requires quite a lot of keeping things in kilter. The cell wall must be maintained, and the correct chemicals in the correct proportion have to be kept within the cell wall and some others have to be kept out, which requires adjustments to the rate at which they travel in or out across the cell wall. Meanwhile, if it is an algal cell, it has to adjust to varying amounts of light and carbon dioxide, and it has to prevent waste products, such as oxygen, from building up too much. Vastly more internal chemical and physical processes than those mentioned here have to be monitored and kept in order, requiring constant adjustments. These adjustments involve feedback systems, such that when something starts to go wrong, this triggers a corrective response. Such and much more a single cell has to do to stay alive. A more complicated living being, such as a human, has vastly more to do. As well as keeping its cells going, or enough of them, it has to regulate such matters as temperature, blood pressure, insulin–blood sugar balance, digestive fluids, salt levels, and so on: Merely to mention a few regulatory functions wrongly suggests that they are few enough to be enumerated. The more biomedical science looks for regulatory functions, the more it finds, from the multitudes in a human cell to the megamultitudes we are still discovering in humans.

At this point we have somewhat narrowed and sharpened the focus in inquiry into life. We can reasonably say of life that it is a process, one that takes place in dissipative thermodynamically open systems and that incorporates a vast number of self-regulatory feedback loops. As it happens, though, there are also nonliving dissipative open systems that incorporate self-correcting feedback systems. A thermostat is an example. The one in the refrigerator starts the cooling process when the interior gets too warm, and it turns it off when the interior is cool enough. So long as the electricity keeps flowing and the thermostat system works, the refrigerator is able to maintain itself in the right temperature range. Again, "smart" missiles are able to home in even on moving targets, correcting their course as they go. Self-correcting systems can get considerably more complex than that. There are computer programs that can do marvelous things along those lines. None of them, though, have achieved anything like the complexity of feedback, self-regulation, and self-maintenance achieved by a single living cell, let alone a human being.

This suggests the possibility that life is best characterized as dissipative thermodynamically open systems with *very high* levels of self-regulation and self-maintenance. Kenneth Sayre offers the following definition:

> The typifying mark of a living system ... appears to be its persistent state of low entropy, sustained by metabolic processes for accumulating energy, and maintained in equilibrium with its environment by homeostatic feedback devices. (Kenneth Sayre, *Cybernetics and the Philosophy of Mind*)[9]

Here I would offer a few comments on terminology. *Metabolic* processes are those by which living beings create, maintain, and, as needs be, dismantle ordered structure. It seems circular therefore to use the term, characterizing life in terms of life. I suggest that it would be better just to delete the term without replacement in the definition. (Metabolic processes can subsequently be characterized as those that accumulate energy, maintain order, and so on, to a high enough degree – or as those that do so in living beings.) Another problematic term here is *homeostatic*. It is a term that is sanctioned by usage, but it is profoundly misleading. From the Greek word *homeo*, same, plus *stasis*, standing, it suggests that what these feedback devices do is to maintain the living being in the same condition, a static condition. Nothing could be further from the biological truth. Life is process and revolves around change and maintaining itself in the face of change. Our life processes – temperature, blood pressure, blood-sugar level, carbon dioxide–oxygen balance, and so on, from the subcellular level all the way up – these are not maintained at *exactly* the same level. Rather, they fluctuate within or around a range of values conducive to our effective functioning. When we start to drift too far out of the appropriate range of values, as living systems we take steps to get ourselves back into the appropriate range. We may, for instance, shiver or pull on a jumper if too cold, we may sweat if too hot, our blood vessels may contract or expand, and various other responses help us to get back into a suitable temperature range. Nevertheless, it is a range, not one static temperature. Numerous and varied other conditions may trigger other responses, whether conscious or, much more commonly, unconscious. In each case, our drifting out of our appropriate range of conditions triggers a response that moves the system back toward its appropriate range. It may be a broad range or a very narrow one, depending on the particular biological function. Instead of the term *homeostatic*, a much better term would be *homeorhetic*. Though this term is much less familiar, it is far more accurate. From the word *rheos*, referring to current or flow, a

9 Kenneth Sayre, *Cybernetics and the Philosophy of Mind* (London: Routeledge & Kegan Paul, 1976), p. 91.

homeorhetic system is one that maintains a sufficiently even flow. The flow is corrected when it becomes too great or too little.[10]

In light of this information, I offer the following statement as a characterization of life:

A living being is an ongoing process, occurring in a dissipative thermodynamically open system, organizing and maintaining itself in near equilibrium with its environment by means of high levels of homeorhetic feedback subsystems.

This is a broad characterization of life, but I offer it as a reasonably serviceable one, and one that is adequate for our purposes.[11] It includes or excludes pretty much what we would want to include or exclude and does so on the basis of what seems on consideration to be a plausible rationale. I think that we would be reluctant to recognize as being alive any being, earthly or otherwise, that failed to meet the characterization. (I suggest too that the equivocal cases, such as viruses, are equivocal for the right reasons. They really are on the line.) An extraterrestrial being, however strange, that did meet the characterization would likely be accepted as being alive. (That is, if we realized what was going on. That might prove difficult in practice. The movie character E.T. was far more humanoid than we might reasonably expect of an extraterrestrial.)

We have already noted that self-maintenance is an important characteristic of life. I also stress that self-organization is a remarkable and central character of living entities. It is not just that they maintain themselves; they bring about that very being (or state of being) that they act so as to maintain. A thermostat cannot make itself, and it would be too much of a stretch of the imagination to claim that a flame or a hurricane does. In a suitable environment, flames and hurricanes occur and grow, and they move toward fairly predictable end states. However, they do not take corrective action when they drift out of the range of conditions conducive to a particular end state. A living being, in contrast, has quite high levels of homeorhesis that serve not only to maintain it but to keep it on course toward that which is implicit within itself to become. As is evident, immature living entities, such as seedlings and embryos, are particularly oriented toward developing their self-organization. Older beings tend more toward

---

[10] This point was made, and terminology proposed, by Dorion Sagan and Lynn Margulis in their "The Gaian Perspective of Ecology," *The Ecologist* 13 (1983): 160–167. The term is first used on p. 161.

[11] The question has been put to me of whether spiritual beings – God, angels, ghosts, or whatever – would be alive according to this definition. Inasmuch as such beings are presumably not material beings, and therefore not bound by the laws of thermodynamics or other physical laws, they would not meet my characterization of life. However, if some of the things said of such beings are true, then there might be some significantly related sense in which they could be said to be alive. I do not know enough about such beings to be able to say. I suspect (or is it only a prejudice?) that any such beings would be better thought of as processes than as things.

self-maintenance per se, but even there the cells are constantly building and rebuilding themselves. You may recall that Plato (*Phaedo* 8ob) described the living body as "never constant nor abiding true to itself." In truth, it is not constant, yet it has great constancy and does abide true to itself. If it did not, it could not be alive. More than that, being true to itself in this way is what being alive is. The Chilean biologists, Humberto Maturana and Francisco Varela, coined the term *autopoiesis,* from the word *auto,* self, plus *poiesis,* making.[12] An autopoietic system is continuously self-making. It is continuously self-maintaining and self-organizing. Autopoiesis is a characteristic of ongoing systems as wholes, rather than a characteristic of their components at any particular time. Life is autopoietic. Furthermore, being autopoietic, being self-maintaining and self-organizing, to a high enough degree of complexity, *is* being alive.

In my proposed characterization I refer to *near* equilibrium for reasons that I have already stated in connection with my rejection of the concept of homeostasis. Life is always a fluctuating matter of more or less. Another relative term is *high levels.* As things stand now, there is huge gap between the level of homeorhesis, self-organizing and self-maintaining, of even the most sophisticated human contrivance, and the vastly higher levels of even the simplest living being. In future years that gap will certainly narrow and may vanish entirely. That we humans might eventually be able to create artificial life is not contrary to my conception of life (though I would worry about what we might do with such a life). Certainly I am quite ready to accept the idea implicit here that the difference between living and nonliving, like that between day and night, is a matter of degree. *Of course* there are gray areas, with any precise lines being negotiable and somewhat arbitrary. Kauffman persuades me that in its origin, life came about gradually and as a matter of degree. That it might be a matter of degree in its current occurrence, as well, does not seem at all implausible or improbable. The lower ranges of life may well fade out into viruses, prions, or who knows what. Life is not a matter of some magic *élan vital* that is either there or else is not. Indeed, such absolutes would be quite out of character for life. Not only is the difference between living and nonliving a matter of degree, but it is also true, as I consider subsequently, that the difference between life and death is a matter of degree and without exact boundary lines – a point of considerable significance in bioethics.

The Openness of Life

What is also of bioethical importance is the fact that life, as a living process, is in continuous interaction with its environment. Otherwise it could not be

---

[12] Much has been written, by many writers, on autopoiesis. A good source is Humberto Maturana and Francisco J. Varela, *Autopoiesis and Cognition: The Realization of the Living* (Dordrecht: Reidel, 1980).

an *open* system, and a dissipative one at that. Its activities of self-organization and self-maintenance require it to continuously interact with its surroundings. This is a logical necessity, not just a contingent fact that might conceivably have been otherwise. Our life processes are part of an interconnected web of processes that extend far beyond ourselves or what we think of as ourselves. Our very breathing is part of the world cycle of carbon dioxide and oxygen, a cycle that depends on and is part of the being of innumerable hordes of living beings. That cycle is only one of the many interactions in which we, as living processes, intermingle our life processes with those of others. For that matter, we are highly dependent on certain bacteria in our intestines. From our dietary needs and activities to our social needs and activities, we are interactive parts of the living world. These life processes, from bacteria to biosphere, are part of our own life process and part of what we are. I believe that this interconnection, or interbeing, of life has profound implications for the ethics of our dealings with our environment, but that is beside the point here. In application to human bioethics, the point is that a living human being as an entity separate from its surroundings, particularly its living surroundings, is as impossible as the catless grin of the Cheshire cat.

The interflowing of life runs far more deeply than what I have thus far suggested. To develop a topic with reference to humans, I first turn to lichen. A lichen is a living being, usually green, often found growing on rocks, trees, and roofs. Many people confuse lichen with moss, or take it to be a low-grade plant of some other sort. Actually, a lichen is a symbiotic union – beings living together for mutual benefit – formed of two quite radically different organisms, alga and fungus.[13] Only the alga is a plant; the fungus is a member of a quite different kingdom of life. The alga performs photosynthesis, making food for both partners from carbon dioxide, water, and solar energy. The fungus serves to provide water and other useful minerals and to anchor the lichen to whatever it is attached. The lichen is not just a conglomerate of different living things. It lives as an organism in its own right, having characteristics possessed by neither alga nor fungus, and living where they cannot. (There are even lichen growing on the barren rocks of Antarctica, and they would be capable of surviving on Mars.) Distinct life processes flow together to form another life process, one with its own identity different from either alga or fungus. Yet within the lichen, the algae and fungi remain what they are. If we look through a microscope

---

[13] There are many different types of algae and fungi that may be combined in lichen. Sometimes the fungus is partnered by cyanobacteria instead of algae. Like algae, cyanobacteria carry on photosynthesis; formerly, they were considered to be blue-green algae, but it has since been determined that they are not algae. They are not plants at all. They are living beings of a quite different sort, of a different domain. However, this does not affect my overall point.

we can see distinct algal and fungal cells, the former easily distinguished by their color.

If we look more closely through the microscope, we see the particles within the algal cells (or those of the cyanobacteria) that make them green: the chloroplasts. This is where the photosynthesis actually goes on. The chloroplasts are contained within their individual membranes, and they have their own quite different DNA that is transmitted separately in reproduction. These particles, organelles, are virtually distinct organisms. Indeed, biologists have concluded that their ancestors once were. Apparently their ancestors once entered the ancestral cells of plants, either as parasites or as undigested food, and some were able to take up residence there. This led to a lasting beneficial union, symbiosis, with all of the world's green plants stemming from that union of different lives. Also within the algal cells, and the cells of other plants and also animals, are mitochondria. These are organelles of another kind, having a different function. They are involved with the release of energy. In our human cells, you and I also have them. Every beat of our heart, nearly everything in our body that requires the release of energy, requires them. Were they somehow magically removed, we would be dead in a split second.[14] They too are contained within their own membrane and have their distinct DNA that is transmitted separately in reproduction. Like chloroplasts, mitochondria reproduce asexually, by division in the manner of bacteria. Biologists have likewise concluded that these organelles originated as independent organisms that became included in our ancestral cells and formed symbiotic unions. Of course, this was a very long time before our ancestors were anywhere near being human. Even before that, the evidence suggests, lives were coming together to form new kinds of life.

We are eukaryotes. Each of our body cells contains our DNA within a cell nucleus, separated by a membrane from the rest of the cell. Such cells are said to be *eukaryotic* (from the Greek word meaning "well nucleated"). As well as humans, all other animals, and also plants and fungi, have eukaryotic cells. In contrast, bacterial cells, lacking such a nucleus, are *prokaryotic* (before nucleation). All living beings having cells are either eukaryotic or prokaryotic. In prokaryotes, the genetic material is dispersed throughout the cell and so is more likely to come in contact with the outside world. Bacteria exchange genes with one another rather promiscuously and rapidly. In this way bacteria are – at the negligible cost of astronomical numbers of individual lives – able to change to fit conditions in the rapidly fluctuating world that confronts it. There always seems to be some new strain of infectious bacteria to confound the efforts of health-care professionals. The evolutionary strategy of prokaryotes has been fairly successful. Even so, we eukaryotes have some things going for us. We keep our DNA in long,

[14] In point of fact, that is pretty much how cyanide poisoning works and why it works so fast.

ordered sequences, our chromosomes. Except for the highly ordered give and take of sexual reproduction, our genetic material is protected within the nuclear membrane. This allows us to develop the more complex bodily structures, on the basis of more complex DNA, that is typical of eukaryotes. The rapidly interchanging genetic kaleidoscope of prokaryotic life would tend to preclude that. The evolutionary strategy of prokaryotes has been quite successful within their own environmental niches, and our strategy within ours. In our origins, we eukaryotes seem to have developed from symbiosis between prokaryotes. First our very early ancestors ate or parasitized one another; then some of them came to join in mutually beneficial associations that evolved into eukaryotes.[15]

We humans stem from symbioses building on other symbioses, many life processes joining together to form new life with its own character and interests. Biologically, life is prone to do that and it is evidently part of the earliest origins of *Homo sapiens*. For that matter, life joining with life to form more lives happens whenever sperm meets ovum. From the past, our life processes stem from countless others of diverse kinds. In the present, our life processes mingle with those of the entire world, interacting and reciprocally affecting one another. None of this is to deny our identity as individuals, with our own unique character and moral importance. We are each unique and morally important. That our life processes intermingle with other life processes, that they do so in the particular ways they do, and that there are no precise boundaries in space and time is part of the character of our own life process. We are still individual centers of self-organizing and self-maintaining life, with our individual character and our individual moral importance. Having definite and precise boundaries is not necessary in order to be an individual something. A nonliving case in point we have already noted is the planet Jupiter. Closer to home (and very much ongoing dissipative processes) are hurricanes. Like other eddies occurring in other fluids, a hurricane is a process that continues for a time and, while continuing, overlaps other processes, and that throughout lacks precise boundaries. Nonetheless, a hurricane certainly is something and certainly it has an impact in the world, and it can be distinguished from other hurricanes. In these ways we living beings are similar, however we may otherwise differ.

Boundary questions still have their uses. Sometimes there are important bioethical questions that arise along the gray edges. When does a particular life stop? Is that the same point where being a person stops, or is it some other point? When does a particular life (or a particular person) start? Do the life processes shared by an embryo and its mother imply that the embryo

[15] Lynn Margulis did much of the pioneering work concerning the development of new forms of life out of symbiosis. She explains this in very accessible form in her book (with her son Dorion Sagan) *What Is Life?*, which was quoted earlier; see footnote 5, this chapter.

is not a separate being? Even though it has a distinct genetic identity? More generally, if the life processes, and to that extent the selves, of different individuals overlap, how do we determine moral priorities? Bioethical discussions have been tackling such questions for years. I will not be able fully to answer every one of those questions, but I hope to offer a different perspective and a more productive approach to those questions through the biocentric view.

Before we tackle those questions, or try to determine just what is riding on them, we would do well to take a further look at that question of what our good is – and of what constitutes injury to a human at one stage or another of her or his life. As living beings we are life processes carrying on, different lives carrying on in different ways. Whatever our particular character, each of us is a life that continually acts to organize or maintain itself within ranges of states determined by the character of that individual life (ranges that themselves change over time). Life acts to cohere with itself, each life as the sort of life it is, and to maintain itself. Some of our character stems from our heredity or our environment, and some we make for ourselves. To ask what is our good is to ask what is good for the life process we are. In light of that, we would have to say that at least part of the answer is that what is bad for us is to fail to maintain ourselves within our optimal range of states, whereas our good lies in maintaining ourselves within our optimal range. Perhaps there are other things that are good, such as acting morally past the point of self-sacrifice, or devotion to God or to some great ideal. Still, our own good, in the sense of our personal welfare, lies in maintaining our own life in all of its aspects, innate or acquired, in healthy operating condition – coherently in what we are and viably in our ongoingness. That is where our own immediate interests lie. Broadly but accurately, we can say that the good for us is our overall health. In Chapter 7 I attempt to elaborate on the concept of *health*, in a sense encompassing our whole being.

A few more words on matters of degree: There are some notably similar gradations of degree to be noted here. One might think of (possibly) living beings as occurring along a spectrum[16] of instances, from beings that are clearly not alive at one end of the scale through beings at the other end that are clearly and often richly and complexly alive. Wherever we draw the line between living and nonliving being, there will be some beings that are almost but not quite instances of life and others that are just barely instances of life. For that matter, life evidently evolved along a similar spectrum. Not only is there no need for any *élan vital*, we need not invoke God or any transcendent Truth or Purpose for these spectra of instances to exist.

---

[16] What I am calling a *spectrum* may not be a proper continuum, though it is certainly a gradation.

Similarly, we might think of the interests of living beings as falling along a spectrum from none at all, or not much even for a not-much being, on up to the most highly developed. We might likewise say, in a quite respectable sense of *purpose*, that purposes fall along a spectrum from not much to quite a lot by means of intermediate points, all without the need for outside intervention. It is in my interests to have adequate insulin and it is a purpose of the Islets of Langerhans in my pancreas to supply it. For that matter, it is the purpose of certain features of a virus to allow it to locate a cell suitable for reproduction. Here we have natural purposes arrived at by natural selection. There is no need for any external purpose giver, or for a conscious human, to have conscious purposes for all the many things his or her body is doing. Obviously we do sometimes intervene with conscious purposes. Whether there is occasional intervention from some external purpose giver is a matter we can ponder at our leisure.

7

Being Healthy

So far, I have ventured the conclusion that our good as living beings lies in our coherently maintaining ourselves in a healthily functional condition as what we, in our whole being, are. What is good for us, we might fairly though broadly say, is to live a *healthy* life. But what is health? Like life itself, health is a familiar thing that we nevertheless find difficult to define. Generally, it is far more difficult to determine that a being is healthy, or that it is not, than it is to determine whether it is alive, so we are all the more in need of a workable characterization of health. It would be lovely if we could find some definition that was clear, simple, unambiguous, precise, and accurate. Such definitions are to be found in mathematics, but the living world tends to be not as neat as that. Health, like life, is a matter of ambiguity and imprecision, and it is a matter of more and less. In such matters as this, the simplest answers often tend not to be the most correct. What it is to be healthy is also determined in some part by the environment in which the living being occurs, as well as by the condition of that being itself. The nature of health is more a matter of factual discovery (and sometimes of choice of priorities) than it is of theoretical definition. My endeavor here is to develop a conception of health that is workable and adequate for our purposes. As Aristotle correctly observed,

[o]ur discussion will be adequate if it has as much clearness as the subject-matter admits of, for precision is not to be sought for alike in all discussions ... it is the mark of an educated [person] to look for precision in each class of things just as far as the nature of the subject admits. (Aristotle, *Nicomachean Ethics*, 1094b)

I would extend that (I believe in the spirit of Aristotle) to note that we must look for the *sort* of precision and accuracy appropriate to a given subject matter. Life is to be understood, if at all, only in its own terms. Nonetheless – indeed, all the more so – there are important matters about life and health to be considered, and we should not use Aristotle's disclaimer as an excuse for vaguing out.

As life is a very complex matter, health can be no less so. It is particularly complex for us humans. Each of us is not just one life process but a complexly interconnected system of a great many processes. Things can go well or poorly for us in a great many differing and often very different ways. We may suffer from anything from cancer to psychoses, by way of athlete's foot and cultural alienation. In contrast to health, such specific conditions are easier to characterize and identify. It is usually far easier for us to notice something's being wrong than it is to notice something's not being wrong. Accordingly, perhaps the easiest way would be to characterize health in terms of the absence of specific adverse conditions, or in terms of not having them in too high of a degree.

As individuals we do often tend to think of our health in terms of departures from it, rather than in terms of what it is, and as communities, we frequently think along similar lines. It is easier to notice things going wrong than going right. Such an approach accords well with the temper of our times and is useful for many purposes. We like to get outcomes of a definite character, and departures from health seem far more definite than do nondepartures.[1] In our individual lives, the need for particular cure is often far more likely to engage our attention than is the need for general prevention. This tendency is more a fault of our ways of thinking and measuring than it is a fault of negative definition as such. Nonetheless, there is an additional fundamental flaw in our thinking, one that leads to the inappropriate measurement of results and assessment of alternatives, one that very much does undermine the utility and cogency of a definition of health in terms of the absence of adverse conditions. That flaw lies in conducting our thinking in terms of criteria that are limited and largely disconnected, a list of states not to be in and conditions not to have, rather than on some sort of a condition to have. This approach is yet another one of those dubious elements from our Enlightenment heritage. In our hunger for exactitude, we focus on the several measurable aspects rather than on the broader whole. This gives us an obscured view, whether in terms of health in the community or

---

[1] We also, as communities with public budgets, like to get verifiably good returns for our effort and expenditure. In an age of economic rationalism, there is a premium on measurement, specificity, and outcome. It is very impressive if we can present figures that show that for *x* dollars we can effectively and verifiably alleviate or cure some adverse condition some specific and well-confirmed percentage of the time. This way of thinking, however, has its drawbacks. Nonhappenings can be quite as important as happenings, though they are far less definite and specific. Nonetheless, we still tend to gravitate toward exact and tangible outcomes in disproportionate preference. We confront them with more immediacy. Doing something about some exact number of heart attacks that have actually occurred is more definite and measurable than is lessening the incidence of heart attacks. Prevention may save more lives for less money, and we may have substantial reason for believing that to be so, but the lives saved are neither specific in identity nor precise in number. Accordingly, the priority in our culture is likely to go to alleviation rather than to prevention as alleviation offers more immediacy and more precision.

in terms of the health of the individual. Health is a way of being or, rather, a range of ways of being. It is not a matter of not being this or not being that.

To be sure, noting concrete examples of unhealthy conditions can help us gain insight into the differences between health and ill health. The central difficulty with the tactic of defining health in terms of the absence of ill health is not that it is negative but that it cannot get us where we need to go. Were there a complete *independent* definition of ill health to be found, we could go on from there. Without an independent definition, defining health in terms of the absence of ill health traps us in circularity. *Ill health, disease, adverse condition* (adverse to what?): Such terms can really be defined only in terms of health or in terms of some concept derivative from that of health. We can hold the circularity at arm's length by defining some (progressively larger) number of standard factors that must be kept with an acceptable range of states, with ill health (or whatever we call it) being a deviation from the standard range that is greater than the acceptable one. Nonetheless, the acceptable range of states overtly or covertly refers us back to health.

In a perfectly respectable, albeit predefinitional, sense, a number of specific conditions are clearly unhealthy and can be identified as such. It is easy enough to decide in the case of cancer and the common cold – but what about obesity (defined how?), or flat feet, or crooked teeth, or homosexuality, or having some percentage of sickle-shaped blood cells? What we need now is a rationale for determining whether and why some condition is or is not an adverse condition. This obviously cannot be purely a matter of arbitrary decision. Nor will it do to cast our definitions in terms of *normality*, for some abnormal conditions, such as having musical talent, or an ability to run a four-minute mile, or having a high IQ, are presumably not unhealthy. What we need is a clearer understanding of why adverse conditions are adverse, and of what it is they detract from. Instead of focusing on a number of detached conceptual particulars such as the having or not having of Condition A, B, or C, we need to think of good or poor health *in terms of the whole and individual person, and of the life that individual leads in that person's particular circumstances.*[2] The sickle cells that might cause debility for one person might be a life saver for another in another part of the world where malaria is endemic (because the sickle-cell trait shields against it). The homosexuality that might be very gratifying in San Francisco might be crushingly frustrating or else fatal in Tehran. There are values at work, to be sure, but not pure subjectivity. The values are *the values implicit in that person's life.*

---

[2] I should stress that health is a matter of what is required by *that* person in his or her circumstances. Membership in a culture or species is part of a person's circumstances, but what is characteristic of other members of the species or society is relevant only incidentally, if at all, to the nature and needs of *that* person's health.

Certainly at least a broad and general characterization of good and poor health emerges from the conceptions of life and interests that we have been developing. If being alive is to maintain oneself within a range of favorable states, with one's interests lying in that which contributes to one's coherent and effective functioning as an ongoing life process, then it seems appropriate to conclude that being healthy is being an ongoing life process that is capable of coherently maintaining itself within a range of states favorable to its continuation as a coherent and viable ongoing life process of the particular kind that it is. I prefer the usage "being healthy is . . . " rather than "health is a state of . . . " because the latter wrongly suggests something static. Being healthy requires being able to maintain oneself over time, and this is a matter of unceasing adjustment. Life, as we will recall, is a matter not of homeostasis but of homeorhesis. Instead of being precisely constant, life is *persistent*, maintaining itself, when healthy, within its changing range of appropriate ranges. It has a sort of *momentum*, resisting perturbations, internal and external, and it has *elasticity*, tending to recover after perturbation. We have what we might (as a first approximation) think of as a *cyclic stability* as we oscillate around a favored range of states. Our life has trajectory *stability*, as we maintain ourselves while moving through various phases of our lives from the womb to the tomb. There is a real sort of constancy here but by no means one of stasis. Nor is it properly cyclic. What may seem at first like cycles on closer inspection may best be thought of as spirals stretching out through time, wheeling about the long trajectory of our lives. As life goes on, we never return to just the same state.[3] We live by maintaining our life processes as we flow through time, we are in good or poor health as we are able to do this well or poorly, and the final collapse of our ability to do so is our death.

Accordingly, we may appropriately describe physical and mental illnesses (and maladjustments) as being instances of some breakdown in our coherent effective functioning, of breakdown in our ability to maintain ourselves within our own range of favorable states. Diabetes, for instance, is a breakdown in our ability to internally monitor and respond appropriately to our blood-sugar levels. Neuroses are another form of breakdown in our ability to respond to things appropriately. Psychoses are instances of inability to track the reality around us adequately. Cancer is an inability to monitor and control cell division – and so on. Anything that did not in some way have a negative impact on our ability to maintain our self within our

---

[3] This is true not only of human life but also of life in general. It applies even to the very different life of a holistic entity, such as an ecosystem. Concerning the latter point, see Holmes Rolston, III, *Conserving Natural Value* (New York: Columbia University Press, 1994), and Gordon H. Orians, "Diversity, Maturity, and Stability in Natural Ecosystems," in W. H. van Dobben and R. H. Lowe McConnell, eds., *Unifying Concepts in Ecology* (The Hague: Dr. W. Junk B. V. Publishers, 1975, pp. 139–150).

then-current range of favorable states would for that reason not be an adverse condition.

Clearly, this characterization of health is quite broad. I do not consider this in itself to be a defect, as health is a very broad matter. There can be no a priori one-size-fits-all characterization of health that is also adequate and detailed. There are many kinds of people, and we all have many aspects, with many ways in which things may go well or go ill for any one of us. The proffered characterization leaves the emphasis where it should be: not on detailed formal precision but on living reality and factual discovery. It is through factual discovery that we can better come to understand health. We are still ignorant about much of human life biologically, psychologically, and socially, and we are not even sure what the other areas are. We are also ignorant, beyond a point, about the particular character of our own individual lives. Individually and collectively we do not even know what we do not know. That being so, we need to discover far more about what it is for us to be able to coherently maintain our self within a range of states favorable to our continuation as a coherent and viable ongoing life process of the particular kind that we are. We need to discover far more about what it is for *us* to be healthy.

I have stressed the need for *coherence* in our health. Mere survival, even long-term survival, is not health. People may, for instance, suffer for years from a painful and debilitating condition, arthritis perhaps, or schizophrenia, which does not shorten their life by one little bit. Nevertheless, in such a condition, the life they live falls short of what it is implicit in their life to be. They lose function, and their pain goes far beyond pain's proper role of impelling us to rectify whatever adverse condition causes the pain. In such a case one aspect of our being has turned against another, and thereby we lose some degree of our coherent functioning. There is a lack of wholeness, a lessening of personal integrity, a departure from that which it is in one's overall nature to be. Departures from health need not be anywhere near as severe as arthritis or schizophrenia, but they are still departures. Not only is health not measurable in terms of survival, it cannot be measured in terms of pain, be it physical or mental. Our health varies along more than just one or two gradients, and not even in principle could any single numerical scale accurately represent our health. Health no more than life is one simple thing. Rather, it has to do with all of our many aspects. Health is our whole life's coherent functioning.

Before we go on I would like to stress that in the conception of health I am developing, health is not merely an instrumental good, a means to such goods as pleasure, love, artistic achievement, or whatever. What is good for us is not pleasure (or love or whatever) per se but first our having the capacity to pursue and find fulfillment in such things and second having those capacities fulfilled. Just having those capacities is good for us, though, of course, having them perpetually frustrated would not be. What is good is not the *x* or just our possessing *x*, as if that could happen in a vacuum, but our engaging with it. In sum, our good, our health, is a matter not just of what we have but of what we are.

Normalcy and Health

Somehow, health seems to have something to do (but, as we shall see, not everything to do) with normalcy and departures from normalcy. At this point I explore some matters about normalcy before returning to issues about health and individuality. We will recall that in Aristotle's conception, the healthy condition of body and soul lies on a Golden Mean between excess and deficiency. This is not a mean in the sense of some arithmetical midpoint between extremes; nor is it an average over the human race. What is excessive in the case of one person may be too little in the case of another. Rather, the Golden Mean is determined by the needs (as distinct from desires) of the individual person. It should be borne in mind that the Golden Mean, neither significantly more nor less than just the right or best amount, does not invariably lie *between* more and less. Intelligence is not improved by being below some maximum; neither is cruelty improved by being more than the minimum possible. In such matters, the best amount lies at an extreme.

Any mean determined with reference to humankind in general, although it may often be suggestive, applies to the individual only to the extent that the given individual approximates to humankind in general. The physician understands human health in general. The excellent physician is able to apply his or her understanding to the case of that individual, striving to attain just the right balance in that particular case. In broad terms, this was the approach to health followed from before the time of Aristotle and for many centuries thereafter.

Somewhat prior to Aristotle was Hippocrates: healer, teacher, and author of the Hippocratic Oath. As he explained it,

> The human body contains blood, phlegm, yellow bile, and black bile. These are the things that make up its constitution and cause its pains and health. Health is primarily that state in which these constituent substances are in the correct proportion to each other, both in strength and in quantity, and are well mixed. Pain occurs when one of the substances presents either a deficiency or an excess, or is separated in the body and not mixed with the others. It is inevitable that when one of these is separated from the rest and stands by itself, not only the part from which it has come, but also that where it collects and is present in excess, should become diseased, and because it contains too much of the particular substance, cause pain and distress. (Hippocrates, *Hippocratic Writings*, p. 262)

This general conception, that of a properly proportionate balance of elements, held sway during the classical era. This was true not only in Greece but, thanks to such Greco-Roman teachers as Galen, also throughout the Roman Empire. The four bodily substances (corresponding to the four elements, air, water, fire, and earth) came to be known as the four *humors*, from the Latin, *humor*, meaning moisture or fluid. The basic personality types were conceived of as being sanguine, phlegmatic, choleric, or melancholic, accordingly as blood, phlegm, choler (yellow bile), or melancholy (black bile) predominated in the person. Moreover, if one or another humor got too far out of balance in some way, in the body as a whole or in a particular organ, then one or another illness was the result. With the support of the Church and the authority of classical antiquity, this scheme of thought was accepted through the Middle Ages. It was part of the shared world view of Shakespeare's day. Hamlet, for instance, the melancholy Dane, was not a well man:

> I have of late – but
> wherefore I know not – lost all my mirth, forgone all
> custom of exercises, and indeed it goes so heavily
> with my disposition that this goodly frame, the
> earth, seems to me a sterile promontory, the most
> excellent canopy, the air, look you, this brave
> o'erhanging firmament, this majestical roof fretted
> with golden fire, why, it appears no other thing to
> me than a foul and pestilent congregation of vapours.
>
> (William Shakespeare, *Hamlet*,
> Act II, Scene ii, Lines 303–311)

For the Elizabethan audience, the diagnosis was abundantly clear: Hamlet had far too much of the black (*melan*) bile (*cholia*). In contrast, Marcus Brutus, a supremely good man, was eulogized by even his deadly enemy, Mark Antony, as one whose humors ("elements") were in proper balance:

> This was the noblest Roman of them all . . .
> His life was so gentle; and the elements
> So mix'd in him that Nature might stand up
> And say to all the world, "This was a man!"
>
> (William Shakespeare,
> *Julius Caesar*, Act V,
> Scene v, Lines 69–76)

Though fundamentally concerned with the body as a whole, Hippocrates and his followers were quite aware that individual organs sometimes became diseased or otherwise malfunctioned. According to the classical conception, this was because the organ in question had too much or too little of one or more of the humors. Unless that particular organ was the one whose role it was to produce the relevant humor, the cause of the illness was in the system as a whole, and it was the system as a whole that was the appropriate subject of treatment. In the Enlightenment era, our conception of health started to change profoundly. From around the end of the eighteenth century, there started to be a move away from understanding health primarily in terms of a balance of humors and toward understanding it terms of particular malfunctioning organs. It came to be thought that illnesses, for the most part, arose through perturbations of particular organs (such as tissues) and that, usually, particular organs served more appropriately as subjects for diagnosis and treatment.[4] Accordingly, we needed to help the malfunctioning organ return from its pathological condition to its appropriate condition.

Yet we might well ask what establishes what the appropriate condition is for an organ or for the body as a whole. What constitutes normalcy in health? What sets the norm? Is it whatever condition is average for that sort of organ? Averages might be determined statistically, but is the average condition necessarily the right standard? Or is there some sort of inherent standard for a given sort of organ – or even for that individual organ? Such a standard would be more difficult to validate. Perhaps these possibilities are in some way related. A complicating factor is that the terms *normal* and *norm*, with their derivative terms, have meant different things at different times and to different people. Moreover, they have acquired connotations involving both fact and value. Whatever health and normalcy might have to do with each other, their relationship, as we shall see, is neither simple nor straightforward. Here I try to offer some clarification of what health has to do with normalcy.

The term *normal* entered the English language from the Latin language.[5] In that language, a *norma* is a carpenter's square, an implement for verifying that the corner of something forms a right angle. This term had elements of evaluation as well as description as a square corner was usually the desired outcome. Prior to its appearance in Latin texts, the term appears to have had Indo-European roots concerning recognizing and knowing, and it seems to be distantly related to our word *know*. By extension, the term for a carpenter's square came in Latin to be used for a standard of assessment – much as in English, reference is made to the *yardstick* for some quality. The term *normal* initially entered English in senses having to do with some mathematical line's being at right angles to some other line. They form a square corner, as it were. Of course, there seems to be something correct about such an angle, something that meets standard. It is a *right* angle. In the course of time, and central to our purposes, *normal* came to describe something that is the way that things of its sort are supposed to be. It meets some standard, specification, or *norm*. In contrast, something that is defective is one that

---

[4] In an attempt to avoid distracting verbal entanglements, I will use the term *organ* broadly here to include systems, tissues, or whatever.

[5] A fascinating and highly informative account of *normal*, from the term *norma* on, is given by Ian Hacking, *The Emergence of Probability: A Philosophical Study of Early Ideas about Probability* (Cambridge: Cambridge University Press, 1990).

is not up to standard. Here we have a term that is evidently right on the cusp, seemingly factually descriptive yet normative as well. If an organ, temporarily or permanently, is not as it should be, indeed, is in a pathological condition, then there must be some way that it should be but is not. The obvious thing to do is investigate organs that are not in a pathological condition and determine as well as we can just what they are like. We then look for what makes the difference.

Our bodily organs work at least acceptably well enough of the time. Otherwise, the human race would not have survived. When an organ is in a pathological condition, it is dysfunctional to a significant degree, and it is therefore not close enough to being in the sufficiently functional condition for organs of its sort. If organs in their normal, usual, or average condition are healthy, with unhealthy organs not being normal, usual, or average, then it seems quite plausible to equate the health of an organ with its being in a condition that is normal, usual, or average for organs of its sort. Presumably the average would cover a range of states rather than one exact condition, but the pathological would be outside of that range and thereby abnormal. According to this understanding, the normal range is indicated by the *normal curve*, also called a bell curve, a characteristically bell-shaped curve that is an expression of the mean and deviation from the mean. As so indicated, the normal comes to feature in derived laws of medical science. The normal or average is no longer considered an artefact of statistics, a compendious way of talking about numerous measurements. Rather, it becomes understood as a reality in its own right, one of causal efficacy and central importance. On this basis we can find scientific laws where none were found before. The normal thereby becomes the biomedical norm.

Over the past two centuries a great amount of theorizing in medicine and the social sciences has revolved around the idea that the normal, as understood in terms of the normal curve, determines the norm. In this view, to establish what is normal is to establish what is right and proper. Accordingly, one school of thought has held that the task of medical science is to determine what is normal (in that sense) for a particular sort of organ, to find means of determining the condition of an individual person's organ, and to devise means of maintaining it in or returning it to a normal condition. Beyond doubt, our having such knowledge is valuable in practice as well as in theory. Even so, if normalcy in that sense is to be used as the measuring square of health, we may still ask whether that statistical averageness is what health *is*. After all, corners are not square, and square corners are not important, merely *because* they fit a norma. Roman carpenters would have been quite aware that there were good normae and defective ones.

An alternative line of thought is that health and averageness are not synonymous, that they are only partially and contingently related. Although bodily conditions that are very unhealthy are precluded by mortality from becoming average, the inherent nature of an organ may indicate an optimal state of health that is by no means average. According to this point of view, there is a norm implicit in an organ that establishes what is normal for it. The nature of a tooth, for instance, indicates that the norm for a tooth is to have sound enamel, to lack cavities, and to be imbedded in a healthy gum. This is so even though the average tooth may not live up to that norm (and certainly the average set of teeth is only indifferently healthy). Were we to plot the condition of teeth on a graph, a normal curve would take shape, but the healthiest teeth would be out at an extreme rather than clustered around the mediocre average. More generally, in this point of view the norm for something is for it to function well as the sort of thing that it is. The body of a fit and well-developed athlete is healthy but by no means average.

The biocentric conceptions that I have been concerned to develop certainly favor the principle that the norm for the healthy condition for a living entity – person, organ, or whatever – is inherent in the makeup of that entity. In general orientation this line of thought clearly owes a great deal to Aristotle. A healthy entity does well whatever an entity of its sort does. What a living entity does, that is, its function, is, at least largely, determined by its own character. (In contrast, what, if any, function other things have depends entirely on what they are made or used for. One and the same object might be a good paperweight or a poor clock.) This is much like Aristotelian teleology, but for Aristotle, the telos of an entity was something fairly specific. As we saw earlier, the ultimate end for a fully developed person was to live a life of disinterested philosophical contemplation. The rest of our makeup is of importance but only insofar as it is oriented toward that end. As I have maintained, in contrast to this Aristotelian conception, our good is more a matter of our overall well-being, or well-functioning, and can take a wide variety of different forms. I will certainly concede that having our intellect well developed, by its own appropriate standards, is part of having a well-lived life. Nonetheless, one need not live an intellectual life to live a good one. Similarly, our various organs do various things for us, often more than one thing, but there is no absolutely exact way that organs have to be to be healthy. Not only is it a matter of ranges of states, it also is a matter of how the organ fits into our lives, our life-styles, our circumstances, what we choose to make of ourselves, and our time of life. It only belabors the obvious to point out that what would be an unhealthy amount of fat for one person might be very healthy for one who has to spend a lot of time in extremely cold weather or who is a sumo wrestler.

On Wholeness

That the health of a person is a matter of that person's whole being, and not just individual aspects of it, has often been recognized in principle, if not always implemented or even borne in mind in practice. In this connection

I elaborate on a very influential characterization of health. I agree with this declaration, as far as it goes, by the World Health Organization (WHO):

Health . . . is a state of complete physical, mental and social wellbeing, and not merely the absence of disease or infirmity. (WHO, Declaration of Alma-Ata, 1978)[6]

It is fair to note that this brief characterization of health is in need of considerable augmentation. Less justly, it has sometimes been criticized for a feature that I consider to be one of its great strengths. In its explicit recognition that health spans all of our multifaceted being, the WHO declaration has been accused of setting a standard that is impossible to fulfill. If health is a matter of complete well-being, then no one could ever be perfectly healthy. For my part, I have no trouble accepting that health is a matter of degree. It is a matter of degree along not just one gradient but along a great many, and it is not at all an absurdity to conclude that no one could possibly be 100.000% healthy in all respects. I am not sure that such a thing as *perfect* health would even be conceptually possible. Life is, after all, a matter of maintaining ourselves closely enough within a range of favorable states. It is always a matter of returning toward but never of being exactly in balance – and that can only be a matter of degree. Life fluctuates. An absence of fluctuation is death. Stasis is death. One need not be perfectly healthy to remain alive, to live a life that is fulfilling and, in round terms, healthy. Indeed, I would offer the observation that some things are better than perfection, and that life is among them.

An excellent feature of the Declaration of Alma-Ata is that it recognizes that we do not live as isolated beings. As thermodynamically open systems, it is quite impossible for us to live in isolation. As living beings, moreover, we are necessarily *very* open systems – and these are only two of several interrelated layers of significance to the fundamental truth that we do not live in isolation. As the sort of beings we are, we are necessarily dependent on, and live in reciprocity with, other living beings. No biosphere, no us. It is not just that we are dependent on other living beings as an external resource: Our very lives mingle with them; it is part of our identity. Substantially and inherently, our life processes are part of the processes of the wider world. For our lives to go well and be healthy there are things that must go well around us. In saying this I am *not* making the trite and absurdly simplistic claim that the health of the part *requires* the health of the entire whole. Counterexamples are easy to come by, from a healthy parasite in a diseased body to a healthy human in a degraded ecosystem. Nonetheless, a living system can be healthy only if, and only so long as, it is taking place within a wider system that is able to support its healthy functioning. To start with, though only to start with, we need to obtain food, air, and water from the

---

[6] WHO, Declaration of Alma-Ata, presented at the International Conference on Primary Health Care, Alma-Ata, USSR, September 6–12, 1978.

world going on around us. The food must be adequately nutritious, and the air and water wholesome. People cannot be healthy if they live in an environment rife with toxic chemicals and disease-causing organisms. In addition to input, as dissipative systems we need surroundings that can soak up and deal with our throughput. If we are to be healthy, we need a materially adequate environment as well as medical care when the need arises and adequate health care to lessen our need for medical care. We might conceivably get along without the latter two items but never without the first.

Moreover, we are social beings and our social needs are part of our health needs. We evolved as social beings; in evolutionary history, we were social beings long before we were human beings.[7] Having good relations with significant others is part of a healthy life. Sociality, like nearly everything about us, is clearly a matter of degree, both in terms of intensity of relationships and in terms of numbers related to. Some of us need more or less social interaction than do others. Even so, a totally asocial human – a person who was or tried to be an island entirely unto himself or herself – would not be living the life, having the fulfillment, that is in our human character to have. Perhaps a hard-core hermit has deteriorated to a state wherein she or he is now best left alone. Nevertheless, to be healthy, we need a social life of some sort, one that is adequately fulfilling to our needs. Otherwise, and to that extent, our life is not in optimal health. Optimal would be to live a healthy and life-affirming life in a society supportive of such a life. Such a society would itself be life affirming. No doubt there are many ways in which a society could be healthy and life affirming, yet no society is fully so, and a great many fall a very long way short. In our body and in our community, we must do the best we can with what there is.

An implication of this inherent relatedness in our lives is that to a considerable extent, our health is conditional on our surroundings, both materially and socially. Materially, this is obviously true in that such things as famine, pollution, and plague epidemics are hazardous to our health. So too is loneliness. Nor, whatever their bodily condition, can children be healthy in an abusive and depriving home – any more than they can be healthy in an atmosphere rife with carbon monoxide fumes. Nor is it just a matter of how we adapt or fail to adapt in response to our environment. Having a substantial proportion of sickle-shaped blood cells may be very healthy in a malarial area and somewhat unhealthy elsewhere. So too a particular sort of personality might be more functional in one sort of a situation than in another. Elderly people may be in good mental health in the familiar surroundings of their long-accustomed home, yet be quite dysfunctional

---

[7] Jean-Jacques Rousseau's myth about individuals in a presocial "state of nature" voluntarily getting together and forming a society is a pleasant story and can be a useful way of thinking about certain political issues. Nonetheless, it is a myth. Even the first humans, as well as a long line of prehumans of various sorts, were already living in social groups.

and mentally ill when moved, likely against their will, to new surroundings. (Often enough, they largely recover if returned home.) The problem is not really that they are slow to adjust, any more than a fish is slow to adjust to being dumped on a desert peak. Nor is it accurate to dismiss these and other far less obvious factors as being merely *external* matters that affect our health, which is itself an *internal* matter. External and internal can never be fully separate, and much of our living *is* our interaction over boundary areas. A bad interaction between our environment and us is not healthy, and the environment with which we must cope is part of our own life.

Openness

As much as I applaud the WHO statement for recognizing our social needs as being part of our health needs, I believe that the statement falls short by recognizing only the social aspect of our need to relate to something of value beyond our own limited selves. Our needs, certainly as I conceive them, go beyond that. Setting the boundaries of our relational needs as being coextensive with our social boundaries appears to me to be yet one more expression of the tired old idea that the world is divided into subjects and objects, with only subjects (that is, humans) being worth relating to, with objects being mere things. Is that really a view that is true to us and to our experience of the world? I doubt it. We evolved as social beings and are that, but we evolved to relate to more than other people.

For example, some people feel an attachment to an area of land, an attachment that goes beyond any material (or social) benefit that might come from it. Some people identify with it to the point of feeling that they and the land are one inseparable being. Much ill health among Aboriginal Australians can be attributed to a severing of bonds with their homeland, the *country* of which they consider themselves to be a part. Their country is not just real estate; it incorporates all living and nonliving beings and their interrelationships. Some evidence, though not considered to be conclusive, suggests that in general, we humans have come to have an inherent tendency, everything else being equal, to prefer landscapes of a sort congenial to the welfare of our Pleistocene ancestors – landscapes having such features as grass, water, and trees. What is conclusively known is that our surroundings do have a significant influence on our overall well-being, with some making us feel better and some worse.

Mary Midgley has pointed out that we evolved not only as social beings but also as beings living in mixed communities with nonhumans as well as with other humans.[8] We have preyed on other animals, often with the help of yet other animals; sometimes we have been prey ourselves; and we have long tended animals in some degree of domesticity as a resource. In all of these

[8] Mary Midgley, *Heart and Mind: The Varieties of Moral Experience* (London: Harvester Press, 1981).

varying cases we were relating to other living beings. A significant part of our lives, our thoughts, and our energies was devoted to doing so. It seems quite plausible that we have come to have an inherent tendency to enter into, and conduct with care, relationships with other living beings, nonhuman as well as human. The biologist E. O. Wilson has argued persuasively (in his *Biophilia*, 1984) that it is an almost universal human trait to find joy, or at least comfort, in the presence of other living beings; he calls this trait *biophilia*. This he describes

as the innate tendency to focus on life and lifelike processes. . . .

[T]o explore and affiliate with life is a deep and complicated process in mental development. To an extent still undervalued in philosophy and religion, our existence depends on this propensity, our spirit is woven from it, hope rises on its currents. (E. O. Wilson, *Biophilia*)[9]

People do like trees, and flowers, and grassy lawns or native bush. It is good to see ducks on the pond and to hear frogs chirping in the evening. Even when we do not have time to visit the park, we like driving by it on the way to the office. In Antarctica, a beautiful place but one where life is far less in evidence, the most common wall decorations (after sexually explicit pictures of women, in the case of men in outposts there) are color photographs of lush rainforests and similar scenes. We like pets, our own or other people's, and we may go to considerable inconvenience to keep one. When I see even the poorest of pensioners keeping a geranium in a jar on the windowsill, I am indeed convinced that biophilia is a human trait. Are there no exceptions? Of course there are. Some people actually do seem to have zero interest in living things, or at least in nonhuman living things. About whether such a life can ever be healthy I am skeptical, but I leave it as a moot point. For a great many people it could not possibly be healthy. Certainly I do believe that a fully moral life requires a respect for life beyond human life and that this would contribute positively to its health.

There is another aspect of relating outward that I believe to be important. Some people find a need for, and gratification from, a relationship with – pick your term – God, Allah, Gaia, the Tao, the Atman–Brahman, the Absolute, the Great Unnamed, or whatever else. Then again, some people scoff at such ideas entirely. Whether any of the associated beliefs are actually true – whether or not there is anything at the other end of the relationship – is not a matter that need concern us here. What is manifestly true is that many people find such a relationship vital to their well-being. (Conversely, as certain misguided sects have illustrated, a bad relationship with whatever there might or might not be can turn out to be very destructive to one's personal well-being.) Our discussion here could well explode into a cosmos of possibilities. *Perhaps* seeking such a relationship is a psychological tactic

9 E. O. Wilson, *Biophilia: The Human Bond with Other Species* (Cambridge, MA: Harvard University Press, 1984), p. 1.

for rationalizing and coping with the scary things and with the possibilities and the unknowns that surround us. *Perhaps*, as Pascal thought, we were created with a God-shaped hole in our heart. *Perhaps* what we think of as our self is only a fragment of a whole being that goes far beyond that limited "self," with the implication that a really healthy life is a matter of our integrating into our greater self, often thought of as *the* Self. *Perhaps* something else is true. These possibilities are not necessarily mutually exclusive. For many people, though, transcendental relationships of some sort are a felt necessity.

Even so, for some people, the lack of religious or spiritual beliefs and practices causes no evident loss of well-being whatsoever. However, can we, being as we are, have a healthy life that does not contain an element of what I call *openness*, some relationship with something beyond ourselves that is related to and valued for its own sake? I very much doubt that we can. Consider the instance of John Stuart Mill (1806–1873). He was given a remarkable education by his father James Mill (1773–1836), who was a noted thinker in his own right and an associate of that leading utilitarian, Jeremy Bentham. Such were the younger Mill's capacities that he was able to learn to read a bit of Greek (as well as English) at three years of age. He was exposed to a wide variety of ideas, particularly the progressively modern ones of that era. He was taught by his hedonistic utilitarian father that pleasure was the one intrinsic good, and that anything else is of value, if at all, only as an instrumentality toward pleasure. Accordingly, the young John Stuart Mill tried to live so as to maximize the amount of pleasure, overall and in the long run. To be sure, he felt concern for the pleasure of others, as well as for his own. In many ways, things seemed to go very well for him. But why then was life starting to seem so gray? Why so pointless? As reported in his *Autobiography*, he evidently came to have what used to be called a nervous breakdown, or something like one. Certainly it was not at all pleasurable. Ultimately, he came to the conclusion that he would be better off were he to value some things for themselves – things other than pleasure and that are valued without regard for some maximization of utility. Life went much better for him after that. In his own way he had come to something analogous to the Buddha's conclusion that ignorant ego attachment is the root of our sufferings.

Mill's case is anecdotal material and not definitive proof of anything at all. There are known correlations, though, between one's personal well-being and the exercise of openness. It is no surprise, for instance, to learn that a genial dog making the rounds at a nursing home can have a beneficial effect on the residents.[10] It is also true that married men tend to live longer than

---

[10] There is a massive amount of literature on the value of therapy dogs. Two books I would mention in particular are *Pets and the Elderly: The Therapeutic Bond*, by Odean Cusack and Elaine Smith (Binghamton, NY: Haworth Press, 1984) and *Creature Comfort: Animals that Heal* by Bernie Graham (New York: Prometheus Books, 2000).

men living on their own.[11] Whether it is dogs, God, other people, or tending one's geranium, there is considerable evidence that, in general, people with good relations beyond themselves do tend to live longer and have better physical condition and happier mental condition. This is not to say that any one thing to which we might relate is as good for us as any other, but it is to say that we do very poorly not to relate to anyone or anything else at all. The WHO Declaration recognizes this need for openness to some extent when it recognizes our need for social well-being. Still, I doubt whether that goes far enough. Perhaps some people can exercise a healthy level of openness through social relationships with other people, or perhaps also with some animals considered as associate members of the human race. We all need good social relationships, but some people need good relationships of other sorts as well. Be it God, or their garden, or something else, a great many people do have a health need for something in addition to human relationships. Accordingly, I would want to widen the WHO characterization so as to encompass not just our social well-being but also our well-being with regard to relationships oriented beyond humans. For some people that is very much part of their health.

Another response might be to include such needs under the heading of psychological well-being. Relationships with God, nature, or whatever else, it might be held, are of benefit to our health to whatever extent they contribute to our psychological well-being. If it makes us feel good to collect old bottle caps, include that too. It is true that trivial and evidently pointless pursuits, as well as loftier ones, can be of psychological benefit to us. It is also true that our social relationships contribute greatly to our psychological well-being. Evidently, the WHO and certainly many others of us feel uncomfortable with taking the value of our social relationships as consisting fundamentally in their contribution to our own psychological well-being. They certainly do contribute to our psychological well-being, but to take that as their principal value would seemingly be to take other people merely as instrumentalities toward our own ends. Perhaps we have learned something from the young Mill. We should take other people as ends in themselves, as being of intrinsic value in their own right. They are *subjects*, not objects, and it is part of our own health needs to relate to them on that basis. For my own part, I am not comfortable with the assumption that our relational needs are entirely a matter of our mental and social needs. Moreover, I cannot accept the assumption, seemingly implicit, that our relational needs are entirely a matter of social relations with other people. I would want to broaden our categories to allow for other possible relationships with entities that are, or are taken as being, ends in themselves, of value in their own right. If

---

[11] This is true even if we statistically correct for the fact that unhealthy people are less likely to become married. See Lee A. Lillard and C. W. A. Panis, "Marital Status and Mortality: The Role of Health," *Demography* 33 (1996): 313–327.

(contrary to fact, as I believe) no such relationships do or might contribute to our overall health, then the widening of our categories is actually vacuous, with no harm done. However, if some of us do have health needs for good relationships with beings, in addition to other than humans, recognized as ends in themselves – as I am convinced some of us in fact do – then it is better to have broader categories that allow for that fact about our health needs.

However, there is a risk in drawing up lists of categories. We can become tied to them. It is very much to the WHO's credit that it recognizes that health is a matter of our whole being in its many aspects. We should follow through on that insight by not interpreting its characterization of health as implying that physical, mental, and social well-being are *distinct* elements of our health. We must never allow ourselves to think as if our life and health involved certain disjoint slots that relevant things and events fitted into, as if we had three or some other number of separate health needs. We are not a collection of components but one whole person. What affects us, for good or for ill, in one aspect of our being may, and most probably will, affect us in our other aspects as well. Our mental, physical, and social states, however complex they may be, with however many distinctive features, cannot be fully separated.

Nevertheless, there might also be possible pitfalls in considering health broadly, in terms of one well-being. If physical health, mental health, social health, and whatever else are all subsumed under the same heading, perhaps we are then allowing one term to conflate a number of different things. To go to an absurd extreme, we can refer to healthy bank balances – but bank balances are not healthy or unhealthy as people are. Social health and physical health differ considerably from one another. Metaphors, though, can only go so far. We may wonder whether the various aspects of our health are too dissimilar to be considered as aspects of one comprehensive condition.

Mind and Matter: Matters in Process

That people can be mentally well but physically unhealthy, or vice versa, hardly needs remarking. Even so, it is also a truism that mental malfunctions often have physical causes, or at least contributing physical factors, and that states of mind affect our physical conditions for better or for worse. (And we might daydream about some sort of a meditational technique, or some sort of a pill, that would make us happy and everything all right.) It is, in short, common knowledge that physical health and mental health have quite a lot to do with one another – yet they also seem to be very different things. How are we to reconcile these points, both of which are true? This sounds like Descartes' problem with dualism all over again, and we would struggle fruitlessly with the same old problems were we to take mind and matter as being two radically different things, or as being one thing. Once again, I suggest that it is better to think in terms of processes rather than in terms of things. We have already noted that life – being alive – is better thought of as an ongoing process. It would also be preferable (that is, more useful and more accurate) to think of mind, consciousness, and self in terms of their being processes. That is true no matter how much we may wish to identify them with matter (or with one another), or how much we may wish to distinguish between them. That the mind or self is to be thought of as an ongoing process is not some strange new idea I am proposing here. Rather, it has roots going back centuries, to luminaries such as William James, Immanuel Kant, David Hume, and Nagarjuna of India, though I do not explore those historical roots here. With the decline (and fall) of the credibility of dualism, it is an idea that has found renewed favor.

These days it is fashionable in academic and popular circles to explain the mind–body relationship in terms of a program being run by a computer. The program is not the computer; nor is it any other thing. It is an activity that the computer is doing. Nor is it possible to equate any one particular state of the running program with any one particular state of the computer. Similarly, it is thought that our mind is an ongoing process taking place in our central nervous system, mostly in the brain, though it is neither the central nervous system nor any other thing. It is something our body does, though it is not possible to equate any one particular state of the mind with any one particular state of the central nervous system (or any of the rest of the body). This is a useful analogy, but we have to be careful not to be too carried away by any analogy. At one time in the early twentieth century the mind was frequently explained in terms of a telephone exchange, and at times before that, often in terms of clockwork. The computer-program analogy, like the others, only goes so far and, like the others, it obscures some differences. The mind functions differently than does any known computer program.[12] Nor does the mind relate to the body as the program to the machine. For one important thing, a bad program cannot physically injure a computer, however much it might injure the rest of the computer's programming (that being one difference between a virus and a computer virus). In contrast, a bad mind-set can not only impede the functionality of our thinking in many other areas, it can also cause the erosion of our physical condition. A good mind-set can improve it. Moreover, the mind, unlike the computer program, is not a process taking place in some thing. Rather, it is a process taking part in a broader process, the life as a whole. That processes can go on in other processes does not raise the difficulties of Descartes' dualism, and one process going on in another is not at all

---

[12] Certainly there are a number of technical differences, such as – one among many – that the mind does far more parallel (as opposed to linear) processing.

uncommon. A relatively trivial example is a television signal conveying both sound and picture. A person is a far more complex example.

An Aside on Spirituality and Survival

One might perhaps make conjecture about what implications, if any, the account that I have given of life and health may have concerning spiritual matters or the possibility of some form of life after death. Does the conception of the self as being a complex of ongoing processes, spanning both what we think of as our bodily aspects and what we think of as our mental (or whatever other) aspects, imply, presuppose, or maybe preclude anything about such matters? My answer is that this conception of the self is consistent with a wide range of possibilities and beliefs, though some views might have to be somewhat reinterpreted. Despite possible first impressions, it offers an alternative that is quite compatible with spiritual beliefs. However, it does not demand them, and it does not demand problematic metaphysics. It does admit the possibility that there are other ways of looking at things.

In a great deal of the Western spiritual tradition, the spirit or soul is thought of as being something radically distinct from the body and capable of surviving it. Such views teamed up well with Descartes' dualism, according to which mind–soul was inherently different from body, associated with it only contingently, and capable of surviving its dissolution. The eclipse of dualism as a conception of reality made associated spiritual beliefs less attractive and evidently less tenable. If there were only one sort of thing and no more, then it would follow that we are made of the same sort of thing as rocks, and dirt, and insects. Obviously we are organized differently, but when we cease to function as living beings, it would seem that we must decompose into our constituent materials. What would be left to go to heaven or to enter into union with God? For my own part, I would prefer to avoid metaphysical speculation. A better approach to such issues, I believe, would be to stop thinking about selves in terms of any sort of *thing* at all, material or otherwise. Like lives, selves are better thought of in terms of processes. Certainly it seems true that the more we know about the world, the more central importance there seems to be to the way things are organized and interrelate and interact and the less there seems to be on the substances of which they are composed.

An interesting thing about processes is that some of them can go from one medium to another. A voice carried first through the air can subsequently be conveyed via wires and optical fibers, sent through space to and from a satellite, and then reformed as a recognizable human voice at the other end. A computer program, or a computer virus, can (under appropriate circumstances) travel from one computer to another. It is conceivable that a self, or some centrally important portion of one, might carry on in some way, in some other medium, when one's bodily processes come to an end.

I do not know whether this is true – and perhaps would not comment if I did believe I knew – but it is possible, and no one can say that it is not true. Nothing I write here either presupposes or precludes any beliefs (suitably formulated) about such matters, and it is not a matter I intend to pursue. What I do want to stress is that our health needs and well-being are a matter of our whole being, in all of its aspects, and that we neglect any aspect of our being only at our peril.

Health and Our Good: Being True to Oneself

Our good, living a healthy life in the broadest sense, is fundamentally a matter of being true to ourselves.[13] Whatever might be involved in our living a good life, we cannot live a truly good life unless we live it in a way that is true to what we are. It is only the baldly obvious that for a life to be good it has to be what it is for *that* life to be good. Much less obvious is the answer to the question of how we are to fulfill that. "Know thyself" read the motto at the entrance to the Oracle of Delphi, advice as easy to give as it is vital yet exceedingly difficult to follow. In the midst of all the many wrong answers, there is no uniquely right answer. At best we can arrive at *a* fairly right answer for ourself. Human nature is not one specific thing, and we are not individually some definite thing, once and for all. As ongoing processes of the general sort we are, it is in our nature to develop and change as we go. In some part, what we are and what is needful for our well-being is a matter of what we are born as and, in some part, it is a result of our choices and of the vicissitudes of life. That this is so has important implications for bioethics.

In Chapter 4 we noted that the mere fact that we value or desire something, even after long and careful thought, does not necessarily mean that it is good for us. We can and do make mistakes. Nonetheless, it is also true that through our choices we give more determinate shape to what or who we are and to what constitutes our good. As Jean-Paul Sartre puts it (1943/1992),[14] we have *being for itself* rather than *being in itself*. A mere thing, a rock for instance, has being in itself. It just is, and is just as it is. In contrast, a person has being for itself. In large part, we shape ourselves and make ourselves what we are through our choices. Through choice or accident, we may acquire one set of interests or aversions rather than another. Think how different "identical" twins can become. Seemingly trivial first steps may

---

[13] This is not to say that there is no more to goodness than the mere satisfaction of self-interest. An unrewarded act of kindness is good. Even so, as I would suggest, it is better, more fulfilling, for one to be a person of a sort inclined to do such acts.

[14] Jean-Paul Sartre, *Being and Nothingness: A Phenomenological Essay on Ontology* (New York: Washington Square Press, 1992; originally published 1943; English translation originally published 1956).

snowball into a different career or a different life than might otherwise have been the case. It might be only a matter of whether we see a particular item on television or what book we read, or of whether we randomly turn left or right at a corner, therefore meeting or not meeting a particular person. We acquire different interests, different fulfillment and vulnerabilities, and thereby acquire a somewhat different identity with a different well-being to be served.

What is true of our choices and the incidents of our history is also true of the accidents of our birth. Well known is the case of Temple Grandin, a very gifted woman born with autism. Accordingly, she has difficulties with social interactions and in understanding the feelings of others. However, she is very sensitive to touch and sound and is able to "think in pictures" with remarkable visualization skills. Her particular mental characteristics allow her to think herself into the mind and experience of a cow. She is able to achieve a high level of understanding of how cattle experience feedlots and other cattle-handling installations, and she has thereby helped to bring about important improvements in design. Temple Grandin has contributed to great progress in the cattle industry. She has also shed an immense amount of light on the nature of autism. Furthermore, her autism has been essential not only to what she has done but to her being who and what she is. That being so, she has stated that she would not agree to stop being autistic, even were that somehow possible.

In his marvelous book, *The Man Who Mistook his Wife for a Hat*, Oliver Sacks tells of a man, "Witty Ticcy Ray" who had Tourette's syndrome.[15] Individuals with this syndrome have excessive nervous energy and tend to be subject to sudden strange movements, such as facial and vocal tics, and to sudden strange ideas. These effects often tend to surprise the people around them. Some with the syndrome are better able than others to integrate it into a functional life. It gave Ray a witty, spontaneous, and quite unpredictable sense of humor. It also allowed him to make sudden and brilliant improvisations as a jazz drummer and as a ping-pong player. Still, it was a hindrance to his social life, and it made it nearly impossible for him to keep a job. Eventually, it became possible to suppress his symptoms by means of a new drug. He was able to make the difficult transition to a new form of life and, free of the effects of Tourette's, he was able to hold a valued job and develop a more satisfactory social life. Nevertheless, he missed being the old witty and spontaneous Ray. Some of his friends from the old days also missed the former Ray. He decided to go off the drug on weekends and subsequently had much the best of both worlds. He thought that it would be better not to have Tourette's at all, so that he would not have to oscillate between the "Witty Ticcy" state and the drug-sober state,

---

[15] Oliver Sacks, *The Man Who Mistook His Wife for a Hat* (New York: Simon & Schuster, 1970).

or to have to choose between them. As it was, though, he was able to take what was a liability and turn it into a valuable part of his life.

At this point I would like to interject an additional perspective on the matter of being true to ourselves, to whom and what we are. What is it to be *true?* We can repose confidence in things that are true. A true diamond, say, or a true friend is as purported to be. You can rely on them to be so when the test comes. A true statement is faithful to the facts. We can depend on things being as they are said to be. The Modern English word *true* derives from Middle English *trewe* and thereby from the Old English *treowe* (meaning "loyal, trusty"). This is connected with Old English *treow* (meaning "loyalty, fidelity"), and both of these are connected with *treo* and *treow*, which are the etymological roots (as it were) of the modern word *tree*. This association is cognitively appropriate as well as poetically pleasing, not least because trees and truth certainly do seem to have something important and striking in common. Firm, solid, reliable, and durable, there is something tree-like about truth, something true about trees. Now, let us ask, what are trees like? Not all trees are alike. Some trees appear to be trying to follow a preordained pattern. The model seems to be calling for them, however well they comply, to be straight up and down, and symmetrical. Such is the stereotypical Christmas tree. Again, some trees, like Australian gum trees, or eucalypts, are very irregular in form. Each gum tree is an expression of its own particular character, history, and environment. Gums too are firm, solid, reliable, and durable. They are also beautiful. Something I very much love about gums is that you actually have to look at each particular tree to know what it looks like.

Gum trees appear to me to offer a better simile for truth than do those trees that are straight up and down and symmetrical. Truth is not characteristically a matter of meeting some preestablished standard. In actual living communication a language user says something about something, referring to some subject matter and describing it in a way that is relative to that subject matter, to the circumstances, and to the intents and purposes of the language user and the intended audience. The statement is true if what is described is as described, with respect to the operative intents and purposes. Truth is not about detached standards but about communication between actual people in actual instances. It is a matter of individual cases. That, however, is another story (which those who wish to do so may pursue in my earlier work).[16] Here we are concerned with being true to ourselves.

Gum trees also seem to me to offer a good simile for our health. What we are and what is good for us is a matter of what we start with, like the gum seed: our environment and our history (what happens to us and, unlike the gum tree, our choices in life). Our health, and what is required for

---

[16] Lawrence E. Johnson, *Focusing on Truth* (New York: Routledge, 1992).

our well-being, is not something that can be determined merely by reference to some detached standard; it can only be determined with reference to our own particular history and character. Oliver Sacks tells of identical twins, born with identical brain malfunction, who had an immense amount of psychological deficits and incapacities. Even the simplest things of life were beyond them. They were, of course, institutionalized. Nevertheless, they had some very remarkable qualities. They could recite the principal events of any given day of their lives from about the age of four onward, though reciting in a way that was very low in cognitive understanding and entirely detached emotionally. They could see, not count, just *see* numerical amounts at a glance (e.g., promptly noting that exactly 111 matches had fallen from a box). Moreover, they were able promptly to state the day of the week of any date within 40,000 years of the present. It was not that they were lightening calculators. They were not *calculators* at all. Even the simplest of multiplication and division processes were incomprehensible to them as processes. Evidently they were able to directly grasp numerical relationships with some sort of an inner sense. They might see the quality of one-hundred-elevenness as readily as I see the quality of threeness. Their inner life was radically different from ours but richly complex in its own way. They delighted in numerical communication, doing such things as citing prime numbers of six or more digits, each for the other's delectation, and engaged in other forms of numerical communication opaque to outsiders.

It was eventually decided to separate the twins so that they could better learn to cope with the outside world. Living under close supervision in halfway houses, they were taught to keep themselves more-or-less clean and clothed and to do menial jobs – much like the Epsilons in *Brave New World*. In this way, they were able to fit into the "real" world in the role of suitably trained and functional morons. Out of contact with one another, they no longer had their numerical communication and gradually their capacity for it dwindled. Of course, they missed one another very much. Still, they were as close to a normal healthy human life as they could come and much closer than they were before. But is a healthy normal life what should have been the goal? I think not. To start with, they could never get anywhere near actually attaining a healthy normal life. Instead of our trying to get them that little bit closer to an impossible objective, a preferable goal would be that of helping them attain a maximally healthy *abnormal* life, one more suited to their very abnormal makeup. They needed to live lives that were more normal for them, according to their own inherent norms. To be sure, they could never have a fully healthy life by even their own standards as their incapacities would not permit it. Nonetheless, the healthiest life possible *for them* would be to continue to live in their numerical world and continue to share delightful numbers with each other. It is not just that they would have had more pleasure in life, though they would have. Their lives would have been more whole, more true to what those individuals happened to be. In trying to help them, the authorities were applying the wrong standard of health, doing them grave injury in the process.

Where once the emphasis in approaches to mental health was predominantly on the normal in terms of the more-or-less average or usual, now the trend is strongly toward the normal in terms of that which is determined by the nature of the individual and his or her needs. I strongly approve of that trend. Abnormality and normality taken in the former sense can be an invaluable indicator and diagnostic tool but, ultimately, it is the nature of the individual that sets the norm. Accordingly, in most countries these days, the twins would not have been separated. Few of us are such extreme cases as the numerical twins, or Witty Ticcy Ray, or Temple Grandin. Nonetheless, each of us is uniquely ourself, and within each of us – however opaque it might often be to ourself or to others – is the true standard of our health and well-being. Knowing ourself is a major and difficult challenge in life, and being true to ourself is a measure of our success in life.

For the moment, let us again consider physical health. Precisely what the norm of physical good health should be is clearly something that must vary, a little or a lot, with the individual's body and life-style. Just as clearly, however, there are sometimes serious departures from the norm that have to be dealt with. Some, pneumonia for instance, can be entirely cured if things go well. With others, diabetes for instance, we have to cope with the disorder and build health around it as best we can. With proper diet and exercise, insulin, and drugs that increase the production or utilization of insulin, we can deal to some degree or other with diabetes and leave the rest of us with pretty much the same inherent bodily norms and personal values. Even so, improved physical habits might possibly lead to adjusted values. More bushwalking and less barhopping might do that. However, there is still a fairly (though broadly) adequate model of what the bodily norms should be. When it comes to *mental* disorders, a greater reshaping may well be required of our inherent norms and values, of who and what we are.

Mental disorders are more like diabetes than like pneumonia in that, characteristically, they have to be coped with on an ongoing basis. We may cope with them poorly or perhaps very successfully but rarely if ever do they disappear without a trace. Like a gum tree that loses a branch, as happens often enough, we have to build good health around the sore spot while keeping the healthy bits intact. An important thing is to sort out just what our priorities are and how we are to achieve them in spite of whatever obstacles there might be.[17] If a person is convinced that strangers are beaming evil thoughts at him when he goes out in public, telling him to stop being silly is not going to help, not if things have gotten to the

---

[17] Indeed, this is a valuable undertaking for all of us. A brush with poor mental health constructively handled can accordingly yield some very real benefits.

point where he is in therapy. Helping him to find ways to go to work, go shopping, or go wherever else he would want to go with minimal discomfort and maximal gratification is far more useful. This may provide a foundation for a healthier mind-set. A bonus may be that, with successful coping, the conviction that strangers are beaming evil thoughts may diminish.

Regretfully, sometimes treatment has to depart from the ideal of talking things over calmly, insightfully, and constructively with the patient. The patient's autonomy may have to be overridden. Sometimes a patient who threatens harm to self or others must be restrained. Sometimes directly biological interventions must be employed. A person with anorexia might have to be force-fed both to prevent irreparable deterioration to physical health and also to bring the patient's bodily mass up to a point where suspended functions of the endocrine system are able to resume. This in turn better enables the anorexic patient to get a better grip on things. In addition, of course, there is a large and expanding pharmacopeia of drugs to enhance, inhibit, or alter various things going on (or not going on) in a patient's brain. Sometimes, regrettably, the overriding of the patient's autonomy may be permanent or at least indefinite. There are the criminally insane and there are those who just cannot get their act together. From cancer to schizophrenia, healing has its limits. Always, though, the ideal must be that of acting to nurture the patient's autonomy. This must be autonomy in the most fundamental sense. This may not be what the patient *does* choose but what the patient would choose were he or she in self-command and with a realistic conception of what would contribute to his or her healthy and effective living. A successful outcome would be for what the person does choose to characteristically be in accordance with his or her true autonomy. What the person's true autonomy is, we must always remember, like the shape of the gum tree is a matter of the particular individual.

We must draw on the art of human living to successfully answer questions about just what one's priorities are and how one ought to go about achieving them. One who would help needy others also must draw on the art of human living. Science and medical history are useful and even indispensable resources, but for neither therapist nor subject do they or could they provide fully determinate guidance. Whether we are attempting to create a beautiful work of art or a beautiful life, there is no by-the-numbers way to do it. Determining how the right priorities are to be achieved is no easy thing either conceptually or in practice, and how we are to determine what the right priorities are in the first place is no easier. What the person needs (reckoned how?) and what the person wants can be very different things. The priorities given by society or some other external authority can be as wrong-headed as our own individual mistakes.

It was not so long ago that homosexuality was considered to be a mental illness. Certain mental health professionals undertook to provide therapy and were able to claim cure rates of one level or another. Nevertheless, many homosexuals did not want to be made normal in such a sense, believing that their homosexual inclinations were perfectly normal *for them*. It was who they were. Many homosexuals have been keen to establish that their sexual orientation is genetically predetermined, and perhaps it is. But if choice or happenstance has a role, is it any the less who they are? If choices were made, and if we could in some way establish that they were not good life-affirming choices (which would be no easy task), it could still be argued that homosexuality is part of who they are *now*. Would it not do violence to them to try to roll back time and make them into different people? What, however, if a homosexual person does not live in a liberal society? Perhaps he lives where a person might be penalized or even killed if there is the slightest hint of his having such inclinations. What if his deepest religious convictions tell him that he will suffer in Hell forever if he gives in to such inclinations? Should we try to help him lose his religious convictions or help him to reshape his sexuality? Perhaps this should not be *our* choice to make.[18]

In her *Regeneration* trilogy, Pat Barker presents a well-researched fictionalized account of World War I and what battle did to people.[19] It incorporates in fictionalized form such real-life characters as the British army psychologist W. H. R. Rivers and the soldier-poet Siegfried Sassoon. When soldiers suffered psychological trauma and collapse in the face of the horrors of trench warfare, they were sent to Craiglockhart War Hospital. There the goal of therapy and its sole criterion of success was for the soldier to be able (whatever might be his condition otherwise) to return to the trenches of the Western Front.

Here we are alluding to some quite extreme instances. The Hippocratic Oath calls on therapists to act above all for the good of their patients, and few are knowingly concerned to pursue agendas contrary to their patient's best interests. What, however, are their best interests? What the patients believe are in their best interests may not be the priorities that actually drive their lives. Their needs, real or supposed, may have gotten ravelled into

---

[18] Complicating matters, suppose something like pedophilia (or some other nasty possibility) is part of who one is. Juxtaposition here is not to indicate that I equate homosexuality and pedophilia. I do not. Nor am I supposing that it is morally wrong to have such inclinations. It is obvious that Lewis Carroll (Charles Dodgson) had such inclinations. He did not act on them, and he is not held in disrepute. Nonetheless, if active pedophilia, serial murder, or other such activity is part of who one is, then changes are required. Even if one can avoid retribution for such behavior, a life of brutalizing others, or being brutally indifferent to their welfare, can never be a healthy well-lived life. One might hope that society might provide means of keeping things from coming to such a pass and also of making life even more unpleasant for those who do go to such extremes.

[19] Pat Barker, *Regeneration Trilogy* (London: Penguin Books, 1995; originally published as *Regeneration*, 1991; *The Eye in the Door*, 1993; and *The Ghost Road*, 1995).

such a hopelessly conflicting tangle that they can find no way out and just cannot cope. The therapist's objective is to help them order their priorities and help them cope. The therapist's temptation is to promote, perhaps tacitly and unconsciously, some particular ordering of priorities. Neither the temptation nor some degree of succumbing to it can be entirely avoided. The patient and the healer each has his or her perception of what reality is and how it works, and they both live in a society that is highly pervasive in its influence with its demands and expectations. On the basis of science and in the face of distorting influences, the art of psychological healing is in finding the best way that therapist and patient can manage to achieve for that person the ability to live his or her life in the best way achievable for that individual life. Indeed, that properly is the aim for us all.

8

Health and Virtue

It will be evident by now that, in my conceptions, it is a truism that health is good for us. (Indeed, who would deny that it is good for us to live a life that is as healthy as possible?) Living a life that is healthy in the fullest and most complete sense is what I take our personal good to be. As we have observed, health in the straightforward physical sense is only part of the story. It is very much a cliché that a person may suffer from poor physical health yet live a better life, all told, than another person with very good physical health. I take the former person to be the one with, overall, the better health. Nor is the healthy life, the good life, merely one of pleasures or having gratified desires or other positive mental states, though all of these things can contribute greatly to a good life. Life is far broader than that, and deeper, and a good life is not just a matter of having more or less of some particular thing. Broadly speaking, having (being) a good life is having (being) a life that is coherently and effectively functioning as the sort of life that *that* life happens to be. It is good or healthy for us to develop in accordance with our own particular character, and to have our various aspects be well integrated and functioning well together. We are in ill health to some degree when we are not in such a condition, be it a departure from a fully healthy condition that is trivial and unnoticeable, or be it cancer or neuroses. These things, in their varying degree, are matters of departures from our appropriate homeorhetic balance.

There are ethical implications that flow from such a conception of our good. This is true in terms of our dealings with others and also in terms of living our own life. A good understanding of what constitutes living well is vital for treating others and our own selves well. Obviously, if we are to respect the good of others, having a clearer conception of the good of others will facilitate our doing so. Unless we have some real insight into the nature, needs, and vulnerabilities of others, our capacity to frame (or even to follow) appropriate laws, rules, and guidelines must be severely restricted. Appropriate rules can be very useful but for the best results in respecting the good of others, we need insight into what their good is. If we are to respect others for what they individually are, then we must take into account their individual needs and character, and general rules for behavior toward others can only carry us so far. Moreover, unless we had some insight and empathy, our following of the rules would be of only a minimally moral character, if that. Following even the best of rules out of mere convenience or self-interest is not the most moral of motivations. Nor is mere rule following an approach sufficiently sensitive to bring about the best possible results in our dealings with others, even when our intentions are good. In the conception of our good as health, we may find some amount of guidance in how to care about and for others. We also may come to a better understanding of why it is well for ourselves to do so – and, more broadly, how to live well.

I make the controversial claim that of central importance to our well-being is our having the quality – as I see it, the virtue – of being life affirming. I believe that this is a contingent truth about us humans, a fact that, although true, might conceivably have been otherwise. By *life affirming*, I mean valuing and respecting the health and wholeness of life, not just valuing or respecting its existence or continuation. This refers not only to our own life but to life around us. In holding this conviction, I adopt (and advocate) what is a form of virtue ethic – which, of course, I undertake to inform through biocentric conceptions. Central to being life affirming is to affirm one's own life – which is itself an ethical matter. That is not the same as being selfish, greedy, or predatory. Indeed, such traits in humans are characteristically manifestations of an unhealthy character. That is, they are vices. Closer to the mark is flourishing and being true to oneself, having what Rousseau called *amour de soi*. To affirm one's life is to develop and maintain one's integrity, one's integrated wholeness, and to be true to the core values implicit in one's life. By no means is it just a matter of pursuing one's desires. Centrally, one must get one's desires into proper order. Affirming one's life does not require hanging on to life at all costs and it may even be, in some instances, that sacrificing it is an affirmation of the core values of that life – as when a parent gives up her life for her child. *Amour de soi* is in contrast to *amour-propre*, which is a mere narrow self-fixation. This latter is a result of maladjustment to life around us and to ourselves. It is ultimately self-stultifying.

Eudaimonia and Virtue

Virtue ethics, as mentioned earlier, is one of those ideas with roots going back to Aristotle and others among the ancients. I am not going to advocate any ancient system nor rely on ancient authority. Time and human understanding have since progressed. However, the general approach of virtue ethics has considerable fundamental merit, and I explore it further on the basis of material developed in the pages since its last mention. I begin by sketching Aristotle's position in broad outline as a means of leading into an explication of the position that I do advocate.

We will recall that Aristotle held that our self is a complex hierarchical entity, organized and oriented toward its own inherent good. Our good, our *eudaimonia*,[1] lies in our functioning well as a being of the sort that we are. To live well – that is, to do a good job of living – we need to develop and maintain the sort of character that has the ability to do that well. In particular, we have to develop and maintain the sort of character that enables us to live well as a *human* being. The kinds of lives that we have as humans, as well as the character we develop for ourselves, shape what it is for us to live well. I am quite pleased with Aristotle's conception that well-being is *an activity of the soul in accordance with virtue* (*Nicomachean Ethics* 1098a). Good is not something we *have*. A good life is something we *do*.

So, how are we to go about living a good life? It is something we have to learn. Aristotle tells us (1103a–1103b) this:

[W]e are constituted by nature to receive [the moral virtues], but their full development in us is due to habit.... [T]he virtues we do acquire by first exercising them, just as happens in the arts. Anything that we have to learn to do we learn by the actual doing of it: people become builders by building.... Similarly we become just by performing just acts.

But how do we know which sorts of actions are the virtuous ones that we should be practicing? The simplest answer is that virtuous actions are those that are done by virtuous people. As we learn to build well by doing what good builders do, so we learn to be virtuous by acting as virtuous people do. We can look to them for instructive example (so long as they remain virtuous). Nevertheless, this simple answer may be too simplistic. Are virtuous actions virtuous because they are done by virtuous people? Or are virtuous people virtuous because they act virtuously? Or, as the challenge is widely put: Who is to say? Who is to say what is good or right or virtuous? Were ethics merely a matter of some rule-making authority arbitrarily drawing up a set of rules, then there would be no very good reason for behaving morally other than fear of running afoul of authority. In truth, too often the rules are proclaimed by those in power to suit their own inclinations and, so far as possible, to justify themselves. Is that, then, all there is to it? Are virtuous acts virtuous merely because they are practiced and recommended by people in authority?

The idea of virtue flowing from the Aristotelian tradition has much more to be said for it than that. In principle, virtue is not fundamentally a matter of

---

[1] Ευδαιμονια, or eudaimonia, derives from *eu*, meaning good or well, and *daimonia*, referring to a spirit or person. It is often translated as *happiness* or, I believe preferably, as *well-being*. It refers to the overall good condition, or *health* – to use the term I prefer – of the entire person.

prescription by authority, however constituted. Rather, a virtuous character is one that is conducive to our overall well-being. We look to those who do a good job of living. On the whole, those with healthier, more functional characters tend to live better lives. In most societies, including Aristotle's Greece, there are those whom other people look up to and (rightly or wrongly) regard as being good models. We can perhaps learn from them. It is a matter of factual inquiry to determine what sort of a character it is best to develop to live well. There are facts here, and we can understand them well or poorly. If we understand them well, we have a better chance of living well. If we get things wrong, our life cannot go right.

As having a virtuous character is a precondition of eudaimonia, one who would attain eudaimonia must work at cultivating virtue. One may cultivate virtue by doing virtuous acts for the sake of eudaimonia, yet that is only part of the story. Being virtuous does not consist of doing acts of the sort done by virtuous people, or even of doing virtuous acts per se, but in having the sort of character of which such acts are the natural expression. Similarly, being healthy does not consist of doing healthy things, though doing them may help us become or remain healthy. Being healthy consists of having a healthy constitution, of which doing healthy things is a natural expression. As I interpret Aristotle, the virtuous character is fundamental to eudaimonia *and* to doing virtuous acts. Having eudaimonia, living well as a human being, requires having a whole and healthy character, a virtuous character. That such acts are the expressions of a virtuous character is what makes virtuous acts virtuous. Although one may try to develop and maintain a whole and healthy character by doing virtuous acts, it is not the acts but the disposition to do them that is virtuous in the primary sense. It is that disposition that is vital to our eudaimonia.

One who is significantly defective in character cannot have true well-being, however prosperous and physically fit he or she might be. Of course virtuous people can suffer major misfortune. Virtuous Socrates was put to death by his fellow Athenians. Nonetheless, on the Socratic principle that no harm can come to a good person, the Stoics, who were also virtue ethicists, held that so long as one retains one's virtue, one has well-being. Material misfortune can never compel us to lose our virtue or, therefore, our well-being. Accordingly, the Stoics aspired to be indifferent to material circumstances. That might be going a bit far. In contrast, Aristotle held that there is more to our well-being than our own personal character. Poverty can deprive us of the leisure or minimal material sustenance needed for living a good life. Material misfortune can erode our well-being. (Aristotle, for his part, once fled Athens in time of peril lest the Athenians "sin twice against philosophy.") In his view, virtue is a necessary but not a sufficient condition for our eudaimonia. We need at least a minimum of supportive surroundings.

Of central importance is the point that virtue of virtuous acts is not an inherent property of those acts in themselves; it derives from their role in the character of those living *humanly* good lives. Acts of radically different sorts might be virtuous with respect to lives of other sorts. For a crocodile, to eat whatever it can find to eat, including baby crocodiles, is quite virtuous – so far as crocodiles go. Unlike crocodiles, we humans are social beings or, as Aristotle has it, political beings. It is our nature to live in a community, a *polis*, with other people. The good life involves, among other things, getting on well with others. On this point, Aristotle was more correct than he could have known at the time. Evolutionary biology and paleontology confirm that sociality was central to the development of humanity. It is characteristic of humans to desire human company and to value cooperation and good relations with other people. We suffer when there is not enough of this in our life. To be sure, some people's lives have led them to desire only the company of pets or to be hermits entirely, and perhaps at that stage in their lives, this is the best option that remains for them, but it is hard to conceive that a life could arrive at such a stage healthily. Misanthropy certainly is a symptom of poor health of character. Little healthier is callousness. An attitude of openness toward and affirmation of other human life is a much healthier sign.

As Aristotle pointed out, however, there is considerably more to the good life than a concern for others and good relations with them. A minimum of material conditions is required and, very importantly, we also need to develop a character that is well integrated and able to function well, which includes being able to get along with itself. All of these factors must be united. Maintaining an appropriate balance in life is central to eudaimonia, and a virtuous character is one that has a disposition to choose actions that maintain an appropriate mean between excess and deficiency, with an appropriate avoidance of extremes. That we should find the right balance has been called the doctrine of the Golden Mean. The virtuous person has acquired the skill to make the appropriate choice and has the disposition to do so. The appropriate mean is relative to person and circumstances, and it cannot be determined by a precise formula. Certainly the mean is not determined by the extremes, as if we could somehow add them up and divide by two. Rather, the extremes are extreme because they are excessive departures from an appropriate range of actions and a disposition to act within that range. Moreover, the appropriate action might well be (or appear to us to be) nearer one extreme than another. What is appropriate or inappropriate for a person is relative to the functioning of that person's life, as a human being and as that particular individual, and to the situation at hand. These things are true of all the virtues. A courageous man, for example, is one who has a realistic awareness of danger and is neither insensitive to it nor rashly disregarding of it, nor yet craven before it. In the face of danger, he behaves as he ought to. Again, temperance is self-control, balanced between self-indulgence and insensibility. Magnanimity requires an appropriate and realistic self-esteem, neither too high nor too low. Being

TABLE 8.1. *Table of Aristotelian Virtures*

Sphere of Action or Feeling	Excess	Mean	Deficiency
Fear and confidence	Rashness	Courage	Cowardice
Pleasure and pain	Licentiousness	Temperance	Insensibility
Getting and spending (minor)	Prodigality	Liberality	Illiberality
Getting and spending (major)	Vulgarity	Magnificence	Pettiness
Honor and dishonor (minor)	[Excess] Ambition	Proper ambition	Unambitiousness
Honor and dishonor (major)	Vanity	Magnanimity	Pusillanimity
Anger	Irascibility	Patience	Lack of spirit
Self-expression	Boastfulness	Truthfulness	Understatement
Conversation	Buffoonery	Wittiness	Boorishness
Social conduct	Obsequiousness	Friendliness	Cantankerousness
Flattery			
Shame	Shyness	Modesty	Shamelessness
Indignation	Envy	Righteous indignation	Malicious enjoyment

a just person is being equitable, giving others their due, and so on. We may summarize this in tabular form, as shown in Table 8.1.[2]

Similar patterns apply to justice and injustice, and to all of the intellectual virtues. Every virtue requires an ability to find a mean between extremes, a mean appropriate to that person's makeup in that person's own circumstances.[3]

---

[2] Here I very slightly modify the presentation of the table on p. 104 of the Penguin edition of *Aristotle's Ethics* (London: Penguin Books, 1953).

[3] The medieval Christian Church eventually adopted, when modified to suit its purposes, large amounts of Aristotelianism, including the general conception of virtue ethics. To be sure, the virtues identified by the Church differed from those identified by Aristotle. Like Aristotle, the Church held that having the virtues are not always sufficient to obtain worldly well-being, though unlike Aristotle, the Church promised otherworldly compensation. Aristotle and Church alike put the emphasis in morality on the nature and intentions of the person acting rather than on the nature of the person's acts per se or on their results. Even acts, such as murder, that are inherently bad are wrong only for us moral agents. The man-eating crocodile is sinless. For moral agents, some rules (being God's commands) are absolute but,

This activity of maintaining an appropriate balance is clearly very much parallel to the way in which we maintain our biological good health. Our biological well-being is a matter of maintaining one's life processes within a range of states favorable to one's particular life and its circumstances, without going to extremes in any direction. (What is the optimal pulse rate? That will vary according to person and circumstance; nevertheless, we are not apt to find it by taking the average of zero and the maximum possible.) That there is this parallelism is by no means a mere coincidence. It is the nature of life.

Up to here, I am largely in agreement with Aristotle. I believe that he is right about our being complex wholes, and that our good is a matter of our overall health as the sort of life we are. I agree that moral virtue is an aspect of overall virtue and conducive to our well-being. However, taking advantage of several centuries of hindsight, I do believe Aristotle to be wrong in his more detailed account of where our highest good lies. According to Aristotle, as humans, our highest nature is rationality, so our highest good lies in its exercise. After all, it is obviously the function of the lower part of our nature to serve the higher. So, in his view (*Nicomachean Ethics*, 1177a),

If happiness is activity in accordance with virtue, it is reasonable to assume that it is in accordance with the highest virtue, and this will be the virtue of the best part of us.

The best part of us, as Aristotle thought, is our rationality. He went on to point out that the gods lack nothing and face no dangers, and so they would lack occasion for courage, temperance, or liberality, or for any other of the virtues associated with human fallibility. What is good for a god could only be disinterested contemplation, and such would be the highest and most godlike condition for a human. The opening sentence of his *Metaphysics* proclaims that "All men by nature desire to know" (980a). Our highest good consists of the contemplation of knowledge for its own sake, with the various other levels of our being functioning together well so that we may live a life of contemplation securely and without distraction. It is preferable that our material needs be securely satisfied so that we need not waste time, effort, and intellectual capacity on lower pursuits, but these lower things are properly for the sake of the higher. Lesser beings, such as slaves, animals, women, and children, cannot possess true well-being as they lack the capacity or opportunity for contemplation. (Though, perhaps more often than Aristotle realized, it was only opportunity that a slave or woman lacked. A child too might have well-being relative to its then nature at that point in its development.) The good life as described by Aristotle

ultimately, it is in terms of their character (including their spiritual condition) rather than their actions that moral agents are to be assessed.

seems remarkably like that of an Athenian philosopher. For my own part, I firmly believe that he is greatly underestimating the importance to our well-being of the nonrational elements in our makeup.

We might now, drawing on conceptions not available to Aristotle, ask whether the rest of our life is there to support our rationality or whether it might be at least partially the other way around. In evolutionary terms "we" – that is, our human lineage – were living sentient beings well before we developed higher levels of rationality. Even were we to accept that evolution is guided by divine providence toward ends encompassing rationality, it seems clear that there was more to our emergence than just the production of rationality. Moreover, however good rationality may be, we might question whether the abstract contemplation favored by Aristotle is necessarily and uniquely our highest good. He offers two reasons for his conclusion, neither of which is adequate. One reason given is that we humans are unique in having reason and, therefore, that exercising it is our highest good. However, it would not really follow that it was good for us at all, let alone that it was our highest good. We humans are most probably unique in murdering one another for religious reasons, but that does not make the activity at all good. The other of Aristotle's reasons seems to me no better. That the exercise of disinterested contemplation is something we, like the gods, do for its own sake does not evidently make it our highest good. There are all manner of things we might do for their own sake, from stamp collecting to nonreproductive sex. A relief from material constraints need not lead one in the direction of dispassionate philosophical contemplation. For that matter, could not one's intellect be satisfied, with a high degree of intellectual virtue, by developing one's skill at various complex and challenging practical pursuits such as farming, cabinet making, or rearing children? Aristotle was perhaps too focused on his own sort of life. If we were *purely* rational beings – is such a being possible? – then rational contemplation might be our highest good, but the fact is, there is more to us humans than that.

Though I disagree with Aristotle about what is most central and important to human life, I very much agree with him that our well-being lies in our functioning well (coherently, viably, and so on) as the sort of life we are. I agree heartily that a good life is a matter of doing rather than having, and that doing well is a matter of acting and maintaining ourselves within an appropriate range of states. All beings have inherent well-being needs or interests and thus an inherent good for which to strive. This is true whether they be philosophical Socrates or a boor with limited intelligence and coarse appetites. In all cases, their good counts morally in proportion to the degree of their interests.[4] Of course, Aristotle is quite right in insisting that we are social beings, and that we live well only by relating well to others and taking

---

4 Once again we tiptoe past the issue of why the interests of animals ought to be left out of account morally, merely by reason of species membership.

their good into account. So it is that virtue, having a healthy living character, becomes a matter of virtue *ethics*. A truly good life is an ethical life, and a good ethic is one that affirms life. All the more must this be so when it comes to bioethics.

Affirming Life

Virtue ethicists, ancient and modern, have taught us that having a decent respect for others as ends in themselves is part of our living a healthy human life. It is better for us not to be exclusively intent on pursuing our own good. All else being equal, one who does not care about others does not have a life as healthy and as well worth living as one who does care. Theories of virtue ethics (and there are different ones) certainly do not make the claim that treating others decently is *all* there is to having a healthy character. Nor do they make the fatuous claim that life always works out well for virtuous people. Both of these things are clearly untrue. We are not complete in ourselves, and we do need sufficiently supportive surroundings. Moreover, at least to appearances, the wicked often do flourish as the green bay tree. Even so, having a wicked character is not the internally healthiest way to live. Indeed, I wonder if such a life, even with pleasure and self-satisfaction, would be worth living. Much less would it be a life worth choosing.

It is a truism of biology that no living being is or could be complete in itself and entirely self-sufficient. Were there no other considerations, life's continuing battle with the Second Law of Thermodynamics would guarantee that. From this fact in isolation, no moral conclusions follow. It does not follow that a living being does or ought to care about anything at all. At most, it would imply that a being that was conscious and capable of forethought should, for practical reasons, avoid doing anything that would interfere with its ambient life-support systems or their continued support. This is on the usually true assumption that it has an interest in continuing to live. Fermenting yeast, had they such foresight, would know to not reproduce so fast and create so much alcohol that they committed collective suicide.

I make the further claim that even though it is certainly not a truism I hold to be true, we humans have a need to care about and interrelate with life beyond ourselves. We have already noted that we have evolved as social beings. We are dependent on one another, but that in itself does not mean that we care about or relate morally to one another. Ants do not do those things, nor could they, but they are social (or at least communal insects). However, social beings of the sort we are do these things. Our need to live in such a way may be underfulfilled, and our capacity to fulfill it might become atrophied, but it is nonetheless a part of a healthy human life. Relating well with other people is part of living well.

Other beings, which are not human and have lives of very different sorts, might live their lives well yet live them in very different ways. Kindness has no part in the makeup of a crocodile, and it is possible to be a very healthy crocodile without a trace of it. Indeed, its presence would conflict with crocodilian nature. The difference between us and crocodiles is not merely that we are more intelligent. There is no logical inconsistency between intelligence and a total lack of compassion, and some intelligent people do lack it. Aristotle correctly pointed out that we are social (and political and moral) beings, but he did not fully realize that we are social beings of the sort that we are, and with all that goes with that, not because we are rational beings but because we are human beings.[5] For compassion we do indeed require intelligence and insight of a level and type not possessed by crocodiles, but compassion has such role as it does in our lives because of the nature of our lives as humans. I accept the principle that compassion or, more broadly, a level of concern for the welfare of others is a necessary part of a fully healthy human life.

Part of living a healthy human life is having an openness to the world around us. Certainly we need a healthy openness of some sort to other human life. It may well go beyond that. Mary Midgley notes that not only did we evolve as social beings, we also evolved in mixed communities with nonhumans.[6] In terms of our survival, our extraspecific partnerships have been tantamount to symbiosis. Our partnership with *Canis familiaris*, of most venerable antiquity, certainly amounted to that. As for prey animals, they or their spirit-beings were related to personally by early hunters and, in some ethnic groups, still are. Animals were kin to whom we were beholden for life and to be treated with respect. Indeed, even plant life was often seen in such a light. James G. Frazer's book, *The Golden Bough*, offers some fascinating examples and insights on these points.[7]

As the years went on, we learned to live with, understand, and relate to a variety of domestic animals. Midgley notes that although our relationships with animals may have been exploitative, we still had to relate to them as beings with their own personalities and ways of thinking. One cannot successfully relate to animals by treating them as machines. She notes too that we, most of us, still like to relate to animals. E. O. Wilson, in his *Biophilia*,[8] goes so far as to argue that as a result of our evolutionary background,

---

[5] Instead of thinking of rationality as the apex of an Aristotelian pyramid, I suggest that we think of our cognitive thought, and our feeling, as being on or near the conscious surface of a multidimensional organism.

[6] Mary Midgley, *Animals and Why They Matter: A Journey around the Species Barrier* (Harmondsworth: Penguin Books, 1983), Chapter 10.

[7] Sir James George Frazer, *The Golden Bough: A Study in Magic and Religion* (New Delhi: Cosmo Publications, 2005; originally published 1900).

[8] E. O. Wilson, *Biophilia: The Human Bond with Other Species* (Cambridge, MA: Harvard University Press, 1984).

we have come to have, characteristically, a love for life around us and a psychological need for it to be there. According to Wilson, that need is not satisfied by human life only. Flora and fauna as well are presences we need in our lives. He also remarks that, other things being equal, we tend to prefer landscapes similar to those of our evolutionary past. There is still some debate over whether biophilia is innate or an acquired taste, but it does appear to be a human characteristic. For my own part, I thoroughly agree with Wilson that it is innate. In any case, biophilia seems difficult to deny when one sees a poor pensioner share a last morsel with an adopted stray cat, or even a sullen recluse nurturing a geranium on the window sill. Whatever we conclude about our need to relate to nonhuman life, however, the operative point here is our need to relate well to other people. This is a matter of the first importance for bioethics. Our need to relate well to life in general is, I quite believe, of the first importance for ethics in general.

Here I would mention the Paradox of Selfishness. A phenomenon that I and many others have long noted is that those who have a very uncaring and exploitative attitude toward others generally do not live lives as well worth living as those who do care. Certainly their human relationships are not so good. By using others only as means to their own gratifications, they usually receive far less benefit from others than if they did care about them for themselves. Not only do they cut themselves off from the joys of others, they also deny real and vital parts of themselves. They may accumulate immense wealth, but they do not fashion lives well worth living. Whether we call it paradox or poetic justice, it certainly appears true that one derives more personal benefit from unselfishness than from selfishness.

It is not only true that it is important to care for others for their own sake; it is also true that we do better not to be overly concerned with achieving ultimate goals. This is a lesson that John Stuart Mill learned to his cost. From his earliest years, his father, James Mill, had educated him as a utilitarian. His intellectual capacities became very highly developed, and he was trained to use his abilities to further the overall welfare of humankind. The young John Stuart Mill was a very talented and dedicated high achiever and certainly not selfish or exploitative. He and the other nineteenth-century utilitarians brought about some fine results. Nevertheless, as related in his autobiography, and as I touched on in Chapter 7, life started to go very gray for him. He did indeed suffer something akin to a nervous breakdown. Eventually he came to the conclusion that he needed to widen his horizons quite considerably. It is better for us, he came to understand, if we value some things for their own sake and not just as instrumentalities for the achievement of utility.

Affirming life, I maintain, life around us as well as our own, is an essential component part of living a truly healthy life. It is also an essential element in a community, as a community, living a healthy life. It is also essential to our living an ethical life, individually and as a community. Indeed, a life that is quite unconcerned with ethical considerations cannot be life affirming and healthy. Certainly life affirmation must be central in our consideration of bioethical issues. I am not attempting to propose life affirmation as a radically new virtue that is the key and previously unknown element in addressing bioethical issues. Were I to attempt to do so, it would be more than a little suspect and probably downright ridiculous, rather as if I claimed to know a fourth primary color that had hitherto gone unnoticed. The virtue of life affirmation is not my personal and recent discovery, and it does not supersede the traditional medical virtues. Rather, I take life affirmation as being the central virtue, and central to healthy living, of which the other virtues are aspects or manifestations. It is the virtue through which we implement them.

The four traditional virtues (as given by Beauchamp and Childress)[9] of nonmaleficence, benevolence, respect for autonomy, and justice may be expanded with the addition of such additional virtues as honesty, veracity, confidentiality, and possibly others. These may be held to be implicit in a shorter list. In contrast, they may all be held to be implicit in the one fundamental virtue of respecting ourselves and others as ends in ourselves – which is a central feature of life affirmation. Whether we have a long list of virtues, though, or a short one, what is important is that we arrive at life-affirming resolutions of bioethical issues. Cultivating the listed virtues is a means, but it is the fundamental virtue of life affirmation that gives these central virtues their core significance. The various other virtues, such as benevolence, courage, and justice, are all – not coincidentally – like life itself a matter of keeping a balance between one extreme or the other. To affirm our own life is not a matter of more or less but a matter of the more the better, the better we live. Furthermore, to affirm life around us is to free ourselves from some of the limitations of our own life and well-being.

In discussing life and interests, and such related topics as autonomy and what it is to be a person, I have endeavored to shed further light on what life affirmation is and what it is to affirm life in bioethical decision making. These concepts have depth as well as specious surface, and only by doing them more than superficial justice can we aspire to more than superficially adequate decision making. Life ought to be lived not only affirmatively but wisely.

A Cautionary Note on Advice

Once again, I would offer a cautionary note. We humans have always had a concern for health, yet after all these centuries, we are still learning what good health is and how to attain, maintain, and restore it. We still find that

9 Thomas L. Beauchamp and James F. Childress, *Principles of Biomedical Ethics* (New York: Oxford University Press, 1979).

ill health is easier than health to identify and define, but even ill health we are yet not able to identify with full precision. As for good health, we know neither just what it is nor quite how to achieve it. Our uncertainty about how to live well or healthily creates a vacuum that human nature abhors. There is any amount of advice available about how to live a healthy life, ranging in quality from the superb to the ridiculous and the potentially catastrophic. Knowledge and ignorance, foolishness and wisdom, benevolence or crassly exploitative self-interest may any or all of them be at work behind the advice we are given. The advice may center narrowly on a particular condition or it may attempt to take into account the whole person. Confronted with so much advice, so often conflicting, it would seem that the only certainty we have is the certainty that much of the proffered advice is wrong. Nonetheless, we also can be certain that there is such a thing as health – such a thing as a range of states wherein our life processes go well for us, and that it is well for us to live within that range. There might even be such a thing as good advice concerning it.

These things are true not only of our physical health but also of our mental and emotional health – of our overall health and so our virtue as human beings. The problem is severely compounded by the advertising industry, which skillfully strives to sell us not only junk food but junk nostrums and junk life-styles. With so much conflicting advice, so much of it bad, we might well wonder how we are to find any sound rationale in the light of which we may live well. As Aristotle noted, we may look for a model in the lives of those who live well, or who are thought to. Therein lays a well-known yet nonetheless very effective trap. For whatever reasons, often poor ones, we are commonly provided with models that do not properly serve our interests and that do serve the interests of others. Mary Wollstonecraft, in 1792, long ago pointed out how women have been victimized by ideal conceptions of fulfilling womanhood that have been imposed upon them.[10] They have been taught that their highest fulfillment lies in service, the act of nurturing, self-sacrifice, and the denial of further aspirations. To be sure, this was the sort of life likely to be forced upon a woman whether or not she liked it, particularly in those days, so perhaps she would be better off learning to like it. Still, this conception seems to be one that serves the interests of men and of a largely male-dominated society. More generally, it frequently seems the case that the ideals and rules that are promoted in a society are those that suit the interests of those people who dominate in that society. Whether this is fundamentally for economic reasons, as Marx argued, or whether it is, as I believe, due to a far wider complexity of reasons, it does happen and has long been noted. Vested interests, outmoded tradition, and just poor thinking are all prominent contributory causes of our getting poor advice.

[10] Mary Wollstonecraft, *A Vindication of the Rights of Woman* (London: Joseph Johnson, 1792).

We have to make do as best we can. Nonetheless, it is possible to live well or poorly just as it is possible to have better or worse physical health.

Objections to Virtue Ethics

Implicit in the foregoing discussion is an objection commonly urged against virtue ethics, that what is taught as virtue is relative to a particular time and society. There are a number of issues to be distinguished here. Not only is society the source from which we get much advice (good, bad, or indifferent) about how to live well, society and its demands are also the milieu in which we live. Certain values and personal qualities may be more conducive to a good life in some societies than they would be in others, where they may even detract from a good life. Moreover, some societies, for whatever reason, may not give us good teachings about how to live well. Different societies have different approaches to exercise, health care, and diet, and some approaches are better than others. We are still trying to work out how to live well on even the most physical level, but it is simply not true that all things are relative and that any answer is as good as any other.[11] More broadly, we are still learning how to affirm life well and properly and live good lives. No doubt, there is more than one way to live a life about as well as we can live one, though with no way at all to live a life without imperfection.

For purposes of illustration, let us look to ancient China. Traditionally, the Chinese have believed that we ought to follow the Dao, that is, the Way, of Heaven in our own lives here on earth. If we follow the dao or way of human life properly, our life will go well, in accordance with the Dao or Way of Heaven – which one might think of as the Way of Nature or the Way of Reality. In seeking to live their dao, the Chinese have been virtue ethicists, and Chinese thinkers have generated a vast amount of advice about how to think and act virtuously. Too much, one might suspect. Chinese life has often seemed – not least to a great many Chinese – as being excessively bound by elaborate, detailed, and overly rigid rules and conventions. A noble Chinese lady once perished in a burning building rather than go outside without an attendant. For her in that society, going out unattended would have been utterly unthinkable. She was just not *that* sort of a woman. To be sure, no few Chinese would have thoroughly agreed that this was manifestly ridiculous. This may be one reason why today's Chinese society is changing so rapidly. Surely what is important are not the rules per se but the reasons behind the rules, if indeed there are any. As I discuss further in a subsequent chapter, a persistent countercurrent in Chinese thought has been that our being true to ourselves is more important and more fundamental than our being

---

[11] Of course, material circumstances often vary relevantly. High-fat diets, for instance, work much better within the polar circles.

true to some role society would impose upon us. Nonetheless, the question remains, if we are social beings (and we are), then must not our developing a healthy life involve developing healthy social relationships? That would not demand that we stand around in burning buildings – but how are we to balance our individual and our social aspects and their needs?

In the West, Jean-Jacques Rousseau was also quite concerned about the distorting and injurious effects of social requirements and conventions on the individual. "Man was born free," he proclaimed in *The Social Contract*, "and he is everywhere in chains." Society then puts garlands of flowers over our chains and tells us how lucky we are to wear them. Passionately, from his own bruised self, he stressed the need for society and its institutions to protect and nurture the wholeness of the individual. Rousseau idealized the "Noble Savage" – whom he thought of as being both male and individual – in the State of Nature. Nonetheless, it would seem to me that Rousseau, like those who followed the dao, had a severe problem in reconciling what we ought to render unto Caesar with what we ought to render unto ourselves.[12] To both Rousseau and Daoist, I would suggest that part of the solution lies in the recognition that society is not some alien entity that only threatens us. Society is necessarily a feature of whom and what we are. To live well means to live well socially and individually, inseparably. Saying that is not to solve the problem of how to live well, it is only to state the problem somewhat more adequately. How we are to be who we are, and to develop compatibly with what we are, is something we are still learning – as women, as men, as people, and as societies. All life has to be lived in whatever circumstances we are in (or can make for ourselves) and, therefore, if it is lived well at all, it must be lived well in those circumstances. The central virtue I advocate is that of life affirmation and that is necessarily a matter of affirming life in whatever circumstances in which we live it. But living well with other people does not require us always to accept the advice society would give us – as the Chinese lady failed to see. It is *our* life we have to live in society. Like gum trees, right answers are sure to be varied, individual, and unexpected.

Another standard criticism of virtue ethics – valid, I believe, against some versions – is that it is too self-centered. It is charged that in virtue ethics, instead of taking a morally appropriate concern for the welfare of others, we are preoccupied with our own righteousness. Indeed, if a self-righteous concern for our own perfection is our core value, then the criticism has merit. However, in the form of virtue ethics that I advocate, the key virtue is

---

[12] In Chapter 16 on Asian approaches to bioethics, I note that, among some Asian communities (those of a Confucianist background in particular), matters of life and death, including active and passive steps, are considered to be more of a matter for the entire family than it is in Western societies. Which society has it right or wrong? Perhaps that is not a question to ask. It might be that in one set of familial and cultural circumstances, one decision, or means of decision making, is more life affirming whereas in another set of familial and cultural circumstances, another decision is more life affirming.

the affirmation of life, our own and that around us. We affirm life around us not because it is causally conducive to affirming our own life but because to truly affirm our own life is to affirm life. Once we understand it, we see that a selfish ethic of life affirmation is self-inconsistent.

A further criticism of virtue ethics is that it is not fully action guiding, that it does not offer us a rule telling us what to do in each instance. It should be clear by now that (and why) I reject this as a criticism and take it instead as a strength of virtue ethics. Some sets of moral principles may tell us what to do in every instance but *no* set of moral principles is able to do so adequately, with there being no possible horrible anomalies. Cases not adequately covered by existing rules do arise, and they arise with significant frequency in bioethics. Virtue ethics based on life affirmation can offer us a set of ideals and attitudes by means of which we may endeavor to deal with instances not covered by the rule books. Will such a system allow us to find the right answer each time? No; nothing will do that. It will, however, provide us with illumination with which we can better search.

Since ancient days it has been recommended that we learn from the example of people who have lived life well. There are some obvious problems here. How can we tell that they had a truly well-lived life? Indeed, how do we weed out the phonies? In any case, what is right for them in their circumstances is not necessarily good for us in ours. Still, with care we can learn from well-lived lives or perhaps from how people have handled particular circumstances well or poorly. Good ball players or writers characteristically learn from those who were skilled in their endeavors. One does well not to slavishly imitate but rather to adapt to one's own self and circumstances. When it comes to bioethics, we might learn from those who have shown insight, factual awareness, and an admirable attitude. What conclusions have they reached and why? Were those who willingly availed themselves of euthanasia, or declined to, acting wisely or foolishly? The questions go on. This will not give us all the right answers, but it can help us get better ones. It can also help us grow.

Why Is the Affirmation of Life a Virtue?

I have made the strong claim that the quality of being life affirming is a virtue, that it is a feature of a healthy well-lived life. Nonetheless, I cannot claim that this is a logical necessity, for it is not. Nor is it a consequence of our being rational beings. As Hume pointed out, reason on its own can give us no motive for valuing anything or for doing anything at all. If rational beings have motivation, it does not logically follow that the motivation is benign. One can imagine highly rational beings with quite nasty dispositions. The works of science fiction are replete with examples, of whatever degree of plausibility, of such beings. The annals of crime and the daily papers are loaded with examples of the doings of real people whose failings often seem to concern their morality far more than their rationality. Bad people often do stupid things, certainly, and good people often do clever things, but there is no evident parity, or even a close correlation, between morality and rationality. It is also true that our rationality is imperfect and serves our self-interest, even when we know what that is, only imperfectly. However, even the most perfect rationality would not necessarily have moral motivation. More is needed than logic. An essential element is *caring.* A genuine concern for others is required and a recognition of their needs as meriting our moral concern.

I think it is *closer* to the truth to suggest that life affirmation's being a feature of the well-lived life has to do with our being social beings – but that is not quite it either. Ants are intensely social beings, and so are sincere rabid racists (as opposed to the insincere sort who take up just any old excuse to be nasty to people). Robots of an appropriately designed sort may be social beings as well. I cannot say just what would motivate the robots, but the ants, bees, and termites of fact are not motivated by moral considerations. It is not just that they are genetic robots programmed to do certain things and to not do others. I could accept robots as moral beings if they were capable of having and programmed to act on such feelings as those of caring, empathy, and respect – so long as they were genuine feelings and not merely behavioral simulacra. Whether or not robots could ever have such feelings, ants do not have them. Morality requires such motivation.

Sincere racists do have *some* elements of morality – forgive me for saying so – insofar as they care for some others, even though they care for too few others and they care (or restrict their caring) for the wrong reasons. Caring about others is central to our morality, certainly, and our evolutionary background has preequipped us to be social beings who, unlike ants, do care about our fellows. A closely related factor is that our evolutionary background has made us mammals that nourish and care for our young. Moreover, we as a species became genetically adapted to division of labor and reciprocal sharing. Contributing to this was not only our increasingly social life-styles but also our sexual dimorphism, with males and females developing living relationships with mutual interchange. Most of this is also true of ants but, in our case, cooperation is managed not by blind reflex but through our reason and our feelings. We are able to weigh things and make choices. That there were utilitarian evolutionary reasons for the development of our capacity to care does not deprive caring of its moral dimension any more than the practical evolutionary reasons for the development of vision means that the visual arts are a fraud.

The biocentric system of ethics I advocate holds that those we ought to care about are those who can meaningfully be cared about for their own sake – those who have interests. The reason why we ought to care about them is that it does matter what happens to them. Nevertheless, it is easier to care about those with whom we can identify. Those who look like us, think like us, speak the same language as we do, or worship in the same way are easiest to identify with. This can be a good start. We have to learn the way we humans learn things, and certainly no child could grow to live a morally advanced life who has not first had experience of kindness and consideration in particular and limited instances close at hand. However, if we are to advance morally, we must go beyond particular and limited instances – if not to more abstract principles, then at least to wider and better applications. Other things being equal, the better or worse we do this, the better or worse for our own integration of character.

We look for wider rules, usually in terms of current usage and customary rights and expectations. There are bad and good ways to do this. Racists and other bigots widen their moral applications along narrow lines expressing, or expressed by, their narrow minds. People are evaluated and respected accordingly as they meet presupposed norms. We need to find ways forward that are less biased and haphazard. We also need to ask what makes moral rules moral. Still, there is some merit in the idea of using as our reference point that with which we are most familiar and with which we can most sympathize. Around the world there has been recognition of the moral insight that we ought to act toward others as we would have them act toward us in like circumstances. Kant's idea was that we ought to follow only moral rules that we can accept in universal form, without private or other exception, and also that we ought to treat each person as an end in herself or himself. Rawls offered the idea that we should imagine what principles we should follow were we entirely unaware of what particular characteristics we (would) have. All those things with which we might personally identify but that are irrelevant to the makeup of moral principles are to be set aside. Rawls has something importantly right here. We have the moral status we do, and so do all others, because we have interests, because we can be hurt or benefited.

This is by no means to say that our individual characteristics are morally irrelevant. That would be to say that our life, any life, is morally irrelevant. It is not that our particular characteristics might give our own interests priority over the interests of others; it is because the particular character of our life determines *that* life, *our* life, and at the same time determines what our interests are. It is by virtue of our interests, in proportion to our interests, that our life has its own unique nature and value. This is so for us and so for all. We have a truer and more realistic grasp of our own nature and a healthier and more complete awareness of our own value when we are aware of this. I am reminded here of the thoughts of Albert Schweitzer, who took as his starting point his awareness of the following principle:

"I am a life which wills to live, and I exist in the midst of life which wills to live." . . . Just as in my own will-to-live there is a yearning for life . . . so the same obtains in all the will to live around me, equally whether it can express itself to my comprehension or whether it remains unvoiced.

Ethics thus consists in this, that I experience the necessity of practicing the same reverence for life toward all will-to-live, as toward my own. Therein I have already the needed fundamental principle of morality. It is *good* to maintain and cherish life; it is *evil* to destroy and check life.

As a matter of fact, everything which in the usual ethical valuation of inter-human relations is looked upon as good can be traced back to the material and spiritual maintenance of human life and to the effort to raise it to its highest level of value. And contrariwise . . . evil, is in the final analysis found to be material or spiritual destruction or checking of human life . . . man is really ethical only when he obeys the constraint laid on him to help all life which he is able to succour, and . . . to avoid injuring anything living. (Albert Schweitzer, 1923)[13]

You are of value not because of your racial, social, psychological (or any other kind of) characteristics but because you are a living being with living interests. To affirm the true value of your life on its true basis is to affirm life. To do justice to yourself leads on to doing justice to all.

To a point, this line of reasoning seems very persuasive. Nonetheless, we might remain skeptical when we recall that genes, though not literally selfish, are selected on the basis of how well they contribute to their own replication. Living systems are selected for similarly, with the replication of their genes being the driving force. Is it not then too much like Pollyanna to try to erect an ethic of life affirmation on such a foundation? The trouble with such a line of objection as this is that if it could establish anything at all, it would establish *too* much. It would tell us that on a genetic foundation, all we could ever do would be to directly or indirectly pursue our reproductive success. That is blatantly, factually false.

We do value things other than having the maximum number of children, and we value those things in their own right and for their own sake. Some we want for ourselves, and sometimes we are willing to make unselfish sacrifices for the sake of values beyond ourselves and our own utility (let alone our genetic utility). We value ourselves. We may just let it go at that, as many do. But if we are to engage with the world and consider our place in it, we come to a crucial point: If we are to affirm our own life as *being* of value – and not just valued by us – we have to recognize that others also are of value. There is a material and moral continuity between us and the rest of the world. If I *am* of value, so are they. Instead of an infantile fixation on being the center of value, or a slightly less infantile disappointment at not being so, the morally more mature response is one of joy at being of value in a world of value. So how did we come to be aware of value, our own or that of others? Can it just be a fluke of the greater capacity and flexibility of human genes? If it is just

[13] Albert Schweitzer, *Civilization and Ethics* (London: Adam and Charles Black, 1923), pp. 253–255.

a fluke of nature, it remains true that we do value ourselves and that the best and healthiest way to value ourselves is through a realistic awareness of whom and what we are. From there, it is no fluke that we can truly affirm our own life only by affirming the life of others around us.

* * * * *

For my own part, I believe that our capacity for self-awareness and recognizing value is the result of something like purpose at work in our world. To go into all of that in detail would require a number of additional books. Here I will offer only a sketch of my views and reasons, these being superfluous to the main development. Those not interested in such matters may safely skip this section. I know, though, that many people do find such matters of interest – particularly when they find themselves caught up in bioethical situations. I sketch these ideas in the thought that some people might find them thought-provoking for their own thinking. To start with, when I say that there is *purpose* at work in the universe, I do not mean the purpose of some intending mind. It is something more primordial than that. Purpose is prior to minds, consciousness, and persons. (Certainly the idea of an *infinite person* is a contradiction in terms.) I see purpose and value as foundational to being. Let me here pose what may at first seem an absurd question: Why is there *anything* at all? Obviously there is a lot of stuff – we all know and take for granted that there is. *But why*? Why is there matter, or energy, or even (as space itself is a sort of something) empty space? If it all comes from the Big Bang, why did that happen? As I think of it, it *necessarily* happened. Utter nonexistence is logically or perhaps it is ontologically unstable.

Inherent in being, I believe, is purpose and value. At this point let us ask why the universe should be one that can support our (or any) life. It did not have to be like this. Physicists have pointed out that were any of the several fundamental constants of physics even slightly different, the universe would be unable to support any form of life. In that case, certainly, the question of life would not arise because there would be no mind in which it could arise. However, it is such a *very* long shot that I believe – I am not claiming to be able to *prove* this – that purpose moved it in the direction of life and, eventually, intelligent value-recognizing life. This is not necessarily to say *human* life. Evolution might well have proceeded differently, and on other planets out there somewhere quite different forms of intelligent value-recognizing life must surely have been arrived at. If and when we meet them, our life-affirming morals will be put to an important test. In the meantime we seem to have enough trouble affirming our own life sensibly.

A Further Note on Desires and Interests

Here I offer some further reflections on the topic of in what way and to what extent a human who is no longer capable of having desires is capable of having morally significant interests. In elaborating on this, we might start by noting that in evolutionary terms, life arises and develops gradually. In terms of an individual living being, life develops gradually from a bare beginning. Interests likewise develop gradually and they do so in parallel. This is not a contingent fact about interests that might have been otherwise. It is a necessary feature of what interests are to life. My own position is that *all* interests of *all* living beings are, in their widely varying degree, morally significant. However, that controversial issue is quite beside the point so far as this book is concerned. Here we are concerned only with the interests of human life and the conditions under which they are morally significant. Are they morally significant when desires and consciousness are not possible?

We might note that a person's last will and testament is accorded great importance not because the dead are thought of as having interests but because we, the living, value the institution of honoring wills because of our concern for the future of what we now value. Much the same can be said of so-called living wills wherein people specify how they want to be treated under possible circumstances wherein they are no longer capable of giving direction. As well as wanting to safeguard future personal well-being, a person may wish to make provision for what remains of the biological life of his or her body when there is no longer a person there. Either way, there is a strong concern for those who are still around and able to have and express their desires. The person's advance directives may give us guidance concerning what we are to do for him or her under possible circumstances, but those directives may still do well or poorly in terms of alleviating suffering or giving the person the best chance of reviving. There are interests there to be served and these are not generated by the directives.

Nonetheless, can a person who can never regain consciousness be capable of having morally significant interests? Desires? Such a person might be claimed to have *dispositional desires*, that is, desires he or she would have were he or she conscious enough to have them. These pretty much amount to prudent desires and I would urge the same fundamental point concerning them: They are supposed to stipulate our good because we do or would have them. Such a view is only a ghost of our liberal Enlightenment presumption that we must be allowed to legislate our own good. For legal wills of whatever sort, such a presumption is very salutary. Nonetheless, the truth is that our desires of whatever sort do not define our good and may not reflect it. Furthermore, some things may be good or bad for us that our desires of whatever sort take no notice of. Setting aside supposed desires, then, can a person who is permanently unconscious have morally significant interests?

Certainly such a person has interests. Where there is life there are interests. That includes living human bodies with any degree of disability whatsoever. That is true whether or not there is still a person there. Just what the being's interests are and just how important they are is a matter of cases.

Some of the person's antecedent interests may no longer hold for the continuing entity. In the event of brain death, the person's prior preferences would no longer be in the interests of *that* entity, which would have only the most minimal interests in such things as oxygen and water. These interests, I believe, would be of virtually no moral significance. A person or human in a persistent vegetative state or otherwise in a permanent coma might, however, have unconscious cognitive processes of various sorts continuing on. Such a being might have enough of its character left to have values as a particular life, not just *a* life. Certainly, where there is cognition, there are values of some sort, even if it is unconscious cognition. Respecting the values implicit in a life that still maintains significant elements of personhood demands that we treat its interests as having moral significance, in a way appropriate to those interests in those circumstances. Although our consciousness and our decisions clearly go a long way toward determining what our interests are, they arise in life to serve our interests. Their moral significance does not lie in their arising but in what they arise to serve. It is not a by-product. It would seem bizarre to impute the intrinsic value in our lives only to mental states or the satisfaction of desire when mental states and desires are created by life to serve the deeper values of life. In the case of such a life, I would think there might still be the odious possibility of unconscious rape, whereas if there were brain death, the charge would be something like unlawful interference with human remains. Clearly, however, the absence of consciousness vitiates many of our interests.

I might add that I have sometimes thought the term *vegetative condition* might perhaps be a bit insulting – to vegetables. After all, a vegetative life can be quite sound and healthy, as may be the case with a rose bush or a pine tree. In contrast, a human living a vegetative life is not in a sound and healthy condition. To keep alive and to bear seeds, and the like, is what the good life for a vegetable is. For a human, a vegetative life is the frustration of what it is implicit in a human life to be, with our more highly developed capacities cut off at the root. Better for such a life to die, I would most certainly think, than to live on with hopelessly frustrated interests. Full death or full brain death would not be as bad for the being as it would be to live on in a persistent vegetative condition with a residual level of perpetually nonconscious mental activity and perpetually frustrated residual interests.

9

Death and Life

Thus far I have been concerned with laying the foundations for a biocentrically focused and biologically informed approach to bioethics. Actual bioethical issues have been touched on only briefly and in passing. Now I address certain central issues in bioethics more directly, doing so on the basis of the understanding of life and interests that we have been developing. I start with that which is most vital to bioethics, life itself. First, let us ask what the value, is for us, of our life or death. Though I have previously provided a characterization of life, I have not yet provided one of death. For the time being, however, let us assume that death is what happens when life stops. In a later chapter, after I have developed more material, I shall offer a more thorough account of death and of where life gives way to death, if such a point can be identified. We will also need to ask *what* dies. Now, though, our question is this: What might be the value of life or death? I ask this question in continuation of the preceding discussion of the nature of life.

I agree with virtually everyone that death is normally contrary to the interests of people and other living beings. Perhaps more surprising, I argue that death in some instances can be in a person's best interests. However, I first argue that death is normally *not* in one's best interests. This may seem so self-evident as not to require argument. It takes no ghost from beyond the grave to tell us that. Still, if we look for reasons why this should be so, we may find it surprisingly difficult to find them. Is our usual aversion to death perhaps an expression of instinct rather than a conclusion of fact or of reason? Is it a mere arational prejudice? My concern here is to argue that this conclusion really is true and, more important, in so doing, to indicate *why* it is true. The why of it has important implications concerning not only the disvalue of death but also the value of one's life, and the moral conclusions we ought to draw therefrom.

Unlike pain, including the possible pains of dying, death itself is not something we can ever experience. So long as we are experiencing, we are not dead. Why then fear death or regard it as being contrary to our best interests? Epicurus, in the fourth to third centuries B.C., thus argued for the conclusion that we need not fear death as being injurious to us:

Death is nothing to us. . . . It is nothing . . . either to the living or to the dead, for with the living it is not, and the dead exist no longer. (Epicurus, *Letter to Menoeceus*)

Some centuries later in his *De Rerum Natura* (On the Nature of Things), his literary and philosophical follower Lucretius said this, concerning the person who fears death:

Subconsciously his heart is stabbed by a secret dread, . . . that after death he will still experience sensation . . . he . . . makes something of himself linger on. . . . He does not see that there will be no other self alive to mourn his own decease. (Lucretius, *De Rerum Natura*, Book 3, 86ff.)

According to this view, death is not bad for us because it can never happen to us. That being so, mortal fears need never disturb our peace of mind.

I am in the majority in not allowing such considerations to dissuade me from taking evasive action in the face of avoidable death. As well as instinct, which provides neither reason nor reliability, I offer reasons for believing that death is normally contrary to one's interests. I base my argument on the premise that a living entity is an ongoing process rather than a thing of any description. If a living being were a thing of any sort, then that thing's not existing – however painful might be the process of that coming about – would not in itself be bad for that thing. There would be nothing for it to be bad for. The nonexistence of some thing is not an adverse condition of that thing. There is nothing left to have any condition. Epicurus certainly had that much right.

Standard responses to the challenge posed by Epicurus typically invoke a utilitarian style of argument to the effect that death would forestall possible future utility (whatever one takes the good or goods to be) and so would be bad for a living being. However, this, of course, begs the question of whether anyone or any thing is deprived of that utility. This is not all that is doubtful about this line of argument: This argument seems to presume that the criterion of the worthwhileness of a life is the extent of the utility that comes to it. This approach seems to take not our life in itself but the utility that it might have as being what constitutes value about the life. Our life evidently only has instrumental value as the receptacle for that utility. This is a familiar objection made against utilitarian ethical theorists that instead of taking us as ends in ourselves, they treat us as a means toward maximizing something.[1] I would also note the doubtful implication, which is implicit,

---

[1] To be sure, some utilitarians may take the loftier view that some things, for instance, Beauty itself (as distinct from our experiences of it), are what is of value. That, however, is no argument against Epicurus' point that death is no loss to *us*.

that a life that is not gratifying can never be worthwhile for the one who lives it.

In principle, if the value of a life were the gratifications it generated, it would be acceptable to kill a person having a happy life, if that served as a means to that individual's being replaced by some other person having a life equally or more happy. So long, seemingly, as we are not lessening the amount of good, then we do no harm. Some utilitarians, such as Singer, accept that conclusion in principle. Logically, they have no choice. However, they hasten to point out that any policy of treating people in such a manner would lead to massive public fears and other disutilities, and so it would have to be ruled out on utilitarian grounds. I welcome the conclusion but I get the feeling, as I have in other instances, that utilitarianism is relying on contingent considerations to rule out something that ought to be ruled out on principle.

A deontological ethicist might value the person as an end in himself or herself. However, does that respect the person's life as an end in itself? Or is it just the person whose life it is that is the end in itself? If the latter, then it might possibly be that, in some circumstances, killing the person (in a way that did not infringe on her or his interests) would not be to negate it as an end in itself. It might even be to affirm it as an end in itself. For our own part, we might deem it good that ends in themselves should exist, or we might find it convenient to get rid of one. Either way, to act on such a preference would be to use the end in itself as a *means* to our own ends. Now, as Kant himself stressed, treating an end as a means is quite legitimate so long as we do not treat that being a means to the *exclusion* of treating it as an end. If death is no injury, then killing a being without causing pain or fear, or other adverse effect, need be contrary neither to a deontological ethic nor to a utilitarian ethic. Perhaps, with tongue very much in cheek, we might even propose killing people harmlessly as being an innocent and acceptable pastime, one that is the logical complement of bringing a people into existence because we happen to love children.

However we account for it, we must accept that being killed would be contrary to the desires of most people. According to the prudent-desire utilitarian Singer, this is decisive:

[A]n action contrary to the preference of any being is, unless this preference is outweighed by contrary preferences, wrong. Killing a person who prefers to continue living is therefore wrong, other things being equal. That the victims are not around after the act to lament the fact that their preferences have been disregarded is irrelevant. (Peter Singer, *Practical Ethics*)[2]

I have rejected the idea that our desires, or some portion of them, fundamentally determine our good. More generally, it is the other way around.

---

[2] Peter Singer, *Practical Ethics* (New York: Cambridge University Press, 1993), pp. 70–71.

Even so, having our desires frustrated is usually bad for us, as is having things done to us against our will. Certainly the process of being killed can cause pain, fear, and a feeling of frustration, often in high degree, particularly when it is occurring against our will. Nonetheless, when we are dead, we are suffering none of those things. Nothing is then being done to us against our will. We have to *be* to be done to. Nor, when dead, do we have any frustrated desires or other pains. Even if, as I deny, our good were determined by our desires, that the desire were no longer held by a living being – and was therefore, at most, a former desire – would make it of suspect relevance to anyone's good.

I am not trying to argue that death is not contrary to our interests. Usually it is. Sometimes it is not, which is well worth noting, but that is much less commonly the case. My concern here is to develop a clearer understanding of *why* death is usually contrary to our interests. It is contrary to our interests neither just because of the possible pains of dying or the possible benefits we forsake nor because of our previous desires. These things are morally significant, but our interest in not dying runs far deeper. It is not a matter of what happens to us, but of what we are.

The key point – and here is where the biocentric conception eludes the argument of Epicurus – is that a living being is not a thing of any kind. Death is of importance to us not so much as a matter of what happens to us as of what we are. A living being, in particular a living person, is an ongoing process, one that incorporates a truly vast number of subprocesses, the great bulk of which revolve around keeping that living person within a range of states favorable to its continuation into the future along lines implicit in that particular life. We are a future-oriented process. Continuation toward our ends will generally (though not always) require our continuation. Our life processes include various biological and psychological subprocesses carrying on over time and utilizing varying combinations of physical matter during our lives. We carry on through a multitude of particular states of affairs and events and, as we do, we undergo sensations, memories, emotions, pleasures, pains, thoughts, urges, preferences, aversions, and so on. Our interests are implicit in this continuing process, not as something it has but as features of what our life process is. Whatever else we might be, as living beings, it is central to our identity that we maintain ourselves over time within a range of favored states, tracking our goals. That is, as living processes, it is part of our identity that we act – that we are action – to maintain ourselves as the kind of being we are. We are not just a thing, existing. As living processes, our present stems from our past, and we have, are, a drive into the future. We are a coherent organic whole and a thrust to maintain ourselves as such. Therein we differ from mere things. Death is not only a termination of this process; it is the frustration of one's being as a self-organizing and self-maintaining process. More generally, we have an interest in whatever maintains the coherent functioning of our life. Only when life has broken down to the point where self-maintenance can no longer be carried on within a suitable range is (the hastening of) death in our interests.

So far, this seems like a very trivial implication. If our interests are in our carrying on as coherent ongoing life processes of the particular sort that we are, then *of course* continuing to live is in our interests. Except for when it is not. Not only can biocentric conceptions provide us with actual *reasons*, not just widely shared prejudices, as to why death is normally contrary to our interests, biocentric conceptions also provide us with viable reasons why death may sometimes be in our best interests. Our interests are determined by the sort of being we are, and our being may have other priorities. To start with nonhuman and, therefore, less controversial examples, consider a salmon swimming upstream to spawn. Far from being a life that has lost its purpose, the salmon's life is full of intense purpose. It maintains itself within a favorable range of states as it follows its internal imperative, fighting its way up cataracts and on to its spawning grounds. Eating would be only distraction for it. In fact, it cannot eat because its digestive organs have already atrophied, leaving it to achieve its end on the strength of stored body fat. Staying alive for the time being helps it to achieve its end, but its life is subordinate to its reproductive end, and not vice versa. Once spawning has occurred, that life process has no further end implicit within it. Continuing to be alive is no longer something toward which its life is oriented, and death no longer matters to what remains of that process.[3] Accordingly, its life process promptly falls apart. Again, some insects cannot eat during their adult life, having no organs for doing so. Their imperative is to mate. Once they have accomplished their reproductive duties, their death is irrelevant to them. For their part, praying mantises can certainly eat. Female mantises often eat the male after (or even while) mating with him. Unless he could get away and mate with another female, it would be in the best interests of the male mantis to be eaten. The protein from his body would go into the production of young mantises, helping his own genes to proliferate. For that matter, salmon carcasses are a highly valuable source of nutrients for baby salmon, supplying phosphorus and nitrogen from the sea.

Even so, we are neither salmon nor insects, and death is normally contrary to our best interests. The vindication of this hardly novel conclusion, as we

---

[3] Might a reflective salmon think, "Hey, I don't want to be in this! I'd rather go back out to sea and spend a few years contemplating the meaning of life"? A salmon's goals are imbedded in its whole being, from its digestive organs to its gonads, and not just in whatever consciousness it has. A being that could think like that just would not be a salmon or anything like one. In any case, if it did desire to retreat to the sea, its failing organs would debar it from doing so. Perhaps a human's goals are more highly developed (complex, integrated) than a salmon's, but the latter's coherent functioning and its good lies in its doing what is inherent in a salmon to do irrespective of longevity.

saw, requires the recognition that each of us is an ongoing life process with ends implicit in itself and with a drive to maintain itself as a coherent functional whole oriented toward its implicit ends. This recognition is also a key to understanding why *sometimes* death is not contrary to our best interests. We must also bear in mind that life is not a single process but rather an integrated complex weaving of subprocesses. Neither our life nor our interests are simple and unitary. Some of our subprocesses can carry on better than others. Some can get out of balance with the others, conflict with them, or cease entirely. Our lives and interests may heal or unravel. Within ourselves, life may conflict with itself, and interests may conflict with other interests. In some cases, death is in our best interests if our life is no longer able to maintain itself adequately within a range of favorable states and only frustration is possible.

That people can be so ill, terminally, or so deteriorated from age that death can be a benefit for them is an almost universally accepted truth. (It is universally accepted in the case of animals.) Debates about the morality of human euthanasia display nowhere near such agreement, but even those individuals most adamantly opposed to active euthanasia can readily agree that death can be a blessing for some people in some circumstances. When death is a benefit for us, the reason is not that we are in those circumstances things in some adverse condition. Rather, we are in those adverse circumstances as the ongoing life processes we are, self-organizing and self-maintaining. For various reasons, our life process may no longer be able to maintain our self adequately as that which it is central to our own identity to be. We then suffer perpetual frustration as we strive to maintain ourselves as that which we can no longer be. Death is the ultimate collapse of our ability to maintain ourselves. Nonetheless, that ultimate collapse can be to our benefit. This is so when the highest level of interest satisfaction we can attain lies in the cutting short of the frustration of our interests. Our life thrust continues to be toward maintaining ourselves as best we can – and death may be the best we can do. Being delivered from the perpetual frustration of the perpetual striving that is life can be, in the absence of mitigating benefits, preferable to our continuing as a goal-orientated process in perpetual frustration.

I am not by any means trying to say that death is invariably in our best interests when our life is in advanced or terminal deterioration. One would hope that, over the years, we have acquired compensations as well as loss. Maturity and poise may go with wrinkles or arthritis, or much worse, and we may have acquired projects, priorities, and affections that can still offer us immense satisfactions. It is part of a healthy life to acquire such interests, and the gratifications they offer are of great importance to us. Even in the face of misery and death this can be so. Life can have meaning under even horrific conditions. I would again note that in considerable measure, our good is determined by our choices. We may commit to values that call for us to live on in spite of our suffering. We may choose other values. Two people in the same situation might reach opposite conclusions, their individual choosing making each choice correct. We shape and build our own good to a remarkable extent despite the fact that sometimes we choose wrongly.

While life goes on, with whatever pain and suffering, we may have good reason to live on. There may be a loved one to whom one should say goodbye or become reconciled. There may be projects to be completed. We may find value in finishing a book, reading or writing it, or in seeing our team play in the Grand Final. Or in seeing a grandchild married. Or in reconciling with God or in otherwise furthering our spiritual development. Many have found profound insight or comfort on the very brink of death. One good thing one can say about cancer – and there are not many – is that it allows people time for such things (often too much time).

It is also true that some people, as they grow older, come to have a growing equanimity or even indifference in the face of death. Most of life's goals are behind them or, at least, those they rate highly. Death is neither feared nor desired. (Do salmon perhaps feel something like that?) People may be content to live from day to day, for day-to-day gratifications. They also may eventually come to the conclusion that it is time for them to go, or at least that there is no compelling reason for them to stay. Our imperatives change with our life, and the changes in our life are also part of our life.

For most of our lives, at least, death is usually not in our best interests, and as we have noted, it may well be contrary to our interests even in very adverse circumstances. Even so, we must recognize that death is *sometimes* in the best interests of a person. If we were to claim that death is *always* contrary to the best interests of a person, then we would be flying in the face of the promptings of both compassion and common sense, and we would be committed to the conclusion that it would always be wrong to issue, or allow, Do Not Resuscitate (known as DNR) orders. At least it would be wrong in cases wherein we had a duty to act in defense of the person's best interests. Indeed, we would then have to use every available measure to prolong life. People's lives would have to be maintained, and even if they found life tedious and unwelcome, they would have to be repeatedly dragged back to it for their own good. If death is always against a person's interests, then scarcely better than a DNR policy would be to allow relief from agony by so-called *pharmacological oblivion*, keeping patients in or near a coma until death occurs. Death or oblivion would forestall whatever good their life supposedly might be for them then. In truth, such options as DNR or oblivion often are quite inappropriate, yet there can come a time when goodbyes have all been said and everything that can be accomplished has been or must forever go unaccomplished. The expiring person is physically, mentally, and emotionally beyond all gratifications, beyond all but suffering and the indignity of being the mockery of what it is in her or his character to be. Oblivion would then be an ally, and death a deliverance.

This brings us to some very explosive issues, issues that have become explosive in political arenas and in the public consciousness, as well as in the debates of philosophers. Euthanasia is certainly a matter of intense concern for a great many people. Abortion is also an intensely debated topic on which the value of a life, for the one living it, has considerable bearing. The moral significance and value of death also becomes relevant to issues about the allocation of medical resources. Although biocentric conceptions can give us no magic formula by means of which we can systematically churn out clearly right answers, they can give us a better purchase on the issues and help us to find better answers.

Concerning Euthanasia

The term *euthanasia*, again from the Greek, *eu*, meaning "good or well," and *thanatos*, meaning "death," has more than one possible meaning. It can mean a good death, as compared with a bad one, or it can mean a death that is good *for* the person dying – which is not at all the same thing. Again, it can mean dying well rather than poorly, as one might be able to do with even a very bad death. As we shall be concerned with it, in all cases it refers to death caused in advance of material necessity or to the causing of it. Many different ways of causing death have been called euthanasia, some though not all of them being highly and uncontroversially immoral. Moreover, laboratory animals are sometimes said to be euthanized in the course of a scientific experiment or shortly thereafter. Often the animal might otherwise have lived happily for some time to come. Again, animals that make excessive nuisances of themselves are sometimes eliminated through what is said to be euthanasia. In such instances it simply seems to mean killing without causing excessive pain. The question of whether death itself is in the interests of the animal is thought to be beside the point. However, our concern here is with euthanasia in application to humans.

Euthanasia was given a very bad name by the Nazis – though it is by no means clear that what they did actually constituted euthanasia, in practice or in intention. Very many people who, in the Nazis' far-from-expert opinion were grossly inferior, mentally or physically, were killed. The goal was to keep them from being a burden on society and to prevent them from proliferating their inadequacies into future generations. Like the laboratory rats, they were eliminated because their remaining alive was inconvenient to those individuals in power. Whether death was in the best interests of those killed was not thought to be a relevant consideration. Neither did the Nazis make much of an effort to minimize the sufferings of those killed. To describe it as euthanasia is to use a euphemism for mass murder. It is also wrong to impeach by innuendo the concept of euthanasia as proposed by people who advocate very different actions from far nobler motives. For our purposes here, let us take euthanasia, good death, as referring to the causing, by act or omission, of a death that is good for the person killed and that is caused *for* that person's benefit. This is the sense that is of central relevance to human bioethics. The term as so understood could also meaningfully be applied under some circumstances to the killing of animals. More than once it has been my sadness to be a party to a well-loved dog's being killed for its own good. The beneficiary was the dog. Note, however, that when animals are killed, even painlessly but not for their own benefit, then that is not euthanasia according to this conception. For my own part, I would prefer that some other term be invented for such killing. Nor in my conception could capital punishment be deemed euthanasia, however painless or justified it might be. In the following paragraphs, I am concerned only with euthanasia in application to humans, and I take the concept to apply *only when the killing is done for the sake of the one killed.*

Concerning euthanasia, a number of important or seemingly important distinctions have been made. As we are attempting to navigate through issues that are complex philosophically and that are politically, socially, and emotionally incendiary, it would be well for us to be clear about what we are talking about. To start with, there are distinctions between voluntary, nonvoluntary, and involuntary euthanasia. When death is brought about for the good of the person killed, at that person's desire, this is *voluntary euthanasia.* However, it may be that a person is unable to have any desires on the subject, one way or another. Such would be the condition of a person in a permanent vegetative state, or a neonate, or someone with little mental capacity but great agony. When death is brought about in a person who is incapable of having desires about it, and for the good of that person, this is *nonvoluntary euthanasia.* A third category is theoretically possible, the repulsive one of *involuntary euthanasia.* In that conception, a person is killed against his or her will but for his or her own good. Once again, the term *murder* springs to mind. It should be stressed that those who advocate legalized euthanasia are normally referring to voluntary euthanasia. Virtually none of them, if any at all, advocate involuntary euthanasia.

Another distinction is that between *active* and *passive.* Active euthanasia would involve taking active steps to bring about the person's death, for instance by administering a lethal injection. Passive euthanasia involves not taking steps to prevent death where it can readily be prevented. Allowing a person to die under a DNR code or failing to give full medical care to a defective neonate would be instances, so long as the omission is for the benefit of the one dying. Things of this nature happen legally and frequently. Many people would object to using the term *passive euthanasia,* even when a person is allowed to die for his or her own benefit. Usually this disquietude about the term seems to be on the part of those who admit that some instances of allowing people to die are morally justified, yet who find the term *euthanasia* offensive. They would prefer that the term be reserved for the active form. I intend to discuss both passive and active forms of euthanasia, distinguishing as necessary. Active or passive, what is or is not done is for the benefit of the one dying. The Principle of Double Effect also arises here. The distinction is made between actions intended to bring about a certain effect, and actions, perhaps the same actions, wherein that effect is foreseen but unintended.[4] A relevant instance would be that of a physician who gives a terminally ill patient heavy sedation for the purpose of relieving suffering, knowing but not intending that death would be accelerated. In contrast would be another physician who gives a similarly ill patient an equivalent dose, intending not only the alleviation of suffering through sedation but also the elimination of it through death. According to the Principle of Double Effect, even though the physicians did identical things, the former was acting benevolently and righteously as a healer, whereas the latter was committing euthanasia or murder. The principle is also invoked in connection with whether or not a particular act is one of suicide. I stress that in this discussion I am trying only to state the categories, and I make no presuppositions about the morality or immorality of any of these alternatives.

Certainly there are moral issues to be raised in connection with euthanasia. Is there any form of euthanasia that society ought to allow to be carried out under some circumstances? In the instance of active voluntary euthanasia, at least, there is a prima facie case that it ought to be allowed. That is, if death were in a person's best interests – as we have reason to believe is possible – and if that person wanted his or her own death to be brought about (and if that person were properly informed, clear headed, and so on), then it would seem that this person should be allowed to have that happen. Indeed, that it should be that person's *right* would seem to be implicit in a right to bodily autonomy. This would seem like a very persuasive argument, *unless* there were substantial reasons to the contrary.

Certainly there have been many arguments to the contrary, whether or not they have been sufficiently persuasive ones. It might be alleged that death can never be in a person's best interests, or that if it could be, we cannot be sufficiently certain that it is in a person's best interests in a particular case. Therefore, runs the argument, we should not risk making an irrevocable mistake. Another line of argument is that whether or not euthanasia might be in a person's best interests in a particular case, euthanasia is inherently immoral for some reason. Maybe it is *always* wrong to kill a person, at least an innocent person. Perhaps killing, even killing a person who wants to be killed and who would benefit from it, constitutes a negation of that person as an end in himself or herself, a failure to respect that person's humanity. Perhaps voluntary euthanasia amounts to suicide, the committing or abetting of which might be held to always be wrong. Another line

---

4 Later, I discuss the principle at greater length, at which point I shall elaborate on the complexities of the formal statement of the principle.

of argument is that irrespective of whether euthanasia is justified in particular instances, it ought never to be allowed because to do so would lead to adverse consequences of various sorts: people developing disrespect for human life and perhaps developing vested interests in euthanasia, other people coming to fear being killed, and the like. This sort of argument, it should be noted, is consequentialist, not addressing any intrinsic moral character of the act itself. Let us now turn to a discussion of the morality of euthanasia.

Active and Passive

Active voluntary euthanasia is probably the most publicly controversial form of euthanasia. Many opponents of active euthanasia have maintained that an actively caused death is never in the best interests of a person. Many opponents have maintained that even if euthanasia could be in a person's interests, it ought never to be allowed because of the possibility of our making an irreversible error. ("How would you feel if you were a party to someone's being euthanized and the next morning a wonderful cure were announced?") It should be noted that, on this point, active and passive forms of euthanasia are on an exact par. Whatever moral differences between active and passive there might be – a matter of considerable debate – *both* forms of euthanasia presuppose that death can be in a person's interests, and that sometimes we can identify such an instance with adequate certainty. Both forms presuppose that possibilities to the contrary can become vanishingly small. If we accept DNR policies and other forms of letting die, that is, if we admit any form of passive euthanasia, then we are committed to the truth of these presuppositions. That is so whether we like it or not. ("How would you feel if you were a party to someone's dying under a DNR order and the next morning a wonderful cure were announced?" For that matter, one might well ask, "How would you feel if you allowed someone to have a long and agonized death when the hoped-for miracle did not come through?")

As the possibility of there being such a thing as beneficial death is tacitly agreed to by anyone who agrees to DNR orders or any other form of compassionate letting die (which is nearly everyone), as there are no known plausible arguments to the contrary, and as I have already given reasons in favor of that conclusion, on the basis of our discussions of life and interests, I shall proceed on the assumption that death can be in a person's own best interests in some circumstances. Still, this does not quite settle the question of whether euthanasia can be in one's best interests. It might be that death by natural causes may be in a person's best interests on occasion, whereas an actively induced death never is. (This is a distinct question from that of whether it is always wrong to be a willing party to someone's being killed, a question to be considered later.)

Why might it be that a natural death can be good for a person, whereas an induced death can never be? It may perhaps be that God, or karma, has numbered our days and would have us live to just the appointed hour, for our spiritual well-being, suffering the flesh for the sake of our soul. For our span to be cut short would be to deprive us of the opportunity to make further spiritual progress toward God, or to burn off bad karma, or something else of that sort. It is presumed, of course, that whomever or whatever sets the measure of our life is able to take into account the future state of medical science, for the length of our days may be greatly influenced by the nature and availability of medical treatment. Presumably it would not be beyond the range of God, or the principle of karma, to take that into account. One supposes that the party when we had our first cigarette would also be taken into account, and the time when we became convinced of the value of exercise and a good diet. It is a comforting thought that our lives are so well monitored by divine providence. Would it now follow on this presumption that DNR orders and other forms of letting die are *never* appropriate? Perhaps life ought to go on until some appointed moment that coincides with the moment when all possible efforts to sustain life fail; until that time, we must resuscitate whenever possible, no matter how seemingly futile or distressing for the person. It seems very strange that divine providence – we are presuming that it works for our good, aren't we? – would allow for all other contingencies but not for a compassionate act of letting die in the face of painful futility. If such a position actually were consistently maintained, with such callousness being required of us, then it must be confessed that it could not be refuted, any more than we can refute the claim that divine providence has arranged things so that it is always wrong to step on cracks in the sidewalk. I think I will offend no one by rejecting any such position out of hand.

Virtually everyone not in the grip of some emotion, including those most committed to the idea that there is a divine providence, will agree that in some instances a compassionate act of letting die is appropriate. Presumably a benevolent divine providence factors that into the dying person's term of life or otherwise makes appropriate provision. Then would a benevolent power not also factor in a compassionate act of active euthanasia, determining a person's allotted time accordingly? That would be no more beyond the powers of divine providence than it would be to make allowance for passive voluntary euthanasia. It seems very strange indeed that a benevolent power could foresee both active and passive euthanasia yet would take only the latter into account in numbering our days – unless there were some very good reason for it. The only even slightly plausible reason I can imagine, and so far as I know, the only one anyone has *ever* thought of, is that divine providence is operating on the principle that active euthanasia is wrong under every circumstance – and that the goodness of that power would preclude its making such an accommodation to evil. Accordingly, let us bypass speculation about a preordained number of our days and put the focus where it properly should be: on the moral character of the act of active euthanasia itself and of its consequences.

Active euthanasia is an act of doing something. Specifically, it is an act of killing someone, which is always an extremely serious matter. In contrast, passive euthanasia is not doing something, though it may well have the same effect. Seemingly clear, the difference between active and passive is not always so clear in practice. If we switch off the life-support system for a hopelessly terminal patient, are we actively killing the person, or are we passively not preventing nature from taking its course? Does it make a difference if we decline to switch it on in the first place? Nor can any moral difference between them be a simple matter in which nonaction is always morally unimpeachable. We cannot keep our hands clean so easily, for a failure to act can be a grossly immoral dereliction of duty. We would harshly judge a physician who failed to resuscitate a young patient who was basically fairly healthy and who, once past the need of resuscitation, would be able to live well for many years. Were I to see a toddler fall face down into a fishpond and then stand around doing nothing, I would be utterly vile. I, and the remiss physician, could have prevented great harm yet failed to do so. By the same token, a DNR order is only properly applied to people who will be benefited by death or at least not harmed. We are under no obligation to prevent something that is not a harm. Yet why must one be under an obligation not to cause what one is under no moral obligation to prevent?

We will recall that according to a utilitarian ethic, the moral character of an act is determined by its intended material consequences. As it is impossible to distinguish morally between active and passive merely in terms of what one is causing or preventing, the utilitarian will morally equate active or passive euthanasia when the foreseen consequences are the same. If we are to distinguish morally between active and passive, it must be on the basis of a system of ethics that distinguishes on the basis of the character of the act itself. This means that if we are to distinguish between active and passive euthanasia – which not everyone would care to do – it would have to be on the basis of deontological ethics, or perhaps virtue ethics, if we consider virtue ethics to be in a different category.

Thou Shalt Not Kill

The principle that we must not kill our fellow humans has much to be said for it. Many people would be severely wronged were they to suffer death at the whim of another. Not just injured, but *wronged*. It seems that the principle is a good one, and we are often told that it has been given divine sanction by the religious commandment, "Thou shalt not kill." As one presumes that God acts only for the good, we must assume that killing is forbidden because it is morally wrong and not wrong merely because it is forbidden. God sees into things far better than we can, but we can know that God would not command something, such as gratuitous cruelty, that is morally wrong. However, if we do assume that God (or karma, or whatever) has forbidden us to kill, just how are we to interpret that edict? Does it mean that we are never to kill *anything*? Some people have accepted just that view. The Jains of India believe that killing anything for any reason is wrong. Accordingly, good Jains will not only refrain from killing people, they will also not eat meat, kill mice, or swat mosquitoes. Very good ones will sweep the path before them as they walk, so that they will not accidentally tread on any living thing. They will not drink in the dark for fear of ingesting an errant insect. They wear gauze masks to avoid accidentally inhaling one. Highly advanced Jain saints will even starve themselves to death to avoid injuring plants that they would otherwise eat. Although they do not go that far, many Buddhists find it abhorrent to kill any animal life or, at least, any sentient life.

In the Judeo-Christian-Islamic tradition, the prohibition on killing has almost universally been interpreted as referring only to humans, with there being much scriptural support for the view that killing animals is not forbidden or wrong. Does the prohibition mean then that we are *never* to kill *humans*? Some have interpreted it this way. We are never to go to war, nor to kill someone in self-defense, nor to execute a criminal. If one does take such an absolutist position, holding that any human reasoning is inferior to the Higher Wisdom that has so commanded, then one cannot be refuted. The dire consequences of inaction cannot be a justification for killing as no consideration of consequences can override the moral law. Yet there are circumstances under which such an absolute rule seems most inappropriate and quite pernicious. (To take a stock extreme example, suppose a vicious killer is on the loose. He has killed several people, including one of your own children, and he is trying to make a clean sweep. The only way to stop him is to shoot him, and you do not have an opportunity to aim for a nonvital spot.) Moreover, there is a massive amount of scriptural support for the belief that some killing of humans is not forbidden or wrong when it is done under appropriate circumstances. Most thinkers within the Judeo-Christian-Islamic tradition have accordingly held some version of that belief.

Perhaps the rule, together with whatever exceptions, can be derived from divine authority without our knowing or being able to know the reasons behind it. Still, if there were exceptions to a blanket ban, it would be very useful to know why they are exceptions, so that we may better recognize them in practice. Furthermore, if we were to take the moral law into our hearts, as every religion calls on us to do, then it would be highly useful to have an awareness of why it is that killing is (usually) wrong. I make no claim to be able to interpret or understand the divine mind. In the following paragraphs, I try to develop as good a grasp as I, one human, can get of why killing is (usually) wrong and of whether euthanasia or other biomedical applications might sometimes constitute morally appropriate exceptions.

The case against killing is quite straightforward: To kill a person is usually to injure that person in the worst possible way. That person is negated as a moral end in himself or herself. People killed have their aspirations shattered, their being violated, their very value profaned and obliterated. It is an injury that can never be recompensed. Nevertheless, we can still ask whether killing always negates the person as a moral end in himself or herself. If a person benefits from being killed, asks or agrees to be killed, and the killing is carried out for that person's benefit in a caring and considerate way, is the person negated? Clearly it is a negation of the existence of that end in itself. Does it follow, though, that it is a negation of that end in itself *as* an end in itself, as the being it is? There is a point of view that holds that acting in a way that benefits that person, and is intended to, is an act of respect for that person as an end in herself or himself. We may even arguably be considered selfish for refusing to give that person the needed help: Are we trying to keep our own hands clean in appearance, at the cost of another's suffering? What is it truly to respect people as moral ends in themselves?

In treating people as an end in themselves, we are not to treat people merely as being of instrumental value. The seeming alternative is to treat people as being of *intrinsic* value. What is it for someone or something to be of intrinsic value? We must be careful here, for there are different things it may mean. Something might be of intrinsic value *for me*. If I were a hedonist, then I would take pleasure (specifically, my own) as being of value in its own right for me. I would believe that our respective pleasure is of intrinsic value for me and for others, whether or not we recognize it. In this account, though, the goodness of my experience is a matter of its being good *for me*. As distinct from that, I might believe that it is intrinsically good that there should exist beings experiencing pleasure, and that if none such existed, it would be better if some did. More broadly, there is a sense in which it might be maintained that something is of intrinsic value if its existence is good, whether or not its existence is good for anyone. Beauty, love, and rationality might be examples. Perhaps a beautiful sunset on an uninhabited planet is of intrinsic value in itself. Perhaps the existence of human beings is of intrinsic value. Perhaps the existence of any one particular human being is of intrinsic value, this being the value of making the world a somewhat better place by being in it. That person's death then is a loss of value.

What if life is no longer of intrinsic value *for* a particular person? If we force that person to remain alive contrary to her or his best interests, bringing about what is of intrinsic *dis*value for that person, is that not to treat that person as a means to some further end rather than as an end in herself or himself? Or are we to say that the intrinsic disvalue for that person of remaining alive is outweighed for *that* person by the existence value of there being one more person? I find it pretty hard to swallow that one. It seems to me that this amounts to an excuse for overriding someone's interests as a means to some supposed greater good. Furthermore, if anyone were to take such a line consistently, they would also have to condemn all acts of benevolent letting die. (Even further, they would have to advocate all useful measures to bring about huge populations.) This is a fundamentally misguided approach.

To take a person as an end in herself or himself is not to take the person as being of value for us or for the universe, though these things may well be true in addition. Indeed, to take a person's moral significance as being dependent on her or his being of value for anything else is not to give the person her or his due moral respect. To take people as ends in themselves is to take them as each being a center of value, one to be respected. Our respecting others as centers of value may well be of intrinsic value, but a person is quite literally invaluable.

Here I would like to point out what is wrong with one of the better known, though certainly not one of the better, arguments used in connection with euthanasia: *Who do you think you are, or anyone is, to declare that another human life is worthless?* Usually there are further rhetorical flourishes, often suggesting that proponents of euthanasia have an ambition to play God. This is an argument that owes far more to rhetoric than to reason. The only proper response to that is that we are *never* to declare another human life worthless. Neither you nor I nor anyone else is to do so, not for ourselves and not for others. Life is *never* worthless. It is the frustration and dissolution of life that one may appropriately wish to reject. Euthanasia, according to the concept being considered here, does not consider human life to be worthless. On the contrary, the objective, the intention, is to help our fellow humans to fulfill what is, for them at that time, their best interests. Instead of declaring human lives worthless, the principle is that each human life is worthy of respect in its own right and has a moral call on us for our help or forbearance when the need arises. We may debate whether euthanasia is ever the right answer, and I am not presupposing at this point that it is. Nevertheless, I am stating that any line of thought that declares that any human life is worthless, or not worthy of moral respect, is not intending euthanasia. The intent of euthanasia is to respect and benefit the one dying. To use the term to disguise the elimination of those deemed worthless, superfluous, or undesirable is to borrow a term implying benevolent intentions in order to dissemble the despicable.

Even if performing active euthanasia is not to negate a person as an end in herself or himself, there may still conceivably be reasons why it is inherently wrong. The field of possible reasons has been narrowed down by the recognition that death can be a benefit for the person dying, but perhaps some beneficial acts can still be inherently wrong. Virtue ethics may suggest a possible line of thought. However similar they might be in effects and intended outcomes, there is still a psychological difference, often a huge one, between doing something and not doing something. We cannot prevent every death, but we can certainly keep from actively and intentionally causing human death. Perhaps we are better off, or the world in general is, if we have an inhibition against taking life, or at least against taking innocent life. Obviously, if everyone had such an inhibition, the murder rate and the rate of wars would plummet, and the world would be a much better place. The justification of the principle, though, is not in its material consequences but in making one a better person for having internalized the principle as a feature of her or his very living. Certainly we all know that rewriting or making exceptions to moral principles is a dangerous thing to do and often dishonest and self-serving. Still, we may well wonder if we had the right principle to start with. Instead of *Never kill an innocent person*, perhaps the principle we ought to incorporate as part of our character is *Never harm an innocent person by killing her or him*. This would rule out nearly all the same things, and the same self-serving exceptions would still be rubbish. This proposed principle also has further virtues. It would not require us to take only insufficient steps in cases wherein death is in someone's interests and requested by that person. It would not require us to keep our hands morally clean at the cost of another person's alleviable but unalleviated suffering. The principle of never killing seems to presuppose an assumption that is almost always true, the assumption that to kill is to harm. The principle of never harming by killing comes closer to the optimal principle in that it recognizes that this assumption is not always true and does not require us to withhold wanted and needed help. Thereby it makes a better fit with what is regarded as another very important virtue: benevolence.

Nonvoluntary Euthanasia

Not all forms of passive euthanasia are voluntary on the part of those dying. DNR policies or other forms of letting die may be instituted in those cases in which patients lack the mental capacity to have any wishes on the subject. Perhaps they are neonates or in a persistent vegetative condition. It also sometimes happens with patients who, were they asked, might have and express desires of a sort. It may be that they are not asked because their mental condition is such that they cannot have coherent responses or sensible desires, while asking them, if possible at all, would only upset them further. We, from our more detached position and superior knowledge, know that steps to forestall inevitable death would only prolong suffering without compensating benefit. Of course there always remains a minuscule theoretical possibility that some last-minute eventuality might save the day. Even so, in these cases of passive nonvoluntary euthanasia, it is deemed that allowing or forcing a person to endure inevitable future suffering is not justified by such a vanishingly faint hope.

The following is from an official medical report of an actual case that is in no way unusual and is taken from among huge numbers of similar cases[5]:

This 71 year old man was [admitted to institution] on [date] following a left cortical infarction resulting in a right hemiparesis and dysarthria. He had a previous stroke in [previous year] and there was a history of hypertension, ischaemic heart disease requiring bypass surgery, and non-insulin dependent diabetes mellitus. He made a fair recovery from this recent stroke, continuing to live at home with minor help from his wife for activities of daily living.

He was re-admitted to [institution] on [date], after suffering another stroke due to cerebral infarction of the right internal capsule the same day. The diagnosis was confirmed by CT scan. His major impairment was a pseudobulbar palsy causing severe dysphagia and dysarthria. He required insertion of a per-cutaneous gastrostomy for feeding but his conscious level gradually deteriorated and he developed a bronchopneumonia. In view of his disability and after discussion with his wife it was decided to treat the latter problem conservatively and he died on [date], presumably from pneumonia. An autopsy was not performed.

In this case, consent for letting the patient die (treating "conservatively") was obtained from the man's wife, acting on his behalf. As there was no consent from the patient himself, it was nonvoluntary euthanasia. It was passive, as no active steps were taken to cause death. As in all genuine cases of euthanasia, the course of action was (so one presumes) taken for the benefit of the one doing the dying.

Nonvoluntary euthanasia is also practiced in application to much younger patients. Neonates with severe birth defects are sometimes treated conservatively. They are given nutrition, water, and palliative care. However, necessary surgery and the use of life-support systems may be underutilized and infections treated conservatively or not at all. Were the neonate normal, such treatment would be grossly negligent or vilely malevolent and probably legally actionable. What makes the difference is that normal neonates have good prospects, whereas afflicted neonates are thought to have very poor prospects in terms of their quality or length of life. This letting die is passive nonvoluntary euthanasia *if* it is motivated by an intention to benefit the neonate. Sometimes it is quite evident that the child has no prospects of benefit to it in living. Of course, we may sometimes be incorrect in our assessment of the child's prospects – and, in any case, there is still the morality of this form of euthanasia to be considered – but passive nonvoluntary euthanasia is what it is if the child's benefit is the motivating concern.

Were the afflicted child to continue to live, it is not the only one whose quality of life might be expected to suffer. Obviously the parents would be in for a very rough time. Indeed, if they had difficulty in coping, that might result in the child's quality of life becoming all the worse. Might the

---

5 The case is taken from the files of a well-reputed hospital. Identifying details, obviously, have been deleted for both legal and moral reasons.

welfare of the parents themselves be the motivating consideration? Perhaps they are appalled by the demands to be made of them, even if the child lives only a short while. Perhaps they know that they would collapse under the strain. Wishful and fearful thinking may well distort their judgment. Even so, if they opt for letting die in the honest conviction that death is of benefit to the child, whatever other benefits it might have, it is passive nonvoluntary euthanasia. Of course, however, those moral questions remain and the question of the accuracy of the assessments of the prospects and interests of all those involved.

Sometimes a severely afflicted neonate does have a potential for living a life well worth living. Severely mentally retarded people, for instance those with Down's syndrome, may yet have good lives. I have personally known instances of that. I have also known instances to the contrary. Either way, there are considerable burdens on those around them. When such defects are detected prior to birth, abortion is often resorted to. Of those who are born so afflicted, a few are left to die. Down's syndrome in itself is not fatal nor, generally, are other forms of mental retardation. Nonetheless, these conditions are often associated with other debilitating conditions. For unknown reasons, about 10 percent of Down's syndrome neonates have an intestinal blockage (duodenal atresia in most cases) that permits the food nowhere to go. An even higher proportion of them have cardiac problems. In such cases, it is possible to treat the condition conservatively – giving palliative care to the neonate but otherwise allowing it to die. This course of action is not primarily taken for the benefit of the neonate but for the overall greatest good for the greatest number. Or, at least, it is taken for the greater good of the other family members. As it is not for the benefit of the one dying, it is not euthanasia. Although palliation might allow the neonate a better death than it would have without palliation, it is no more euthanasia than it is in the case of the laboratory rat dispensed with as surplus to requirements. To call it euthanasia would be to employ a euphemism for something else. Whether we should therefore condemn such letting die as murder, or condemn it at all, is a further issue. Indeed, it is a complex of both legal and moral issues. Currently, the climate of opinion on such matters seems to be quite volatile and wildly fluctuating. Certainly some people are persuaded, with supporting rationale, that infanticide can be morally justifiable under some circumstances.[6] Whatever the morality of that, it is a different matter from the morality of euthanasia.

[6] Notably, Peter Singer has made some highly impassioned enemies by suggesting that infanticide, including active infanticide, can be morally justified under *some* circumstances; see Helga Kuhse and Peter Singer, *Should the Baby Live? The Problem of Handicapped Infants* (New York: Oxford University Press, 1985). There are real issues here. For my own part, I suggest that those who condemn Singer morally ought first to get clear on just what he does and does not say, and on just why he says what he does say.

Involuntary Euthanasia

Thus far we have considered voluntary and involuntary euthanasia. More briefly, we have noted euphemistic uses of the term *euthanasia* in connection with surplus animals or, in some of the most repugnant events of the twentieth century, perpetrated by some of its most repulsive people, in connection with other people held to have objectionable characteristics. Such actions in application to people would be better described as cold-blooded murder. Indeed, *involuntary euthanasia* is generally dismissed as being a contradiction in terms. Though sometimes people are killed involuntarily by way of murder, accident, self-defense, capital punishment, war, or whatever else, having death imposed upon them against their will is not thought to be in their best interests. There are sometimes occasions when a person's will might properly be overridden for that person's own good. Nonetheless, it seems just too bizarre that having death forced on an unwilling person could be other than a gross infringement on self and well-being. In the interests of intellectual honesty, though, let us ask whether any action ever could properly be described as being one of involuntary euthanasia. I am not at all happy to raise the possibility. Much less would I want anyone to act upon it. Logically, however, the question is there. For an act to be one of involuntary euthanasia, it would have to be preferable to any viable alternative, and it would have to be to the benefit of the person killed and done for that purpose. Could there be any such thing? Yes, I do believe there could. Could it ever be morally justified? That is more problematic. If it were ever morally justifiable, would it be moral or prudent to provide for it in our laws and institutions? That too is problematic. Some slopes can be slippery.

First, that involuntary euthanasia is a logical possibility. Sometimes people do not track their own good adequately. If death is in a person's best interests, and it can be, it may be that the person is unable to cope with that truth. One might have acquired responses that are not appropriate to one's current situation. Perhaps one might just mishandle a particular extreme situation. To be sure, having one's desires overridden, particularly a very strong desire such as a desire for life is apt to be, is in itself that much contrary to a person's interests. Even so, it might possibly be that a person actually is better off having a swift and relatively painless death rather than a long agonized death. It might *possibly* be that someone else intervenes, killing the sufferer, or stands by and does nothing to prevent death, doing one or the other for the supposed good of the sufferer. The morality of involuntary euthanasia, active or passive, in such a situation is a further issue.

Consider the following situation as a possible example of passive involuntary euthanasia. Suppose that a patient in a hospital is in a very bad way. The suffering is intense, and it is made worse by the patient's intense fear of death. The patient begs all within earshot not to let him or her die. Die he or she shall, though, and in the relatively near future, whatever anyone's desires might be. The patient is motivated by terror, not by any desire for future gratifications. (Let us assume that there are no considerations of family, unfinished business, or other such things.) We may come to believe that this terror on the patient's part is irrational, but terror is no less real for being irrational. Nor is consent to death any the less withheld. Remember, too, that denial of consent does not lapse when the patient is unconscious, whether it is due to palliative sedation or something else. It might perhaps be that the patient is allowed to die because the requisite medical resources are vitally needed elsewhere. That would not be a matter of euthanasia per se as in such a case the patient's well-being is not the decisive consideration. However, perhaps the medical staff (possibly in consultation with the next of kin) decides to follow a policy of DNR or conservative treatment, doing so in the conviction that more active treatment could only prolong the agony – and doing so in the knowledge that this course of action was against the patient's strong desire. As a result, the patient dies sooner rather than later. Indeed, perhaps the patient might have lived on indefinitely, with medical support, though living only in a wretched condition. There is therefore a time when the patient is dead (against his or her will) but would have been alive had not the staff acted in the conviction that death would be the preferable possible outcome. In effect, the medical staff (with or without agreement from the family) has appointed itself guardian of the patient's well-being and overridden the patient's desire for continued life, doing so for the patient's own good. At that time (and therefore at all subsequent times), an instance of passive involuntary euthanasia has occurred. In point of fact, passive involuntary euthanasia is widely accepted and not at all an unusual occurrence.[7] Ought it to be accepted?

As patients, or as prospective patients, we would all like to have the assurance that everything will be done to keep us alive so long as we want to stay alive. Accordingly, medical staff will usually strive well past hope. Sometimes this continuation of effort is to the distress of the patient. If the patient's stated wishes are that all life-maintaining steps be taken, should these steps continue to be taken even past the point when it becomes crystal clear to all who can see with clarity that this can only postpone the inevitable at the price of prolonged suffering? One may be convinced that if the patient knew the relevant facts and were thinking clearly, she or he would consent

---

[7] Certainly, it has been found beyond doubt that in many cases, DNR and "No Extraordinary Measures" have been interpreted to allow more inaction than was called for or intended by the signatories. In one particular nursing home, a survey was made concerning ninety-six patients who had died after having previously given written advance instructions about the care they were to be given in extremis. It was found that eighteen of these patients were given less life-extending care than they had explicitly requested. For a broader discussion of the phenomenon of excessive inaction, see Jim Stone, "Advance Directives, Autonomy and Unintended Death," *Monash Bioethics Review* 15, 1996: 16–33.

to the cessation of all but palliative care – but, in point of fact, her or his known wishes are to the contrary. Are members of a medical staff morally obligated to continue doing the useless at the price of suffering? Sometimes we do override a person's wishes, doing so for their own good. We may take active steps for the purpose of preventing a person's irrational desire to end his or her own life from being fulfilled. May we make omissions for the purpose of preventing a person's irrational desire to live longer than could possibly be good for that person from being fulfilled?

It would obviously be desirable for there to be *advance directives* that were as clear and comprehensive as possible and that were made on the basis of fully informed consent freely given. Beyond that, there is a role for a *medical power of attorney* whereby a trusted person is empowered by the patient to make decisions on the patient's behalf. Still, the question just will not go away: Can things ever get to the point where those on the clinical care staff are justified, whatever patients or next of kin might request or demand, in ceasing to attempt to do the impossible? My own conviction is that in the messy world of human affairs, sometimes it is justified. Sometimes, in the name of compassion, it is morally requisite.

* * * * *

Now we come to the most repulsive topic of them all: *active* involuntary euthanasia. The question is whether actively killing a person against his or her will, but for that person's intended benefit, can be morally acceptable. The most persuasive illustrations of the possibility of active involuntary euthanasia are drawn from war. In his *Seven Pillars of Wisdom*, T. E. Lawrence (i.e., Lawrence of Arabia) tells of the aftermath of one armed conflict:

Salem would have been dead, for the Turks did not take Arab prisoners. Indeed, they used to kill them horribly, so, in mercy, we were finishing those of our badly wounded who would have to be left helpless on abandoned ground. (T. E. Lawrence, *Seven Pillars of Wisdom*)[8]

Consent was clearly not a relevant consideration.

What would be the right thing to do under such circumstances? What would I do were I to face the choice in actual fact? It is difficult to answer either of those two questions. On balance I would prefer to not kill a person contrary to that person's clear wishes (setting aside cases of self-defense and the like). Nonetheless, I would be most distressed, to say the least, by a fellow human being, perhaps a close friend, dying in a needless agony from which I could relieve him. Even so, I am inclined to think that we ought to respect her or his wishes, even misguided ones. That is part of the cost of having

---

[8] T. E. Lawrence, *Seven Pillars of Wisdom: A Triumph* (Hertfordshire: Wordsworth, 1997; originally published 1926), p. 363.

consciousness and choice. That there is a down side to consciousness and choice we must long since have realized.

Would I then not kill the hopelessly injured soldier on the field of battle? Perhaps I would be overcome by strong emotions of compassion, and revulsion at his suffering, and put him out of his misery – perhaps finally doing so on a split-second impulse. Would I be acting well, or would I be succumbing to temptation? I do not know how I would act in such a situation. What I do know for certain is that were some other person to kill him, and were I convinced that the situation truly was hopeless and that the killing was done from compassion, then I would not care to raise my voice in condemnation.[9] However we assess such matters, though, I do come to the distasteful conclusion that the concept of active involuntary euthanasia cannot just be dismissed by philosophical fiat. There is some real meaning here, with real problems. That the concept does have meaning, more meaning than we humans in our frailty can be trusted to handle well, is part of its terror.

That the concept of involuntary euthanasia might have application is a dangerous conclusion, too highly dangerous for application to human bioethics. Even if we could conclude that involuntary euthanasia were a good thing in particular cases – an *if* of very large proportions – any good consequences we might hope to obtain through a willingness to act on that conclusion quite likely would be outweighed by the overall bad consequences that would follow from any such precedent. For example, many people would be terrified about other people making lethal judgments about them. A particular occasion of terror would be when people contemplated hospitalization. More broadly, any recognition of legitimacy for involuntary euthanasia could and therefore would be used as a specious pretext by some individuals pursuing selfish ends. Moreover, we in our presumed wisdom might get it wrong even when well intended. Perhaps those in extremis still have some hopes, or gratifications, or objectives, or unfinished spiritual pursuits – still something to live for. Or, yes, they might be hopelessly unrealistic in their thinking, suffering from a useless agony that could be relieved. That happens. Still, the choice must be theirs to make, even if they make it unwisely. The overall consequences of our making choices for them might very well be much worse. We too can make mistakes. Even worse, evil people could, and have, used such rationales to dissemble evil intentions and vile deeds. Moreover, it may not be a matter of

---

9 In her *The Eye in the Door* – one part of her *Regeneration* trilogy, which is a factually based fictional account of the physical and psychological effects of World War I trench warfare – Pat Barker tells of a terrified soldier sinking ever deeper into immensely deep mud from which he cannot be rescued. This is right on the front line, where alternatives are lacking. His commanding officer shoots him dead from pity. Several such incidents, I understand, did occur in fact. See Pat Barker, *Regeneration Trilogy* (London: Penguin Books, 1995; originally published as *Regeneration*, 1991; *The Eye in the Door*, 1993; and *The Ghost Road*, 1995).

consequences at all. It may just be that the choice is a person's to make for himself or herself regardless of the consequences. It may be that it is part of the respect we owe them to respect the person's choice, however well or poorly taken, advantageous or otherwise to the person. It may just be that this is part of the sometimes-heavy price we, agent or patient, have to pay for being a person.

* * * * *

Involuntary euthanasia is an unpleasant topic and I have often found thinking and writing about it to be a disagreeable experience. Even so, I must face up to a further disagreeable question in this connection. Whatever my omissions – and I can hardly claim to have said the last word on such matters – I must in some way face up to the moral dimension of *active* and *passive*. Earlier, I ventured the conclusion that, in extremis, passive involuntary euthanasia can sometimes be justified. Sometimes. However, I have come down against allowing active involuntary euthanasia. Many moral philosophers, utilitarians in particular, have poured scorn on any claim that there is a moral distinction between active and passive. Certainly they seem to have a point. If I take a course of action in the thought that a certain result will occur, am I not morally responsible for the outcome whether my course of action is active or passive? If I do nothing (except give palliative care) so that a person's suffering may end the sooner, is that any better than taking an active step to hasten the same inevitable outcome? Indeed, the latter might well be said to be the *more* humane course of action insofar as prolonged suffering could be not just lessened but ended with a painless injection. Perhaps it might be suspected that in not taking that compassionate step, we, like Pontius Pilate, are trying to wash our hands of our own responsibilities in the matter.

Those who put the most stress on a moral distinction between active and passive are those whose ethics center on absolute rules of ought and ought not or shalt and shalt not. For them, the distinction between active and passive euthanasia is of immense significance. For those who do not take such a stance, I can offer another rationale for attaching importance to the distinction. This is not because of the moral strength of the distinction but because of our moral weaknesses as humans. The line between active and passive is one that can be drawn with pragmatically useful effect. It is a line that can be maintained and patrolled as well as or better than other lines, and ruling out active involuntary euthanasia more strongly has the merit of ruling out many things that ought to be ruled out while at least tacitly allowing the possibility of some courses of action that arguably ought to be allowed. No line, however, is without problems, and this one is no exception.

For example, the distinction between active and passive is not always one that can be made with comforting clarity. For instance, is switching off a life-support system an active step, or is it to cease activity and revert to passivity?

If we refuse to turn it on in the first place, that would presumably be a passive course of action (whether right or wrong). Does turning the system on preclude our ever turning it off while the patient lives? If it did, that might possibly make us too cautious about activating the system in the first place. Again, is it passive to withhold a powerful drug that would postpone the inevitable? Is it passive to withhold food? Air?

An even more serious problem is that the active–passive distinction does not very closely approximate the boundary between good and evil. The worst evil is obviously that of killing people for our own purposes rather than (if at all) for their good. Then it is not euthanasia at all, though such a claim might be used as a pretext. Usually, murder can be performed more readily actively than passively, though it usually will be more detectable. Murder by willful omission is no less murder from a moral standpoint, though it might be less serious from a legal one. As those who would murder are more likely to find active means, the active–passive distinction is of some use as a deterrent. Even so, not all of the benign cases of involuntary euthanasia are necessarily on one side of the line. Sometimes it would be the most compassionate and benevolent thing to follow a policy of DNR, or treating conservatively, or going slowly, or whatever else it might be called. Sometimes it would be even more compassionate and benevolent to give the person a shot to speed him or her through the terminal suffering. Drawing the line between active and passive, I suggest, is not a moral absolute. It does, I suggest, have the practical advantage of putting most of the worst cases on the unfavorable side of the line and most of the least objectionable cases on the other side of the line.

I hasten to add that we need further boundaries than just that between active and passive involuntary euthanasia. Not only should the law entirely rule out active involuntary euthanasia, but also only in very exceptional cases should it allow (or turn a blind eye to) passive involuntary euthanasia. Only if it is and is intended to be for the benefit of the dying person, only if further treatment could no more than postpone the inevitable at the cost of further suffering, and perhaps only if the patient has no valid claim to the continued utilization of resources needed by others could we even contemplate allowing such a practice. Pitfalls abound. Where will it all end? An earlier chapter deals with the knotty problem of slippery slopes. In Chapter 11, I offer a further exploration of the motivations of euthanasia in the context of a discussion of the Principle of Double Effect.

10

Drawing Lines with Death

Sooner or later, we have to ask more particularly what death is and, in so doing, to face up to some of the associated bioethical issues. End-of-life decisions can be very difficult, not least when it is difficult to determine when the end of life is. Some of those issues are of biomedical fact, and some go well beyond that. How are we to determine the criteria appropriately applicable to death? Previously we noted that instead of asking what life is, we do better to ask what it is to be alive. Being alive is a process, a going onward of a nexus of life processes. A converse truth is that instead of asking what it is to be dead, we do better to ask what death is. Being dead is not a process, nor is it anything at all in particular. The occurrence of death, to a broad approximation, is the termination of the life process. At most, we can say that dying is a process, the ending, rapidly or otherwise, of the processes of life. When all of the life processes have ceased, then death has occurred to the formerly living being. So far so good, but major problems arise when *some* of the life processes have stopped and some continue.

Issues become complex here. For one thing, the criteria by which we define *conceptually* when death occurs need not be the same as those by means of which we determine *in practice* when it occurs. Those lines that are the most easily drawn are not always the most accurate. We must also bear in mind the possibility that it might not always be appropriate to try to establish precise lines, as death might not occur at any precise point. Furthermore, in the midst of our difficulties in trying to pin things down as well as possible, we must keep a firm grip on the fact that issues about what occurs and when it occurs – and why that rather than something else should count as death – can be resolved soundly and sensibly only on the basis of some sound and sensible resolution of the issues about *what* death occurs to.

Is some living entity about whose death we are inquiring actually a person? What is a person? Whatever the degree of overlap there might be between the two in application, being *human* and being a *person* are conceptually different things. They would be different even if all humans were persons and all persons were humans – which is something we do not at all know (unless we cheat by rigging it into our definition). Whether or not some entity is an instance of human life is a matter of biological fact. DNA can answer that if it is not already obvious. Whether or not some entity is a person is more difficult to determine. From the Latin term *persona*, referring to an actor's mask, and by extension, the character portrayed, a *person* has character, has personality. A person characteristically has thoughts, feelings, attitudes, reactions, and desires, together with a considerable awareness of self and world. Perhaps also involved is some sort of moral capacity. It is quite absurd to ask whether a dolphin is a human being. It could never be. Whatever our answer, though, it is not at all absurd to ask whether a dolphin has the requisite qualities of a person. Our answer will depend on how high we set our criteria for having these qualities, and it also will depend on how highly we assess the abilities of dolphins, but it is a question that sensibly can be asked. We also may ponder the case of chimpanzees, particularly those who have attained some skill in the use of sign language. We can at least imagine cases wherein we would virtually be forced to concede that a nonhuman entity is a person. Science fiction offers a plethora of imaginary examples. In the real world, the existence of SETI projects (the international Search for Extra-Terrestrial Intelligence) shows that we do take the possibility quite seriously. If beings way out there had intelligence, civilization, and the capacity to generate signals that we could pick up from here, they would be persons, though certainly not human persons.

Situations often arise wherein we have what is clearly a human entity, one that is (perhaps with the extensive aid of life-support systems) carrying on what are life processes. This entity may be in terribly bad condition but it is still a living human entity. The question we face is whether there is still a living person there. When does the death occur to a person? Is a person's life some nexus of centrally important bodily processes, such as particular ones of the brain or nervous system? Might some of those bodily processes continue when some others have terminated? Or is there perhaps some other question we should be asking? Years ago, for nearly all practical purposes, it was simply that people were alive or else they were not. We could get by with checking whether the person in question was breathing and had a heart beat. Even then, though, there were occasional ambiguous instances.

Ambiguous instances are more frequent now, and they are often far more ambiguous and longer in duration. With the increasing capacities of modern life-support systems, which are often able to keep cardiopulmonary and certain other functions going for a long while, gray areas are becoming more of a practical problem for us. We must ask more urgently whether the presence or absence of cardiopulmonary (or any other) functions is definitive of life or death, or whether they are merely diagnostic indications.

There are various lines that can be drawn, and which are the right ones (right for what purposes?) cannot be determined just by looking through some microscope. We might possibly agree on the biomedical facts yet draw differing and incompatible conclusions therefrom. We could perhaps narrow our minds, as some do, so that we can only conceive of one answer. There is psychological comfort in such an approach, even though it is inadequate both morally and intellectually. Another form of response that is convenient, conventional, politically correct, and perhaps virtually automatic is to proclaim that there can be no single right answer, with where we draw the line *therefore* being a matter for our individual or our collective decree. Where we are to draw our line on death is said to be a matter of what best suits our intentions, purposes, value judgments, and personal and social situation. Death, when it is not an indisputable positive fact, is thus (to this way of thinking) held to be merely a matter for arbitration and philosophical discussion. It is a social construct, and perhaps a moral conclusion, but we have presumably gone beyond biological and any other facts. I maintain that this approach is too simplistic and in need of major modification. There are limits beyond which we cannot appropriately go with this line of thinking. Things can have fuzzy edges yet robust cores. It is simply false that one answer is just as good as another, so long as they are both consistent with the biomedical facts. It would be, taking an obviously extreme example, very unwise to hold that a patient is still alive so long as *any* of her or his human life processes still continue. After all, some life processes are very persistent. A body can continue to grow hair and nails long after it is dead by virtually any other standard (e.g., when head and body are in different places). This is obviously not the sort of area where real disputes are apt to arise, but real disputes do arise in areas that really do (at least to some of us) seem impenetrably gray. That there is no one precisely right line to be drawn may be true enough, but some lines are better than other lines. Although determining what death is and why it occurs is not a purely biological question, our approach to answering it must be properly informed biologically. Next I illustrate why I believe that some lines are better than other lines.

Practical Cases and Biocentric Approaches

When there are gray areas in the shadow of death, it is widely and appropriately done that the next of kin are consulted. They are presumably best able to speak for the interests of the patient and to know what the patient had wanted or would have wanted. This is generally done, when possible, when there is any question of treating conservatively or instituting DNR orders. It is almost universal policy and practice to consult with the next of kin and defer to their decision when it comes to turning off a life-support system. Not only does following such a policy avoid a lot of legal difficulties, it respects the feelings, dignity, and well-being of the kin. They and, by extension, the one whose life is at issue have some autonomy in the matter. Certainly it is therapeutic for those still among the living to actively make the decision that death really has come to their loved one. Or they may decide that resisting its coming is cruel or futile. Or they might decide that any question of death is now only a matter of bodily functions, the person having already departed. However, things do not always go according to such kindly scenarios. The optimistic hope that matters always can be resolved tactfully and through consensus can lead us into a too-facile dismissal of real and very difficult issues, and perhaps into an abrogation of moral responsibility.

One classic case concerns the late Karen Ann Quinlan, a 21-year-old college student who, after ingesting a combination of drugs and alcohol at a party, sustained severe brain damage. She lived on for an extended period in an irreversible coma, doing so in a hospital by means of a life-support system. It came to be presumed that her damaged brain would never be able to support consciousness, and also that it would not be able to sustain respiration without a life-support system. Eventually her parents asked that the system be switched off. There was a protracted legal (and political) battle that attracted international attention, and eventually the Supreme Court of the U.S. State of New Jersey made this ruling[1]:

Upon the concurrence of the guardian and family of Karen, should the responsible attending physicians conclude ... [and] the hospital "Ethics Committee" ... agrees that there is no reasonable possibility of Karen's ever emerging from her present comatose condition to a cognitive, sapient state, the present life-support system may be withdrawn.

These conditions were duly met, and Karen Ann Quinlan's life-support system was switched off. She (at least her body) continued to breathe and to live on without artificial aid for a surprisingly long while but eventually died. But was it Karen Ann Quinlan who died? Or had she died long before, with only some of her bodily functions continuing on? (A postmortem examination of Quinlan's brain found extensive damage to the bilateral thalamus, rendering conscious personhood impossible.) I am not trying to revisit the issues of euthanasia here. To be sure, such cases might plausibly be considered as instances of nonvoluntary euthanasia. If Karen Ann Quinlan were alive, would it be right to cause or allow her to die?[2] Would death be in her best interests, or would life? In point of fact, the Supreme Court did in

---

[1] Matter of Quinlan 70 N.J. 10, 355A.2d. 647 (N.J. 1976); Supreme Court of New Jersey, USA.
[2] By the way, if we turn off the life-support system, is that an active step of killing, or is it a passive step of letting die by ceasing to take active steps? Is turning off a life-support system any better or worse than not turning it on in the first place?

effect treat it as a matter of passive euthanasia (though the word *euthanasia* was never used), making this declaration:

> We have no hesitancy in deciding . . . that no external compelling interest of the State could compel Karen to endure the unendurable, only to vegetate a few measurable months with no realistic possibility of returning to any semblance of cognitive or sapient life. If a putative decision by Karen to permit this non-cognitive, vegetative existence to terminate by natural forces is regarded as a valuable incident of her right of privacy, as we believe it to be, then it should not be discarded solely on the basis that her condition prevents her conscious exercise of the choice.

The court here was concerned with protecting the rights of Ms. Quinlan as a living person, including the right not to be compelled to "endure the unendurable."

Yet another way of approaching the matter might be to consider whether or not there was still such a person as Karen Ann Quinlan. If Ms. Quinlan had already died previously, then there would be no question of causing or allowing *her* to die. There would be no question of euthanasia, passive or active, with respect to Karen Ann Quinlan. At most, it would be a question of causing or allowing her body, or some lesser subsystems, to die. At what point, we ask, did she die? Whenever her death might be said to have occurred, let us agree that in the end, Karen Ann Quinlan was dead by the time her bodily functions finally and entirely closed down (even if her soul lived on in some form). Virtually everyone would agree that she was dead when her brain functions had finally and entirely closed down. But might Ms. Quinlan's death have occurred prior to her total bodily death or even her total brain death?

How are we to try to answer such a question without resorting to prejudice and bare assertion? With such aid it is lamentably easy, as much debate in that and other cases has made manifest. Part of the problem is that *death* is not an unambiguously biological term referring to a biological event. There is ambiguity even if we are talking about the death of the body. When it is a matter of the death of a person, the ambiguity is all the more. The term *person* is not entirely a biological term, even though some presumptive or possible aspects of personhood, such as sentience, consciousness, and rationality, can be to a considerable degree given a biological footing. If personhood requires having a moral character of some sort, that is not something biology can define for us on its own. When it comes to *soul*, the biological sciences are even less helpful.

There is no biological evidence one way or the other about whether we even have a soul, let alone (if we have one) about when, if ever, it leaves the body. It could be that the soul perishes with (or before) the body. Nor is there a necessary presumption that the soul, if it does dissociate from the body, does so at exactly the moment of biological death (whenever that is). Among some cultural groups, it is thought that the soul lingers in

A Life-Centered Approach to Bioethics

(or with) the body for some while after bodily processes cease. Sensitivity and tact may therefore be called for, particularly if there are questions of autopsy or organ transplantation. In contrast, might the soul depart *prior* to bodily death? Some people have felt that their loved one was no longer there, even though there was some residue of sentience and even low-level consciousness and communication. Things seem to be going on automatic pilot. But who can say? If the criterion for being a person is having a soul or spirit, and if the person as a living entity is properly dead only when the soul or spirit has dissociated from the body, then so far as physical science can tell us, *anything* whatsoever might be a living person. According to some cultures, anything can be – even rocks.

Trying to stay in contact with observable fact as much as possible, let us ask this: If the personality is no longer there, then is the person no longer there? If a person is an entity with properties of particular kinds, then seemingly there is no person present when the properties are no longer present. Nonetheless, even if *person* is to be given a purely material definition, just how it is best to be defined is not a purely material question. Are there, we might ask, some minimal biomedically observable criteria that must be met in order to be a living person?[3] We must note that having human DNA is neither a sufficient nor a necessary condition for being a person. That it is not sufficient is shown by the existence of living cultured human tissue, and that it is not necessary is shown (at least to all but the most narrow-mindedly doctrinaire) by the conceptually possible existence of intelligent and cultured extraterrestrial persons lacking human DNA. Asking about the role of consciousness in personhood seems like more of a step in the right direction – but any plausible criterion revolving around consciousness cannot be a simple one. After all, frogs, dogs, rats, and fish have consciousness, of a sort. Moreover, sometimes we persons do not. However, we do not cease to be persons, and much less do we cease to be alive, when we are asleep. Does death perhaps occur when there is no longer any *possibility* of consciousness? Perhaps Ms. Quinlan's last moment of consciousness was not her last moment of life, with that occurring when she lost even the possibility of resuming consciousness. Again, if not just any level of consciousness is sufficient for being a person (remembering frogs), does one die when one no longer has the capacity to have a high enough level of consciousness to be a person? Or is there some other vital (degree of) capacity along the way that is of critical importance? I will not be pointing to some place that I favor for drawing *the* line. Any

[3] For our purposes, let us assume that unless otherwise indicated, the term *person* refers to those who are biologically living. The dead body of a formerly living person might be said to be *a dead person*, or a dead person may be a person who was once alive but is not now (regardless of whether the body or soul still exists). Persons may perhaps continue after biological death as souls or spirits, but disembodied persons are not our concern here.

biomedically determinable line would have some element of arbitrariness or imprecision, and any precise and nonarbitrary line (e.g., when the soul leaves the body) would not be biomedically determinable. We must also bear in mind that there might be more than one sort of gradient of cases from being unambiguously alive to being unambiguously dead.

Suppose now that the family insists on keeping the person (if person it is) on life support long after there is any possibility of her or him regaining consciousness – perhaps there is not enough brain still alive with which to have consciousness – and that this is being done at great cost to the taxpayer, or at the cost of others not being able to use the medical equipment or the transplantable organs of the subject. Would it be appropriate for society to declare the subject dead? If the person is not dead and has an interest in remaining alive, then the answer must resoundingly be *certainly not!* If the subject were a person in whose best interests it is to remain alive, it would be outrageous to sacrifice her or him for the utility of taxpayers or organ recipients. No amount of utility can override whatever rights the person might have or alter the truth of the matter. However, *is* there a truth of the matter? If there is no one factual and definitive line separating life and death, does that mean that we can always legitimately decide that the person is dead? Or that she or he is still alive?

A possible case in point here would be that of the late Terri (Theresa) Schiavo. In 1990, while in the apartment she shared with her husband, she suffered an apparent heart attack that caused her brain to be starved of oxygen. She thereby incurred brain damage, rendering her unconscious and in a persistent vegetative state. She remained so for approximately fifteen years. During this time, she received water and nutrition via intubation but did not require cardiorespiratory support. Not only was there enough brain function for that, she was also able to yawn, swallow, and have sleep–wake (without consciousness!) cycles. After exhausting all medical alternatives and getting comprehensive medical advice that there was no hope of recovery, her husband, Michael Schiavo, requested that her nutrition and hydration be discontinued. The State of Florida, wherein the events occurred, permits artificial nutrition to be discontinued in the event of a persistent vegetative condition, unless there is an advance directive to the contrary. Her parents strenuously objected in the conviction that Mrs. Schiavo was *not* in a persistent vegetative condition, believing that they detected signs of consciousness on her part. Medical evidence, including brain scans and eventually the autopsy, all supported the conclusion that she did not have enough functional brain to support consciousness. Eventually, after legal and political battles, Terri – or her body – was disconnected and died in consequence.

As in the Quinlan case, legal debate focused on due process of law and on the question of whether life or death was in the best interests of the person thought to be at the center of the situation. The question of whether there actually was a person left at the center, though raised in some quarters, was not the central legal issue. No judicial determination was made as to whether Terri Schiavo was still a living person. I am inclined to think that this, perhaps wisely, avoided the morally fundamental issues. At some future time, I think it might be useful, appropriate, and perhaps even necessary for us to determine whether there is or was a living person. This is something we will have to face up to intellectually and morally well before we could ever hope to canvass and resolve it adequately in a court of law. As things are, no court would find itself at liberty, even if willing, to address the issues we would here consider morally relevant.

As a thought experiment, let us imagine that a Mr. Ecks suffers catastrophic brain injury. He has not suffered total brain death, as there is enough function in the brain to support his cardiopulmonary functions, though he is supported in this by a life-support system. Nor is he in a persistent vegetative condition, as there are occasional signs of low-level responsiveness. However, Mr. Ecks, as time reveals, is no longer capable of conscious thought on anything like the level of a person. The man who taught English, loved his wife, wrote fairly good poetry, and was a connoisseur of classical music was no longer there. One need not have all of that to be a person, to be sure, but he had virtually nothing. His responses, when present, were more like that of a frog to a nearby sound. Neither the personality nor the capacity for it survived. Mrs. Ecks is given strong and unanimous medical advice that his condition could never improve. At her request, the life-support system is disconnected. Like Ms. Quinlan, however, Mr. Ecks continued breathing. Mrs. Ecks is horrified by the prospect of her husband's body living on bereft of the person she loved. In memory of that person, she kisses those once-beloved lips and smothers him or it with a pillow. Had the body died as a result of the life-support system's disconnection, there would have been no legal problem. However, actively killing a person is against the law. The prosecuting attorney is sympathetic and offers to request only a suspended sentence if Mrs. Ecks pleads guilty to manslaughter. Prudentially, Mrs. Ecks might do well to accept the plea bargain. Nonetheless, she believes strongly that she is not guilty of anything, that she did not kill a person as there was no person there to be killed. It was not even a matter of compassionate euthanasia, as no person was euthanized. She had merely killed whatever life was left in the depersonated body.

How could we argue against her firm conviction that she has killed no person? She points out that being human life is not sufficient for being a person, as is demonstrated by the existence of living cultures of human tissue. Nor is it even necessary, if we accept the conceptual possibility of extraterrestrial persons – though that is beside the current point. She notes too that life can cease to be a person while still alive. After all, the transplantation of live organs from dead people is a routine matter. The legal jurisdiction wherein Mrs. Ecks resides makes no clear and systematic distinction between the death of a person and the death of a human body. That goes for wherever just about any of us reside. Mrs. Ecks believes, and I strongly agree with her, that this is due to great confusion in legal thinking and in the thinking of people in general. Life and death are too often thought of as black and white matters, as if they were a matter of some entity either having some condition or not having it, either being there or not being there. (I offer biocentric conceptions as helping us to go beyond such simplistic thinking.) Compounding the difficulty is ambiguity in our thinking about whether it is a person or a human body that dies. The death of either of these can be a matter of degree, and they do not necessarily go together.

Perhaps we might intrude ourselves into Mrs. Ecks' thoughts here to note that the beginning of a person might also be a matter of degree and vagueness. Are we to feel free to kill neonates with birth defects who are not yet and perhaps could never be actual persons, however much they might be living human beings? Mrs. Ecks takes a deep breath and responds that severely brain-damaged neonates indeed are not persons, and to kill them is not murder. As is so for all living beings, their interests are entitled to appropriate respect, but it might still be morally appropriate to kill one for its own good, or for the general good. (Obviously, for practical reasons, we would have to be very cautious about how we were to proceed, if we were to proceed, but that does not alter the moral truth.) She concedes that she cannot stipulate just where or how to draw the line, but she contends that it is not her responsibility to do so. What she does know is that the case of her husband was well over any morally defensible line. Her husband, the person, had predeceased his body.

I would continue my intrusion into Mrs. Ecks' concerns by explicitly noting my own agreement that not only is death a matter of degree but also that personhood is a matter of degree. There is no one essential quality that all and only persons have. Personhood is a matter of degree; life and death are matters of degree; and therefore interests and their moral significance are matters of degree. Instead of chasing ghosts (in an almost literal sense) about whether the person Mr. Ecks was still there, the more appropriate question would be whether the living interests of the Ecks-entity were appropriately respected.

Another concern we might put to Mrs. Ecks is that were the killing of human nonpersons condoned, people might become worried about their own future prospects were they ever to fall short of someone's standards of personhood. Her response, first, is to point out that some people have advance fears of DNR orders or of having their life-support system disconnected. She herself holds that it would be wrong to kill any person (and likely any post-person) who desires that not to happen, and that it would be just as wrong to do so by passive steps as by active ones. This is not just because either way of doing it might be fear inspiring. Advance directives may sometimes give us guidance in marginal circumstances, but only some-times. However, Mr. Ecks was not capable of having any desires, then or thereafter. (Moreover, Mrs. Ecks is quite certain that the person she knew would have wanted his body not to live on after him.) Were the law to rec-ognize the propriety of killing his body, she affirms, this would not create a precedent that threatened the life or welfare of any person. Yet, in the end, Mrs. Ecks resignedly pleads guilty to manslaughter, doing so on the advice of her attorney, who persuades her that no court would be game to declare that a living human being might not be a person, much less to try to draw a viable line between the living human body and the person.

I refer to Chapter 5 for a further discussion of the logic, difficulties, and moral significance of drawing lines. Such a discussion might be pursued further but now we must go on to other topics.

11

Double Effect

Euthanasia and Proportionality[1]

There is a principle, the Principle of Double Effect (PDE), which is often invoked in connection with a number of bioethical issues, including abortion, the risks of medical experimentation, and, most of all, it seems, with euthanasia. According to this principle there are circumstances under which we may make what are apparently exceptions to absolute moral rules. For a great many people, the prohibitions against suicide or causing or permitting the death of an innocent person are absolute. Should all forms of euthanasia (or, for that matter, suicide) be covered by such an absolute prohibition? Or might the nature of an individual case be counterindicative of an absolute prohibition? The PDE may offer us some needed leeway.

Here I explicate the PDE in concrete application rather than only in the abstract, endeavoring to indicate the reasons for there being such a principle, to indicate some of its weaknesses, and also to indicate its major source of strength – *proportionality* – a feature that is not often properly appreciated. However, though I will be discussing the PDE in application to euthanasia, I will discuss it in such a way as to explicate its rationale and to illuminate its principal strengths and weaknesses as they might arise in any area of application. I argue toward the conclusion that what gives proportionality and the PDE such credibility as they have is that they allow the imperative of life affirmation to have some force in the face of moral absolutism. By life affirmation I mean an attitude of protecting and promoting the integrity and coherent functioning of life. This will be discussed in more detail in a subsequent chapter.

A further aim here is to bring out some of the important features of the motivation, intent, and nature of active voluntary euthanasia that distinguish it from other (and more objectionable or, at least, more problematic) forms of bringing about voluntary death. I believe there are differences that are

---

[1] This chapter is adapted from my article, "Euthanasia, Double Effect, and Proportionality," *Monash Bioethics Review* 22 (2001): 30–45.

morally important and that are of practical importance as we struggle to formulate public policy. I suggest that the central question in consideration of euthanasia is that of whether death can sometimes be life affirming rather than life negating. One need not accept the PDE to accept the conclusions I draw about euthanasia in the light of a consideration in terms of that principle. I am not advocating the PDE; I just want to draw out some logical implications with respect to euthanasia. Those who do accept the PDE will not likely accept the conclusion that application of this principle might ever morally legitimize active euthanasia. By far the greater number of those who accept the PDE take it as a matter of faith – I use that term advisedly – that the PDE may not so be used. Still, if we are to deny that the PDE can support active voluntary euthanasia, we can at least become clearer on what is presupposed by the denial.

The Principle of Double Effect

Before I state the PDE formally, I illustrate why such a principle would arguably fulfill an important need. Suppose, calling on a traditional example, that a woman is trapped on an upper floor of a burning building. She is unable to find a means of escape. Perhaps there is none. Her shrieks for help have not been effectively answered. The flames come closer. The heat and smoke become increasingly unbearable, with her terror compounding her distress. She is at the last window available, but even there she can no longer find breathable air. Eventually, in her terror and her agony, she flings herself out the window – away from the fire and toward a gasp of cool air. She swiftly dies on the paving several stories below. This was a standard example since long before the horrible events of September 11, 2001, provided dramatic factual instances.

Did the woman commit suicide? She would have realized as she went out the window that she could not survive the fall. At that stage, though, she did not think this to be a decisive consideration. It was suicide in one sense, inasmuch as she intentionally took a course of action, knowing that it would result in her death. Shortly thereafter, there were a few minutes when she was dead that, had she not jumped, she might still have been alive. We might just let it go at that – were the term *suicide* not one that we find very troubling. Suicide is usually thought to be more-than-extreme foolishness, or a symptom of severe mental disorder, or an instance of grave moral evil – an irrecoverable dereliction of duty to God or oneself. People who appear likely to commit suicide, or actually make the attempt, are restrained when the situation comes to the attention of responsible authority. In order to want to do such a thing, it is held, one cannot be in one's right mind.

To make such a judgment, though, in the case of the woman who flung herself from the burning building seems quite harsh. She had, we may suppose, no desire to die. She may have had good reasons to live and strongly desired to do so. That she threw herself out of the window was not due to suicidal inclinations on her part; it was due to her pain and to her terror of worse to come. She leapt away from a hideous death and fell into another death. Although she was aware that death awaited her, it was not for the purpose of embracing it that she went out the window.

We may claim that her death was *not* suicide, at least not in any pernicious sense of the term, because her death was not the intended consequence of her action. It was merely a foreseen but unintended consequence, a side effect, of her saving herself from the fire. This is an instance of the PDE at work. It holds that under appropriate circumstances, one is not morally responsible for foreseen but unintended consequences of one's actions. Conditions apply. The PDE is not offered as a license for people to do as they please regardless of the consequences, pleading innocence on the grounds that they did not specifically intend those consequences. It is no defense against a charge of manslaughter that one merely intended to hurry home after an evening's heavy drinking. The conditions are of central importance.

Even with conditions, such a principle will not appeal to everyone. Obviously, it will not appeal to utilitarians, whose very principle is to judge actions by their foreseen consequences. The PDE is most at home in deontological ethical systems, wherein certain actions are prescribed, or proscribed, regardless of their consequences. Religious ethics, with their *thou shalts* and *thou shalt nots*, are characteristically of such a nature. It is from Christianity in particular that the idea of the PDE arose, though the principle has gained wider acceptance. It attempts to address the problem of reconciling the demands of absolute injunctions, such as the commandments of God, with the apparent demands of common sense in particular situations.

The PDE is based on the conception that an act, whether active or passive (i.e., an omission), is morally wrong in any of the following circumstances:

1. It belongs to a class of actions (e.g., blasphemy, theft, adultery) that are evil irrespective of their effects.
2. An evil effect is not merely expected but is intended either as a means or as an end.
3. An intended good depends on one of the evil effects.
4. The evil effects are disproportionate to the good effects.

Accordingly, as explained in the *Encyclopedia of Bioethics*,[2] the principle stipulates that one may rightfully cause evil through an act of choice if four conditions are verified:

1. The act itself, prescinding from the evil caused, is good or at least indifferent.
2. The good effect of the act is what the agent intends directly, only permitting the evil effect.

[2] Warren Thomas Reich, ed., *Encyclopedia of Bioethics* (New York: Simon and Schuster, 1995), Vol. 2, p. 637.

3. The good effect must not come about by means of the evil effect.
4. There must be some proportionately grave reason for permitting the evil effect to occur.

The woman who leapt from the flames, whatever her other troubles, is morally justified in these terms. Although resigned to her death, she was not intending it. Her overall aim was to escape the intense pain.

Consider now a case wherein someone under medical care is suffering from a condition that is painful, incurable, and inevitably fatal. Perhaps it is one of the many forms of cancer that satisfy that description. This, obviously, is the sort of case standardly cited by proponents of the legalization of active euthanasia. In this particular case, however, euthanasia is never considered. The patient is given the best of palliative care until the inevitable end. This involves, among other measures, the use of morphine to alleviate the patient's physical and mental distress. The dosage increases as the patient's condition deteriorates. The patient's death occurs sooner than it otherwise would have, as a side effect of the use of the morphine.

Is there any question here of wrongdoing on the part of anyone involved? The PDE would permit us to answer firmly in the negative. First, the procedure itself, the administration of medication for the relief of suffering, is morally acceptable. Second, what was intended was the relief of suffering, not death. Had it been possible to maintain life and health, patient and physician would have preferred that. Third, death was not the means to the good effect, the relief of suffering. This is the crux of the matter, according to the PDE. Fourth and finally, there is proportionality between the good and bad effects. Were one to provide a form of pain relief that had death as a side effect in the case of a mere toothache, that would be *disproportionate*, amounting to murder or malpractice on the part of the physician (or dentist) and to suicide on the part of a consenting patient. In the case of this cancer patient, the foreseen but unintended acceleration of inevitable death is not disproportionate to the intended end, the relief of severe suffering. Legally and professionally approved guidelines permit the physician to provide such care, and PDE ethicists agree that death-hastening palliative care in such cases is acceptable.

To continue, suppose now that we are dealing with another patient, one suffering from a similar terminal cancer but who experiences things differently. In addition to the physical pain and distress at leaving family and friends, the person is very distressed by helplessness and the sense that things are spinning ever more out of control. The person dislikes and even resents being doped out of her mind.[3] She intensely dislikes having her rationality, awareness, and self-control continuously and irrevocably being

---

[3] I use the feminine pronoun here not only to avoid labored gender neutrality but also because within my own mind I am thinking of a particular woman who had to die in a way she much disliked.

eroded. She feels that her autonomy and her very personhood is being ever diminished, and she looks with fear and disgust on the prospect of dying as something less than the person she holds herself to be. She does not want to die at all, she who has always been so full of life, but at this stage, what she most fears and loathes is the very real possibility of dying in a way she finds depersonalizing. Being told by helpful would-be advisers, "now, now, dear, we mustn't feel that way," she feels is a patronizing put-down and a further insult to her assaulted personal integrity. What she wants is not only relief from suffering but also relief from what she regards as a depersonalizing death. Unlike some others, she does not find suffering, of that variety at any rate, to be a pathway to spiritual growth or fulfillment. She wants active voluntary euthanasia so that, having to die, she can die with dignity and self-control as the person she wants to be. She wishes to leap from the many flames of suffering to the cool air of peace, with personal integrity maintained. To those who would tell her that she is making a mistake, she would reply, "Okay, you die as you please, but allow me the right to die, if die I must, with dignity and integrity, as the person I want to be."

Means

Does her taking this action (or others assisting her to take it) meet the requirements of the PDE? Most of those who advocate that principle, perhaps nearly all, would answer staunchly in the negative. In terms of the actual logic of the PDE, however, I believe that a strong and morally cogent case can be made for the affirmative. I contend that those who wish to undergo active voluntary euthanasia are characteristically *not* seeking death. They are seeking to escape from the suffering that is a manifestation of the severe deterioration of their life.

Clearly, the major difficulty with such a line of argument with respect to the PDE is that principle's third condition, so I will deal with it last. We start from the recognition that the woman, like she who leapt from the flames, is seeking not death but relief from suffering. There is no problem with the second condition. Moreover, there is proportionality between good and bad effects. It is not a matter of death instead of life but of the acceleration of imminent and inevitable death. Death, as such, is accepted rather than desired. As with the previously considered case of palliative care hastening death, there is proportionality between effects. Moreover, as in that case, the procedure itself, the administration of medication for the relief of suffering, is morally acceptable. It might even be the same medication (perhaps morphine), in a dose sufficient for the distress to be relieved.

"Hold it right there!" demands the outraged objector. The medication might be the same but what is done with it is not. In this case, death is the *means* to the relief of suffering, and that is not allowed. In the case of the other cancer patient, or of the woman who leapt from the burning building, death was not intended, only foreseen, and occurred only *after* the relief. It was not the means of bringing it about. The objector is invoking the third condition – and it is only that, if anything, that could call into question whether the PDE is satisfied in application to such a case as this. In contrast, I maintain that in a case of active voluntary euthanasia, such as the one described, death is not the means to the end. Although it may occur as a by-product of the relief, and even be simultaneous with it, death is not the means to the relief. A question that will immediately spring to mind here is that of how this line of thought relates to self-killing, considered more generally. After all, suicide is characteristically a matter of avoiding something thought to be comparatively objectionable. In most cases, at any rate, self-killing is widely (and I think correctly) thought to be inappropriate. Is self-killing, in every form, to be ruled out?

Here let us briefly explore that question, as a means of further issues about euthanasia and the PDE. I shall approach the issues here through a brief bit of historical background, following Edward Gibbon (1776). In Western cultures suicide has a particularly odious reputation – more so than in most other cultures – because it is heavily tainted by imputation of irredeemable sin. This is in addition to whatever suggestion there might be of mental illness or weakness of character. In great part, this moral odium arises from the historically influential teachings of the Catholic Church, which strongly condemns suicide. This was not always so. In the early days, when Christianity was not yet established in the Roman Empire, Christians would sometimes court martyrdom. In some part, martyrdom was in the service of the True Faith. Moreover the promise of a martyr's entry to the eternal felicity of Heaven, with perhaps some earthly glory as well, was a significant inducement. Prospective martyrs would sometimes draw themselves to the attention of authority, demanding to be persecuted through prosecution on the charge of refusing to honor the official Roman deities as well as their own. Those in authority often did not want to be bothered about it. No doubt, some of those in public office occasionally wanted to entertain the crowds with public bloodletting. For the most part, however, officials preferred not to concern themselves with people's religion. They had plenty of things to think about that actually did matter to them. Roman law, moreover, was not designed to deal with defendants who had injured no one and were accused only by themselves. Sometimes whole mobs of Christians would besiege the offices of the magistrates demanding their right to be executed for violating pagan law. In effect, those who succeeded had committed suicide by magistrate – with the magistrates forced into being unenthusiastic participants in the process. Complained one exasperated official (Proconsul Antoninus, to the Christians of Asia):

Unhappy men, unhappy men, if you are thus weary of your lives, is it so difficult for you to find ropes and precipices? (Edward Gibbon, *The History of the Decline and Fall of the Roman Empire*, Chapter xvi)

So eager were so many of the faithful to attain martyrdom that even the Church had to impose some rules. Eventually it decided not to recognize as martyrs those who had provoked the wrath of authority by forcefully overturning the idols of other gods. Such "martyrdom" represented virtually nothing. (These days we refuse the victor's reward to the cheating athlete who is found to have used drugs.)

Once Christianity became the Empire's established religion, in the time of the Emperor Constantine, it was no longer possible for Christians to achieve martyrdom at the hands of the state. Still, some Christians, not favorably impressed with life on earth as compared with their prospective life in Heaven, wanted to cut short the former for the sake of getting to the latter that much earlier. They would take communion and make such other spiritual preparations as they believed useful, following which they would suffer death while (at least, as they thought) in a state of grace. The Church might have had practical reasons to regret this as they were losing pious Christians, and the Roman state, now in partnership with the Church, was losing good citizens. However, the Church officially decided against self-killing not on practical but on theological grounds. *Thou Shalt Not Kill* applies to oneself as well as to others. God has put each of us on earth for some purpose. To kill our self is to frustrate God's plan for us, to derelict our duty to our creator. Only God can dismiss us from our duty. Our job is to cope.

As we have previously noted, life is a matter of dealing with difficulties. We might say that living *is* the process of *coping* with them, maintaining homeorhesis in the face of all that would break it down. From the simplest cell to human levels of complexity, the life of a living system revolves around its maintaining its viability as a coherent integrated ongoing life process, which it maintains by keeping its favorable balances. This it does in the face of substantial and continuing difficulties. What constitutes its ranges of favorable states is determined by its particular makeup as a living being. The affirmation of the living system's life requires not just the dragging out of the process but also maintaining it within or restoring it to the appropriate ranges of that particular life. When we can do that well, life is well worth living. When our overall life deteriorates to a point whereafter it is severely and irremediably incapable of returning to what, in its own terms, it needs to be, then it can be in its own interests to terminate.

Those early Christian cultists, with their eyes on Heaven, or our distressed contemporaries fleeing the problems and frustrations of modern life and their own emotions, held that life does not repay the effort. Depending on our point of view, we might deem their suicide to be sinfulness or sad and wasteful foolishness. These are cases of refusing to cope with life and its demands. Life is coping. Death is ceasing to cope. Now, what about the cancer patient whose life was shortened by palliative care? That patient, far from rejecting life, was distressed by and rejected her body's severe and increasing inability to do that coping that life is. It was the process of dying, not that of living, death rather than life, from which that person was seeking relief. Escape from the process of dying, from the continually diminishing capacity of the whole system to cope and from the suffering that was a manifestation of that noncoping, was not possible. But relief, of a sort and to a point, was possible. The phenomenon of pain, suffering, and distress, which is a manifestation of unrectifiable noncoping, imbalance, and disharmony, can be relieved. This is at the cost of – indeed, by means of – a different sort of imbalance. The process of dying, altered and speeded up, is not the means to relief; nor is it desired or intended. Nor is death the means of relief. The means of relief is an *alteration* in a death process already in train and unavoidable.

That death was inevitable, near at hand, and in the process of occurring ensures that the proportionality condition is met. A feckless youth contemplating suicide because his girlfriend dumped him would not meet the proportionality condition. Nor would he meet the third condition according to the PDE as it is usually interpreted. It would be similar for a person suffering continuing agony from a chronic but nonterminal condition. For my own part, I would (reaching a nonstandard conclusion) accept some instances of the latter sort as meeting the conditions. The fact that the agony is of an indefinite duration rather than a short one does not negate the fact that what the person is concerned to do is to *end* the agony. In the case of the death-hastening palliative care for the terminal patient, we are supposing a case wherein the process of death, already in train, is transformed. We here assume that the PDE can accept, as indeed it must, using an altered (and accelerated) form of the process of dying, already caused and unavoidable, as the means of relief. The unintended product, death, is not itself used as the means of relief.

In the case of the woman's requesting active voluntary euthanasia, was her causing her death the *means* of relief from suffering – or was it just a simultaneous, or nearly simultaneous, by-product? There is clearly a sense in which neither of the aforementioned cancer patients nor the woman in the burning building was causing their death. Death was coming right at them, and it was contrary to their desires yet impossible to avoid. At most, they could delay it slightly. Still, there is also a sense in which it might be said that the woman who leapt from the flames caused her own death on the pavement – though only as an alternative to allowing the fire to cause her death in the building shortly thereafter. For that matter, cancer patients who die earlier as a result of palliative care might be said to have caused their own death by bringing about (directly, via others) a state of affairs wherein they are dead when they would otherwise have been alive. Moreover, the woman who leapt from the flames could be said to have caused her own death, inasmuch as she took a course of action that interrupted the previously prevailing course of events and led to *that* death. Whether or not death in the flames would have occurred later is beside the point. Nevertheless, in causing the death she did meet, she was not acting wrongly. She acted proportionately, and she was *not* using death as the means to relief.

By using morphine or other palliative care, the patient who hastened death acted proportionately and did not use death, which might have occurred some while later, as the means to the relief. Death might have occurred weeks or even months after the arrival of worthwhile relief and certainly not have been the cause of it. Then again, it might not take nearly so long. The hastened death might occur only a week or so later, or just a few days, or even just a few hours. In principle, there is no reason why it might not be just a few minutes, or split seconds. So long as there is pro-portionality, which there would be in these extreme cases, and so long as death is not the actual means of relief, the length or shortness of the time lapse is logically and morally irrelevant, even according to the demands of the PDE.

But what if death is *simultaneous* with the relief? Must it then be the means of relief, or may it still be only a by-product? Actually, that is asking more than we strictly need. Euthanasia will typically result in a death that happens some small amount of time, though perhaps a very small amount, after relief is secured. It is the altered process of dying, not the product, death, which secures relief. However, perhaps it will be thought that this is splitting hairs too finely, that death in such a case follows so soon as to count as being simultaneous with the relief. (Those who wish to provide palliative care without performing active euthanasia will usually take care to ensure that death does not follow *too* soon after the administration of the palliative care that accelerated it – whatever *too* might mean.) So, let us suppose that death is to count as being simultaneous with the relief. Must it then necessarily be the case that death is the means to relief? No. Temporal proximity is no proof of causal connection; nor is it even any very reliable indicator. It is the alteration of dying that is the relief.

Terminally ill people typically desire relief from physical pain as well as from psychological distress of several different sorts. Perhaps we should use the term *anguish* to distinguish it from physical pain, which is often much easier to bear. (Psychological distress need not be only a matter of people's emotions. There is more to the erosion of personhood than how one feels about it.) Palliative care can offer relief to some point or another. So too can euthanasia do that: no pain, no distress, and no physical incapacity, indignity, or personal erosion. Thereby, death *appears* to be the means to the end. I argue, though, that death is not the means but the by-product. Instead of death causing the relief of pain and suffering, the relief itself leads to hastened death (perhaps extremely hastened) as the foreseen but unintended by-product of that relief. Indeed, this is even more so than it was in the case of the woman who leapt from the flames. There it was another death substituted. In the cases of the cancer patients, it is the same death hastened, the same dying process accelerated. Death does not bring about relief but occurs with it.

Proportionality

Patients who, in extreme circumstances, seek euthanasia, a *good* death, are seeking it as an alternative to a bad death, but they are not seeking death per se. They are not fleeing life as one flees who seeks to commit suicide in the face of the slings and arrows, real or imagined, of outrageous fortune. Perhaps they might wish for life without the slings and arrows, but that is to neglect the fact that life *is* coping with slings and arrows. Death is not coping. Those who seek euthanasia are characteristically fleeing not life but death, fleeing the pain and suffering that in their case are not parts of the process of coping, living, but are part of the incapacity to cope, which is dying. If through some magic they could be able to cope and live, free of the sufferings of dying, we could feel quite confident that they would have no desire for death. It was never *death* that they were desiring to begin with.

I have often noticed that people tend to use the terms *suicide* and *euthanasia* differently, applying them differently even with respect to death that is voluntary and self-performed. Although people may not distinguish between them formally or rigorously, many do tend to keep them separate. Not everyone does so, to be sure. Vigorous opponents of euthanasia like to point out that euthanasia is a form of killing, either self-killing or other killing, and so they claim that, accordingly, it is either suicide or murder. They believe that they have scored a point when they make the connection. However, to conflate voluntary euthanasia with suicide or murder is to obscure some important issues.

The unarticulated distinction that so many people implicitly presuppose does indeed have a significant foundation. There is a real distinction to be drawn between desiring to flee the pains of living and desiring to flee the pains of dying. Nonetheless, it is not a precise distinction. Some pains can be coped with as one carries on with life, and it is the business of life to do that. It is wrong (sinful or foolish) not to do that. A good life is not good in the absence of things to be coped with but in spite of them and by means of them. Yet again, some sufferings just cannot be coped with while furthering life. There is a whole spectrum of cases in between, ranging from the routine to the impossible. Toward the latter end of the spectrum, life loses its functional coherence, its capacity to maintain its own integrity. It may be that the difference is like that between day and night where, in the grayness of dusk, no specific and nonarbitrary line can be drawn. However, like the day–night difference, the difference between the ends of the spectrum is quite real. It is a matter of due proportion.

Our good as living beings lies in maintaining our viability as coherent integrated living systems. When our life process falls into collapse and can no longer maintain itself as what its own nature requires of it, things can get to the point at which it is in our best interests, as a living being, to die. More precisely, it is in our interests to obtain relief even at the incidental price of death. We do commonly recognize that when it comes to animals. We may feel sadness, even anguish, when the time comes to put down the family dog. Nonetheless, the dog's condition may, in the light of medical prognosis, compel us to conclude that to keep faith with our loyal companion, we must relieve it of pointless suffering when its life is no longer of value to it. Many have suggested that this is one area, the only one, wherein we are more moral in our dealings with animals than we are with other humans. What would clearly be a vile cruelty in the case of a dog or horse is arguably no less vile or cruel when imposed on an unwilling person.

Yet there is more to a person's life than there is to that of any dog. What there is in a dog's life that is of value to the dog may come to an end before the dog's life and suffering end. A person, though, characteristically has self-consciousness, plans, values, and moral agency. In the face of suffering, it is argued, a person remains a center of values that transcend the merely material contingencies of life and that can rise above the suffering. There are some things for which it is worth suffering. Material things, we are supposing, are all there is in the life of an animal, but a person lives not by bread alone.

Still, there can come a time when it is in a human's best interests to die. (I hasten to add, as if it were necessary to do so, that such a decision ought never to be imposed on an unwilling person. We are not dogs.) Sane and rational people may come to a free and considered decision that their life has had its coherence and integrity eroded to the point where it is in their best interests to discontinue the unnecessary sufferings of the dissolution of life. They might be wrong. Perhaps they are (quite understandably) depressed or overreacting to pain or to the overall situation. Certainly it would be acceptable for us to offer them counseling and help in exploring alternatives. They might, however, also perhaps be right. Perhaps they have reached the end of their capacity to enjoy, or achieve, or give of themselves to others, or to do any of the other things that made their life meaningful. We may admire a heroic stoicism that endures to the bitter end, but we cannot authoritatively tell other people that they are wrong in not wanting to endure such an end themselves.

An inevitable objection arises here, returning us yet again to the vexing matter of suicide: If euthanasia can be defended on the grounds that death is neither the desired end nor the actual means, then seemingly any suicide might be defended on similar grounds. The despondent lover turns to suicide in seeking relief from heartache and the perceived emptiness of life without the beloved, but does not seek death itself. It is only the foreseen, and perhaps regretted, accompaniment of relief from suffering. If death is not the intended means in euthanasia, then neither is it the intended means in suicide. If this is not an adequate rationale for suicide, so it will be argued, then no such rationale can be adequate to justify active euthanasia.

Certainly I must agree that the distinction between appropriate self-performed euthanasia and objectionable suicide is not a precise one. Neither can there be any precise dividing line demarcating when or where DNR policies or other forms of passivity may or may not become appropriate. However, the differences are real, and decisions may well become appropriate. The key desideratum, imprecise but nonetheless critical, is that of whether continuing to live under those circumstances is in the well-being interests of the individual. If it is our role to decide for or against passivity on behalf of someone unable to make her or his own decision, one who has not previously expressed relevant preferences, then it is on the basis of the well-being interests of that individual that we ought to decide. In making those decisions (if only when they are forced upon us), we must try to do our best to keep things in proportion. It is a matter of what is going to happen; what might happen; what our own intentions and motivations are; what the consequences, intended or otherwise, are likely to be; and it is a matter of degree, possibility, and intention – all to be kept in due proportion. Life itself is a matter of keeping things in due proportion. So too, to be viable (if I may be pardoned the foreseen but unintended pun), the PDE must rely on proportion. I see its best wisdom and greatest strength as lying in its third condition, that of proportionality.

Turning from a discussion of the passive to that of the active, I would appeal to the same imprecise but critical desideratum in considering cases of active voluntary euthanasia and suicide. Again, the key issue is that of whether continuing to live under the circumstances is in the well-being interests of the individual. When active voluntary euthanasia actually is in the individual's best interests – and, most assuredly, that is not always the case – it is so because it best serves the interests of that particular life in that particular circumstance, protecting it from the frustration and disintegration of what it is in the character of that life to be. In such a situation, euthanasia can be not life negating but life affirming. In particular, it is affirming of that life. Culpable suicide, in contrast, which is a refusal to cope with that with which it is life's business to cope, is life negating. Specifically, it negates the inherent good of that individual life.

I believe this to be the heart of the matter, that the great wrong is to be life negating. About why it is wrong, there would be a wide diversity of opinion. Perhaps it is contrary to God's plan for our earthly lives. Perhaps it has something to do with *telos* or *dharma*. Perhaps it is a matter of the value of life for that particular life, as turned up by blind chance and evolution. Maybe it is something else. In any case, I would take euthanasia to be wrong (sinful or foolish) when it is life negating and right (morally appropriate or wise) when it is life affirming. In the generality of cases I would take suicide to be wrong because it is life negating.[4] The central question then is that of whether we are affirming or negating life. That is the essential difference between measures being proportionate and their being disproportionate.

In practice there is no place to draw an indisputably correct line between what is life affirming and what is life negating. There is no way to draw such a line either for active or for passive measures. Nevertheless, that does not relieve us of making decisions. Decide we must. We must do things or not do things. The best way to proceed is to keep alert to the proportions in the particular case and always be life affirming in intention. Is the intent behind a contemplated course of action (or of inaction) life negating? Or is the intent to give relief, of an appropriately proportional character in the particular situation, from the dissolution of life? Does one still, as it were, have promises to keep and miles to go before one sleeps? To what extent has the life of the person collapsed from its coherence and viability? Is the person able to maintain enough of the life and consciousness that is an expression of *that* life? Or has it gotten to the point where it is better, more affirming of that life, for that life to cease to suffer the continuing and irrevocable negation of what, by its own nature, it ought to be?

A rhetorical red herring is the following challenge: Who are you, we, or anyone to declare that a human life is worthless? The clear answer to that is that we are not to make this declaration. Not ever. Not for ourselves and not for anyone else. Life is *never* worthless. It is the *frustration and dissolution of life* that one may sometimes appropriately wish to reject. Who are we to make life-or-death decisions *at all*? Who are we to allow them to be made? We are, one would hope, people of reason, sensibility, and good will. In point of fact, we do make such decisions. We make such decisions when we accept life-shortening palliative care, or when we allow it to others or allow it to be offered. We make such decisions for others when we issue, or allow to be issued, Do Not Resuscitate orders. Whether we take active steps or passive nonsteps, either way we do make decisions about whether continuing to live is of value for the one whose life it is when we decide for or against passivity. We would be morally culpable in high degree were we to stand passively by and allow someone to die who could likely make a full and happy recovery. We are still making decisions about the value, for the person concerned, of that person's continuing to live when we decide whether or not to be passive. These can be difficult decisions. Sometimes the wrong decision will

---

4 Whether it is always wrong is another matter. I suspect that suicide might not always be wrong in the case of a person who has no hope of a good life yet is not in a terminal condition. Clearly, such a person needs to search for neglected alternatives. What, however, if the person actually is in the grip of long-term but non-life-threatening agony that cannot be adequately relieved and without realistic possibility of any compensating benefit?

be made, and sometimes no decision, one way or another, will clearly be right or wrong, even in retrospect. The only alternative is to refuse to make such decisions, demanding that human life always and in all circumstances be continued as long as possible, at whatever cost in human suffering.

That is to make a decision of another sort, a very wrong decision. Like it or not, times for decisions do come. We may have to decide what is right for ourselves, and we may have to decide whether to help another person. The time may come when we decide, advisedly, that the dissolution of our own life has proceeded to the point where we can no longer maintain it sufficiently as it ought to be. We ought never to force such a decision on others. Others ought never to force us to remain in the flames while our own life burns to the ground.

An Afternote

Scene

A well-regarded nursing home operated by a mainstream Christian church that is firmly opposed to active euthanasia. (In fact, they seem to not like the E-word at all.) The staff are well trained, compassionately motivated, and give a high level of care. An eighty-four-year-old woman is dying of cancer. She is pleased at the idea of dying and rejoining family and friends in Heaven. She has asked for palliative care only, with no antibiotics for any infections and certainly no resuscitation. Fortunately, her form of cancer causes minimal discomfort. Members of her family are reconciled to her dying, and all good-byes have been said. Granny's Last Christmas came off beautifully. Quite early one morning, her children are called in for what are clearly going to be her last very few hours. She is unconscious, and her breathing is quite heavy from fluid on the lungs. It sounds very much like a coffee percolator and, over the next couple of hours, it gets worse. So do her complexion and her pulse rate. Her children are stroking her brow and saying loving things to her, though she seems unable to experience anything. When fluid from her straining respiratory system starts to dribble from the corner of her mouth, the staff members turn her on her other side and also give her another shot of morphine. She dies a few minutes later, to the relief of all those present.

There is a strong element of voluntary passive euthanasia here, as she had refused all but palliative care. There is also a strong element of Double Effect, as it was foreseen that the morphine would further depress her already overtaxed respiration. Turning her would cause the fluid to move around in her lungs, causing yet further strain on her breathing. These steps are part of normal palliative care, with the hastening of death in this instance presumably being a foreseen but unintended side effect. But were they really palliating her suffering when at that point she was, in fact, experiencing no suffering whatsoever? Could it be that the real purpose of the intervention was to hasten the welcome and inevitable end? All those present (well, all but one) would have been scandalized by the thought that this was *active* euthanasia and perhaps technically murder. Yet was there anything here that was less than loving or other than moral?

12

Concerning Abortion

In light of the foregoing information, and particularly in light of the conclusion that death is usually bad for a living being, how are we to tackle the
moral issues of abortion? On this topic, opinion is sharply divided and often
bitter. When does human life start? What is good or bad for human life?
Is abortion harmful to the aborted? Is it murder? When does human life
have full moral status as a human being – or any moral status at all? What,
if anything, does being a person have to do with it? Of what significance
is it, if any, that (except in vitro) an embryo's life processes overlap with
those of its mother? How are we justly to resolve conflicts of interest? These
are some of the issues we need to consider in connection with abortion,
and biocentric conceptions can give us some help in dealing with them.
My primary concern at this point is not to commence arguing the rights or
wrongs of abortion but to explore some of the background material needed
for a well-grounded consideration of the moral issues of abortion.

The Beginning of Human Life

When does human life start? The factually correct answer is that it has
already started, having done so quite a long while ago. Life comes from life
before it, but never, so far as we have even the slightest reason to believe,
does it now start afresh. Certainly human life does not. Every child, every
embryo, every adult started from a microscopic living cell, a zygote. But life
did not start there. The zygote was formed from a living ovum and a living
sperm cell, each of which formed as part of, then separated from, other
living beings (the parents) – and so on back. If we are creationists, then we
believe that human life comes from previous human life, all the way back
to the Creation. If we accept scientific orthodoxy, then we hold that human
life comes from human life or (a long time ago) from prehuman life, all the
way back in time and back in evolution, to the very first life arising in the

primordial soup. Never at any time since has there been a nonliving stage. The process of life goes on continuously from first until now.[1]

Zygotes, sperm, and ova are not, or not yet, individuated as functioning organisms, but they meet our fundamental criteria for being *alive* (except when they are dead). Certainly there is a sharp difference between their being alive and their not being alive. The fundamental question we must address is not that of when human life starts but that of when a *particular* human life starts. This is a question that arises in discussion of important bioethical issues in connection with abortion, or in tort law in application to prenatal injury. When does a human life start, and what respect is owed to it? As no individual human life has gone on since the beginning of life or the beginning of our species, we want to know when a *particular* life starts. We have to be very careful here about just what we mean by *human life* and what we take to be a human being. In a misleadingly straightforward sense, it is clear what human life is. Biologically and genetically, it can be determined whether an entity is an instance of *Homo sapiens* and is alive. Biology would include in that category not only conscious adults and children but also those who are permanently unconscious, those who have only a brainstem (anencephalic neonates) and so can never have consciousness, and even some who are brain dead. Also included as human life would be human fetuses, embryos, and zygotes[2] from the earliest stages, and sperm and ova that have not joined forces, and also human tissue of various sorts cultured in vitro. All of these are instances of human life. A living being with human DNA is human life of some sort, and distinct DNA indicates a distinct life. That much is unproblematic biology. Very problematic are questions having to do with the moral status of such varied instances of human life, and with the moral implications to be drawn. It by no means follows automatically

---

[1] I am not ruling out the possibility of a separate origin of life on some other planet. (For that matter, it could conceivably arise a second time on this planet but, in all probability, the molecules suitable for the origin of life would be preempted by existing life.) Nor would I think it impossible (whether or not advisable) that we might some day be able to create – I hesitate to use that word – life artificially. Nor would I negate such life morally if it were brought about. Living beings, whatever their origin, and whether or not they could properly be considered to be *artifacts*, have, or would have if they ever came to exist, whatever moral status is appropriate to their character. Extraterrestrials would have a valid claim on our moral respect and so too may some future product of a laboratory.

[2] Strictly speaking, the terms *zygote, embryo,* and *fetus* differ in meaning. The zygote is the single cell formed by the union of ovum and sperm. The embryo is the living entity during the early part of its development but after the zygotic stage. In humans, this is during about the first three months. Between then and birth, the entity is a fetus. Obviously, there are no sharp dividing lines between them. For the time being, I shall generally use the term *embryo* for the prenatal being at all stages, though for reasons that will soon appear, I consider the term unsatisfactory. We might note that anti-abortion forces often prefer the term *baby* for all stages.

that a living being that has human DNA, and that therefore is a human being, is a human being in a morally relevant sense.

Our main concern here is with the embryo, that which might be the subject of abortion. This is a human living being, one that is distinct from its mother, as evidenced by its distinct DNA, even though their life processes considerably overlap. It is only because it is a distinct human life, not a part of any other, that the question of its moral status even arises. It has its own moral status – whatever that happens to be. The central moral issues do not center on any question about whether to kill a human embryo is to kill (distinct) human life. The biological fact is that it is to do so. The moral issues concern how we are to assess the killing of life of that sort. Is it on a moral par with killing human life that is cultured tissue (so what?) or does it amount to murder most foul? Perhaps it is somewhere in between.

For some people, the matter is settled straightaway by the biological fact that a human embryo is human life. To kill it therefore is held to be to kill a human being, an unborn child, a person. To harm it is to harm a person. Morally, any such act is to be judged accordingly. At the other end of the range of opinion is the view that what is killed in abortion is a being that yet lacks the characteristics of a fully fledged human with full moral status. It is not, or not yet, a person. It is not a being with self-consciousness, rational thought, or any but (at most) a very primitive awareness of the world. In early stages, it is a blob of biojelly that has less awareness of the world than does a cockroach. At later stages, it is considerably more developed, but even so, it has less awareness than do a great many nonhuman animals. Does the embryo perhaps merit a moral status commensurate with its level of development? Proponents of legalized abortion are often willing enough to conclude so. Perhaps abortion is not entirely a morally neutral act, they may or may not concede, the embryo having some intermediate status. Still, the living being is not yet a person, and it is therefore not entitled to the moral status of a person and may be sacrificed for the greater good of those (the mother in particular, obviously) who are persons. Or perhaps it can be sacrificed prior to some particular intermediate stage in its development. This all leaves us with some very loose ends with which to cope. Just what is a *person*? Do blobs of human biojelly, or some of them, have a higher moral status than living blobs usually have?

Granted that persons are not necessarily humans, could it still be that all human life from blob-zygote on (setting aside cultured tissue for the time being) is a person? Perhaps embryos are entitled to the moral status of persons because they are potential persons or, which is to make a much stronger claim, because they are already persons, though persons in an early stage of development. Perhaps, unlike other blobs, God has given them a soul. (I shall have a little bit to say about souls somewhat later.) Before we get to considerations such as that, I would like to consider some implications of the fact that human life can develop from its earliest stage to the stage of being fully fledged and unambiguously a person.

We must be wary of language here, for as so often happens, language contributes to confusion of the issues. We lead ourselves astray if we focus on the embryo as being a thing with particular properties, and then try to evaluate abortion in terms of the embryo's moral status as a being with those properties. To speak of an *embryo* (or *zygote* or *fetus*) in the same way as one speaks of a *person* is to fall into conceptual confusion. *Person's body* would be the appropriately correlative term. A person is a complex ongoing life process taking place in a body. (This, it should be obvious by now, is not to posit any sort of Cartesian dualism between person and body. Nor does it preclude spiritual beliefs.) An embryo is also a body, a much less developed one, wherein an embryonic life process is taking place. I therefore prefer the term *embryonic life* for that which might be killed in abortion. That a living being is best understood as an ongoing life process that is happening through time and through various bits of matter is particularly and very strikingly true of embryonic life. The earlier in life we look, the more evident it is. Life is a process with thrust and direction, following a course of development, self-organizing and self-maintaining. To dismiss the human embryo as being only a blob of jelly, having no higher moral status than other blobs of living jelly with similar currently realized capabilities or lack thereof, is to fall into error both morally and biologically. The central questions with which we are concerned here do not revolve primarily around the character and interests of the embryo, the blob, but around the character and interests of the embryonic life going on within the embryo. The blob is not the living being, it is only where the living being is happening.

On Embryonic Life

In this section, I argue that the embryonic life has a plausible claim to *some* moral status, more than that to which the lives happening in blobs of biojelly of other sorts are entitled. (That this is so is not contingent on claims about the embryonic life being a person or having a soul. In the subsequent section, I briefly discuss the question of whether the embryonic life is a person by virtue of having a soul.) Given the aforementioned understanding of the distinction between embryonic life and embryo (and so forth), and given the conception of interests and their significance that we have been developing, I am led to conclude that the embryonic human life is entitled to a higher moral status than is suggested by the current capacities of the embryo in which the embryonic life is taking place. I argue that it has this higher moral status by virtue of the kind of being that it is in the process of developing. It is a further question just how much higher its moral status is.

This is not a traditional argument from potentiality. I am not arguing that, as a potential person, the embryonic human life has the moral status of a person. A potential so-and-so is not a so-and-so, it does not have the same qualities, and it need not be treated in the same way. A ticket in a million-dollar lottery is not a million dollars. Nonetheless, I cannot dismiss arguments from potentiality (in connection with abortion) with quite the same scorn with which I once did. In a confused and inaccurate way, such arguments are on to something. The human embryo is importantly different from other blobs of biojelly by virtue of the importantly different sort of process that is going on there. The embryonic human life is *actually* going on and it is in the actual interests of that life process to realize potentialities of certain sorts implicit within that life process. It is in its interests, for instance, to develop rationality, self-consciousness, awareness of the world, and a functional heart and circulatory system. It may be in its long-term interests to develop potentialities that would find fulfillment in music or mathematics.[3] Being a potential thinker is not to be a thinker but to have the capability of developing into one under favorable circumstances, and an inherent interest in doing so, is a real and current feature of the embryonic human life. (The embryonic life also has the potential to become a serial axe murderer or, for that matter, a smoker with lung cancer. Fulfilling these potentials are not healthy developments for that life.) The embryonic lives going on in nonhuman embryos are somewhat different, or very different, and have different sets of interests. An embryonic mouse life has the interests of only a mouse life to develop, which, although slightly more than nothing at all, are much less than the interests of an embryonic human life and are worthy of much less moral consideration. Not all blobs are equal.

We should note that the interests of embryonic life will vary not only according to the potential outcome but also according to the degree to which the outcome has already been actualized. Not only will the interests of an embryonic human life differ from those of an embryonic mouse life, the interests of the embryonic human life at a particular stage will also differ importantly from its interests at an earlier or later stage of its development. Although the outcomes of the different stages may be nearly the same – only *nearly*, as environmental factors always have an influence – the potentialities are in varying degrees of actualization. Accordingly, interests also change and develop. At earlier stages the embryonic life has an interest in acquiring interests, though it does not yet have those interests. The closer a potentiality of ours is to being actualized, the more of an interest we have in actualizing it. As potentialities become actualized, an actual interest in realizing a potential grows into an actual interest in exercising the actuality. After I became a

[3] The morally significant potentials are those that help the embryonic life develop and satisfy interests conducive to its having a good healthy life. Potentials toward psychosis or mass murder do not have such moral significance.

bushwalker, walking the Northern Territory's Larapinta Trail became more in my best interests than it was when I was born. An embryonic life at a stage when its sensory capacities have recently come into being has an interest in exercising those capacities because doing so will be (come) useful for it and also because at that stage it has an innate drive to do so. Its sensory interests are more highly developed than they were in its earliest stages, though less than those of a postnatal person with experiences, desires, and projects, all flowing from its sensory capacities. The late-term embryonic human life has more to lose than it did earlier, having developed more, so abortion (or any other form of death) is more harmful to it.

I do not expect other people to accept, as I do, the principle that we ought to give respect to the interests of *all* beings (human or nonhuman) that have interests, in proportion to the interests. If other people do share that belief with me, so much the better, but we need not invoke that principle to conclude that the embryonic human life has some nonzero level of moral importance, even if it is not that of a fully developed person. We need only to invoke the less adventurous principle that all human interests are entitled to some level of moral consideration and that interests of equal degree are (other things being equal) entitled to equal degrees of moral consideration. (However, if only the interests of persons count morally, we may well conclude that the pre-person embryonic life lacks moral significance.) If human interests are significant, then embryonic human life will merit more moral respect than is due to it by virtue of its realized capacities, by reason of its interests in developing its potential higher capacities, interests lacked by nonhuman embryonic life. Even if these interests are far from fully developed, they are still interests to a degree. Interests and moral significance develop gradually and neither cuts in suddenly just exactly when consciousness does. The embryonic human life will thus have a higher moral status than a nonhuman embryonic life with a similar level of realized capacities but that lacks an inherent thrust toward (and capacity for) human levels of development.[4]

Nevertheless, this conception cannot support the claim that the embryonic human life has the same moral status as an actual person. Those higher capacities that the embryonic life is in the process of developing, the person actually has. What is in the interests of the former to develop, it is in the interests of the latter to maintain and exercise. The actual person also has

---

[4] We must ask at some point why the more central human interests are more important than nonhuman interests. Why, for instance, is our human interest in having rationality more important than a cheetah's interest in a capacity for speed? Isn't an interest an interest? For one thing, rationality is a far more complex interest. In addition, although a human's rationality and a cheetah's speed are each vital for their respective possessor's survival, rationality lends itself to the existence and pursuit of other interests, many having little or nothing to do with survival. That being said, though, we ought never to lose sight of how marvelous and morally significant are the lives or interests of other beings.

developed a whole web of interests stemming from those capacities, with the projects, ideals, and values that go to frame that person's life. Not least, the person is part of an extended complex of interrelationships with others. Still, we cannot entirely rule out the possibility that, for some other reason, the embryonic human life has the same moral status as an actual person, though to reach *that* conclusion we would require further premises, perhaps of a religious or spiritual nature.

Even if postnatal persons must have the highest moral standing, it certainly does *not* follow that the interest of a person in having an abortion must necessarily outweigh morally the interest of an embryonic human life in not being aborted. The moral universe is not a hierarchy wherein any interest of a higher-ranking being must outweigh every interest of a lower-ranking being. To say that a person has a higher moral status than a being of some other sort is not to say that the person's interests, in whatever degree, are invariably entitled to priority. Sometimes, for instance, it is appropriate for us to go to some inconvenience to respect the welfare of an animal. So far, we have little to go on in morally assessing abortion. On one hand, the embryonic life is (human) life and therefore evidently has some morally considerable interests. On the other hand, we have no answer to the question of whether the embryonic life is a person, though we know that it lacks the interests of a fully developed person. Neither of these points is of itself sufficient to determine whether abortion is morally appropriate in a specific situation. The issues are too complex to be resolved by considerations of bumper-sticker brevity (*Right to Life, Freedom of Choice*, and all that sort of thing). At this point we can conclude only that if death is (as normally it would be) contrary to the interests of the embryonic human life, then, whatever the benefits to us or to others might be, abortion does come at *some* moral cost. Just how high that moral cost is, and just when, if ever, it might or might not be appropriate to incur the cost, are further and as-yet-unresolved questions. Perhaps, on balance, it might sometimes be morally appropriate to pay the moral price, even a high one. Whatever the rationale, though, this ought not to be done lightly. Moreover, some would wish to give some consideration to a further sort of reason why there might be a moral case against abortion.

A Soul Consideration

Some people hold that the embryonic life does not become a person gradually but instead is a person right from the start. In this view, being a person is not having developed capacities meeting some standard. Instead, it is a matter of what one essentially *is*. For whatever reason, this is often linked to the embryonic life's having distinct DNA. It is also often linked to the idea that the embryonic life has, or might have, a soul. (In a later section, I discuss the mystique of the gene, and how DNA often seems to be taken as some sort of a material version of the soul.) That the embryonic life is at all stages a distinct living being, with its own character and moral significance, we have already noted – but that does not establish that it should be due to the moral status of an actual person. If having distinct DNA, being a separate life, is not enough to establish that, perhaps the presence of a soul is a decisive factor.

Unlike DNA, a soul is not something the presence or absence of which can be established objectively. A soul generally seems to be thought of as some sort of a nonmaterial entity somehow associated with the material body. It is thought to be of immense value and morally require our respect and protection, and it is thought to be central to the respect we owe the ensouled infant, child, or adult. It also generally seems to be thought of as either being there or else not being there, with no middle ground possible. Nevertheless, it is not altogether clear what one is supposed to be. Our background ideas about the soul seem to owe a great deal to Platonic and Stoic conceptions of it as being of a divine and spiritual rather than a material nature and also as being of a rational nature or, more properly, as being of the nature of rational essence. At the same time, not incompatibly, our background presumptions also seem to incorporate the Aristotelian conception of the soul as being the form or rationale of the living being, and what makes it alive. This is fairly summarized by the *Catholic Encyclopedia*, which tells us that[5]

The soul may be defined as the ultimate internal principle by which we think, feel, and will, and by which our bodies are animated.

At one time, the idea of the soul as that which gave the body its life was associated with the idea, now discredited in biology, of *élan vital.* This is claimed to be a subtle substance, the presence of which is necessary for matter to take up life. I would observe (later I give further detail) that DNA now seems to be assuming in popular thought some of the mystique of the soul and of *élan vital.*

Just when the soul becomes associated with the body has long been a matter of conjecture. At one time it was thought that the soul entered the body at the *moment of quickening,* the supposed moment when the body acquires the power of motion. It is at this point that the fetus was thought to become *animated* (from *anima,* based on ancient Indo-European roots referring to *life, breath,* and *soul,* that which brings about movement). We now know that muscles and nerves develop and become operational only gradually, the so-called moment of quickening being only when motions become perceptible to the mother. Nor is there any other specific point along the way that strongly recommends itself as a time when the soul

5 Robert C. Broderick, ed., *Catholic Encyclopedia* (Nashville, TN: Thomas Nelson, 1990; available online at http://www.newadvent.org/cathen/14153a.htm).

enters the body. Because that is so, those who, in defense of the innocent soul, are most adamantly opposed to abortion often assume that the soul is present at every stage from conception on. I should note, however, that the Roman Catholic Church, among the foremost of those opposing abortion, does *not* officially proclaim that the soul enters the body at the moment of conception. Rather, the teaching is that the soul could enter the body that early (for all we know to the contrary) and, accordingly, that at *every* stage there is a grave risk that abortion is murder, a mortal sin.[6]

There appear to be three possibilities about when (and how) the soul becomes associated with the body:

1. Perhaps God directly intervenes and puts a soul there at some point, which may or may not be at conception.
2. Perhaps the souls of the parents, through a natural but immaterial process, somehow create a new soul. Then do ova and spermatazoa carry bits of souls that are not souls themselves but that compound to form a soul? We might then wonder whether the loss of the soul bits was of any moral importance. Certainly, if each gamete carried a soul bit, huge numbers of soul bits would be lost in (or even in the absence of) sexual intercourse. But can a soul be a compound of simpler elements?
3. Perhaps preexisting souls find their way to a new home during the course of pregnancy. This view is particularly popular in Eastern philosophies and religions.

It cannot be conclusively demonstrated that there is or is not any such thing as a soul. Nor can it be demonstrated (if there is such a thing) whether or not killing a soul's associated life vehicle is a morally deplorable injury to it. For those who believe that there is a soul present in the embryonic life at every stage, and that it is wrong to kill innocent life (or, more properly, life associated with an innocent soul), abortion is appropriately anathema. However, I shall offer reasons for thinking it unlikely that a soul is present from the beginning of embryonic life. Though there is no one definitive moment we can identify biologically, I suggest that reflection on our greater scientific knowledge will rule out the moment of conception as the moment of ensoulment as surely as it ruled out the moment of quickening. Moreover, I shall offer reasons why it may not be appropriate to conceive of the soul as a thing of any sort, even if there are souls, nor to conceive of it as necessarily being entirely present or entirely absent. In the subsequent section I offer

---

[6] For that matter, if God, with His divine foresight, can foresee that a particular spermatazoon is to join with a particular ovum, might the souls be made present to both of them jointly prior to conception? Souls are not bound by space and presumably God could do that. In which case, what then? Speculation could wander on forever.

reasons why death is not always contrary to the interests of the embryonic life (or its soul).

I think it is worth noting, to start with here, that the "moment of conception" is a myth. There is no such moment. Conception is a process that takes about 20 to 24 hours. That is, it takes about that long from when the spermatozoon reaches the ovum until the time when there is a zygote, with strands of DNA (chromosomes) from each parent aligned with those from the other. And it takes a while longer for the embryonic DNA, as distinct from the maternal, to take over governing the embryonic life. As is the case with all biological processes, conception does not always take place successfully. At what point, if any, is it a matter of a new soul being lost if something goes wrong? Instead of there being one magic moment, we have a gradual process taking twenty-odd hours followed by a gradual process taking about nine months. However, even if we could identify some biological moment with pinpoint accuracy, what warrant is there for assuming that the biological moment is the moment of ensoulment?

It is worth reflecting on the fact that it would be very careless of souls were one to be associated with each embryonic life as soon as conception takes place. For one thing, for embryonic life to survive, the embryo must become implanted in the lining of the mother's womb. That takes nearly a week, and many embryos fail to implant and therefore die.[7] Nor is it all clear sailing after that. A substantial proportion, about 50 percent, of those embryos that are implanted fail to survive, often without the mother's being aware that anything has happened.[8] One standard medical text makes this statement:

Estimates are that as many as 50% of pregnancies end in spontaneous abortion, and that half of these losses are a result of chromosomal abnormalities. These abortions

---

[7] There is a so-called morning-after pill (also known as emergency contraception) that prevents the zygote or early embryo from successfully implanting in the woman's uterus. This it does by means of a dose of the hormone levonorgestrel. Technically, it might be argued that this is not properly an instance of abortion as no implanted embryo is removed. Rather, the embryo is not allowed to implant in the first place. Nothing is directly done to it. For later use, there is RU-486, now known as mifepristone (a synthetic steroid compound), the so-called abortion pill, which works by blocking the action of progesterone in a woman's uterus. In the absence of the effect of that hormone, the lining of the uterus sheds, as in menstruation. When it sloughs off, the embryo is lost. Because this pill is taken after implantation occurred, its use does amount to an active withdrawal of the embryo's life-support system (the woman's reproductive system). Whether or not it is a passive act of letting die, as distinguished from an active act of killing, it is considered by anti-abortionists to be unwarranted and morally culpable. So too is use of the morning-after pill. Nevertheless, it remains true that in the normal course of events, a great many zygotes and early embryos fail to implant successfully with no outside interference.

[8] Conceptually and practically, it is difficult to distinguish sharply between spontaneous abortion and cases wherein the embryo fails to implant successfully. It may be that as many as 60 percent of conceptions fall by the wayside.

are a natural means of screening embryos for birth defects, reducing the incidence of congenital abnormalities. Without this phenomenon, approximately 12% instead of 2% to 3% of infants would have birth defects.[9]

There are some interesting implications here. It seems that screening for birth defects and aborting accordingly is a natural phenomenon and not a human innovation, though it is a natural phenomenon that catches only most but not all birth defects.[10] Moreover, if the early embryo has a soul, then vast numbers of such ensouled beings perish unborn without human intervention. It is also worth noting that about half of those spontaneous abortions are *not* due to chromosomal abnormalities, so about a quarter of all pregnancies end in spontaneous abortion for other reasons. If ensoulment happens at conception, then a substantial number of souls are lost quite early on. Or, at least, the souls lose their embryonic vehicles. If God puts souls there, and if God were good, then the implication would seem to be that the death of the embryonic life is not a very bad thing for the soul. Whether or not we attribute the origin of souls to divine intervention, however, it would appear that either the welfare of the souls is not the primary reason for their entering human life, or else that early death is not bad for the soul – or, alternatively, that the soul does not get there until later.

There are many other problems for the soul-at-conception theory. If an embryo splits into two or three bits, as sometimes happens, resulting in genetically identical embryos and (if all goes well) identical twins or triplets, did the original soul get subdivided? Did God add further ones as the occasion arose? If one of the resulting fragments dies, as often happens, is that a person who dies, a soul deprived of a body? Again, sometimes two of the fragments recombine, forming a single embryo resulting in a single baby. Did two souls merge into one? Did one soul die? Or depart? Does the baby have two souls? For those who can answer these questions, I have an even tougher poser. There are cases known to medical science, very rare but actual, where two embryos that are *not* genetically identical fuse to form a single embryo, resulting in a single baby.[11] Usually the two embryos, if both

---

9 T. W. Sadler, *Langman's Essential Medical Embryology* (Philadelphia: Lippincott Williams & Wilkins, 2004), pp. 44–45.

10 Is it that God is setting a precedent for us by terminating (all?) those pregnancies that ought to be deleted? One might or might not welcome the precedent – but why does God let anencephalic fetuses through? Is it perhaps just that some wombs and some embryonic lives are workable combinations and some are not? There seems no persuasive reason from that to conclude that those that suit the womb are exactly those that ought to be born. When the plague strikes, as it rarely does now, some people survive and some do not. It used to be that some people thought we should just leave it to God and not try to interfere – God's will be done. However, perhaps instead of trying to guess about God, we should try to use our head to do what is right.

11 Claire Ainsworth, "The Stranger Within," *New Scientist* 180(2421) (2003): 34. The resulting embryo is said to be *tetragametic*, as it results from four gametes, via the two embryos. As

survived, would have resulted in fraternal (as distinguished from identical) twins. Presumably they would have a soul apiece. Would the baby resulting from the amalgamated embryo have two souls? Did the two different souls merge? Or what? One can generate such questions well beyond the point of being sadistic to the opposition. I reject the soul-at-conception theory as being just too simplistic to do the work required of it. Like the theory of the soul at the moment of quickening, it just cannot cope with the biological facts.

We humans do have a liking for finding simple and definite answers. The eternal risk is that we might settle on answers simpler and more definite than truth and reality happens to be. In quest of definitude and simplicity, we may hastily identify one hoped-for simple and definite fact, the start of being a person, with another (more-or-less) simple and definite fact, the start of being a human living being. In testimony before a U.S. Senate inquiry concerning abortion nearly thirty years ago, a professor of law who was also a medical doctor asserted, supposedly on the basis of his expertise, that

the exact moment of the beginning of personhood and of the human body is at the moment of conception.[12]

I can at least applaud his not claiming that that is when *life* starts. As we have already noted, life is continuous, having started very long ago. What happens at conception is not the beginning of life but, at most, the beginning of an individual living system. What begins is not life but, at most, individuality, as marked by its new combination of DNA. Actually, it takes a little while for that particular DNA to take control of the embryonic life, and environmental factors also have their influence. However, as an approximation, let us accept that the *individual* living system starts at the time indicated by the learned professor. But why must we take it as a scientific fact that this is when being a *person* begins? If it is a fact at all, it is not a scientific one. If we have found a definitive point for the beginning of individual human life, that is no sufficient reason to believe that we have found the longed-for definitive starting point for its being a person.

of the date of the *New Scientist* article, there were known to be about forty people having such origins, though it was suspected that there are many more. These have all occurred naturally and not as the result of some bizarre experimental procedure. It is known that there are animals as well as people that have tetragametic origins. Scientists have adopted the term *chimera* for such entities, human or animal, based on the monster in ancient Greek mythology that resembled a lion in the forepart, a goat in the middle, and a dragon behind. (As applied to humans, this seems to me a rather tactless terminology.)

[12] Professor McCarthy de Mere, of the University of Tennessee, testifying before a U.S. Senate Judiciary Subcommittee held April 23–24, 1981. (This citation is taken from http://www.roevwade.org/upl, an anti-abortion Web site.)

If its being human life with distinct DNA logically implies that a life has a soul or that on some other grounds it is a person, then the implications would be quite bizarre. Under laboratory conditions, living human cells of many types, from many parts of the body, can be kept alive and able to reproduce themselves pretty much indefinitely. As an instance of life, the cultured tissue may perhaps have moral status of some sort, but it does not have the moral status of a person. This is true even if the tissue is genetically unique, as it may well be if the tissue donor has since died. There is more to our moral status then being alive with human DNA. Terminating the cultured tissue would not be homicide – though terminating one of a pair of genetically identical twins would be. Moreover, if a person were created as a product of cloning technology as the genetic duplicate of a preexisting person, it would be morally monstrous to take that as lessening the clone's (or the original's) moral status as an end in himself or herself. These things being so, not only is genetic uniqueness not sufficient for human moral status, it also is not even necessary.

Is it perhaps that what is needed for a living entity to have the moral status of a person is that it be, or have the potential to develop into, what is unambiguously a postnatal person? That would rule in the clone and the embryonic life as persons but apparently rule out the cultured tissue. Tissue is composed of differentiated *somatic* cells, those that have acquired a specific character and taken up a particular role – as liver cells or whatever. Liver cells do not grow into people. Evidently, we can rule somatic cells out as people. To be distinguished from somatic cells are undifferentiated *stem* cells, which under suitable conditions can, through cellular division and subsequent specialization, develop into any and all of the body's more than two hundred different types of cell. A special sort of stem cell is the *zygote*, formed by the union of ovum and spermatozoon. Perhaps it is zygotes and their subsequent embryos that have souls or that are people because of some other attribute. We might note those who ethically object to the use of stem cells in research characteristically object on the grounds that embryos, potential persons, are destroyed when stem cells are obtained. However, if technology were developed whereby any stem cell could be developed into a person, then presumably the range of beings with moral standing would extend further. One conclusion would appear to be that potential must be enabled and shaped by surrounding possibility. Perhaps cells that are not zygotes can be given a future.

This brings us to Dolly. I am referring to the famous sheep, a clone that arose from a somatic cell. More specifically, what are we to think in view of the process whereby Dolly was created? A cell was taken from the udder of an adult ewe and, after some preparatory treatment, was inserted into an ovum, taken from another ewe, from which the gene-bearing nucleus had been removed. After further treatment, the ovum with its genetic transplant – which we might think of as now being a concocted zygote – was implanted in the womb of a surrogate mother – and eventually became Dolly. She was a genetic copy of her "mother" (the somatic cell donor), Dolly's cells having the genetic makeup of the ancestral somatic cell from which she developed.[13]

To be sure, people do not generally worry about whether sheep have souls. However, what if cloning in a similar manner created a human baby? A storm of controversy would erupt and many people would be outraged. Clearly there would (and ought to) be questions about the wisdom, morality, and legality of allowing such a thing to happen. (Furthermore, what about the clone attempts that fail to survive? It took several – 277 – attempts to get Dolly.) Still, if it did in fact happen in the case of humans (as likely it eventually shall), would the clone be a person? Would it have a soul? One would assume that, like Dolly, the human clone would be as sentient and as aware of its surroundings as other members of its species. Whether it has a soul or not, it would presumably be wrong to be cruel to the clone. However, if it lacked a soul, would the lack of a soul in some way compromise the clone's moral status? Would it be morally permissible to painlessly kill a soulless clone to harvest organs for transplantation? In contrast, if it did have a soul – as one would imagine that any decent god would see to it that the clone did – when did she or he acquire it? Was it back when that bit of life was going on in the yet-to-be-cloned somatic cell? Then did the cell next to it in the body also have a soul? Or, if the soul is not added until later, why are souls not also added later in the case of zygotes?

If a soul were attached to every cell with the potential to develop into an adult or infant human being, then seemingly every cell in a human body would have a soul as any cell might conceivably be cloned. I would then be causing death to multitudes of innocent souls every time I go bushwalking and leave a bit of my skin on rocks or vegetation along the way (as happens

---

[13] It might be noted that Dolly did not have *exactly* the same genetic makeup as the ewe from which she received the great bulk of her genetic makeup. Although she got the genes in the DNA that came from the nucleus of the "mother" cell, she also got some of the genes in the DNA of the mitochondria of the other ewe's ovum. All animal cells (except spermatozoa) contain mitochondria, which are tiny organelles outside of the cell's nucleus. They play an important role in the release of energy in metabolism. Though most of an animal's genes are in the chromosomes of each cell's nucleus, some are in its mitochondria. Mitochondria have their own DNA, of a distinctive sort, which is transmitted separately in reproduction through the mother's ovum. Mitochondrial genes also affect our characteristics, and some abnormalities in mitochondrial DNA can have serious consequences. In Dolly's case, when the ovum was scooped out to make way for the inserted cell, some of the mitochondria remained behind in the shell of the ovum and contributed their own DNA to Dolly's genetic makeup. Thereby she inherited both mitochondrial and nuclear DNA from the ewe that donated the udder cell together with some mitochondrial DNA from the ewe who donated the ovum. However, for our purposes here, we might easily imagine there being a refinement in the process, whereby the mitochondrial DNA of the ovum would be entirely replaced.

often enough).[14] If we assume that God is not so profligate and wasteful of souls as that, that there is not one soul per cell, and if we accept that the postnatal infant or adult clone does have a soul as much as any other person, then there is a question of how that could possibly come about. (It is a benefit of the prevention of human cloning that it would help us avoid being confronted by such a poser in practice, but even if human cloning never happens, the logical issues remain.) There seem to be few possibilities:

1. Perhaps God was enabled by divine foresight to know which particular somatic cell was destined to be cloned and gave that individual cell, though not neighboring cells, a soul. If that is what God does, we might ask whether God would use the same foresight to withhold a soul from any embryo destined not to implant in the womb, to be aborted, to be expended in research, or otherwise to die before birth.
2. Perhaps there is no such thing as a soul, with the embryonic life gradually attaining moral significance to the extent that it acquires the characteristics of a person. This conclusion would be acceptable to some people and quite unacceptable to others.
3. Perhaps the soul comes in at some unknown time, subsequent to the time when there first exists a genetic assemblage with the potential to develop into a person's body. Does the soul perhaps enter only after the central streak (the first foundation of the nervous system) starts to form at about the fourteenth day? Here, the embryonic life is starting to function as an individual organism. Nevertheless, it is still far short of having the characteristics of a person, having only characteristics that an embryonic fish or tadpole might have to a far higher degree. If God, or wherever souls come from, waits that long, why not wait until there is something more nearly like a person into which to insert a soul? One might expect a well-intended God to do that.
4. Perhaps the soul enters *gradually*, to the extent that the embryonic life acquires the characteristics of a person. (For my own part, I find it very difficult to believe, or even imagine, that a soul could be a spiritual thing somehow attached to a physical thing. A life is an ongoing process, not an assemblage of cells, and I suspect that a soul would likewise be a process. If so, it could enter into or arise in a life process gradually.)

However we figure it, though, there is no necessity to hold that every speck of life with the capacity to develop into the body of a human person is itself a person or that it has a soul. If we did hold that view, then we would also have to accept that every living human is full of a vast number

[14] I understand that the adult human body contains about 100,000,000,000,000 cells, but the exact number of zeros does not really matter.

of souls, almost all of which (or of whom?) are doomed to an early death. I believe that souls should be thought of in some other way, if thought of at all.

Some people deny that there are any souls at all. For those who deny that there are any, there would seem to be no insuperable barrier to accepting the principle that the embryonic life has varying degrees of moral significance, according to its varying degree of development. If being a person is not a matter of some intangible whatever-it-is somehow attached to a bodily entity, then being a person might quite plausibly be a matter of degree that increases during the embryonic life.

* * * * *

The principle that embryonic lives have varying degrees of moral significance, according to their varying degree of development, need not be rejected even if it is assumed that there are souls. I make no claim to be able to state definitively what a soul is, and I distrust the proclamations of those who do so claim. However, I do feel confident in asserting that much of our thinking about such matters is contaminated by outmoded conceptual baggage, which we have inherited from the past. One of the most problematic legacies is the presumed duality between the material body on the one hand and mind or soul on the other. This has led some contemptuously to dismiss the latter as "the ghost in the machine." There is no ghost, they believe, no soul, with mind being only an activity or organ of the body. Others stubbornly insist that there *is* a ghost in the machine, the ghost being who we really are. Better, I believe, is to reject the supposed duality between radically different sorts of things.

An important part of the difficulty is that our conceptual schemes predispose us to think in terms of *things*. Our Western languages revolve around nouns, with verbs and other parts of speech describing nouns and their adventures. What are presumed to be real are things of various sorts, doing or being done to. Other languages revolve around verbs, taking reality to be composed of happenings. If we think in such terms, a thing is just a state of affairs at a particular time. Both sorts of languages have their virtues, and both (perhaps with strenuous effort) can express pretty much the same content. Verb-centered languages lend themselves well to discourse concerning life and living systems, these things being processes. Perhaps our noun-centered languages tend to obscure from us the possibility that the *soul* is best thought of as being a process of some sort. Such a view is compatible with most religious traditions, Eastern and Western. (In the West, process theology perhaps comes the most readily to mind, but it is far from being the only instance. In the East there are numerous examples.) It is also compatible with modern science, which has been eroding the matter side of the mind–matter dualism. Certainly there is no logical problem about a process going from one medium to another. A passage from one medium to another might be gradual. A medium might itself be a process. A mundane (as it were) example would be a spoken utterance going from one telephone to another via a satellite relay.

I prefer not to go further into religious and related conjecture. My concern here is only to suggest the idea that a soul might arise gradually, or it might gradually come to associate with a life. That being so, late-term abortion might do more to disaccommodate a soul than would early-term abortion. That would accord well with the idea that the moral cost of abortion continually increases the more the embryonic life develops. At the other end of life, the suggestion that ensoulment is a matter of degree also accords well with the idea that some people, near death, are only partially here and are partially elsewhere. That would allow an alternative to the view that it is merely that there is not much left of them at all. Let us speculate no further. Now I would like to indicate how abortion is not always harmful to the aborted embryonic life.

Beneficent Abortion

We have already noted that death is not invariably contrary to the interests of a living being. That can include the death by abortion of embryonic human life. The particular nature of an individual living being, each with its own particular nature, determines what its interests are. Broadly, as we have noted, the interests of a living being lie in that which contributes to its overall well-being as an effectively functional ongoing living being. Just what its interests are in detail will obviously vary from one instance to another. Usually, though, staying alive will be paramount among its interests, being prerequisite to all other interests. Abortion usually will be very much contrary to the interests of an embryonic life. Even so, life can get to a condition wherein the chronic frustration of its interests, rather than their fulfillment, becomes the only future possible for it. Life becomes only suffering and living becomes dying. To cease to live may then be in the interests of the living being, death being the best outcome actually possible for that being in that particular situation.

What I propose therefore is that abortion can be a beneficent form of in utero euthanasia in some circumstances. If the embryonic human life's nature is such that to be is to be irremediably frustrated in the pursuit of its inherent interests, then it is better for it not to be. Better *for it* not to be. One would presume that a high proportion of those many spontaneous abortions that occur naturally as a result of genetic abnormality are, in effect, naturally beneficent. Were we able, moreover, to determine that a pregnancy would result in the birth of an anencephalic child, then it would be fair to conclude that abortion was in the best interests of that embryonic life as well as most probably in the interests of the pregnant woman. Anencephaly invariably proves fatal shortly after birth, if not before, but it is becoming increasingly possible to keep anencephalic children alive for longer periods. (In what amounts to passive euthanasia, such means are almost invariably withheld.) There are other conditions in which a child with a savagely incapacitating birth defect may live indefinitely – to its own distress as well as that of those around it. There are yet other conditions that lead to lives that are brief and of negative value for the child himself or herself. A case in point would be Tay-Sachs syndrome.[15] Far better would it be for all were such embryonic lives (those that cannot be lived with benefit for those individual lives) to come to an end well before birth.

The question of whether life would be of benefit to the embryonic life is usually not one that can be entirely determined on the basis of the character of the embryonic life itself. Life just does not happen in itself. What is also to be considered is the character of the circumstances into which it would be born. It might be in its interests to live if it were to be born into (or adopted into) a loving, supportive, and functional family situation, for instance, but not if it were to be born into an unloving and dysfunctional family situation. It might not be able to flourish under certain socioeconomic conditions. Quite apart from abortion, there are moral questions about whether such socioeconomic conditions should be allowed to arise or persist, but the fact is that they do arise and persist. If that were the only life available to the embryonic life, then it could well be that continuing to live would not be in that being's interests.

It is also true that the question of whether life would be of benefit to the embryonic life is usually not one that can be answered with full accuracy and precision. It is not just that usually we will not know all the relevant facts – though that is certainly true. Even with every relevant fact conceivable, we could not draw a line between *yes* and *no* in any way that was clearly exact and correct. Any line could be offset, with plausible reason, somewhat to one side or the other. For that matter, so much is true of night and day. Still, we may sometimes declare, with absolute certainty, that it is night or that it is not. When it comes to whether continuing to live is in the interests of the embryonic life, though, the difficulty is more severe. The difference between night and day is virtually a one-dimensional gradation, whereas questions of whether continuing to live is in the interests of the embryonic life are multidimensional. There are many factors to be considered, many of which are difficult or impossible to compare on a sound rationale. Nonetheless, we can say these things about questions of what is or is not a "good" place to have a picnic. Many instances will be impossible to decide beyond reasonable doubt – whether we are deciding about picnics or about abortion. Even so, there are many cases wherein we can say with certainty that continuing to

---

[15] In the first few months after birth, children with this condition suffer inevitable mental and physical deterioration. The child becomes deaf, blind, and unable to swallow, with paralysis and dementia setting in. Death usually occurs by age four.

live is in the best interests of an embryonic life – and sometimes we can say with certainty that it is contrary to its interests. I would conclude that in *some* cases we would have an obligation to the embryonic human life, in full recognition of its moral importance to abort it.

I would add that although we may or may not decide that the interests of the embryonic life are the decisive consideration, we certainly should keep in mind the truth that the life of an individual living being is the standard by means of which its interests are identified. Down syndrome (or Down's syndrome), widely associated with cognitive dysfunction, is a daunting prospect for parents-to-be. It requires them to strive harder and with many inconveniences and to have lower ambitions for their child. Nevertheless, the Down syndrome child might be able to have a life that is, on its terms, quite fulfilling. Many children with this syndrome have had such a life. It is irrelevant to argue that without the condition, the child might have more highly developed fulfillments. That would be someone else. What is relevant is that for that child with that condition, it is possible to have a life that is worth living. (Something similar might be of those who, at some stage in their life, suffer brain damage through misadventure.) However, these considerations only pose an ethical dilemma. They do not solve one.

Conflicting Interests

According to the nature of a particular embryonic life and the prospects it faces, death may be a major injury to it, or a major boon, or it may be of any degree of positive or negative benefit in between. Most of the time, to be sure, the embryonic life does have an interest, a strong one, in continuing to live. Nevertheless, the embryonic life is not the only life with a stake in the matter. Usually the prospective parents keenly desire that it continue to live, and they take joy at the prospective birth. Unfortunately, as we all know, life is not invariably as happy and straightforward as that. Different beings have different interests, which interlock with and affect one another, and the sad fact is that there can be conflicts of interest between living beings, human living beings not least of all. A pregnant woman's interests may vary as widely as those of an embryonic life, and instances often arise in which abortion might be in the best interests of the pregnant woman but not in the best interests of the embryonic life.[16] Certainly it would be morally preferable that such situations not arise. However, whether from

---

[16] There are other logically possible, if improbable, cases wherein we might be certain that an embryo had an interest in being aborted, but the prospective parent(s) would have an interest in its being born anyway. (This might be for some legal or economic reason, or perhaps for a religious one.) Maybe the child would necessarily suffer from Tay-Sachs Syndrome, though its birth might allow the parents to claim an inheritance. Maybe the parents (perhaps a bit substandard themselves) want to get some more welfare money. How

negligence in antecedent forms of birth control, or whether they are due to other causes, conflicts of interest do arise. Moral decisions about abortion have to be made – yet it might perhaps be that we can never be absolutely certain of a way of making them all on a sound moral basis. Certainly there is no decision procedure by means of which we can determine which is the most life-affirming conclusion. Still, we are obliged to make our moral decisions as morally best we can.

On the one hand, there is asserted to be a right to life on the part of the "unborn child." On the other, there is asserted to be a right of women to control their own bodies. Even if the fetus is not technically part of the body of the pregnant woman, being genetically and physiologically distinct, the embryonic human life is going on there. Many of that embryonic life's life processes, such as those of the circulation of oxygen and nutrients, the removal of wastes, and the maintenance of innumerable other chemical and physical balances, are intermingled with and derivative from the life processes of the woman. Likewise their interests mingle, even when in conflict. How then are we to adjudicate between their evidently conflicting rights? Should we instead turn away from rights and assess individual cases on some utilitarian basis? That would raise a host of issues about whose utility is to be assessed and on what basis. On the assumption that all human interests would have to be recognized as having some moral weight, we would have to work out how the interests of the embryonic human life are to be assessed in comparison with those of adult people. That puts us into the "apples and oranges" problem of weighing rival interests of quite differing character.

Even were we to develop a scheme for assessing and comparing interests, though, we might well be skeptical about whether we ought to repose our moral trust in utilitarian assessments in every application, even if there were a correct and possible way to add it all up. We have previously noted that in some applications, utilitarian assessments seem very doubtful – yet we might also be skeptical about whether an ethic revolving around exact rules or rigid rights can do the job well enough. Rights and rules seem too often to be subject to exceptional instances wherein their being put into force would evidently be morally unacceptable. We have already noted this as well. When it comes to abortion, we could settle on a particular system of rules and rights – and try to turn a blind eye to anomalies. But can we avoid anomalies? We might perhaps add some qualifications to the rules in an attempt to do so. If we have a rule against abortion, perhaps it could be amended to allow

do we decide what is best here? One suspects that the morality of not aborting in such instances will be a matter of particular cases, depending on just what was riding on it for the various parties. That an embryonic life faces quite bad prospects may not always give it a *right* to be aborted. Nonetheless, we can at least imagine that the law might be modified or interpreted so that civil or criminal suit might be brought on behalf of the child against those responsible for forcing it to be born against its evident best interests. It has long been possible for a child to sue for damages resulting from other forms of prenatal injury.

for abortion when pregnancy is due to forcible and incestuous rape of a minor, or when there is strong evidence that the baby would suffer severe brain damage. If we approve of abortion being allowed in general, perhaps in honor of women's right to choice, we might temper our approval if it were a matter of a late-term abortion of a healthy fetus performed merely to spite the woman's mother-in-law. (Yet some acts of petty spite we would just shrug off as being within a person's right to choose, so why not that one?) We may fine-tune our statutes or our moral precepts to screen out as many moral anomalies as we can, yet even if we succeeded to a great extent, such an approach might well be merely ad hoc and lacking in clear rationale. Moreover, the infinite variability and interwovenness of interests, circumstances, and life prospects render the prospect of *entirely* screening out anomalies highly unlikely and certainly unrealized. Such an approach might do for developing a more-or-less adequate set of ad hoc statutes, but a moral rationale requires something more coherent.

One might think that instead of trying to map a complex moral reality with complex moral rules, we might do better to look for simpler and more general laws. Why not in morality as in physics, where a highly complex reality is described by a few basic principles? Unfortunately, the prospects of achieving such an outcome in moral philosophy do not appear at all bright. As we have noted, rights and rules do not seem to have a universal and exact fit with moral reality. Even so noble and universal a principle as that one ought always to treat others as ends in themselves, and never as means only, faces anomalies. In some instances the stark choice is between using the mother as means in the service of the embryonic life, overriding her moral status as an end in herself, or else sacrificing the embryonic life for the sake of the mother, negating it as an end in itself. A failure to choose between ends in themselves may result in one being selected by chance and the other sacrificed, and it might even result in death or severe injury to both mother and embryonic life. Though in none of these cases would we be actively sacrificing one of these beings for the sake of the other, we may well be *allowing* additional injury to one or both as a sacrificial means to our own end of avoiding the making of such moral choices. That the inviolability of the rights of ends in themselves can lead to moral grotesqueries we have already noted in connection with *McFall* v. *Shimp*. So too we have noted that utilitarianism can lead to moral grotesqueries. Deontological and utilitarian moral systems alike can be too strict to be moral. Perhaps we need to take a different approach.

Perhaps we need to make our decisions on a case-by-case basis instead of trying to force them all onto the Procrustean bed of a particular system of ethics. On what basis, however, do we assess individual cases? If we do not have an ethical system on the basis of which to make our case-by-case decisions, how can we make them – except with arbitrariness in proportion to our departure from system? That is a fair question, and it would be a decisive objection if acting morally were only a matter of acting in accordance with a (valid) moral system. In an earlier chapter, though, I argued that moral systems, when valid, are validated by moral reality. In this view, moral systems are to morally good behavior pretty much what maps are to successful navigation. Nonetheless, no map can be completely accurate or complete to the finest detail. Sometimes we may strike an obstacle that has been charted inaccurately or not at all. Sometimes, not least in bioethics, we must traverse uncharted terrain. To find our way with the best chance of success, we must be sensitive to the terrain itself and try to follow it as carefully as possible.

How then are we to go about getting the right moral answers? Sometimes it is easy, but obviously it is the tough issues with which we have difficulties. The real-world fact is that we cannot always get an unambiguously right answer. That *is* one of the messy things about the real world. Rules and principles can help, so long as they are not relied on excessively. Nevertheless, sometimes they do not offer enough help and, sometimes, when we are legislators or members of ethics committees, we have to draw up rules, regulations, or guidelines ourselves. So, how are we to proceed in the face of moral uncertainty? There are people, as we have all observed, who do seem well able to cope with difficult moral issues; some people do better than others. This requires skill and insight, and certainly it involves caring. People who do this well have the quality of being, as I would think of it, life affirming. They affirm life. Now, as a principle, "affirm life" gets us approximately nowhere. Recommending it as a principle would be on a par with telling a painter or a novelist to create beautiful and meaningful works. What is needed is to be able to do that successfully in practice. We cannot just paint by the numbers and expect to be good artists. To be life affirming is to have the inclination to respect the health and wholeness of life, to protect it, and, when appropriate, to seek to enhance it. This, of course, requires some insight into lives and their needs, and to be effectively life affirming requires a developed measure of skill. Rules and principles may be used to enhance one's skill, but they cannot adequately replace it. This skilled regard for life is expressive of a healthy strength of character, a virtue. This virtue is one that may give us good service when abortion is under consideration.

Affirming life does not invariably entail adherence to a supposed "right to life." There is more to affirming life than just life *or* death. As we have been developing the idea, it is a matter of quality in a very encompassing sense. Continuing to live, as we have noted, may be quite contrary to the interests of an embryonic life. Alternatively, it might be so marginally in the interests of the embryonic life that it would be absurd to take it as an absolute that trumped all other considerations. There are other lives to be considered that might be affected for better or for worse. The embryonic life at whatever degree of development is not all that must be considered;

nor, for that matter, is the mother's life as well as its own all that matters. Moreover, the affirmation of life is not something that can be measured and calibrated on some linear scale. It is not a matter of trying to maximize the amount of some particular property a life has, any more than achieving beauty in painting a picture is a matter of trying to maximize the amount of some particular property it has. To affirm life is not to affirm what life has but what life *is*. It is to respect and cherish its wholeness, what I have called *health*, in a broad sense, and, as appropriate, to enhance it and not impoverish it. Unless we affirm life, we humans cannot, I maintain, sufficiently well affirm our own lives. Life affirmation has many applications, not least of which concern abortion.

Biocentric conceptions remind us that being a living being is a matter of degree and that having interests is likewise a matter of degree. They remind us that, to whatever degree, all the interests of living beings merit appropriate moral consideration and that this moral significance is not restricted to rational life or thinking life. Affirming life on the basis of biocentric conceptions can offer us a working basis for approaching bioethical issues. However, doing so cannot provide us an algorithm for finding infallibly correct ethical answers. But, then, neither can anything else. So where do we draw our lines? Line questions refuse to go away, as I attempted to explain in the chapter on elusive lines, even if we cannot draw our lines with precise justification. I will close with some thoughts concerning abortion decisions.

* * * * *

A woman deciding whether to proceed with an unplanned pregnancy might well in her ponderings and decisions manifest an affirmation of life, one which goes well beyond a calculation of self-interests or a consideration of who has which rights. For illustration, consider the following possible cameos (fictitious instances abstracted from real ones).

Case I

Abigail is a twenty-eight-year-old mother with a six-year-old child, and she has a partner with whom her relationship is problematic and only partially satisfactory. She finds herself with an unplanned pregnancy and is uncertain what to think or do about it. So far as she is able to estimate, her life will no more (or less) probably be better as a consequence of having another baby than it will as a consequence of having an abortion. Her life would certainly be different, but she finds no reason to think that it would be any better one way than the other. Life, she reckons, is more or less okay, on the whole, but is nothing marvelous. If she did not have an abortion, the resulting child would probably, she reckons, have a life that would be worth living, though not greatly so. Neither her prospects nor those of the prospective child would be particularly bright, given the condition of the world and her situation in it. Although life would be worth living in a mediocre sort of way, it would not be human life at anything close to its best. Abigail reckons that life ought to take a much richer form and is (or would be, if she knew of them) appalled by Derek Parfit's scenarios of huge populations having lives that are just barely worth having.[17] Abigail believes that the world or life or humanity (or whatever one calls it) would be better off for there not being one more marginal life, whereas no one would be better off if there were. After thinking it over, she proceeds to have an abortion.

Case II

Bernice, a childless professional woman of thirty, had no definite plans to have children and, indeed, did not feel particularly interested in doing so. Certainly she had not planned to fall pregnant just then, and when she found out that she was it was a disagreeable surprise. This was particularly inconvenient inasmuch as she was planning a very special overseas holiday later in the year, plans incompatible with continuing her pregnancy. On the whole, Bernice finds life quite enjoyable, and she both wants and expects to continue to do so. She feels some qualms about abortion, but she believes that at its early stage the fetus really would not suffer. She would suffer more by losing her holiday. A happy and childless life stretching indefinitely into the future is an attractive and realistic prospect. However, Bernice starts to wonder whether there might be more to life than that. Were she to have the child and care for it, her life would not be more pleasant. Nevertheless, she thinks, were she to love and share with a child, she would be taking part in something that was richer and more meaningful. This might or might not be better for her, she reckons, and in many ways it would be worse. Still, she would be bringing about and taking part in something that was better. With less taking in life and more giving and sharing, her life would still be quite good. Accordingly, Bernice decides to cancel her holiday and proceeds toward maternity.

In their differing circumstances and in their differing ways, both Abigail and Bernice were, in effect, trying to enrich the fabric of human life – or perhaps we should say that Bernice was, whereas Abigail was trying to lessen its impoverishment. Either way, each wanted to contribute to life's (and not just her own life) being fuller, healthier, better. That is what their choices

---

[17] There might be more *total* utility from there being *huge* numbers of people having lives slightly worth living – but is that good? Derek Parfit, in "Personal Identity and Rationality," *Synthese* 53 (1982): 227–241, and *Reasons and Persons* (Oxford: Oxford University Press, 1984), finds these scenarios very disturbing but does not provide a full defense against arguments that such outcomes are not morally objectionable. I present my arguments to the contrary in the chapter in this book on genetic engineering, concerning the question of whether an act can be harmful when no individual is harmed by it.

amounted to, though they may not have thought of them in quite those terms.

Although Abigail and Bernice both made decisions that were not based entirely on their own self-interest, it also would be fair to say that through their decisions, they each shaped what their interests were to be in the future. In our decisions we do more than shape, partially, what happens to us. We shape (still partially) who we are, what our values are, what is good for us, and what we become. Out of various possibilities we develop some and ignore or repress others, a continuous process of creating ourselves. We may make ourselves better, worse, or just different. Abigail and Bernice made decisions about whom and what they were and wanted to be and, on the basis of those decisions, they came to have different interests and satisfactions, becoming somewhat different people from what they had been. They might have made different decisions. Had Abigail decided to continue her pregnancy, she would have been ordering her values and priorities differently; perhaps for that differing Abigail, it would have been a decision that was just as suitable for her best interests as the one Abigail did make, though her interests would then have been somewhat different. (Of course we can never be quite sure how well things will work out in practice.) Had Bernice, for her part, decided that her holiday and individual gratifications were more important, then abortion would have been even more in her self-interest. By choosing to go beyond her self-interest, she changed herself and changed her self-interest. Each of these women, though, in reaching her moral decision, reached it on the basis of a wider view than just that of self-interest, general utility, or abstract rights. Each was affirming life. I would regard each woman's choice as being morally acceptable. For each, a conscientious choice to the contrary also might have been morally acceptable and also might have been life affirming.

13

The Gene, Part I

The Mystique

It is only to state the well known and the obvious to remark that mentions of DNA and genes are every bit as central to innumerable contemporary discussions of bioethical issues as DNA and genes are central to life itself. *Gene,* and *DNA* are terms that light up like neon in the modern consciousness. Like neon, they often produce a striking effect without producing much by way of actual illumination. In the minds of a great many people, there is a mixture of information and misinformation about genes and DNA. This has had, and continues to have, a severely distorting influence on many discussions of diverse issues, not least bioethical issues. Difficulties are often further compounded by murky ideas about evolution and natural selection. Matters get all the more confused when we go to consider matters of genetic engineering. Although no one could hope to offer a complete and definitive discussion of such matters, I try to identify and clarify some of the problematic elements in the widely shared assumptions that many of us have about genes and DNA. I point out that many beliefs widely and firmly held about genes are actually incorrect. My intention is that this will lead to a clearer view of some important bioethical issues.

As well as with bioethical issues, genes are connected with some other very contentious issues as well, ranging from the agricultural to the social and political. Some contentious issues, for instance, concern whether there are inherent differences (other than the obvious) between the sexes or between the races (if, indeed, there actually are races). If there are such differences, so what? Extremely contentious issues concern the possibility that genes might affect our behavior, and these issues become all the more explosive when such hypothetical differences are linked with race or gender. To what extent can, or ought, the effect of genes that influence our behavior be modified by our life conditions and experiences? Furthermore, if there are genetic predispositions toward (supposedly) problematic behavior x – violence, substance abuse, schizophrenia, homosexuality, or whatever – to what extent are people responsible for their own behavior? What are society's rights and responsibilities concerning people with such (suppos-edly) problematic genes? These various matters tie in with a multitude of diverse social and ethical issues, a great many of which have a bioethical dimension. Certainly this is so whenever there is any possibility of the way in which people are treated being altered for the worse because other people have knowledge of their genetic makeup. This ties in with questions about how we should treat embryos in response to supposedly problematic genetic factors. Should we provide prenatal therapy? Perform abortion? Make our genetic selection prior to conception? Take some other proactive course? Beyond these, there are further issues that arise when we as a society con-template allowing (or requiring) any alteration in the genetic makeup of human beings, individually or as a species.

More broadly, we must ask what we are to do with a knowledge of genes once we have it (to some level). We may wonder if there is some deep wisdom infused into the human genome by God or by nature with which it would be unwise or immoral for us to interfere. *Natural* is a comforting word, whereas *unnatural* can be scary. Again, there is the question of what it is to be a person and of what our genes or DNA might have to do with our being one. (This too is of possible relevance to the ethics of abortion, and it might perhaps shed some light on the question of just when does a person, if and as distinguished from a body, die.) Perhaps closest to home, the question confronts us, seemingly with increasing insistence, of what our own individual edition of DNA has to do with *whom* and *what* we are. What do our genes *mean*? What *power* do genes or DNA have over us and in our lives? Just what, for that matter, *is* a gene? On the one hand, DNA or genes often seem to be cast in a role similar to that traditionally assigned to the soul, though appearing in secular and more material form. They are thought to have meaning and purpose, and somehow to encapsulate who and what we are. On the other hand – or maybe it is the same hand – genes often seem to be thought of as controlling us, mind and body, in what would amount to some form of biological determinism. Like the soul, genes seem to be in league with good or with evil, with our fate in the balance.

Selection and Evolution

To start with, let us note a few points about evolution, which is presumably the process by means of which our human genes came about. Back in the days before we knew anything about DNA, when there was only the most vague of ideas about how heritable traits were carried from one generation to the next, the concept of *selection* even then caused us immense difficulties. In *The Origin of Species*, Charles Darwin proposed that heritable traits tend to become more or less widespread in a population, or to drop out entirely, accordingly, as they help or hinder the beings whose traits they are as they struggle to survive and reproduce. Chance in its many forms may and does intervene, and there are no guarantees, but those heritable traits that give their possessors some competitive advantage will have a better chance of increasing their incidence within a population. Novel traits may become established; unsuccessful ones may be eliminated. Over long periods of time, this *natural selection* has the effect of altering the characteristics of succeeding generations, with more adaptive species eventually developing. A great many people have wondered whether in conjunction with natural selection there might be natural goals or natural purposes of some sort, implementing some sort of natural values. What implications might that have for us? This is a question that remains of great concern to many people.

As we humans practice it, selection revolves around goals and purposes. Despite the occasional coin flip, when we select one thing or one course of action over another, this is characteristically because we prefer some outcomes to others. Certainly this includes biological outcomes. We have long practiced our own form of selection as we have shaped breeds of animals and plants to better serve human purposes. We did not until recently know how heritable traits were passed on to offspring (though we told ourselves some imaginative and wonderful stories about how they were passed on, stories about good or bad blood, or Johnson blood, or whatever). Nonetheless, we did realize that certain traits were heritable, and we purposefully selected plants and animals (and marital partners, for that matter) for reproduction accordingly. Even though things did not always go according to plan, we did in fact make enormous changes in living beings, adapting them to suit our human advantage.

Many people have been inclined to suppose that natural selection takes place in accordance with natural criteria that somehow distinguish one alternative as being *better* than another. *Evolution* has been widely understood as change that is, moreover, progress toward something better. "Survival of the fittest" proclaimed Herbert Spencer, in a turn of phrase frequently but wrongly attributed to Darwin.[1] According to this conception, defective organisms are eliminated, whereas those with superior qualities live on and reproduce. Species are improved and new ones are developed. Evolution started with slime and ended with us, so obviously it is going in the right direction. It is a comforting thought that there is a law of perpetual progress, a force that leads things to work out for the best in the end. Here we evidently have a biological cognate of divine providence or of something like Aristotle's final cause acting toward which nature does nothing in vain. Indeed, it need not be secular: Many have seen in evolution the hand of a purposeful God implementing intelligent design.

---

[1] Herbert Spencer, "A Theory of Population, Deduced from the General Law of Animal Fertility," *Westminster Review* 57 (1852): 468–501. This was seven years before the publication of *The Origin of Species*, at a time when Darwin was best known for his work on barnacles.

Nonetheless, as Darwin himself carefully explicated, evolution through natural selection can give the appearance of design without design actually being required. According to Darwinian theory, natural selection proceeds on the basis of the extent to which genes are replicated into further generations. This process does not require or create merit in any broader or more evaluative sense. Evolution does not necessarily involve progressive improvement, certainly not in any comfortingly robust sense. To the extent that genes for being faster, smarter, or less susceptible to infection get proliferated more widely, to that same extent those genes are naturally selected. To the extent that genes for qualities that strike us as less admirable get proliferated, to just that extent they too are naturally selected – admirability in any greater sense having nothing to do with it. Cockroach genes evidently proliferate at least as well as human genes (and better than those of Neanderthal humans). The fact is that evolution often takes directions that evidently favor no value beyond that of gene survival, and that may even seem quite degenerate. About one-third of living species have evolved as parasites, for instance, with adaptations suiting them to such a role. E. O. Wilson explains how some ant species parasitize other ant species.[2] In advanced cases of parasitism, the parasitic species loses those traits superfluous to successful parasitism. The size of the brain may diminish and the species may lose the physical or behavioral ability to perform many tasks (such as the individual's feeding itself). The worker caste may dwindle or be lost entirely. This is a matter of genes for larger brains, and so on, being selected against. What the species develops and retains is the capacity to parasitize its host, thereby enhancing the likelihood of its naturally selected set of genes being further replicated. Otherwise, there is a lessening or total loss of traits that would contribute to the makeup of a functional ant.

It is worth noting that not only have genes no imperative to improve their species, they also have no imperative to assist the organism whose genes they are to survive. Survival of the individual and improvement of the species do not matter except insofar as they lend themselves to the replication of the genes (either directly by reproduction or indirectly by the organism's being of assistance to related organisms bearing a high proportion of the same genes). Otherwise, so far as evolution, natural selection, or any genetic imperatives go, neither the survival, much less the welfare, of the organism nor the improvement of the species is at all relevant. In many invertebrate species, for instance, the female eats the male after (or even during) copulation. His genes are passed on, and the protein from his body may contribute to the development of the eggs, which is to his posthumous genetic

---

[2] Bert Hölldobler and E. O. Wilson, *The Ants* (Cambridge, MA: Harvard University Press), 1990).

advantage, but the well-being of the father itself is totally irrelevant. Social insects provide further striking examples of the irrelevance to the gene of anything beyond genetic replication. It is not out of self-interest (or a sense of duty, or an avoidance of shame) that the ant, bee, or termite gives its life to defend the colony. The defender does not have goals that it pursues or ideals that it reveres. Nor does its DNA. The insect responds to stimuli in specific ways, as determined by its genes. It was not out of any concern for the individual that those genes were naturally selected but only in consequence of such responses on the part of such organisms being conducive to the replication of those same genes (through the very closely interrelated colony as a whole). Apart from genetic proliferation, natural selection has no imperative. Some people have remarked that an organism is DNA's way of producing more DNA (and that is certainly not an *intention* on the part of the DNA). In this connection, we might well note that some of our DNA, the so-called junk DNA, produces no bodily effects of any sort whatsoever. It has just developed the capacity to freeload, getting itself reproduced along with the rest of our DNA.

Not only does natural selection not necessarily favor individual survival, it also does not necessarily favor survival of the species. To the extent that genes are able to proliferate into succeeding generations, to that extent they tend to become more frequent and predominate in a population. This remains true even if the genes are detrimental to the long-term prospects of the species. The Irish deer and the Argos pheasant are notable cases in point. In each case, the females select males for breeding, doing so on the basis of secondary sexual characteristics. In many species, including to some degree our own, individuals make sexual selection on the basis of secondary sexual characteristics (e.g., male strength and female breasts). However, in the cases of the Irish deer and Argos pheasant, the traits selected for, size of antlers and length of secondary wing feathers, respectively, make it more difficult for those that have those traits to survive in a dangerous world. Such long display feathers make evasion and flight far more difficult, and antlers seven feet wide are less than useless when trying to run through the forest. Nonetheless, it is in the interest of the female to ally her own genes with the problematic genes. This is so because her own male offspring would then have a better chance of having offspring. This is to say that it is in her genetic interests to select for genes that are detrimental to the long-term prospects of her own species, just as it is in his genetic interests to have them. The Irish deer has become totally extinct and the Argos pheasant survive mostly in captivity. If it were true to say that genes had purposes, or intentions, or were selfish – none of which is actually true or perhaps even meaningful – then it would be true to say that genes can be quite remarkably stupid. So much for the supposed wisdom of genes. Now let us ask more directly what DNA and genes are.

What Are Genes?

In asking what DNA and genes are, I think it best to start with what they are materially. Then we might better be able to explore some of their significance and implications. The term *gene* (from the Greek, meaning *birth*) was introduced as a name for units of heredity. That there were some such units of heredity seemed evident as some traits are undeniably hereditary. Early on, though, no one knew just what those units were and little was known of how they functioned. Eventually we learned that they evidently had something to do with chromosomes – those long wiggly strands that are found in the nuclei of cells and that divide and recombine during reproduction – but little was known of their composition or operation. In the mid-twentieth century, it was determined that the material of genes was *deoxyribonucleic acid,* or *DNA* for short, which is a substance found in chromosomes. At the time, it was not known in detail just what deoxyribonucleic acid was or how it was structured. In 1953, Crick and Watson discovered DNA's structure. It comes in parallel strands, with interconnecting links, which take the form of the now-famous double helix. Those strands are composed of subunits, *nucleotides,* which are combinations of atoms. There are four varieties of nucleotides, that is, adenine, cytosine, guanine, and thymine, referred to as *A, C, G,* and *T.* These occur in sequences of differing elements and differing lengths.

What a gene, an assemblage of nucleotides, actually *does* is to start a chemical reaction leading to the production of a particular sort of protein. Differing proteins result from differing combinations of nucleotides. However, a particular gene can trigger the production of its characteristic protein only in the presence of a suitable variety of other chemicals, including ribonucleic acid (see the subsequent text)[3] and appropriate chemical building blocks. Without these, nothing happens. With them, something might happen. The resulting protein, in the presence of many other things, may produce a particular bodily result. However, what happens, the protein or the bodily result, is not the *intended meaning* of the gene, any more than the intended meaning of the flame of a cigarette lighter is cancer or a loud pop (depending on whether it is applied to a cigarette or to the fuse of a fire cracker). In themselves, they do not have intended meanings.

A complication is that though we know why firecrackers pop, and though we have at least a fair idea of why smoking leads to cancer, we usually have no more than a foggy idea (if that) of the chemical pathways by which a gene does its work. At best, we know that a certain sequence of nucleotides goes into some chemical black box (containing unknown causal machinery) and out the other end (usually) comes a particular result. We discover this

[3] Ribonucleic acid functions to copy sections of DNA and so help carry the replication process further.

backward when we discover it at all. When there is Huntington's disease, there is always a particular sort of sequence of nucleotides, so they must be an essential part of the chemical processes leading to Huntington's disease. And just what chemical processes are those? It will be a long time before we can even start to answer questions like that. In the meantime, we know that the sequence CAG repeated an excessive number of times on chromosome 4 leads to Huntington's disease, just as primitive fisherfolk knew that a particular phase of the moon means a particular sort of tide even though they did not know how it came about. In some stories the moon god intends certain results. In other stories, genes embody some intended purpose.

It is worth noting that we routinely and quite correctly use attributions of purpose to span causal black boxes. The last time you turned the page of a book, what caused the page to turn? The short and accurate answer (barring peculiar exceptions) is that your fingers did it in response to your intention that they do so. Nonetheless, you probably do not have a much better idea than I do of the causal pathway involving brain cells, nerves, chemicals, and muscles. Still, the short answer is correct. Not only did your decision *mean* the turn of the page much as red skies at night are likely to mean fair weather, it is a further and essential part of the story that you *meant* for the page to turn, that you did it on purpose (even if it was only a semiconscious purpose). In presumed parallel, it is easy (but wrong) to go on to think of genes as not just meaning in the sense of portending (à la lunar phase) a particular outcome, but as being the encapsulation of some sort of an intention that it come about.

Explanations of DNA and genes, in popular expositions, frequently describe A, C, G, and T as being characters in a four-letter alphabet. Different instances of DNA, of course, have differing combinations of A, C, G, and T. These "letters" are said to be formed together into three-letter "words," with genes being "sentences" of such words. These, in turn, are said to constitute a blueprint or a set of instructions by means of which our body is told how to develop and what form to take. (Have blue eyes. Be susceptible to schizophrenia.) We are said to have genes *for* various traits, good, bad, or indifferent. As an expository device, such a scheme of explanation can be very useful. However, it is only a metaphor, and a very dangerous one, for here there is no language in the sense in which human languages are languages, and there is no meaning intended in the occurrence of a gene. Taking the analogy literally can be profoundly misleading, encouraging us to draw conclusions that are quite unwarranted about meaning, purpose, or intention in connection with genes. Many people, scientists and philosophers among them, have in fact been profoundly misled.

A gene does, in a sense, convey information. The relevant sense of *information* is that mentioned earlier in connection with Schrödinger's discussion of the minimal requirements for life to occur. It concerns complexity. A gene is a particular differentiation in DNA and (in suitable circumstances) has the effect of conveying into further media a complexity and differentiation without which, as Schrödinger noted, life would be quite impossible. The ability to preserve a particular complexity and differentiation and convey it onward is a necessary condition for life, and it is also a necessary condition for language. Both life and language employ complexity, and an ability to preserve it intact, to maintain continuity of their required sorts and, indeed, to bring about their particular sorts of result. Nevertheless, life and language each requires more than the preservation and conveyance of complexity, and they require different things. Whereas genes convey complexity, and thus information in the specified sense, they are not words, sentences, or instructions. In no literal way do genes express purpose, intention, or meaning; nor do they depend for their effect on systems that are oriented in such terms.

Genes are able to convey an immense amount of complexity and differentiation. Our genome has gradually evolved to become a highly sophisticated information storage, processing, and retrieval system. It is central to the workings of our life, and when it functions well, life can go well. When it is dysfunctional, our lives suffer. There are any number of possible combinations of A, C, G, and T, and different sequences may bring about different results. Seemingly minor differences in DNA can bring about very major differences in outcome. Out of many thousand nucleotides, one single T in place of the usual A in a particular gene connected with hemoglobin can result in sickle-cell anemia. A sequence of too many CAGs at another place leads to Huntington's disease. (If no CAGs at all occur at that place, then the outcome is Wolf-Hirschhorn syndrome, which is invariably fatal quite early. Ironically, no one seems very sure just what the CAG assembly does when it is all in order.) An anomalous gene on chromosome 7 leads to cystic fibrosis. Other outcomes may stem from multiple genes, occurring in combination. Some outcomes may or may not occur at all, depending on nongenetic factors that may range from environmental influences to personal choice.

More and different "information" is required for a living being to come about than is contained in all of its many genes. Vital roles are played by RNA (ribonucleic acid). This is a simpler chemical that is chemically akin to DNA, to which it may have been an evolutionary precursor. One of its functions is to provide so-called messenger RNA that copies the structure of the genes and carries it into onward trains of chemical events. To do this "transcribing," it must have its own chemical structure of the appropriate sort. Of course, the appropriate additional chemical compounds must be present for the transcription to happen. In the absence of any of those things, the sequence of chemical events would fizzle out. Of course the DNA will carry the instructions for making the RNA to "read" it, but we need to have the RNA first in order to make use of that. It is not quite a matter of the chicken and the egg, but it takes more than a set of genes to make a chick. The DNA is obviously a vital link in the causal chain, but the information needed to create a human or other living being is scattered through the entire system.

Suppose that through some bizarre chain of events, a well-thumbed copy of *Hamlet* were to come into the possession of some highly intelligent extra-galactic civilization that otherwise knew nothing of us or our planet. They would no doubt conclude that it was an artifact of some more-or-less intelligent life form – but would they be able to read it? Theoretically, there are an infinite number of languages into which that collection of marks could be translated. Moreover, there would be more than one way in which those marks could be rendered into whatever language they use. However, those beings would not have the cultural presumptions we take to *Hamlet*, nor would they have the equivalent concepts. In the absence of further information about the earth and its inhabitants, and our customs and beliefs, they would not be able to acquire the appropriate concepts, even if they had intellects of the sort that could entertain them. Lacking the conceptual apparatus, they would be unable to distinguish *Hamlet* from a handbook on motorcycle maintenance.

Perhaps their forensic scientists would be able to help out by carefully examining the human thumbprints on the manuscript. They might be able to find interesting traces of biochemicals, enabling them to draw some conclusions about our form of life. They might even chance to find some dried skin cells and deduce that the bizarre double-helix molecules found in the middle of the cells are part of some sort of an information storage and retrieval system used in the construction and maintenance of (what is to them) alien life. They might then stand back in awe (if they are the sort of beings who might do such things) and think, "Gee, if we only knew how to read and follow the recipe, we would be able to make a real space alien!" Alas, lacking a correct key, they would not be able to know which, of an infinitude of ways of reading the DNA, would be a right way. The information needed to build a human being is not entirely to be found in the DNA. It is encrypted through a whole living system.[4]

* * * * *

I believe that it would be useful at this point to offer a few brief remarks about *real* words, and about meaning. It is worth noting that even those very different things that actually are words do not have any meaning in their own right. To put it in capsule form, words do not mean. Rather, people

---

4 For more on these points, see Daniel C. Dennett, *Darwin's Dangerous Idea: Evolution and the Meanings of Life* (New York: Simon & Schuster, 1995), pp. 113–118. Dennett points out that even had we an intact set of dinosaur DNA, we would be unable to create Jurassic Park because we would be unable to "read" it.

mean, using words as tools for organizing and indicating what they mean. In broad terms we can say that a word is used as a sign for something, used within the general framework of some language system and intended, by some language user doing the intending, as a device for indicating her or his intended meaning. The word *rain* is a sign for rain, being conventionally correlated with what it is to be about. Other words might equally well have been used, and in other languages they are. In contrast, a dark nimbus cloud is not a sign *for* rain. It may be an important part of a causal chain leading to rain. For the alert observer of weather, it is a sign *of* rain, but it is not a sign *for* rain. We might say that the cloud "means" rain – but this is meaning in a radically different sense from that in which words have meaning. There is no language user (except for one who uses Indian smoke signals) for whom clouds function as words. A gene has significance in the manner of rain clouds and not in the manner of words. A sufficiently keen and knowledgeable observer may see in a particular set of genes one or more signs of blue eyes to come or of an impending onset of Huntington's disease, but the gene is not a word. Like the cloud, it is part of a causal chain that may, depending on many other factors, result in a particular effect. There is no language user, and the gene expresses no intended meaning.

A Bad Inheritance

Genes or, more accurately, ideas about them have been involved in some of the nastiest events of the twentieth century and in some of the most bitter and acrimonious of controversies. They also have been central to some of the most futile controversies. What is it that best explains what we are, *nature* or *nurture*? On the one hand, it is often suggested, our human character is principally determined by our human genetic makeup, stemming from our long evolutionary background and augmented by such particular genes as we have acquired from various ancestors. Our human DNA gives us human nature and our own particular edition of it gives us our own individual nature. If we are programmed by nature for Huntington's disease, musical genius, or territorial aggression, then that's the way things are and that's that. This way of putting it is perhaps a bit of a caricature, but such caricatures (and worse) have been accepted and asserted in literal earnest. They also have been put to uses that are, to say the least, problematic – and sometimes downright evil.

There are antecedents to these events and controversies that go back to far distant years. They spring from a time well before anything was known of the existence of genes, and following the discovery that there are genes of some sort, the controversies and associated events were all too often fueled, muddled, and emotionally intensified by half-baked ideas about genes and what they are. We might recall the eugenics movement of the early part of the past century when restrictive laws about marriage and immigration were often coupled with enforced sterilizations. Even worse is when groups of people are stereotyped as naturally having particular inherent characteristics and are then treated in accordance with those stereotypes. These are almost invariably positive in our own case, and often negative when concerning others. During one regrettable era in Central Europe, this went well beyond sterilization to mass murder on an industrial scale. Nor are such events something we have entirely put behind us. Improper and sometimes downright vicious actions based on ethnic stereotyping have often occurred since, and to this must be added the injustices of gender stereotyping. An additional worry is that one's favored socioeconomic ideas (be they in support of the status quo or some nasty innovation) can be defended on the grounds that it is only the natural way of things. We humans, or our group, or some other group, are just a certain way because of our or their natural makeup.

The conception of a "nature red in tooth and claw"[5] was and is still being used to support laissez-faire capitalism, entrenched elites, and minimalist government (or, at least, governments that provide minimal benefits for the governed). According to Spencer,

... the poverty of the incapable, the distresses that come upon the imprudent, the starvations of the ideal ... are the decrees of a large, far-seeing benevolence ... under the natural order of things society is constantly excreting its unhealthy, imbecile, slow, vacillating, faithless members, ... (Herbert Spencer, as cited in Coser)[6]

This was also written prior to Darwin's publication of *The Origin of Species*. One is reminded of Adam Smith's Invisible Hand (from *The Theory of Moral Sentiments*, written in 1759) whereby the pursuit of individual self-interest in the capitalist free market is supposed to lead to the general good. Along similar lines, the megacapitalist, monopolist, and ruthless competitor John D. Rockefeller once explained to a Sunday school class that

The growth of a large business is merely a survival of the fittest.... The American Beauty Rose can be produced in the splendour and fragrance which bring cheer to its beholder only by sacrificing the early buds which grow up around it. This is not an evil tendency in business. It is merely the working out of a law of nature and a law of God. (John D. Rockefeller, as reported in Hofstadter)[7]

---

[5] This turn of phrase is frequently associated with Darwin and sometimes attributed to him. Actually, it is from Tennyson's poem *In Memoriam*, canto 56 (1850), which, like Spencer's "survival of the fittest," predated *The Origin of Species*. The poet was reflecting a view of nature that was common in his own industrial society. Darwin himself was aware that in evolution, as in life generally, there is mutual benefit as well as exploitation.

[6] Lewis A. Coser, *Masters of Sociological Thought: Ideas in Historical and Social Context* (New York: Harcourt Brace Jovanovich, 1977), pp. 99–101.

[7] Richard Hofstadter, *Social Darwinism in American Thought* (1860–1915) (Philadelphia: University of Pennsylvania Press, 1944). Reprinted 1992 (Boston: Beacon Press).

More recently we have been treated to popular expositions suggesting that our evolutionary success is at least in large part due to our nature and genetic background as ruthless predators – "Man, the Killer Ape" and all that sort of thing. In some part, this has been further fueled by misunderstandings of Richard Dawkins' metaphor of the selfish gene.[8] In his *The Selfish Gene*, Dawkins uses the metaphor to convey his point that genes do not act so as to benefit those organisms whose genes they are, nor to benefit anything else. Indeed, genes do not even act to benefit themselves or for any purpose whatsoever. They have whatever effect they might have, and those genes tend to proliferate, which happen to bring about results conducive to their own proliferation. However, Dawkins' explanatory metaphor has often been misinterpreted as indicating that these molecular components are literally selfish, and perhaps even that we have a gene *for* selfishness. These suggestions seem rather repugnant as well as unfounded, but they have been taken as providing support for a ruthlessly competitive dog-eat-dog view of the world. There may be, in consequence, a strong and morally plausible impulse in response to throw up our hands in horror and reject all hereditarian views. We might note, though, that genes do not *demand* selfish behavior on our part. Indeed, genes might be favorably selected for by environmental circumstances that favor social behavior and altruism, and even love. All it would require is that populations that have those genes proliferate themselves and, therefore, their genes, better than do populations that lack such a gene. Social wolves do better than lone wolves.

Instead of the view that we are inherently selfish and determined by our genes, a more attractive alternative would seem to be that we are what we are because of the social and other environmental conditions that made us that way. These circumstances can be changed for the better. The trouble here, as so often with either–or conceptions, is that the opposite can be just as bad. We might easily point to programs of social determinism as conducted in the old Soviet Union or East Germany. There, too, evil flourished under the banners of ideology. Rather than choosing sides in some sort of nature-versus-nurture dilemma, we would do far better to keep our heads and decline any such choice. It is not a matter of one thing *or* the other; nor is it a matter of two different things in some proportion. As we have seen, genes are what they are and do what they do only in an environmental context, and variation in either genes or environment may well lead to different results. Always it is nature *and* nurture, heredity *in* environment, and there is a very wide range of cases, from those wherein the hereditary components are quite rigid to those wherein they are highly flexible to those wherein they are almost infinitely malleable. It is a matter of cases

[8] Richard Dawkins, *The Selfish Gene* (Oxford: Oxford University Press, 1989; originally published 1976).

and a matter of degree. Toward one far end of the spectrum, we locate ants and their instinctive behavior, though even with them, different particular circumstances trigger different genetically programmed responses (for example, eat, dig, fight, flee, and so on). Environmental factors even determine whether a particular egg develops into a worker or a queen. Yet we can fairly say that ants mindlessly adopt their role in life and perform their various tasks as determined by genes and triggering stimuli. We do well to reject with scorn any suggestion that we are so much prisoners and puppets of our genes as that. Theirs is not our own end of the spectrum.

But are we on the same spectrum with ants at all? Before we commit ourselves to an answer to that, let us first note that there are many instances in which genetic influences are not nearly as hard-wired as they are in ants. There are ranges of intermediate alternatives. Coyotes, for example, are highly intelligent animals. They make decisions, learn, adapt to circumstances, and have individual personalities. Different packs of coyotes behave differently. Nevertheless, their ways of doing things are recognizably canine and, more specifically, recognizably coyote-like. Parallel things could be said about lions. A pride of lions will have feline and leonine behavioral patterns characteristically and mostly predictably different from those of any coyotes. In a more subtle way, their behavior will differ from that of other lions. Animals of both of those sorts are adapting the expression of their genetic makeup as they shape their own lives in their environment.

Clearly, if our genes affect our behavior at all, we humans, with our greater intelligence, greater awareness of the world, and greater cultural resources, are even further from being in ant-like bondage to genetic imperatives. Humans deliberate and choose, selecting, refining, or rejecting goals and means to them. We think about how we react to situations, about how to interact with other people, and we assess and often choose to alter how we feel about things. It seems quite repugnant to think that genes can prevent us from controlling and altering our decisions, institutions, and ways of doing things. Many times, undeniably, ignorance and poverty have been overcome by education and opportunity, and even genetically caused physical conditions such as phenylketonuria have successfully been countered by diet and medication. Again, conducive circumstances, as well as will and talent, contributed to Mozart's career. He might possibly not have gotten nearly so far had he been born into deprived and very unmusical surroundings.

Genes gave Mozart musical abilities, and they gave nearly all of us minds and bodies capable of thought and speech, and of doing various other things, but have they any more influence on our behavior than that? Whether they do have more influence is still a matter of bitter dispute, though the trend has been strongly toward the affirmative, which I certainly believe is the correct answer. However, I would observe that any such dispute is substantially beside the point. If genes do influence our behavior, we still have an immense amount of flexibility in how we respond. We can make decisions, order our values, and shape our societies and institutions. If our genes do push us in certain directions, it is not absolutely mandatory that we comply; nor is there necessarily any "wisdom" in "Mother Nature" indicating that it is preferable for us that we do comply. We need not be like the Irish deer. Moreover, conditions that led genes to proliferate, or not to proliferate, may no longer be relevant. A striking, or possibly amusing, example concerns our toilet habits. As we are the descendants of free-swinging apes who could let things fall where they might, toilet training does not come nearly as easily to human infants as it does to puppies and kittens. The latter get the idea fairly early and comparatively easily and, after that, barring the odd accident, they are not much trouble in that regard. Human infants require a great deal of effort in training them to overcome their natural inclinations. Nonetheless, clearly it is possible for us to overcome our genes and preferable that we should do so.[9]

Aggression may well be a case in point of a tendency in need of tempering. Certainly aggression is not something to be allowed to go out of control. This is so even if, as many believe, humans (or possibly but improbably only male humans) have innate aggressive tendencies. Aggression is still dangerous and not just physically. Even if it comes naturally, aggression, like our toilet habits, has to be controlled. Perhaps it can be turned into harmless channels (e.g., sports) or even into useful ones (e.g., competitive striving for creative excellence). If we do have such inclinations, we cannot afford to deny their existence on the ideological grounds that we ought not and therefore just *cannot* have such natural features. Nor can we afford to shrug off the thought of curtailing them, on the grounds that they are *natural*. Inclinations that might (arguably) have served to protect our ancestral clans during the early hours of the Pleistocene era can be too destructive, individually and collectively, to be allowed to go unchecked under modern conditions and with modern technologies. Carrying the point further, suppose it were true, as has sometimes been suggested, that in general men, more than women, have innate tendencies toward aggression and domination, and that women more than men tend to be compliant. This would not justify forcing those who did not fit these stereotypes to comply. These stereotypes are harmful to men and women both. Even if, contrary to fact, all men and all women did fit those stereotypes, injustice would still be injustice and could and ought to be guarded against. We would be foolish indeed, and most probably harmful to others and ourselves, were we to acquiesce in the presumption that hereditary influences are or ought to be destiny. If, and it is still an *if*, aggressive inclinations, like diabetes, have genetic roots, they are no

---

[9] I owe this example to one of the great many authors who wrote about sociobiology, but I cannot now recall or rediscover who it was.

more than diabetes to be accepted as being good or inevitable because they are natural. As with diabetes (not to mention our bowel movements), we should take appropriate steps to control their manifestation and ameliorate their impact. Understanding those genetic roots, and the causal pathways through which they might come to be manifested, could help us to achieve control.

Our concern here is with bioethical issues rather than wider sociopolitical issues. Yet here again the truth is the same: Our genetic inheritance is not necessarily our destiny. In some instances, certainly, we have not (yet) found any means to dodge the genetic bullet. There is no way known to rescue those with Huntington's genetic disorder from Huntington's disease. Such cases are very determinate. Sometimes from our genetic inheritance there is a little less determinacy, or a lot less, or virtually none. I have had the disturbing experience of being in contact with a young person whom I was told was about twenty years old. What I found disturbing was not the contact but seeing what had happened to her. At first appearance, she looked about six, though from closer range her face looked older, in a disagreeable way. Her mental capacities were far less than those of a normal six-year-old child, and her body was as poorly coordinated as it was poorly proportioned. This unfortunate girl had phenylketonuria (PKU). On her twelfth chromosome she had, one from each parent, a matched pair of defective genes. The non-defective genes she should have had would have led to the production of phenylalanine hydroxylase. This is an enzyme that governs the metabolism of phenylalanine, which is needed for growth. Without the enzyme, phenylalanine builds up in the body to severely toxic levels, resulting in mental retardation, organ damage, and misshapen posture. This poor girl was doubly unfortunate. In addition to her genetic misfortune, she was unlucky in that her condition had not been diagnosed in time. Had it been, proper treatment and diet (one very low in phenylalanine) would have allowed her to live an approximately normal life with her full capacities. A differing environment would have led to a very different and far better outcome.

There are other outcomes of genetic influences that are much less determinate. Asthma is a case in point. More properly we should say that it is a matter of several cases, for there seem to be not only many sorts of asthma but also many genes involved. Genes (or rather their expressions in the body) may in turn interact with various possible antagonists that might be present in the environment in variable degree and under varying circumstances. How people respond to antagonists is a factor, and another factor can be the *absence* of antagonists. There can evidently be such a thing as being *too* hygienic. It seems that children reared in an environment that is too clean may not have their immune systems sufficiently stimulated and so may develop susceptibilities later in life. We must say then that genes are only part of the stories concerned with various outcomes. Not only do genes not contain any deep primordial wisdom, they also are not chemical transcriptions of our soul and they are not little nuggets of inevitable destiny. Even the Huntington's gene can do its dirty work only as part of an encompassing system, and it might conceivably be balked. Some day, one would hope, we shall learn how to do that.

14

The Gene, Part II

Manipulation

Beyond doubt, we could improve the human condition by forestalling or ameliorating the effects of problematic genes. Might it also be a good strategy to entirely replace defective genes with better ones? The prospect of genetic modification, *genetic engineering*, is one that is becoming more and more inescapable. Nevertheless, it is not entirely clear just which things would come under this wide and ill-defined heading. Neither are the central ethical issues sufficiently clear or adequately addressed. There are few topics that lead to more widespread debate or that stir more intense feelings. There is fear of our creating (or becoming) monsters, of maniacs cloning multiple copies of themselves, of our disrupting the very fabric of human life, or of our turning loose new organisms, unnatural and genetically modified, to destroy ourselves or our biosphere. What else, we might wonder, might there be to fear? However, there is hope that advances in genetic modification might lead to means for alleviating or preventing some of the most horrific adversities we humans face. Perhaps we can find ways to improve our health and the health and makeup of our children or to provide nutritious food to feed malnourished billions. We are fearfully and hopefully aware that we are prying open the unknown and that, in whatever form, important consequences are bound to ensue.

As with previous matters, I cannot offer a general formula for resolving all ethical problems that might arise in connection with genetic engineering. Indeed, I believe that only a fool or a charlatan would promise that. This is due both to the expanding width and amorphous nature of the subject matter and to the limitations of formulae. Nonetheless, I offer the general considerations we have canvassed as allowing us to develop useful insights for dealing with such matters. Among other points, I argue that those approaches to ethics that concentrate on living things rather than on living processes, and that moreover focus exclusively on discrete individuals, are at a disadvantage in dealing with the ethics of genetic engineering. They should be supplemented with broader conceptions, centering on the interests of living processes. I go on to suggest that we need to take a broader look at the nature of humanity.

One difficulty in dealing with the moral issues of genetic engineering is the now-familiar one that there is a vast array of cases, ranging from those in which genetic modification appears to be morally appropriate and highly desirable to those in which the modification would appear to be utterly evil. Again, we can find a whole rainbow spectrum of intermediate cases with no clear place to draw a definitive moral line. Indeed, we can find spectra, for there is more than one spectrum of possibilities. A frequent and understandable reaction is to just throw up one's hands in horror and shout *No!* How dare we interfere with the essence of life or of human life? How dare we play God? By presuming to do what humankind was not meant to do, we would run the risk of opening a Pandora's box of vast, incalculable, and uncontrollable evils. As a prudential warning that cautions us to be wary of unforeseen consequences, there is undoubtedly some merit in this response.

Even so, we might begin by asking whether it is *intrinsically* wrong to genetically modify a living organism. It is all too easy to envision maniacs turning killer plagues loose on the world, or some such thing, but does the enormity of such horrors ensue from some inherent wrongness in genetic modification in itself? We can just as well point to instances of genetic modification that are evidently beneficent rather than evil. For instance, vats of genetically modified bacteria in pharmaceutical plants produce huge amounts of insulin for the treatment of diabetes. Other genetically modified bacteria produce other life-saving products. Unless, for no clear reason, all forms of genetic modification are always to be taboo, or unless we take a very extreme view about the rights of bacteria, there would seem to be nothing objectionable about the production of insulin and other valuable products by such means. It is the use of genetic technology to bring about bad consequences that we would have to guard against.

Is there a moral problem with inserting genes from human beings into the pharmaceutical-producing bacteria? Extremely misinformed people often seem to have some sort of an occult view according to which a human gene somehow encapsulates a portion of the human soul. Taken to its logical conclusion, this suggests that human insulin genes ought not to be inserted into bacteria or otherwise given nonhuman treatment. Note, though, that we share more than 98 percent of our genes with chimpanzees and various other percentages with various other animals and even with plants. A particular sequence of atoms might be a human gene, a chimpanzee gene, or any of a number of other things, but on its own, it is not anything in particular – not even a gene. Genes can function only as genes, can *be* only genes, within a larger encompassing system. They are human genes only when they are part of a human living system. Let us then focus our concentration on what actually is a moral issue, that of whether it can ever be right to modify the genetic makeup of a human system (or to genetically select who is to become a human being). However we might dread potentially slippery slopes, there are some possible instances of genetic modification that would appear to be not only morally acceptable but salutary as well.

Benign Genetic Engineering

Let us start with what would appear to be the most unobjectionable form of genetic engineering, that of selecting out defective genes in vitro prior to conception. It is becoming increasingly possible to identify defective genes and possibly do something about them. For present purposes, let us for now set aside questions of just what is or is not defective and think about genes that clearly are. Huntington's disease and hemophilia are two among many conditions resulting from a genetic defect. In the case of hemophilia, the defective gene occurs on the X chromosome. If the person is a woman, therefore having two X chromosomes, the normal gene on the other X chromosome will keep the defective gene from manifesting itself. That is, the hemophilic gene is *recessive* while the normal gene is *dominant.* (A woman would have to have a hemophilic gene on both of her X chromosomes to have hemophilia, which would be most improbable.) However, men only have one X chromosome, which is paired with a Y chromosome. The latter lacks a gene to override the hemophilic gene. Accordingly, a man may develop hemophilia from a defective gene on his single X chromosome, inherited from his nonhemophilic mother (only one of whose two X chromosomes carries the hemophilic gene). With hemophilia, one is subject to uncontrollable bleeding, which is quite debilitating for the person and often fatal. Huntington's disease, as we will recall, is invariably fatal, though its onset is much later. Nor is there any reason to think that the presence of these genes is of any benefit to humanity as a whole, even under the most irregular of conditions. What interventions might we appropriately allow here? We may well feel apprehensive at this point, for this is the sort of place where slippery slopes often get started.

One point of view might hold that genes were created by God, or by Mother Nature, and that they are intended for some wise purpose beyond our ken with which it would be wrong to interfere. Although this belief cannot be absolutely and definitively falsified, it certainly cannot be verified, and it suggests that we ought also to accept small pox, tetanus, and diphtheria as expressions of superhuman wisdom. Short of going to that extreme, let us assume that, in principle, there is no reason why we ought not to eliminate hemophilia or Huntington's disease if we can do so by acceptable means. There are prospective ways of doing so, by means that would certainly appear unobjectionable, though the means are not yet perfected in practice. One possible way would be to discard any gamete that carried a gene for the condition. Even those who oppose abortion without exception would not have to object to an unfertilized gamete being left to remain so. (As the hemophilic gene is carried only by the woman, only the ova need be screened for that. The Huntington's gene is carried by both males and females but, as it is recessive and so cannot take effect unless it is inherited from both parents, we could prevent Huntington's disease from occurring by screening just the ova. That would save us time and money. However, that could allow some of the offspring to carry the Huntington's gene even though they do not manifest Huntington's disease. We could go a step further, at some additional expense, by screening spermatozoa.)

Tissue Typing for Transplantation: An Early Venture in Genetic Engineering

This sort of screening is still in the future, albeit a rapidly nearing future. Nonetheless, genetic engineering is no longer exclusively a matter of future speculation and abstract controversy. To a point it is already with us. We are doing it when we screen for birth defects such as Down syndrome and abort accordingly. (In some societies, being female is considered a birth defect.) As well as screening against undesirable (at least undesired) characteristics, there is one instance of current genetic engineering that screens out quite healthy prospects that would be unsuitable for external objectives. In this section, we consider some of the central issues that might be raised by such a procedure. Our concern here is with the form of genetic engineering that is put into practice when parents bring about, or attempt to bring about, children intended to be able to fill a specific beneficial role. Here we are not contemplating the creation of highly talented wonder kids (or untalented drudges), or offspring designed to be resistant to environmental hazards or to fill particular occupational roles. Rather, it is a matter of parents trying to bring about a child intended to be a tissue donor for a chronically ill older sibling. It might perhaps be that bone marrow of the right sort is needed for an existing child who would otherwise die. This is the sort of donation McFall needed from Shimp and could not get. To the goal of creating the donor child, embryos are tested in vitro, and only one with a tissue type suitable for donation is selected for implantation in the womb of the mother to be. Other embryos are discarded.

Ethical issues proliferate here. If we are to focus on the moral issues specific to this form of genetic engineering – that of bringing about babies of particular tissue types as potential tissue donors – then we must separate them from the no-less-real moral issues of abortion. The abortion issues are intensified by the fact that in the in vitro procedure, embryonic lives are brought into being intentionally, with the thought that most of them would be left to die. Is this a properly respectful attitude toward life? It does not seem very respectful of the foreshortened embryonic lives – whatever we are to make of that. Alternatively (though not easily), a naturally conceived embryo may be typed in utero and aborted if unsuitable. The parents could then try again. Fewer embryonic lives are lost but, either way, we are faced with the moral issues of abortion. Perhaps in the future we will be able to avoid the abortion issues. Let us suppose that we could somehow inspect ova and sperm separately and introduce them to one another only if they would result in an embryo of the requisite tissue type. Abortion then would not be an issue. What then would be the relevant issues?

The procedure of selecting an embryo for tissue type certainly does respect the life of the older sibling and arguably those of the other (post-natal) members of the family. But are we respecting the special-purpose child to be born? Is this a matter of creating a child designed and condemned to be exploited as a means to an end other than itself? Most assuredly, it would be highly objectionable were the child to be utilized merely as a source of biological components and otherwise treated as a nonperson by the rest of the family. This, however, really seems more than a bit absurd. We have already noted that it is possible to treat a person as both a means *and* an end. Most of us treat other people that way on a daily basis. Let us make the reasonable assumption that the prospective child would be loved for itself, as the elder child is evidently loved. Certainly, it seems very plausible that children in this family are loved and valued highly. The prospective child might even have honored status because of his or her life-saving role. Moreover, let us assume that as with most children, there is no probable reason to think that the child would not have a life worth living. If it is likely to have a life worth living, then its being brought into existence does not injure it.

Once the child is brought into being, neither is it necessarily true that being caused to give a donation would be an injustice to her or him. It might or might not be. The central question is whether the procedure would fail to respect the child as an end in itself. Even if we can be said to create the child – and that is a big if – that does not mean that we own the child or are entitled to do with her or him as we like.[1] Certainly, siblings that are born without genetic aforethought are often called upon to be tissue donors without that being thought morally outrageous and without its having unusually adverse consequences. As with any child, predesigned

---

[1] To be sure, we have here another instance of contingent existence. For the designed child, if it were not born to be a donor, the chances are infinitesimal that it would have come into existence at all. Nor would its nonexistence have been an injury to it. Once born, however, it has the same moral status as any other child and is under no *special* obligation to be a donor. Those who maintain otherwise put me in mind of those who once held that it was acceptable to use plantation-born blacks as slaves, as they were born to it, even though it was wrong to import freeborn blacks from Africa. In Kazuo Ishiguro's *Never Let Me Go* (New York: Knopf, 2005), p. 207, clones who were created and educated to do so give their organs and ultimately their lives willingly because "[a]fter all, it's what we're *supposed* to be doing, isn't it?"

or not, the question – which may have an answer in either the affirmative or the negative – is whether a tissue donation is the appropriate choice in the prevailing circumstances. A heart transplant would obviously be going too far, but it may well be that a lesser donation, such as that of a kidney, would be compatible with the interests of both donor and donee.

Of clear moral concern are the effects of the contemplated procedures on any person, child or adult, who might be affected. If, however improbably it might be, there were effects on society as a whole or on the human race, then they too would be of moral concern. Central to it all are the motivations by which we act in such matters. If we act with love and with respect, we can still make mistakes. We can always make mistakes, whatever we do and whatever we do not do. Nonetheless, if it is done with love and respect, there seems no plausible reason why the procedure of tissue-type selection and tissue donation should be a mistake.[2]

While we are at it, we would do well to note that similar questions arise whenever we contemplate having children. People routinely do have children, and their motivations are not usually subjected to moral scrutiny when they do so, but having children is nonetheless a matter of moral significance and raises moral issues even if they are not addressed or even noticed. People may have children for just about any reason or for no reason at all, and I doubt whether there could be any clear-cut method that determined whether a particular instance of childbearing is more life affirming than life negating. Normally, though, one supposes it is life affirming.[3] One can, however, imagine horror scenarios to the contrary, which might be of at least speculative interest. In some countries, impoverished parents may sell a child into slavery or prostitution in an attempt to relieve the distress of the rest of the family. Perhaps they produce another child or two as a provision against extreme distress. Other parents, of beggar families, may provide a child with a career by blinding or laming it. I find it offensive that such things happen in the world in which I live, and it disgusts me that there exist those who would willingly exploit (or even tolerate) slavery or child prostitution.[4] However, can we entirely blame parents who feel driven to such expedients? Yes, it is all too easy for those of us in the affluent West

---

[2] Love and respect are clearly central to the virtue of life affirmation. Respect must go beyond a punctilious respect for rights and prohibitions and extend to a caring attitude such as that called for by Nel Noddings in *Caring: A Feminine Approach to Ethics and Moral Education* (Berkeley: University of California Press, 1984). With a virtue of life affirmation, we want to care for and nurture (as may be appropriate in the circumstances) life around us.

[3] My father was one of seven children in a farming family that utilized their labor. Nonetheless, they cared for one another greatly, and none appeared to have been wronged by being brought into existence.

[4] Need I add that we would do well to aid people, and societies, to allow them not to be driven to such expedients?

to do so. We might indeed be justified, were the parents' actions primarily self-interested. Perhaps sometimes they are, but we might well doubt whether this is always or even usually the case. It may be that the parents hold the culturally supported conviction that the individual belongs to the family, and that in extremis, the part can be sacrificed for the greater good of the whole. Perhaps it really is the only alternative to ruin for all. Whatever degree of validity there is to such reasoning – and no doubt it usually will be a matter of degree – would be at most the degree to which it rose above crass self-interest. Seemingly far more easily justified and less problematic would be a one-off tissue donation for the older child.

Toward Designer Babies and Other Problems

Also causing alarm bells to ring is the realistic prospect that as technology gets better and less expensive, both of which are happening at a rapid rate, it might be possible for intending parents to become highly selective about which of their own gametes they wish to introduce to each other in the first place. Instead of selective abortion, it would be selective conception. Suppose a married couple with adequate funds goes to an in vitro fertilization lab, where she has several ova harvested and he produces semen containing several million spermatozoa. As well as selecting out anything with a gene for such defects as Huntington's or hemophilia, they might get quite a lot more selective. Perhaps they might decide to select against any spermatozoon with a Y chromosome, as they want to have a little girl. Does society have a right or duty to keep the gender balance from being overly skewed by parental selection? The prospective parents might also want to see to it that she has hair and eyes of preferred colors. The more technology improves, the more detail would become possible. As there would likely be numerous spermatozoa and a few ova available that meet these initial criteria, the couple might screen for additional optional extras or avoid features that they consider unattractive. Complex questions about the public good arise here, going well beyond issues of gender balance. Does society have any rights about which genes become more or less frequent in its gene pool, and who gets to have them? Or is gender and genetic selection the parents' inalienable right? It is widely held that people have a right to have or not have children, as they see fit,[5] and with that would *seem* to go a right to be selective about the conditions under which they would be willing to undertake parenthood. Who has the right to tell people what genes they may or may not select for their parenting?

Past programs of abridging people's reproductive rights have been at best controversial and at worst utterly abhorrent. There would have to be some very strong reason for overriding that presumptive right. The supposed

---

5 Is there truly such a right? What about times of catastrophic overpopulation?

best interests of the prospective child might possibly be such a reason. The supposed best interests of society also might be a reason (perhaps a very bad reason or, at least, a very problematic one). Another consideration is that of whether we would all (not just the privileged) get a fair chance to enhance our children. Such issues as start to emerge here will become all the more pressing when it becomes possible not only for parents to select from among their own genes but also to select from some sort of a catalogue of genes available for implantation. For example, should wealthy people be able to buy as much genetic selection, for and against, as they are willing and able to pay for? Perhaps their children, but not ours, could have very high levels of intelligence plus various other talents and a high level of drive to succeed. Their children would presumably prosper ahead of our own and so in turn would their children – and so on.

The technology for adding and subtracting individual genes from a chromosome is already being developed and, in some instances, its implementation would be unproblematically beneficial. We might, for instance, wish to do something for those many people already born who have hemophilia. The current course of research suggests that it may become possible to treat the illness by employing some means of causing an alternative gene – one that fits into the appropriate spot on the X chromosome but that was nonhemophilic – to replace or override the hemophilic gene. To treat a person with hemophilia would require the development of some means of altering the genetic makeup of many trillions of the body's cells. That obviously would be impossible if we had to treat each cell individually. What we clearly need is some biological means of treating cells on a wholesale basis.

Promising lines of research suggest that this indeed might become possible. The first step, of course, is to locate a copy of the gene with which we want to replace the defective gene. In some cases, this may be far easier said than done. In the case of hemophilia, we would locate the normal alternative to the hemophilic gene on some normal X chromosome we might have handy. The biological means (restriction enzymes) exist to snip the gene out of the X chromosome. The next step would be to insert the gene into a suitable *retrovirus*. A retrovirus, composed of relatively simple RNA molecules, has the ability to cause its genome to be incorporated into the makeup of some suitable host's DNA. When the human host becomes infected with the modified retrovirus, the virus multiplies and goes around inserting the nonhemophilic gene into the patient's genome, curing the person of hemophilia. That is the idea, anyway, though there is some way to go before this can be done in practice. As a safety precaution, the virus has to be disabled so that the modified virus cannot spread through the community. Moreover, a virus may affect only certain tissues or organs, leaving alone the ones we want affected. There are other practical problems. This sort of treatment for hemophilia is still only a distant prospect, yet it is still a real prospect on the horizon. Similarly, and I would stress speculatively, it may someday become possible to treat cancer by tinkering with the genetic makeup of those cells that are reproducing cancerously or to prevent cancer by replacing or overriding genes that tend toward it. There might be similar possibilities for helping people who carry the Huntington's gene. The latter intervention would be a matter of seeing to it that there is just the right number of CAG assemblies in just the right place. I explore some attendant issues later in this chapter. We will certainly come to have to explore them further in practice.

There is an important distinction to be noted here, one that becomes more important as we consider ever more adventurous forms of genetic engineering. This is distinction between *somatic-* (bodily) *cell gene therapy* and *germ-line gene therapy*. If we are altering the genetic makeup of some or all of an individual's bodily cells, as in the aforementioned scenario concerning hemophilia, we are doing the former. If we are making genetic alterations that get forwarded into future generations, we are doing the latter. Somatic therapy that includes genetic alteration of what is or will become the cells of the individual's reproductive system is therefore also germ-line therapy. It is more directly germ-line therapy if we are modifying the gametes (or zygote) prospectively developing into a person. The moral stakes become higher in connection with germ-line therapy, if only because we are potentially affecting a great many more people than we would be in treating the body of one sufferer. Here we would be altering the genetic makeup of every descendent. However, without resorting to obscurantism and obfuscation, it would be hard to find fault with such a procedure in the case of something like hemophilia or Huntington's. If we could also relieve the genetic burden of many existing individuals, then so much the better.

Again, we have started with possibilities that appear morally impeccable. Here too, though, we rapidly come to worrisome issues. The questions just posed about social justice and about the rights of society arise in this context as well. Does society have legitimate rights to decide which genes may or may not be added in to its gene pool or overridden? Ought people be able to buy, or the state to provide, their choice of interventions for their children or for themselves? Conjecture in such matters comes all too easily. My point here is that there is once again a spectrum of cases, one that has no clear dividing point and that will require continuing ethical surveillance. As always, there is the horrible end of the spectrum, with those gruesome science-fiction scenarios about maniacs letting loose on the world diseases that are genetically engineered to affect people with particular sorts of genes, perhaps people in particular ethnic groups. We might encounter ethnic cleansing on a grand scale. Or perhaps the target of psychopaths is *all* humanity. If this were an actual possibility, any research facilitating such outcomes at the very least must be subject to the most strict monitoring and control. Here is a hypothetical quandary: What if research toward targeting cancer genes also lent itself, in some part, to targeting ethnic genes? Any presentable ethic, and not just a life-affirming virtue ethic, would be contrary to genocide and in favor of relieving or preventing cancer. We can all agree on what we want to prevent. The question here is not such a moral issue to be resolved as a practical problem of implementation and avoidance, the very old problem of preventing useful technologies from being put to evil ends.

Now let us turn aside from matters of somatic-cell interventions – be they for therapy or for mass murder, or for whatever other purpose – and concentrate on issues concerning germ-line therapy oriented toward individual humans. Here we find most of the principal issues of bioethics that arise in application to genetic engineering. Suppose that instead of just selecting gametes we start to actively modify them. There are plausible reasons why we might think this an appropriate thing to do. Such procedures are not yet available in routine clinical practice, but no doubt some such procedures will eventually become possible for us in practice. In application to hemophilia, as noted previously, it normally would be possible to select out the defective gene in vitro, without having to resort to genetic modification. In the case of other genetic defects, that might not be possible. Sometimes it is a matter of the afflicted person having a recessive defective gene on each of two paired chromosomes. Huntington's disease would be a case in point. This fatal disease manifests itself in one's middle age after what are normally one's reproductive years. A person subject to the disease though not yet manifesting it, might wish to have children. Unfortunately, any of his sperm or her ova, as the case might be, would have the defective gene. The resulting offspring would not have the disease unless the reproductive cell from the other parent also carried the defective gene. Nevertheless, the offspring would still carry the defective recessive gene. Knowing the potentially devastating effect of the gene, the parents might wish to see to it that the gene was not carried on into later generations.

Let us suppose in particular that we are concerned for a woman who has the Huntington's gene on each of her fourth chromosomes. Therefore, all of her ova carry the gene. She wants to have a child now, when she is twenty. The child will be an adult by the time the woman actually manifests the condition, as inevitably she will do. She and her partner are very concerned not to pass the Huntington's gene on to their offspring. The envisioned line of therapy, again taking place in vitro, would involve snipping out the problematic gene and replacing it with a normal gene (perhaps taken from a normal fourth chromosome in the body of her partner, or from some other gene donor). We are on the verge of being able to do things like that.

Procedurally and morally, we would be going a step further there. Instead of selecting from naturally occurring gametes, choosing one rather than another for reproduction, we are now contemplating the production of gametes whose final composition is artificially constructed (though of naturally occurring genes). Are we starting to go wrong morally? Certainly it would seem morally unproblematic to remove the clearly defective gene from the line of descent in favor of another naturally occurring and far more common gene. In such a scenario nothing alien or novel is added to the human gene pool, and the genes that are promoted are clearly benign. This might set our minds at ease – yet there are interventions answering that description that might well be cause for concern. With increased genetic knowledge and increased technical abilities, for instance, it might well become possible for prospective parents to select from a menu of genes, opting for genes favoring good looks, musical talent, or whatever. Let us assume that it is still not a matter of introducing new genes into the human gene pool but only one of selecting among human genes that already occur naturally. Doing this sort of thing effectively may still be in the future, but it is not so far in the future that we need not give it serious and prompt consideration. Many are keen right now to use such a technology, and many are hard at work trying to develop and provide it. Many are keen to profit financially from it. We do well to ask, now rather than later, whether and in what way anyone would be injured by the implementation of such technology when it does become available (as gradually it must). A further consideration would concern possible attempts to improve the human race by adding genes or combinations of genes that do not occur naturally in the human gene pool. We might think of some plausible improvements. However, what might look good on paper also might work out very poorly in practice or over many generations. Is it just a matter of prospective parents to do as they like so long as they do not injure any person who exists (or perhaps who would exist in any case)?

To attempt to curtail the implementation of genetic engineering would be to carry us onto dangerous ground. For one thing, to effectively curtail its implementation would require us to curtail its development, which would require us to police scientific laboratories, forbidding certain lines of factual enquiry. On top of that, it would require us to exercise increased vigilance over people's reproductive behavior. However, leaving genetic engineering uncontrolled also would carry us onto dangerous ground, with horrible disruptions possible to human lives and to humanity as a whole. We ought not to play God, we will be cautioned – but is it playing God the more to restrict people's reproductive rights or to leave them unfettered? Either way, we have to think about where it all might end. Certainly I am convinced that there is a strong case for caution here. Human history very strongly suggests that we tend to learn to exercise new capabilities sooner than we learn to exercise them wisely and before we learn all of the associated pitfalls. When it comes to something like genetic engineering, it may well be that what we learn the hard way will cost us dearly. Yet still we must ask, who (or what?) stands to be injured by the implementation of such technology? Other questions may follow, but this one is a necessary preliminary.

Whose Interests Are at Stake

Individuals Alone?

The first possibility that comes to mind, of course, is that the resulting child himself or herself might be injured by an injudicious choice of genes or by some clinical procedure that went badly. It would be very wrong for us to run substantial risks of bringing about people who must live bad lives. Much less may we willfully bring about such children, whatever might be our own motivations.[6] It is not inconceivable that some day a child might sue for damages caused by the bungled insertion or poor selection of genes. Suppose, however, that the child were genetically modified in such a way as to have a life that was worth living, but not as good as it would probably have been without the intervention. Arguably, a possible such instance arose in prospect recently when a profoundly deaf couple applied for medical assistance in order to have a profoundly deaf child. I only say that this would have been *arguably* an instance, as the couple and their supporters maintained that being profoundly deaf would actually be of benefit to the child. This was because the parents would be able to relate well to the child and introduce him or her into the special culture of deaf people, who have customs, values, and rewards all of their own. The couple was refused medical assistance on the grounds that this would be against the best interests of the prospective child. Let us leave that assessment as a moot point. Rather, let us ask about some hypothetical case wherein, we can agree, the child would be disadvantaged. Even so, it is possible to argue that no one would be injured by the intervention. The prospective parents might well maintain that the choice is not whether the child has or has not a particular condition. If they cannot have the child they want, they won't have any child at all. They would not be injuring any child by causing it not to exist. Moreover, even if they did bring a child with another makeup into the world, one without the supposed disadvantage, that would be *another* child. With a very different makeup and life experiences, a different person would come about. Thus, there would be no choice between a child's being deaf (or whatever) or else not being that. Rather, the choice would be between

---

[6] That is not as farfetched as it sounds. Obviously, no ethics committee would approve a research proposal calling for children to be born with, let us say, particular combinations of genes leading to severe depression, no matter how productive such research might be. However, my wife, who teaches handicapped children, reports that it is common knowledge (anecdotally) that some welfare parents knowingly produce large numbers of children with severely debilitating conditions, such as Fragile X syndrome, because they like getting the welfare payments. That cannot be declared illegal. However, I have no hesitation in declaring it immoral.

one person coming into existence or else a different person doing so. Each, in the advent, would have a life worth living, and neither would be injured by not being created.

This is what might be called the *Problem of Contingent Existence.*[7] It is an important problem in bioethics as it is in certain other applications. At first, it may seem to be only a philosopher's word game with little to do with practical reality. However, I intend to show that it does have practical importance. Moreover, I intend to show that our difficulties in coping with the problem stem from systematic inadequacies in our traditional approaches to ethics. In the subsequent text, I offer a means of dealing with the Problem of Contingent Existence; I offer it as an account that meshes with common sense and that gives us a way of dealing with what are rapidly becoming practical applications. Not least is this so in connection with genetic engineering. A splendidly disturbing illustration of the problem is provided by Aldous Huxley's fictional future London in the *Brave New World.*[8] As I explained in Chapter 4, in the imaginary society depicted there, behavioral conditioning, cloning, and evidently genetic engineering are used to create different castes of people to fill a variety of social roles. They are well able to fill their assigned roles and quite enjoy doing so. Alphas, assisted by the Betas, do the planning, administration, and supervision. At the other end of the scale (skipping over the Gammas and Deltas) are the Epsilons, physically and mentally stunted, who enjoy doing the mindless drudgery that is their lot in life. As depicted, this is a society of remarkably well adjusted and happy people. Most of us, though, would feel considerable disquietude about this Brave New World.

However we might feel about the Alphas, a matter that also would raise a few questions, most of us feel appalled at the idea of programmatically creating the mentally and physically stunted Epsilons. Yet to whom does their being created do harm? The Epsilons themselves? It is not that they might have been created Alphas or Betas instead. That the Epsilons were made the way they were was a condition of *their* being made at all. Otherwise, very different people would have resulted. For the Epsilons, things could not have been any better. If life is even slightly worth living for them, and if their only alternative were to not exist at all, then it would seem that they have not been injured by their being created. Is the creation of Epsilons then morally neutral or perhaps morally justified by virtue of its benefit for other members of society? Are the qualms we feel about it merely a result

---

[7] This problem is raised and extensively discussed, though not fully resolved, by Derek Parfit. He calls it the "Nonidentity Problem." See his *Reasons and Persons* (Oxford: Oxford University Press, 1984) and also his "Lewis, Perry, and What Matters," in *The Identities of Persons*, ed. Amelie Oksenberg Rorty (Berkeley: University of California Press, 1976), and "Future Generations: Future Problems," *Philosophy and Public Affairs* 11 (1982): 113–172.

[8] Aldous Huxley, *Brave New World* (New York: HarperCollins, 1998; originally published 1932 by Harper & Brothers).

of an irrational prejudice? On a purely individualistic ethic, such a program is very difficult to argue against. We might perhaps contrive some way to argue that some specific and otherwise existent individuals would be made the worse off by such a program. However, even were such an argument to be successful, it would only be to nibble around the edges of the moral issues. From an ethic focusing entirely on individuals, I suspect that nibbling around the edges is the best that we could ever do. Even if no one's rights or welfare were infringed, though, and even were there a general increase in utility, I would still find fault with such a breeding program.

We can get to the ethical heart of the matter, get to what is *really* wrong with an Epsilon-breeding program, only with the recognition that intentionally creating Epsilons would be to make of human life less than human life ought to be. Though not harming the resulting Epsilons, and perhaps benefiting the Alphas, such a program would detract from the well-being of that ongoing life process that is humanity, or *Homo sapiens*, as a whole. I believe humanity to be a morally significant entity in its own right. The creation of Epsilons would make less of human life. It would diminish its coherent integrity, detracting from that which is valuable in human life and from that which human life inherently strives to be.

We might draw a contrast between the case of the Epsilons and that of the worker castes of ants. Various ant species have workers specialized for various tasks such as food gathering or battle with outsiders. However, in their various forms, worker ants are not generated with less than those qualities that go into a healthy functional ant. Not even their reproductive interests are overridden because they proliferate their genes more effectively through the reproduction of their queen-sisters.[9] Even in dying for their colony, they protect their genetic interests. No ant loses what it is in the nature of an ant to be. Nor is it contrary to the interests of their species that it takes these functional forms and, certainly, it does not lose its integrated character.

The Epsilons may contribute to the function of the society depicted in *Brave New World*, but that society, and not just in its requiring Epsilons, is a stunting of what is inherent in humanity to be or to develop toward. Though the Epsilons cannot be other than they are, they are not what it is good for a human to be and they were shaped not for their own good but as a means to exterior ends. It is better for humanity that it not take forms requiring some individuals to live stunted lives. Humanity is capable of doing and being better. I would hope that it would go without saying that those Epsilon-type individuals who do in fact occur naturally in the human population merit our care and moral respect. This is so even though we would do well to take appropriate steps to minimize the rate of occurrence of such individuals.

---

[9] It is implicit in the *haploid* reproduction of ants that workers are more closely related to the queen's daughters than they would be to their own.

I offer the conclusion that we must widen the scope of our moral concern so as to regard *more* than the rights and well-being of individuals. This is true in particular when what we do or do not do has the potential to affect the future welfare of humanity. To be sure, concern for the rights and well-being of individuals is an ethical necessity and always must be rigorously maintained. Nonetheless, that is not the only level on which human life is significant, and such concern cannot in itself do justice to the whole range of human moral issues. That we do need a wider scope of concern emerges forcefully in cases in which the very existence of those individuals primarily affected by an act is itself contingent on the doing of that act, as would be the case with any major genetic modification. A very important and very practical issue with which we must deal is that of the extent to which individual humans are morally obliged to defer to the interests not just of other individuals but also of humanity as a whole. Before we concentrate on that, however, in the next two sections let us further explore the conception of humanity as a living entity in its own right and its significance for genetic engineering and other future-oriented activities.

Homo sapiens *and Other Holistic Entities*

To make it clear, what I am suggesting is that humanity itself has interests, morally significant ones, and that these are not merely the aggregated interests of individual humans. This may seem quite bizarre to some. Perhaps to others it seems plausible, even self-evident. In any case, there are some issues here that do have an important bearing on the issues of genetic engineering, so I will offer this section and the one following in exploration of the issues of whether holistic entities can have their own interests. First, we must ask how humanity could possibly have interests that really were *distinct* from those of individual humans, given that it exists only through their individual lives. In answer, we do well to proceed from the wider biological fact that a living system that spans subsidiary living systems can have interests that are distinct from the aggregated interests of its subsidiary systems. One example of that is the interest some ecosystems have in being burned by fire at appropriate intervals. Most living entities in the system do not themselves benefit, and many are injured in fires, but the ongoing health of the overall ecosystem does benefit. In the absence of fire, some species of plants are unable to reproduce and so are squeezed out, taking with them other species dependent on them. A few species come to dominate, and the ecosystem loses its biodiversity and its resilience. It loses its own particular integrity. This is not to make a case for incendiarism; frequent fires are as bad as no fires, and generally it is the natural frequency of fires that is best. This argument does not *depend* on the assumption that the interests of nonhuman entities are morally significant; that is a very different story. The current point is that the interests of the broader system are distinct from those of its subsidiary living systems.

We should also note that as well as ecosystems, a species also might have interests that are not just the aggregated interests of its species members. A species of plant or animal may flourish over a burned area, though some are burned in the fire and few directly benefit – most of the ones to benefit not then existing. Again, a species (for instance, deer) may benefit from being preyed upon in terms of the overall health of its populace and its fit with the carrying capacity of its habitat. The individual animal does not benefit from being killed with, once more, most of the benefit coming to species members that do not yet exist and to the species itself. This being a book about human bioethics, I shall drop the fascinating (and elsewhere important) subject of ecosystems and concentrate here on species as living systems, asking more closely about what a biological species is. In particular, of course, we shall be asking about *Homo sapiens*.

Traditionally, a species has been thought of as being a collection of relevantly similar organisms, each having specific properties in common with the others. Indeed, it is on the basis of that assumption that we came to use the term *species*. Members of a species are supposed be members of a class of beings that answer to a particular specification. However, life just does not work that way. We would be hard-pressed to find a set of properties, or even a single one, that every last *Homo sapiens* has and that no non-*Homo sapiens* has. Again, which properties do an egg, larva, chrysalis, and Monarch butterfly have in common? Virtually none, save that they are all part of an ongoing Monarch butterfly life process. Moreover, species frequently gain and lose individual members. Specified collections do not do that; nor do they, as species do, change over time, bud off new species, undergo Darwinian evolution, or become extinct. Species can do all of those things. Biological philosopher David Hull makes this point:

Single genes are historical entities existing for short periods of time. The more important notion is that of a *gene lineage*. Gene lineages are also historical entities persisting while changing indefinitely through time.... Like genes, organisms form lineages. The relevant organismal units in evolution are not sets of organisms defined in terms of structural similarity, but lineages formed by the imperfect copying processes of reproduction. Organisms can belong to the same lineage even though they are structurally different from other organisms in that lineage. What is more, continued changes in structure can take place indefinitely.... Single organisms are historical entities, existing for short periods of time. Organism lineages are also historical entities persisting while changing indefinitely through time.[10]

The organism lineage, the species, is an ongoing historical entity that meets our previously developed characterization of a living entity. Instead of taking a species as an assemblage of particular things, it is better to take it as an ongoing life process, a living entity that takes place in but transcends

[10] David Hull, "A Matter of Individuality," *Philosophy of Science* 45 (1978): 335–360; the quotation is from pp. 340–341.

individual living entities. Such I would point out is the case with *Homo sapiens* or humanity, which meets the characterization of life developed in Chapter 6. As a living entity in its own right, it has interests and these are morally significant in their own right.

Biology is rich with fascinating stories of living entities that in one way or another incorporate other living entities. Famous is the slime mold living on the floor of certain South American rainforests. Part of the time, the organisms live as small amoeba-like beings scattered through the leaf litter. Once a year, for reproductive purposes, they flow together to form a much larger organism with properties noticeably different from those of the component organisms. After dispersing its reproductive spores, it disassembles. Is this one organism becoming many? Was it many throughout? Was it always one, sometimes a dispersed one? These questions may not have answers.

Symbiotic (literally, *living together*) entities offer countless examples of living entities composed of living entities. Lichen are symbiotic unions of algae and fungi, organisms of two very different sorts. They live where neither alga nor fungus could live on its own. The algae provide the food through photosynthesis; the fungi provide water, minerals, and other services; they send out reproductive bundles jointly; and, in sum, the whole thing functions as a living entity in its own right. Within their cells, many marine organisms contain other organisms that generate light or provide food or other useful products or services. It is part of their nature to have them, and they cannot live without them. As a different sort of instance, there are the siphonophorans, which are marine entities looking much like jellyfish. However, true jellyfish are single organisms that (like humans) form their organs from mesodermal tissue. The siphonophoran entity has organs – bladder, each tentacle, and so on – composed of individual siphonophorans.

Yet another sort of instance is provided by *chloroplasts*, which are essential to the life of all green plants. It is in these organelles, which occur inside of plant cells, that photosynthesis actually takes place. The chloroplast has DNA of a sort different from that of the surrounding cell, which is transmitted separately when the plant reproduces. Biologists have come to draw the inference that ancestral chloroplasts were separate organisms that long ago formed a successful symbiotic union with the ancestors of modern plants, making modern plants possible. Something very similar is evidently true of *mitochondria*. These organelles are included within the cells of plants and animals, and they are necessary for the release of energy. If, somehow, the many mitochondria in your body were suddenly to die or disappear, you would die before reading to the end of this sentence. The DNA of mitochondria is different from that of the rest of the cell and, in reproduction, it is transmitted separately. Seemingly, ancestral mitochondria formed a symbiosis with the ancestors of plants and animals, a very successful symbiosis that has thrived ever since. This is not to suggest that you are only a collection, one composed of a large number of microorganisms. You are a unique individual. What I am affirming is that a living entity, a living system, can have its own identity and its own interests, though it arises from a number of other living systems. This is a very frequent phenomenon with life. The interests of humanity are compatible with those of individual humans, most of the time, but sometimes they must be considered separately. One of those times is when we are contemplating interfering with the very makeup of humanity.[11]

Still, though it might be granted that species have their own interests in a meaningful sense, the moral conclusions I would draw therefrom might perhaps still be resisted. If humanity, as distinct from individual humans, is not a *conscious* entity, why, it will be demanded, should its interests matter? In an earlier chapter, as I discussed the good for individuals, I noted that we human individuals could have some things in our interests and some things opposed to our interests, even though we were never conscious of it. If a woman were raped while unconscious, or another person defamed behind his back, and neither ever learned of it, this would still be an affront to the personal integrity of the person and therefore contrary to the person's interests. There was also my discussion of the Experience Machine. The conclusion drawn there was that we have consciousness to serve our interests, our having interests being prior to our having consciousness. If individual humans can have morally significant interests and be subject to benefits and interests of which they are never consciously aware, then there is no evident reason why humanity cannot have morally significant interests. That the interests and future prospects of humankind are of moral importance seems intuitively plausible to most of us – at least, once we are aware of it as a distinct consideration.

If we are to take species as morally considerable entities, as I certainly do, there are a few problems or, at least, questions that are posed. For one thing, there are all the issues concerning where we should draw the line to distinguish one species from another closely related one. This is not a huge question in the case of humans. (What about chimpanzees,

[11] These are things that I have pointed out at considerable length elsewhere. Rather than reinventing the wheel here, I refer readers to my earlier works, Lawrence E. Johnson, *A Morally Deep World: An Essay on Moral Significance and Environmental Ethics,* New York: Cambridge University Press, 1991; "Humanity, Holism, and Environmental Ethics," *Environmental Ethics* 5 (1983): 335–343; "Species: On Their Nature and Moral Standing," *Journal of Natural History* 29 (1995): 843–849; and "Future Generations and Contemporary Ethic," *Environmental Values,* 12 (2003); 471–487; and to literature by David Hull, "Are Species Really Individuals?," *Systematic Zoology* 25 (1976): 174–191; "A Matter of Individuality," *Philosophy of Science* 45 (1978): 335–360; and "Kitts & Kitts & Caplan on Species," *Philosophy of Science* 48 (1981): 141–152; as well as Stephen Jay Gould, "The Origin and Function of 'Bizarre' Structures," *Evolution* 4 (1974): 191–220. The idea that species are entities was initially floated by M. T. Ghiselin, *The Economy of Nature and the Evolution of Sex* (Berkeley: University of California Press, 1974).

though?) However, if we are to extend it to species in general, then there are some *very* close cases. Furthermore, what about genera, phyla, and all the other classifications? Then there are ecosystems, which characteristically merge into other ecosystems. Nonetheless, these are problems only if our primary consideration is morally considerable *entities*. Rather, our primary consideration ought to be interests and interacting complexes of interests. Just where we draw the line between complexes would be only of subsidiary interest. What would be of importance is that we give due consideration to all interests according to the degree of the interest. For my own part, I would want to do that over the entire living world.[12] Our concern in this book, though, is with human interests, those of individuals and those of *Homo sapiens*.

The Problem of Future Generations

The moral problem of making provision for contingently existing beings arises in political philosophy and environmental ethics as well as in bioethics. It has become known as the *Problem of Future Generations*. I propose that we take a brief look at that problem for what we might bring back to bioethics. In particular, it has important implications with respect to the ethics of genetic engineering. First let us ask whether it would be morally neutral were we to leave for future generations a world that was highly polluted and with severely depleted resources. The difficulty, obviously, is that those people do not yet exist. As they do not yet exist, there is no one we are harming. So it would seem, on a purely individualistic ethic, that polluting the future would be morally acceptable, inasmuch as there is no one who would be harmed. However, there seems to be a dense air of cheap self-serving moral cop-out about any such line of argument. This line of thought undoubtedly will strike most people, certainly most nonphilosophers, as being silly and selfish. Of course, future generations do not exist *now*. But those people *are* going to exist, and it is not fair for us to muck things up for them before they even get here. Some of the more philosophically inclined might perhaps invoke a Rawlsian idea of intergenerational justice, whereby our position in time does not affect our moral entitlements. The trouble with any such response is that it tacitly assigns to future generations a shadowy sort of existence, or preexistence, as if they were actors waiting in the wings for their eventual entrance. In point of fact, though, there is no one waiting anywhere, no particular *them* for whom matters might be better or worse. Not just nonexistent, they are also indeterminate.

---

[12] I go into this in my *A Morally Deep World: An Essay on Moral Significance and Environmental Ethics* (Cambridge: Cambridge University Press, 1991). I regard this book and that one as twin volumes though with different areas of focus.

Worse even than being indeterminate, their identity is contingent. It tends to depend on (among other things) our actions now that affect future living conditions. The makeup of future generations is certain to be affected by what we do in the present. There is no one set of individuals who will necessarily come to exist. Even the small things we do have rapidly multiplying consequences and will inevitably and radically alter the composition of future generations. In the first place, bear in mind that when an event of conception takes place, there are literally millions of spermatozoa in the area. A different one with its slightly different genetic composition might have gotten there first. Had the prospective parents stayed up to watch the late movie that night or else not done so, as the case might be, a different child would have resulted, or no child. A phone call during the day, even a wrong number, would have slightly altered the sequence of events and so affected which (if any) spermatozoon fertilized the ovum. So would someone unexpectedly changing lanes the week before. All other events or nonevents also multiply in their consequences. If we follow a course of pollution and resource depletion, different things will happen, and different people will meet and have differing children in differing numbers at different times. As well as wars, presidential elections, and what we do about the Kyoto Protocol, a butterfly flapping its wings anywhere on earth can blow away an entire generation and fan another one into existence.

If we follow an environmentally exploitative public policy (or, for that matter, a genetically manipulative one), those who reap the consequences in a hundred years' time will be a completely different set of people than those who would exist had we shown more restraint. If their lives were worth having at all, they would not be the worse for having been brought into existence. Nor can we avoid the unpalatable conclusion on the strength of a utilitarianism that sought to maximize the amount of good. For whom do we maximize it? Remember, there are no particular individuals made worse or better off. Do we then try to bring into existence the greatest *total* amount of good, regardless of who inherits it? Although such a principle might seem appealing to start with, it has been pointed out, by Parfit in particular,[13] that logically this would imply what he calls the "Repugnant Conclusion." We would have to accept the conclusion that adding people to the population would be a good thing to do, so long as the additional people had lives with a balance of good over bad and so long as they did not detract by as much from other people's lives. The optimum would be astronomical numbers of people having lives just barely worth having, inasmuch as their vast numbers, greatly multiplying a small balance of good over bad, would have the greatest possible total balance of good over bad. It seems a depressing thought, all those people grubbing along with lives

---

[13] See Derek Parfit, "Future Generations" and *Reasons and Persons* (footnote 7, this chapter).

hardly worth having, and little hope of betterment in, as I imagine it, a world of plastic, silicon, and soybeans. For whom, though, would that be a bad thing? It is not a question of these people having marginal lives rather than good ones. They either exist with lives slightly worth having or they do not exist at all. These are the only alternatives for those people. Still, there seems little imperative to bring about such a world.

Instead of trying to bring the greatest total amount of good, perhaps the thing to do would be to work toward the greatest *average* amount of happiness. It would seem preferable to have far fewer people having far better lives. (For whom, though, would it be better?) However, the principle that we should maximize the average level of happiness also has unpalatable implications. (It might even raise questions about whether we should eliminate those with unhappy lives, or even those happy people whose happiness was *below* average. But let us set aside considerations of homicide.) As Parfit points out, to maximize the average amount of happiness, we might elect to utilize our environment at an unsustainable rate while lowering our numbers by natural attrition and low birth rates. Thereby we might have very enjoyable lives, happier than if we practiced sustainable life-styles. In the end, we might elect not to reproduce at all, allowing the human race to go extinct (presumably the last happy few would be tended by robots). Bringing this about would then be a utilitarian moral obligation, had we good reason to believe that this course of action would bring about the greatest average happiness. We might query whether this were a possible scenario, a contingently factual question. If this were a conceptual possibility, would the outcome be anything less than a reduction to absurdity of the idea? Remember that we cannot escape by taking the operative principle to be that we ought to maximize the average happiness for those individuals who do or *would* exist anyway. As a result of the indeterminacy and contingent existence of future generations, that would leave only our contemporaries as objects of moral concern. Parfit brings a great deal of ingenuity to bear on this problem but is not able to find a fully adequate solution on the basis of any formulation of a utilitarian ethic. There are indeed limitations on what a utilitarian ethic can do. However, I believe that the problem here runs far deeper than that.

I draw the conclusion that there are some moral issues to deal with which we need to go beyond an exclusive preoccupation with individuals (and their rights or their utility). Certainly when persons are affected, that raises moral issues, yet there is more to morality than individuals or aggregates thereof. This is because there is more to humanity than individuals or aggregates thereof. Humanity, the ongoing flow of human life, can be affected by our actions and ought to be respected as being of moral concern. We certainly do not respect it if we undermine its future health and sustainability. Nor do we respect the best interests of humanity if we act so as to intentionally create

Epsilons or so as to otherwise disrupt the fabric of human life. Bioethics does concern matters that affect the future welfare of humankind.

* * * * *

Addendum

The evident ethical anomalies to which the Problem of Contingent Existence gives rise seem morally preposterous, yet the conclusion that *Homo sapiens* is a holistic entity also may seem mind-boggling to some. One may resile in consternation and ask whether there is any viable alternative within an individualistic ethics. This reaction has been put to me. To this I can only reply as follows:

1. The aforementioned argument implicitly demonstrates the impossibility of any such counterargument being successful within the confines of individualistic ethics.
2. In the years since I first floated a less articulated version of my argument, no serious attempt has been made to refute it (let alone made successfully). Nonetheless, I have been criticized for not addressing such counterarguments. Others and I have made an extensive yet fruitless search of the literature trying to find any such attempt.[14] Meanwhile, many serious thinkers have been convinced.
3. A growing consensus in the biological sciences favors recognition of species as holistic entities.

Individual Interests versus the Interests of Humanity

Most of the time the interests of humanity will not conflict with the interests of individual humans. What if they ever were to come in conflict? Could it ever be morally appropriate to infringe on the latter for the sake of the former? Let us start with what is an obvious and inevitable challenge: If intentionally creating Epsilons would be morally wrong because it would detract from the well-being of humanity, does it follow that we ought to right the wrong by eliminating existing Epsilons or their like, be they created intentionally or incidentally? If that did follow, then it would be a severe moral indictment of the position I have been developing, all the more so because of odious historical precedent. We all know that there was once a regime that sought to protect the health and hygiene of the human race – or, more specifically, of the supposed Master Race – by eliminating those whom they considered to be grossly defective. Even had their diagnoses been correct, which they were not, such actions did not benefit humanity – just the contrary. Now, I must concede that the human race would be better off were natural Epsilons and the like not born, or not so many of them.

---

[14] I would be grateful to any reader who would direct me to such an attempt.

Nonetheless, once they come into existence, they too must be extended appropriate moral consideration. Humanity is injured when an individual life is injured. To the extent that it is possible for them and for us, we ought to help them live worthwhile lives. To harm or be indifferent to them is to brutalize ourselves and to brutalize humanity, to make less of humanity than it could and ought to be. Individually and as humanity, we diminish our health, our virtue. The only *conceivable* justification for eliminating them would be if it were done for their sake; not our own nor that supposed of humanity, but *theirs*. This could be only if being alive truly were a burden to them and they were terminated for that reason. There are clear and deadly dangers here. We might fall into error inadvertently, or we might use claimed good intentions, not for the first time, as cover for sinister motivation. Nonvoluntary euthanasia I discussed in a previous chapter. Here I would just observe that in view of the dangers to society (as well as to other existing individuals), we might perhaps decide that the lesser evil would be to not cut short their supposed suffering, allowing it to continue for fear of allowing worse to happen.

More generally, I believe that we must accept the conclusion that sometimes the interests of humanity ought to have precedence over the interests of particular individuals.[15] Indeed, it is a necessary condition of taking anything as being morally significant that in some circumstances, we ought to defer to its interests. When it is a matter of genetic modifications that affect or may possibly affect the future life of humanity, the possibility of unanticipated and seriously adverse consequences indicates that we ought to follow the *Precautionary Principle*. That is, the future of humankind is not something we can afford to risk for relatively trivial gain in gambles with the imperfectly known. To be sure, I do very much doubt whether anyone would seriously contemplate attempting to breed a race of Epsilons, and I doubt whether they would be allowed to do so if they did try. In passing, I would note that there is not just one but rather two good reasons for not allowing that. Were we to create an ongoing breeding population of Epsilons, doing so would be to do injury as well as insult to the human race. Another reason is that even if it were not a matter of corrupting the human gene pool (if the Epsilons were not allowed to reproduce or were unable to), humanity nonetheless would be injured by being divided and debased in such a way.

---

[15] This is true not only in bioethics but also elsewhere. As alluded to earlier, it certainly applies to many environmental issues. The possibility (I believe certainty) of serious global climate change and numerous other environmental issues affecting humankind put moral constraints, both positive and negative, on us who exist in the present. There are some things we ought to do and some things we ought not to do. In addition, we have obligations in terms of maintaining civilization, civil liberties, and general living conditions. These are obligations to the ongoing life of humanity itself, not to contingent and indeterminate future individuals who may or may not come to exist. However, here is not the place to pursue such matters.

It would be further injuring itself by willfully acting so as to produce such a result. These are reasons of sorts that would apply to things far more likely to happen than the programmatic creation of Epsilons.

Beyond any doubt, though, many prospective parents will try to enhance the genetic makeup of their children, with many of them very probably making the attempt before the means are perfected. There are forceful reasons why they ought not to be allowed an entirely free hand in this, and these go beyond even the need to avoid any nontrivial risk of creating children born to bad lives. There are also issues of social justice involved. We might doubt whether the wealthy should be entirely free to engineer healthy high-achieving children able to out-compete our own children. This might create a whole new form of hereditary and self-perpetuating aristocracy. Nor would the human race necessarily be enhanced by having greatly increased proportions of genetically enhanced go-getters. Balances of various sorts may be of importance for the welfare of humankind. More broadly, we might question whether what are apparently improvements to individuals will always actually be improvements.

There are several aspects to be noted here. It may be that a modification that enhances the genetic makeup of the child detracts from the well-being of humanity or its gene pool, and vice versa. It is also true that we humans, in our arrogance and short-sightedness, often feel certain that we are making improvements when in fact we are doing just the opposite. I am writing this here in Australia, where we have a history of introducing rabbits, foxes, cane toads, and other noxious pests while exterminating the Tasmanian tiger and several other native species. At the same time, we improved the land by destroying wetlands that we are now trying to re-create and cleared native vegetation we are now replanting. These were all seen, when we were doing them, as rationally and self-evidently being improvements. Nor have we humans acted appreciably more wisely on other continents. If fumbling and foolishness have often characterized our attempts to improve nature, what confidence could we have that we would not commit major blunders in trying to improve human nature? Whether it is our own child that we are trying to enhance or the human race as a whole, we could very easily bungle. Here I shall offer some brief speculative sketches of sorts of things that might go wrong.

Some Blunders of Conceivable Sorts

Obviously, I cannot give an exact and detailed example of a blunder we might make because if we knew enough for me to do that, we would know enough to (probably) not make that particular blunder. Instead, I shall sketch a couple of what I hope are plausible scenarios suggesting ways in which things might go wrong. *Not* predictions, these scenarios are intended only as suggestions of the sorts of things that might go wrong. As a possible example, consider a scenario concerning schizophrenia. Many of us have known people afflicted by that terrible condition and know how hard it is on those afflicted and on those around them. It is known that schizophrenia often runs in families, and there seems to be some genetic predispositions to it. This is an area of continuing research. Let us suppose that future research finds that some genes are very often found in people who have schizophrenia and only rarely in those who do not. This would still leave us with many unknowns. For one thing, we do not know the causal pathways by which the genes lead, when they do, to schizophrenia. Nor do we know what other affects with which they might be involved. Something we do know is that genes often work in combinations and that genes are not mere semantic instructions telling us things like "be schizophrenic." They can be involved with many things and many causal chains and under many circumstances, not all of which necessarily lead to bad results. We also know that although *schizophrenia* is a single word, it is one that does not apply to one single thing. There are several forms of schizophrenia, evidently working in several different ways. How many different forms and in what different ways? Those are more things we do not know. We just know, because it is part of our definition, that people with schizophrenia often have a very poor grasp on reality (social or material).

Knowing the terrible toll of schizophrenia on individuals affected and on society as a whole, we might want to do something about it. We might be worried about our own prospective children because the condition runs in our family, or we might hope to do good for humankind as a whole. We might feel greatly heartened by the recent near obliteration of hemophilia and Huntington's disease – remember, we are conjecturing here – and want to do the same with schizophrenia. This aspiration is widely shared and, accordingly, interventions to remove or disable the schizophrenic genes are widely used. The rate of schizophrenia falls considerably and we are well pleased. From the standpoint of later years, though – as we conjecture on – people came to be considerably less pleased. In retrospect, this era (after the near eradication of schizophrenia genes) became seen as one of stagnation and mediocrity even though momentum carried social progress somewhat further. It was hard to entangle the complex factors involved, but eventually the consensus developed that the loss of creative genius was very much correlated with the loss of the schizophrenia genes. Schizophrenics, after all, are people who have radically different conceptions of major aspects of reality than do the rest of us. This is also true, *necessarily*, of the great geniuses of art and science[16] and the great saints as well. Shakespeare's

---

[16] Back in the 1600s, Galileo had this screwy idea that the sun stood still while the earth moved around it. For his contemporaries, *anybody* could see that the sun moved, that it went up in the morning and went down at night. With a head full of (what were then considered) wild theories, Galileo was insensible of palpable fact. The man was obviously nuts. Intellectual

Hamlet is a remarkable illustration of the idea that genius is oft to madness near allied. Come to think of it, Shakespeare seems to have been a bit peculiar himself. In our hypothetical projection, we also might conjecture that the problematic genes are important in other undiscovered connections. Perhaps other psychiatric syndromes start to be noticed, with people becoming unbalanced in other ways (with attendant suffering), and this too is to be attributed to the alterations in the gene pool.

This is all conjecture, neither fact nor prediction. If it could be conclusively demonstrated ahead of time that some particular course of action would be a blunder, we would (one hopes) probably do something else. Our actual blunders no doubt will be more remarkable. Nor by any means do I wish to downplay the sufferings of people with schizophrenia or detract from the importance of finding means of preventing or alleviating the condition. What I am trying to do is illustrate two points. The first is the fairly obvious one that well-intended mistakes can be bad in terms of individual lives. More important for our purposes is the possibility that some genes or combinations of genes might be good for humankind as a whole even though they might be devastating (at least, under some circumstances) for some individuals. It perhaps might be (in terms of our conjecture) that the health or survival of the human race depends on there being a continuing supply of a few creative geniuses, paid for at the cost of there being larger numbers of suffering schizophrenics. In such a case, the thing to do would be to try to retain the benefits while minimizing the human cost.

We might concoct a similar scenario concerning possible genes inclining people toward homosexuality. Of course we are all enlightened liberals who hold that what consenting adults do in private is their own business, and all that. At the same time, some of us may feel *not with my kids you bloody don't!* Prospective parents may believe that it would be in the overall best interests of their child to not have to cope with homosexual inclinations. Perhaps many parents, despite the protests of the gay lobby, would opt to see to it that their own children do not have such genes. This may result in a substantially lowered proportion of homosexuals in the population. One consequence is that those who were homosexual might feel even more isolated. It might also turn out to be the case that genes predisposing toward homosexuality have persisted in the human gene pool because it is of benefit to the human race that they persist. We know that for whatever reason, a disproportionately high level of creative excellence is to be found within the homosexual community. It is also true that various societies have found homosexuals useful, even indispensable, in different roles, spiritual and otherwise. We also might speculate that genes that, in combination,

freedom is one thing, but total absurdity, particularly when tinged with blasphemy, is quite another. Recall that Galileo was tried and found guilty by the Catholic Church (as part of the Inquisition) and spent the end of his life under house arrest.

lend themselves to homosexuality might in other combinations lend themselves to other effects. Some of these might possibly be useful for us. Again, apparent benefits might be offset by hidden or unanticipated costs.

Another conceivable way in which we could well blunder badly might be through trying to create our children as superathletes or supergeniuses. In the attempt, we might well bring about wildly skewed combinations of genes that cannot function well together, let alone live up to parental hopes or expectations. We could imagine vivid conjectural detail of one-dimensional wonders and unbalanced horrors. As I have stressed, these are all only conjectural illustrations, which we might spin indefinitely. The blunders we do make will no doubt be stranger than fiction. Whether it is a matter of possibly misshaping lives or misshaping human life or doing both together, there is a need for caution. Caution and substantial safeguards are clearly needed, particularly as powerful forces tending to erode them. Desire for scientific prestige or commercial gain would clearly be such forces, and another would be a powerful longing to have better children.

Finding Guidelines

In treating patients, the traditional primary principle of medicine since the most ancient of days has been, first, do no harm. Prudently, we must place the protection of health before attempts at enhancement. If patients must be subjected to some risk, we must have excellent reasons for believing that the probable benefits outweigh the potential costs. We must follow some form of a precautionary principle, never undertaking risks of potentially catastrophic consequences. If it is a matter of running risks with the makeup and well-being of the human race, we must be cautious indeed. First, we must not act in such a way as to damage its health. Again, I must confess that I cannot give a detailed set of rules for deciding which sorts of genetic modifications ought to be allowed or forbidden, or for deciding just how we ought to monitor them in application. Indeed, given the amorphous and indeterminate nature of the field of possibilities, I suggest that only a fool would try. However, I think it would be excessively cautious to rule out genetic modification entirely, given the fairly clear benefits of eliminating such conditions as hemophilia or Huntington's disease. To be sure, one could perhaps conjecture that there is some unknown but important service performed by the continued presence of hemophilia or Huntington's genes in the human gene pool. By the same token, we might speculate that such diseases as smallpox and polio might serve some unknown but useful function, so we should allow them to continue also. With absolute caution, one could do absolutely nothing. Nevertheless, if we do decide to allow genetic modification under some conditions, we must somehow face up to a formidable array of slippery-slope and line-drawing problems and to a potential minefield of unanticipated disasters, and we must be able to face up to them in practice as well as principle. These problems would inevitably be made worse by misplaced enthusiasm and vested interests of various sorts.

I would be pessimistic about deriving any adequately workable set of comprehensive guidelines. Certainly I would be pessimistic about doing so on the basis of a traditional (individual-centered) system of ethics. Clearly, we ought to continue to be wary of allowing adverse consequences to individuals and of not respecting them as ends in themselves, but that only goes so far. We travel a useful way forward if we accept the principle that humanity, as well as individual humans, requires our moral concern as an end in itself. Not only is doing so biologically as well as ethically appropriate, it also is necessary in order for us to deal with bioethical issues concerning nonexistent and indeterminate people who might or might not come to exist. With that insight, however, goes further difficulties. Not only must we deal with the supposed right of individuals to upgrade their children, with its range of cases ranging over continua from the obviously benign and salutary to the utterly horrific, we must deal with those enthusiasts who want to improve the human race, by either eliminating genes deemed defective or increasing the proportion of those thought superior. There also will be those zealots who would want to implement genetic novelties. Even so, the principle that humanity as a whole has a morally important stake in such matters gives us some ground on which we can evaluate and regulate what people may or may not do, without just leaving it up to individual choice. Yet there remains the problem of finding the basis on which to draw up our regulations.

Any once-and-for-all set of rules that is adequate, if it could be found at all, will not be found for a good many years. Were we to fall back in horror on a blanket ban on genetic engineering, that once-and-for-all rule would be very inadequate. For one thing, as biological technology continues to advance, as it invariably will do, people inevitably would try to implement some form of genetic engineering in spite of the ban. Perhaps their moral motivation will be of the highest order, as they attempt to prevent such afflictions as hemophilia or Huntington's disease. Indeed, it would be a strong moral indictment of a blanket ban that it would prevent us from ridding the human race of unnecessary and useless suffering. A blanket ban is not the answer morally, and it would be impossible to enforce in practice. So, we must cope as best we may. Our rules and guidelines must be carefully thought out and constructed, and their applications must be carefully monitored. Always, we must stand ready to amend our rules and guidelines in the face of emerging considerations and factual results. A key objective must be to arrive at as much consensus as possible, based on wide consultation. Nevertheless, we must ever be wary of opinion being distorted by commercial or other vested interests. So, proceed we must, driven both by necessity and humanitarian need. Yet, in the face of what might go wrong, we dare proceed only with the greatest of care. In assessing any proposed procedure in connection with genetic engineering, I stress the following five vital considerations:

1. Are the *motivations* of the proposed course of action morally sound?
2. Would the procedure be a danger to humanity as a whole? (It is on this point that a biocentric system of ethics in particular offers us some useful help.)
3. Would individuals suffer as a result?
4. What scope would there be for unanticipated adverse consequences, and what scope would there be for dealing with them adequately?
5. Would costs and benefits be distributed inequitably?

Such questions must be asked – yet here as elsewhere, our ultimate safeguard can be only thoughtful and eternal vigilance.

An Application to Cloning

These points can give us some guidance in application to reproductive cloning, a matter concerning which we are greatly in need of guidance. The idea of cloning provokes considerable thought and an immense amount of emotion. Most of the emotion, I have noticed, takes the form of intense feelings of aversion. I also have noticed that very few people opposed to it are able to give anything even slightly substantial as a reason for their aversion. Nor by any means is it universally understood just what cloning is, even with reference to human reproductive cloning. Nonetheless, it is widely thought to be unnatural, immoral, somehow dangerous, and moti- vated by discreditable aspirations. The often-vague cloud of disquietude around cloning appears to encompass, on the one hand, objections to the occurrence of cloning and, on the other, disquietude about the reasons for which cloning might be done. Both of these aspects must be explored.

First, just what is cloning? The term is used in different ways. As I am using the term here, *cloning* is the production of a living being that has the genetic makeup of another (currently or previously) living being. Some other writers writing about other things sometimes apply the terms *DNA cloning* or *genetic cloning* to the mass production of genes or other fragments of DNA that might be of interest. Though I have no complaints with that usage, my concern here is with the replication of cells or organisms. Of particular concern is *reproductive cloning*, whereby an individual organism is genetically replicated. What mostly worries people is that *people* might be thus replicated. Apart from that, there is the replication by cloning of various sorts of cells in such a way as not to lead to actual organisms. This is where I shall begin my discussion. I adopt the term *cellular cloning* for such procedures as being the least contentious term I can devise.

Cellular cloning has been with us for years – several decades, in fact – without provoking appreciable controversy. In cellular cloning, somatic (bodily) cells of one sort or another are reproduced more or less indefinitely in laboratory cultures. Liver cells, kidney cells, and cells of many other kinds can be replicated as needed for research. An envisioned extension of this technology would be the culturing in vitro of tissues and possibly even entire organs, tissue-typed to be suitable for particular individuals. Such projects are in their infancy but show considerable long-term promise. Perhaps a process involving cellular cloning could grow skin for the relief of burn victims. Perhaps nerve tissue might allow those with spinal injuries to rise from their wheelchairs. Perhaps, some much later day, entire organs could be grown from cells of a particular person to provide replacement organs for implantation in that same person. As well as ensuring availability, this would ensure there being no tissue rejection. No doubt, such a process would be in considerable demand. One ethical concern would be whether such a benefit would be available only to the wealthy. There might be worries about various other possible social consequences. That much could be said about a great many medical innovations. It also could be said about most innovations that they are in some way unnatural, which claim might be raised in this application. So too are cesareans and hip replacements unnatural, as are dental fillings. Far more forceful objections would be raised against the cloning of replacement components if the cultured material took on morally significant characteristics of an actual person. Growing a brain (or a substantial portion of one) in vitro for the purpose of providing a transplant of brain tissue might raise important questions about the moral status of the brain. Still, setting aside other issues, tissue cloning in itself seems morally innocuous.

As we proceed with our research in developing living material for therapeutic purposes, we can go only so far working with somatic cells. Some lines of research intended to lead to therapeutic outcomes require something more flexible. Somatic cells have already settled into a particular form of life, as liver or nerve cells, or whatever, and are set in their ways. We may need stem cells as these still have the capacity to develop in different ways. Stem cells are those that may develop by cellular division into somatic cells of any particular somatic type.[17] Zygotes, obviously, are stem cells, though they are not the only ones. In fact, though, most stem cells used in research are derived from embryos, either those that are aborted or that are left over from in vitro fertilization programs. Conceivably, embryos might even be created especially for use in medical research. Here, obviously, we are on ground that is very contentious ethically.

---

[17] As well, there are various gradations between stem cells and somatic cells. *Multipotent* and *pluripotent* are terms sometimes used for cells that can differentiate in many ways but not in every way.

Certainly there are those issues about the moral status of the embryonic life that surfaced in connection with abortion. Even if the embryos are "leftovers" from in vitro fertilization programs undertaken for reproductive purposes and that would otherwise be discarded, there is still vigorous objection to their being used for research. It would create that much more pressure on the "demand" side and perhaps lead to the increased production of embryos. There might be slippery slopes leading down to objectionable outcomes, perhaps including commercial exploitation. Moreover, using embryos or using embryonic stem cells would be to use human life rather than to treat it with the respect it inherently deserves. If excess embryos cannot be adopted out and must die, then, the argument goes, the remains ought to be disposed of with proper respect.[18] Another range of objections would concern the possibility of using cloning and stem-cell research to influence the path and outcome of human organ or tissue development, bringing about supposed improvements. This brings us again to central issues concerning genetic engineering. Once we set aside issues of sources of cells to be cloned, or possibly objectionable outcomes, I have not been able to discover any objections to cellular or tissue cloning in and of itself. This is far from being the case when it comes to human reproductive cloning. Let us here consider that sort of cloning before going on to consider the cloning of embryonic stem cells or doing research on them.

Human Reproductive Cloning

In the natural world, reproductive cloning happens widely and routinely. It is not some novelty dreamed up by mad scientists in the artificial world of the laboratory. There are many species, both of plants and of animals, that reproduce that way some of the time or all of the time. Some species reproduce mostly through cloning but reproduce sexually every few generations. The interspersing of occasional sexual generations has the effect of reshuffling the genetic deck once in a while, which benefits the species. Because of that benefit, species that reproduce sexually tend to have an evolutionary advantage, but some species have reproduced exclusively by cloning for millions of years. Even for species that normally reproduce sexually, there are advantages to having cloning in their repertoire. It can provide an alternative means of reproduction useful in extreme circumstances. For example, it allows certain plants to regenerate effectively in response to fire. Some species have switched from sexual reproduction to cloning as the sole means of reproduction. Indeed, the entire King holly species, *Lomatia tasmanica*, unique to Tasmania, consists of genetically identical individuals, the proliferation of a single clone that occurred about 43,000 years ago. The

---

[18] This puts me in mind of the stance the Church once took against the dissection, even for purposes of medical research, of human corpses.

individual plants are nowhere near that old but by one possible measure, the cloned life-form could be held to be among the world's oldest living entities.

Human beings are also, though rarely, subject to natural cloning. That is what happens when identical twins (even more rarely, triplets) come into existence. This is the result of a zygote splitting into two (or more) genetically similar parts, a form of cloning. The existence of twin clones might bring about problems, not least for their parents, but their existence is no moral enormity (though some African tribes believe any twins are to be killed at birth). For some mammals, such cloning is not only natural but also normal. Armadillos normally produce four genetically identical offspring (making them of particular interest to scientists studying how genes are manifested under differing circumstances). In these cases, adults (humans or armadillos) produce, through entirely natural (and sexual) means, offspring that are clones of one another yet are genetically different from their parents. These things happen. Yet it would certainly provoke moral controversy were people able to utilize some technology of zygote splitting to be able to give birth to identical twins or triplets on demand. It would be strenuously protested that this was an unnatural procedure with problematic consequences.

Even so, the envisioned sort of cloning that creates most public concern, even though it is not yet a reality, is the sort wherein a child is created that has the same genetic makeup as some preexisting person. Perhaps a woman might give birth to her identical twin daughter. Or she might try to produce a genetic replica of her husband or of some other person. Perhaps the most heart-rending are those cases wherein grieving parents wish to bring about a child who is the clone of a deceased elder sibling – thus giving the previous child a posthumous identical twin. These seem intuitively preferable to possible cases wherein egotistical billionaires want to present the world with multiple copies of themselves, or wherein fanatics want to pursue some religious or political agenda (stock example: hordes of Adolf Hitlers). What are to be our grounds for moral assessment of human reproductive cloning when the time does come?

Before we go on with this topic, there is an important point to be stressed. Cloning is a biological process, and what gets replicated is a genetic makeup, a genotype. One does not get a duplicate person or a duplicate personality. As noted previously, some people seem to think of our DNA as being our very identity, some sort of secular and biological soul. However, that is incorrect and far too simple. DNA is one array of components in the genesis of a person. In addition, there is the biological environment, the material and social environment, the events in one's life, and the choices one makes. That is why experience over centuries has confirmed that identical twins do not become identical personalities. We each become who we are. What would one get if we reared clones of Adolf Hitler? Some years ago, a popular film employed such a scenario. Would one get a crop of people with personality disorders, inadequate artistic talent, and a capacity for cheap psychological manipulation and rabble-rousing? To the extent that these things have a genetic basis – no small *if* here – a clone might develop that way. Nonetheless, one would not get a duplicate of Hitler. With different family, social, and physical environments and different life events, one might have gotten anything from a different sort of madman to a more-or-less okay, more-or-less ordinary sort of person, or a person who was a great credit to his community – and who used his oratorical skills to defend his Jewish friends from anti-Semitic attack.

And what would we get in the case of the replacement child? With loving parents in a similar loving environment, one might well get another wonderful child. Nevertheless, it would not be the *same* child or the same personality. Nor could the child's environment possibly be exactly the same. If nothing else, the parents would be that much older. Moreover, one thing that might be different and cause things to go *very* wrong would be if the parents subjected the younger child to expectations that were preconceived and unrealistic. Even with the same genes, it would be unrealistic as well as morally wrong to try to make the younger child into the same person. Of course, it is also true that parents often have preconceived and unrealistic ambitions for their noncloned children. This is no less morally problematic.

I asked earlier about *when* rather than *if* human reproductive cloning becomes a reality because I find it virtually inconceivable that the technology will not be developed and (legally or otherwise) become available for utilization. How might the development of such technologies possibly be stopped? To be sure, we might pass laws all around the planet against human reproductive cloning, but the laws could not be enforced with absolute efficacy if the technology were to become known. To prevent it becoming known, we might pass laws banning research into methods of reproductive cloning. However, not only would it be impossible to enforce such laws absolutely, it also would be immensely difficult even to give such laws clear and appropriate meaning. To rule out research that might possibly lend itself to human reproductive cloning, we would have to rule out any sort of research into any sort of cloning of any sort of cell, human or otherwise. However different we humans may think ourselves, our cells have a great deal in common with other cells. Furthermore, we could not just stop with prohibitions such as those, for we would have to rule out a vast amount of research having to do with DNA and with the makeup and activity of living cells. Certainly we would have to rigorously prohibit and prevent any research into cellular cloning for therapeutic purposes. Such research might shed light on the technical problems of reproductive cloning. Even if such laws could be framed, an attempt to enforce them would cripple an immense amount of valid and useful research. In any case, such laws could never be effectively enforced, no matter how many inquisitions and witch-hunts we were willing to suffer in the meantime. Human reproductive cloning is certain to come. When it does come, we must be ready to enforce a ban on reproductive cloning or on such forms of it as we wish to ban. Likewise, we ban murder. Even though it continues to happen, we try to discourage it. It would be absurd, though, to try to ban any line of research or inquiry that might yield the means of killing someone.

Yet it will not come all at once. Between now and when human reproductive cloning does become a reliable (whether or not legal) clinical alternative, there are bound to be transitional stages wherein it remains somewhat problematic – with there being varying degrees of "somewhat." Before the bugs in the system are eliminated, there will be ambitious researchers and overly ambitious (or desperate) would-be parents who are willing to risk various moral and material disasters in pursuit of their dreams and obsessions. As things are, mammals of several sorts have been successfully cloned, yet most attempts at cloning have not produced viable offspring. It took 277 attempts get Dolly. The technology has improved since then (1997), but it remains true that even when live newborns have been produced, they have often developed defects and often have relatively short lives. However we might feel about that sort of thing when it is a matter of sheep or mice, we cannot accept that in the case of humans. Those who condemn abortion as being murder will deplore the generation of embryos so very probably condemned to an early death. Others, who are not concerned about insentient embryos per se, will draw the line at bringing about infants born to lives of poor quality. Real risks pose real ethical issues, and for the foreseeable future, attempts at human reproductive cloning ought to be suppressed as being too dangerous. Nonetheless, we should not allow these matters to obscure from our minds the more fundamental question of whether human reproductive cloning is morally wrong in principle.

If it could be undertaken with justifiable confidence in the creation of a child who was properly healthy (and not a menace to the rest of the world), would human reproductive cloning be inherently wrong? In advance of the time when we are forced by events to decide which uses of it we are to attempt to prevent or control, let us continue to ask on which grounds we might decide what are or are not morally objectionable procedures or outcomes. Seemingly, there are only so many moral grounds available. On the basis of a purely individualistic ethic, we might assess whether the greatest good (for whom?) is achieved or whether everyone's rights and moral status have been respected. When there actually is or might be an injured individual, an individualistic ethic can gain some purchase in giving us useful moral guidance. As we have already noted, it would be morally wrong to knowingly create humans of some sort whose lives were less than worth living. We injure them by creating them. Only a moral madman would contemplate creating people with miserable lives, however useful they might be for industry or medical research. Nor should optimism blind us to the fact that an attempt at cloning might well have such consequences.

The considerations of individualistic ethics will always be important, yet it takes a larger arsenal with which to do battle with the complexities of human reproductive cloning. The question of whether there actually is an injured party, a recurrent question in bioethics, is one that faces us here. In some possible applications, no one is injured – in which case an individualistic ethic becomes silent. Virtue ethics, I would suggest, might offer us something of value, and so might a system of ethics recognizing that *Homo sapiens* is a morally significant entity. I believe that we can profitably use all of these perspectives in addressing the complex issues of human reproductive cloning, that we ought not to rely on just one formulaic approach.[19] As we have already seen in connection with the cloned Epsilons of *Brave New World*, an individualistic system of ethics on its own cannot adequately cope with the Problem of Contingent Existence.[20] Even though life was marginally worth living for them, and could not have been appreciably better for them, to intentionally bring about such beings would be to detract from the well-being of humanity as a morally significant entity in its own right. By no means would it be life affirming. It would be morally wrong to create such beings by genetic engineering, and it would be wrong to replicate them by cloning. Nonetheless, on the basis of an individualistic ethic, we cannot validate such a condemnation. No one is having his or her rights violated or otherwise being negated as an end in herself or himself. The Epsilons, such as they are, are not being injured. An individualistic utilitarian system of ethics might even validate an Epsilon project on the grounds of social utility. Evidently, unless we are to accept such outcomes, we must look beyond individualistic ethics.

Widening our system of ethics to incorporate holistic considerations can improve our capacity to address ethical issues, but it does not go nearly so far as a great many people wish to go in condemnation of cloning. This is not to say that everything some people would condemn ought to be condemned, but there are some further questions that must be asked. Suppose, for example, someone did want to run off a genetic copy of herself or himself. We might suspect an ego problem there, but the existence of a genetic duplicate would not be an injury to the human race – no more than if the person had been born with an identical twin. There would be no realistic question of altering the genetic makeup of the human race. Nor is it meaningful to enter a plea on behalf of some "normal" child who is deprived of coming into existence. The self-cloner is not intending to create

---

[19] I am not presupposing that there is a plurality of independent moral principles. It might be that they all ultimately reduce to one single foundation. If so, I would suggest that it is the virtue of life affirmation.

[20] Presumably, the Epsilons of *Brave New World* were created through genetic engineering, prior to their cloning, but we cannot rest our objections to such projects merely on a condemnation of genetic engineering. That would leave open the possibility of cloning naturally occurring Epsilons. Epsilon-like individuals do occur, and they are to be cared for and loved, but not replicated.

a person whose life lessened the overall quality of human life. However, to produce a child for such narrowly egoist purposes would certainly not be indicative of good character and would be to create another person for the purpose of making it an object of self-love. Here, certainly, we should only proceed with caution.

Who would be injured by the creation of a genetic replica of a deceased child? So far as the existence of that combination of genes goes, neither the parents, nor society, nor humankind would be any the worse off than they were when the first child was alive. To avoid extraneous issues, let us assume that there was nothing genetically objectionable about the first child, and that there is no reason to suspect that the replacement child would not have a life worth living. Of course, there is the argument that the child would suffer under the weight of excessive parental expectation (as do many children who are *not* clones). Certainly, though, this is not enough for us to be able to conclude that life could not be not worth living for that child. By now, we will have noted that the possibility of some alternative noncloned child's not having that particular problem is irrelevant to the issue of whether the proposed child would have a worthwhile life. Nor would such an alternative possible nonreplica child have some preexistential right to come into existence. Instead of forbidding the prospective parents to clone, might it be better to just give them solid counseling to the effect that genetic duplication does not entail duplication of personality? Experience with identical twins, over many centuries, has demonstrated that conclusively, and we cannot automatically assume that the prospective parents would fail to grasp that fact. Were we to forbid people to have children of whom they had significant expectations, very few children would be born. I am sure that when the technology for reproductive cloning becomes available, we will have far more serious things to worry about than the cloning of deceased children. In such a case, there would be at least a realistic expectation that the clone, like its deceased sibling, though a different person would be very much loved. Far more objectionable would be reproductive cloning for commercial, ideological, or egoist purposes. Although this could not be entirely prevented, even if prohibited, we could at least frame laws in such a way as to prevent exploitation. We might have laws against certain sorts of commercial operations or against willing or otherwise transferring substantial sums of money to one's clone.

Stem Cell Research

Let us return to the troubling topic of stem cell research. This topic is so very contentious because there is such a great deal riding on it, both in terms of the progress of medical science and in terms of the moral issues thought to be involved. The fact that stem cells can develop into any sort of somatic cell offers marvelous prospects of breathtaking medical advances. If we could learn how to do it, perhaps we could help people with spinal-cord injuries or brain damage by giving them just the right sort of nerve tissue. Perhaps we could give heart tissue to those who have had heart attacks or insulin-producing cells to those afflicted with diabetes. Then there is Huntington's disease, Parkinson's disease, and so on. The wish list could be extended indefinitely. Clearly, though, there is much we have to learn. We will have to learn how properly to administer just the right sort of tissue to the patient once we have learned how to produce it. Critically, we have to learn how to produce it. Of course, we have long known how to grow tissue cultures of various sorts but, for effective therapy, we cannot use just any old nerve (or whatever) tissue. For it to work well, we would need to have tissue that matches the patient's own tissue and DNA type. It is of vital importance, therefore, that we need to learn how to produce such individualized tissue. As things are now, we do not know what conditions govern the development of particular sorts of somatic cells from stem cells. Some genes get switched on, some genes get switched off, and surrounding conditions matter. However, how it all works and how we are to get the results we want are unknowns that stem cell research would have to work on.

But is this the sort of research we are morally at liberty to pursue? What is at issue is *embryonic* stem cell research. After all, this is human life we are dealing with, we are reminded, human life of a very special sort and of very special provenance. Can we avoid this issue? Could we do morally acceptable research of the same value by using *adult stem cells*? Gathering them would not cause the destruction of a human life. Adult stem cells have indeed been found to exist. Seemingly they are scattered through the body to be on hand for various repair jobs. Let us assume, as seems likely, that such cells can be gathered in useful quantities. If they can be gathered and can do an adequate job, then we would no longer have to pay the price of using embryonic stem cells – whether we consider that moral price to be zero or to be something higher. Unfortunately, adult stem cells appear to have a more restricted range of possibilities than do embryonic stem cells, being able to differentiate into some but not all of the different types of somatic cells. If this is so, then they may not be as useful in research and therapy as had been hoped. Perhaps there was wishful thinking on the part of those who are morally opposed to the utilization of embryos. As of this writing, it is still an open question just how far we can advance with adult stem cells in comparison with embryonic stem cells.

It may then turn out that whatever moral issues there are concerning the use of embryonic stem cells cannot be avoided so easily. For our purposes here, let us assume that the use of embryonic stem cells would better serve medical progress for the relief of human suffering, and let us inquire into the moral issues thought to be at stake. Just why is it that embryonic human life is thought to be so special morally? Though all life has *some* moral significance, sometimes its level of significance is quite low, and that includes instances of living cells with human DNA. Is the supposed moral significance of embryonic stem cells a result of their having, unlike somatic cells, the potential to develop into persons? Such an objection would overlook the fact that, a lá Dolly, somatic cells too have that capacity. One must presume that this would be all the more true of adult stem cells. For the most part, what causes the fuss is that embryonic stem cells are normally obtained by breaking up embryos. (Or we could start with the single cell of a zygote, which might be considered even worse, were being worse thought possible.) Embryos utilized are generally obtained from early abortions or from embryos created in vitro. These latter may be surplus to requirements of in vitro fertilization programs, or they may be created specially to serve as a source for embryonic stem cells.[21] Clearly, we return here to issues canvassed previously in connection with abortion together with whatever issues there might be about creating embryos specifically for research purposes.

Previously I have argued at some length that there is no good reason to believe that an embryo, much less a single cell, has a soul and that there appears to be very plausible reasons to the contrary. Nor is there is there good reason to deem such beings to be persons. Such an entity might be a potential person (in common with each of the approximately 100 trillion cells in an adult human body), but a potential person is not a person. Unlike cloned somatic cells, though, embryos can develop into people through *natural* processes. Still, they are no more than potential persons. We might well ask what moral significance rides on that loaded term *natural*. Naturalness is something that it is far easier to invoke than to explicate. Just what is natural for an embryo created artificially in vitro? It could be implanted artificially in a womb. Although the technology employed would be far less complex than that required for cloning a somatic cell, would it be any less *unnatural*? If embryos and somatic cells do have some primitive potential to develop into persons, though they are not yet persons, is it morally monstrous to sacrifice them for the benefit of those who are persons now?

Actually, there would be very little need to create embryos especially for stem cell research. There are many embryos left over from the numerous abortions that occur in any case, and there are leftovers from in vitro fertilization programs. As I already noted, there is the argument that human remains should be disposed of with appropriate respect. Even if we grant that embryos are (unlike other bits of human flesh) human remains to be

---

[21] It is also claimed that placentas and umbilical cords are other possible sources of embryonic stem cells. If they can provide a source of suitable cells, this would evidently give us a way of avoiding the use of embryos. Placentas and umbilical cords, potential persons though their cells may be, have routinely been discarded throughout history, this seemingly being the way of nature. If so, that might be a way to avoid facing up to the ethical issues. For our purposes here, let us proceed on the pessimistic assumption that the moral issues have to be faced up to rather than side-stepped.

disposed of with proper respect, is it any less respectful or appropriate to use them for medical research than it is to use dead adult bodies for medical research? The latter has been accepted for at least a couple of centuries, though it too was once disapproved of for many of the same reasons. As for the argument that using embryos for research would lead to embryos being created especially for the purpose, that argument seems to have things completely the wrong way around. It is the refusal to allow the great many such surplus embryos that there already are to be utilized that creates pressure for embryos to be created especially for research purposes. These things being so, I see no persuasive reason why we ought not to proceed with scientifically well-informed and conducted embryonic stem cell research.

Sometimes attempts are made to find a compromise position. An example of such a proposal came from the United Kingdom's Committee of Inquiry into Human Fertilisation and Embryology (chaired by Dame Mary Warnock) that recommended (via a closely split vote) that researchers be able to use embryos prior to fourteen days after conception. The reason for that is that around the fourteenth day, the embryo starts to form a fold that, eventually, quite some while later, develops into the spinal cord and brain. To be said in favor of drawing the line there is that this is about where the embryonic life begins to function as an individual organism. It could be claimed, then, that this is about the time that a particular human entity starts life as an organism in its own right. Twinning and combination into chimeras are no longer possible. Nonetheless, the embryonic life is nowhere close to being a person. When the fold first forms, the embryonic life does not have anything remotely resembling the sentience, let alone the rationality, of a person. The fold is not actually functioning in any way as a nervous system. The embryonic life at the time has no sentience at all, let alone rationality, and therefore has far lower capabilities than does a fish or a tadpole. The embryonic life is making a start toward developing its potential but is then manifesting only the first trace. In terms of what it then actually is, it has only the most minimally higher level of moral status than it did a few days earlier in its prefold condition. The Inquiry's recommendation seems very much like the work of a committee.

According to popular wisdom, a camel is a horse designed by a committee. This is really quite unfair. A camel is superbly well adapted to survive and flourish in environments and under conditions in which most other things, horses included, cannot. However, it does make a fair point about committees in that they tend to add a bit here and make a change there so that the outcome is something that enough people can agree on even though (unlike a camel) it lacks any clear rationale in itself. Yet arriving at a practically workable compromise can be a very valuable outcome. The Inquiry's recommendation that embryos be used only prior to the fourteenth day provides a cutoff point well before the embryo develops any of the characteristics of a person even though it is undeniably human life.

Therefore, while it will not be acceptable to those who oppose any use of any embryo under any circumstances, it might well be acceptable to those who want to take a less hard-line position still short of dismembering those who recognizably are people, even though they may have no clear idea where they want to place the cutoff point and no clear rationale for why they want to put it somewhere rather than somewhere else. If researchers can get enough embryonic stem cells that way, I would certainly be happy to accept such a provision in the belief that no harm was being done.

I might mention here another ethical problem that rears its troubling head in these matters. Really, it is not so much a new problem as a doubling-up of previous problems. To get tissue implants for a given individual in order to, let us say, repair an injured spinal cord, it is best if we can get tissue that matches as closely as possible the tissue type, ultimately the DNA, of the tissue recipient. We would want to start from a tissue type of just the right sort. How might we procure that? Ultimately, we would do best, were this possible, to start from cells from the patient's own body: Take some nerve tissue to grow more nerve tissue. It may turn out that the most useful starting point for growing replacement tissue for that patient would be adult stem cells procured from that patient. Then, if we knew how, we could grow tissue of exactly the right sort in terms of DNA as well as tissue type – a perfect match. But if we start from stem cells from that patient's own body and start reproducing them, then we have the ethical problems not only of manipulating beings that are potential humans but also of possibly creating the means whereby the patient might be cloned. Yet to stop research that might lead to human reproductive cloning would require us to abandon research offering important possible therapeutic advances. Are we to condemn many millions of people around the world to live with, for instance, diabetes in order to stop some egoist from running off a DNA copy of himself or herself? The latter is almost certain to happen in any case.

15

Ethics and Biomedical Research

Some Applications

Deservedly, biomedical research has a good reputation because of the great benefits it has brought, and promises to bring, to humankind. Nonetheless, it also has a tarnished reputation in the eyes of many people. In part this may be due to irrational fears, but the sad fact is that some things have been done as biomedical research that ought not to have been done. There is a continuing fear that new things, and new sorts of things, might go terribly wrong. To be sure, things can just go wrong, particularly when one is dealing with the unknown, as research characteristically does. However, sometimes things have gone wrong because of moral shortsightedness, or just plain immorality, on the part of the researchers or those controlling them. I will shortly tell a few horror stories in this regard. Furthermore, sometimes situations are so novel and complex that the best and most moral will in the world would have the utmost difficulty in determining the right course of action.

We must bear in mind that moral wrongness does not commonly appear in stark and overt form. In biomedical research, as elsewhere, it frequently arises from ignorance, inadvertence, or misguided priorities. Researchers may be driven by a desire for reputation, or perhaps just by a desire for professional survival, and by visions of the great good to come of it all. Ethical corners may be cut and means justified by ends, all without consciousness that any *real* wrong is or might be done. We humans find it very easy to not see what we do not want to see, as well as to see what we do want to see (even if it is not there).

For our part, we who influence the making of rules or their interpretation are not characteristically faced with the task of taming moral monsters. Rather, our primary concern is with patrolling moral boundaries, gray and indeterminate as they may be, and with keeping alert to possible side effects and implications that have not been thought through. Mostly it is a matter of making sure in particular cases that the interpretation and application of moral rules fit moral reality. It is only occasionally that the rules themselves have to be redrawn or, more commonly, our way of applying them has to be adjusted so as to fit moral reality. Usually this is in response to cases that are anomalous in greater or lesser degree. These require us to do some rethinking. From time to time it is in response to horrendous events. In the following text, I shall begin by discussing some notable horrendous events, doing so for the purpose not only of illustrating what can go wrong but also of how easy it is for us humans to slip into apparently minor violations of major principles. How we make major adjustments in the face of horrendous events sheds some light on how we are to make adjustments in the face of lesser instances. Something I shall *not* do, which would be silly, is to try to provide comprehensive solutions to all the outstanding ethical problems of biomedical research. Any such thing would, in any case, become rapidly out of date. Rather, my objective is to show a way of approaching ethical issues in biomedical research.

Horror Story I: Nuremberg

After the conclusion of World War II, the civilized world was appalled and disgusted as the moral enormities of Nazi activities were revealed. Particularly atrocious were some of the biomedical research projects undertaken at German concentration camps. In response, the Allied forces convened a military tribunal, sitting at Nuremberg, to investigate and try some of those charged with crimes against humanity. An outcome of the Nuremberg hearings was the articulation of some important moral principles, among which is the *Nuremberg Code* for medical experimentation. Also implicitly repudiated, though not explicitly mentioned in the code, is the principle that "just following orders" (following what Hermann Goering called "the Leadership Principle") is not an adequate defense to such charges.

It would be comforting if we could just consign the Leadership Principle to a time, a place, and an ideology safely receding into the depths of history. However, the discomfiting truth is that people more generally have a tendency to defer to authority in their moral judgments and actions, if only to the authority of those around them. This tendency was vividly displayed in a classic series of experiments conducted by Stanley Milgram.[1] People were recruited to take part in what was ostensibly a research project investigating the effect of punishment in learning. Their role, as it developed, was to assist as "'teachers' by administering electric shocks, graded in intensity, to people whom they thought were taking part in the research as

---

[1] See Stanley Milgram, "Behavioral Study of Obedience," *Journal of Abnormal and Social Psychology* 67 (1963): 371–378; and Thomas Blass, *The Man Who Shocked the World: The Life and Legacy of Stanley Milgram* (New York: Basic Books, 2004).

'learners'." Actually, these latter individuals were actors. When the "learners" gave wrong answers, the "teachers" were to administer an electric shock. The level of shock was ostensibly increased by increments of 15 volts over that administered for previous wrong answers. In reality, the apparatus operated by the "teacher" delivered no shock whatsoever, with the actor portraying appropriately increasing levels of pain and distress. At higher apparent voltages, the actor would portray great pain and distress and beg for the experiment to stop. Many of the "teachers" were worried about that and displayed high levels of stress. If they demurred, the experimenter would verbally encourage them to continue and would assume full responsibility for all adverse outcomes. How far were people willing, however reluctantly, to go on with this draconian program? Sixty percent of the people in the role of teacher – the actual subjects of the experiment – followed orders to punish the inadequate "learner" all the way to the end of the 450-volt scale. Not one of them refused before the 300-volt level. Hannah Arendt once remarked on the "banality of evil." Evil creeps up on us by small degrees, through a series of minor compromises, in the guise of the ordinary and with the sanction of recognized authority. There are few of us indeed who are not susceptible and never would have been. This is attested to not only by Milgram's experiments but also by today's newspaper.

At the Nuremberg Tribunal, several individuals who were "just following orders" were sentenced to death. The Nuremberg Code for medical research had as the foremost of its requirements that of informed consent: Research is only to be performed on subjects who consent to take part, without being subject to any form of coercion. Subjects must be given all the relevant information they require prior to giving their consent. The Nazis, of course, routinely performed experiments on subjects who did not give their consent and who were not informed about the nature and purpose, or likely consequences, of the experiment. Moreover, the Nuremberg Code requires that subjects must be able, without penalty, to withdraw at any stage of the experiment (however exasperating that might be for the researchers).[2] Beyond that, the researcher is obligated to terminate, at whatever stage, a subject's participation in an experiment if there comes to be reason to believe that continuation in the experiment would be likely to result in death or injury to the subject (unless the risk is accepted by

---

[2] This clearly raises a few points about the Milgram experiment. Those taking the role of learner tried, so far as those taking the role of teacher were aware, to withdraw from participation in the trial. To continue the trial against their will would be contrary to the Nuremberg Code as well as to supposedly commonsense morality. Moreover, Milgram's actual project was itself contrary to the Code, inasmuch as the subjects ("teachers") were deceived and did not give their informed consent to take part in the experiment in which they actually participated. They did not consent to experience the stress so many of them felt. Did the undoubtedly great value of the experiment outweigh the ethical shortcuts taken?

the patient and held reasonably possible benefits that would outweigh the dangers).

Moreover, research is not to be conducted randomly or on a purely spec-ulative basis but rather only if there is substantial scientific reason to believe that the results would be of significant social benefit. *However* – and this is very much to be stressed – the Nuremberg Code does not explicitly say anything about whether the projected *social* benefit of the research would be a valid reason for asking or allowing prospective experimental subjects to undertake a high level of risk without a prospect of compensating benefit for those individual subjects. Certainly, some experimental procedures can be risky indeed for the subject, but they also may offer compensating possi-bilities of substantial benefit for that particular subject. Many experimental cancer treatments are in this category, and they are generally approved sub-ject to informed consent. However, can we ethically allow a research project to proceed if it poses high levels of risk without possibility of benefit to the subject – whether or not it is on the basis of informed consent? On this point, the Nuremberg Code is silent, yet it is a question that often returns to haunt us. Nor is it the only one.

Horror Stories II and III: Tuskegee and Auckland

If we are to assess the merits of some regime of treatment for a medical condition, it is obviously useful to compare how well the treatment does in comparison with outcomes when no treatment is used. However, this raises some important ethical issues. From 1932 (before the Nuremberg Code) until 1972 (much after its declaration), the United States Public Health Service did a survey on syphilis in treated and untreated cases. Whatever else can be said, certainly it can be said that information gained in the study was of medical and social benefit. Subjects of the survey were black men in a number of the southern U.S. states, centering on Tuskegee, Alabama, who were diagnosed as having syphilis. Some were given treatment, some were given deliberately substandard treatment, and some were given no treatment at all (even though it was known that treatments then available offered some alleviation and, by the late 1940s, penicillin was standard treatment for the disease). Other agencies were prevented from supplying treatment as well; the Public Health Service intended the subjects to not be cured so that the natural progression of the untreated disease could be studied. The course of the disease was followed over the years. Treatment, such as was given, and when given, was by consent, but otherwise the black men did not consent to take part in the survey. About four hundred were not only untreated but were not even informed that they had the disease.[3]

---

[3] For further material on the Tuskegee Syphilis Study, see Fred D. Gray, *The Tuskegee Syphilis Study: The Real Story and Beyond* (Montgomery, AL: NewSouth Books, 2002); James H. Jones,

Unlike so much of what the Nazis did, the problematic part of the project was passive rather than active. Nothing was done *to* the untreated black men; they were not intentionally infected. Yet nothing was done *for* them when they might have been given treatment or at least counsel.[4] We might ask whether the fact that the men were black would be relevant to our moral assessment. In any case, whether or not it was a question of social or racial justice, it was seemingly a question of justice. The men not treated medically were not treated as ends in themselves but only as means to the ends of others. The eventual, albeit long-delayed, outcry over the Tuskegee Syphilis Study led in the United States to the adoption of the recommendations of the Belmont Report. These reaffirmed the principles of justice, beneficence, and respect for persons and, as a consequence, the principle that informed consent necessarily requires a thorough and open assessment of the potential risks and benefits. That would include the risks of doing nothing. There was also an affirmation of a principle of social and individual justice in the selection and treatment of subjects. It is hoped that one will be outraged because of injustices done to defenseless minority groups – yet not conclude that they were injustices just *because* they happened to minorities. Such treatment should never happen to anyone.

We would want to rule out that sort of thing entirely. Indeed, we have made rules against such atrocities. Moreover, around the world, we have mandated institutional ethics committees to oversee experimentation in order to see to it that projects do conform to the rules, both in the letter and in the spirit. Even so, things do not always work out so as to realize our hopes and intentions in formulating rules and instituting committees. Commencing in 1966, Dr. Herbert Green, Professor of Gynecology at the National Women's Hospital, Auckland, New Zealand, sought evidence in support of a strong conviction of his. Specifically, he believed that changes in cervical intraepithelial neoplasia (CIN), when left alone, do not develop into invasive cancer. He conducted a trial following women who were identified as having CIN but who were not offered any treatment. Despite the protests of some doctors within the hospital, the hospital board did nothing to halt the trial or to notify the women. As it turned out, the rate of invasive cancer among those women was a great many times higher than among women who did not show evidence of CIN changes. Several of them died. So, what went wrong – and can it be fixed for the future? Professor Green, of course, had convinced himself that he was not violating the principle of

---

Bad Blood: The Tuskegee Syphilis Experiment (New York: The Free Press, 1993); and S. B. Thomas and S. C. Quinn, "The Tuskegee Syphilis Study, 1932–1972: Implications for HIV Education and AIDS Risk Education Programs in the Black Community," *American Journal of Public Health* 81 (1991): 1393–1394.

4 Again, one wonders how morally significant is the distinction between passive steps of omission and active steps of commission. Is the plea that we do not actually *do* anything appreciably better than the plea of just following orders?

informed consent. As the CIN changes, he believed, were not indicative of risk, there were no risks of which the women were not informed. But of course that ought not to have been his decision to make. Events demonstrated otherwise, and the condition is now described as "precancerous" – *carcinoma* in situ, CIS, rather than CIN.[5]

Our first reaction may be to wonder whether there was an ethics committee there and, if so, what in the world it thought it was doing. There was one, but its procedures in overseeing biomedical research were somewhat lax, to say the least. There was no requirement for the researchers to submit for its inspection a Participant Information Sheet, explaining the nature of the project to prospective participants. Moreover, there was no requirement for the researchers even to submit a copy of the consent form to be signed by participants. Seemingly, many projects (not only Professor Green's) would just be waved through – or should it be "waived" through? – on the grounds that Dr. So-and-So is a competent researcher who knows what she or he is doing. Even in the face of alarmed protest within the hospital, neither the National Women's Hospital Ethics Committee nor its hospital board was willing to allow the boat to be rocked. Thankfully, when this sordid business finally did come to light, there was a major shake-up of how surveillance is conducted in New Zealand.

Obviously, better rules were needed to see to it that the rules were followed. But piling rules about rules on top of rules can only carry us so far. The National Women's Hospital was lax in following its own rules. The Nuremberg Code was being violated. The Hippocratic Oath was being violated, insofar as the researcher was acting for the sake of his research project rather than acting first for the sake of his patients. Rules there were, but rules – however indispensable as tools and guidelines – cannot do it all. Indispensable they clearly are – but as tools and guidelines for people to use. Always there must be people willing, alert, and able to use those tools and guidelines sensibly and morally. Not all rules are good ones, as Nuremberg reminds us, and even the best of rules need to be applied well to practical moral reality. Ethical rules are *about* practical moral reality, they do not comprise it, so ethics can never be merely just about ticking off the right boxes in accordance with the prevailing rules. That is the real lesson they had to learn the hard way at the National Women's Hospital.[6]

5 For further details, see Sandra Coney, *The Unfortunate Experiment: The Full Story behind the Inquiry into Cervical Treatment* (Auckland: Penguin Books New Zealand and Camberwell, Victoria: Penguin Books Australia, 1988); and the report by Judge Silvia Cartwright, that is, the Cartwright Report (Report of the Cervical Cancer Inquiry, August 5, 1988).
6 Somewhere between a minor annoyance and a pet peeve for me is what I so often find in research proposals, on the standard form under Ethical Considerations. One might hope to find there some discussion of actual issues, considerations about impact on participants, informed consent, and the like. Instead, there is often something like "This project was approved by the [Whoever] Ethics Committee" – as if some committee's approval were the

Free Consent

As there is more to morality than ticking boxes, there is much more to consent than just a signature on a consent form. Just what *free* consent is can be a fine question indeed. This is yet another of those matters wherein it is difficult to draw good lines, and wherein it is far easier to rule things out than to rule things in. In practice, lines here can be drawn only with imperfect accuracy and followed only with considerable difficulty. One factor is adequate knowledge of what one is consenting to. Consent is not free when it is obtained by trickery or dishonesty or willful nondisclosure of relevant information. However valuable the Milgram or Auckland experiment was or aspired to be, free consent to take part was not given and would have made the actual experiment impossible. One can freely consent to run risks, but it is not free consent if known risks are undisclosed.

Nor, obviously, is any consent free if it is obtained by threat of violence or suspension of privileges or through any other coercive means. This might be very difficult to determine in practice. Coercion can take many forms, including some supplied by circumstances. A gratuity for taking part in a drug trial might be something I could just shrug off yet be virtually compelling to a cash-strapped student: "My poverty, but not my will consents." (Later in this chapter I return to the question of how poverty can undermine free consent.) At one time, prisoners were often offered time off their sentences for showing public-spiritedness by "volunteering" to be research subjects, thereby repaying some of their debt to society.

Again, even if I am assured that my clinical care would not be compromised, is my consent *entirely* free if I am influenced by a strong desire to stay on good terms with the clinical care team – including nurses who may have been ordered to *consent* the patients? By degrees and gradations, we can go on to other psychological factors and limitations on the capacity to make free choice. Except under very special conditions (and involving only the most minimal risk), the law does not recognize as being free any consent obtained from minors or committed mental patients because those persons are characteristically in dependent relationships and are deemed incapable of thinking adequately about their own welfare in all cases. Yet it is clearly a matter of cases. It is too coarse of an approach just to suppose that people are either competent to make free choice about their own welfare or else they are not competent to do so. In particular instances some minors or mental patients might make very sound judgments, and – a danger area

ethical issue. In the place for a discussion of possible physical side effects, we would certainly want a lot more than just the bare statement that the project was approved by the [Whoever] Drug Committee. The drug committee's opinions, however well taken, are about the likely efficacy and side effects. It does not create or abolish them. Some committee's approval, or that of the Women's Hospital in particular, does not make a project ethical.

in bioethics – in particular instances, some supposedly competent adults might not.

Consider now a recent actual research project, one that raises in my mind questions about whether any cogent line can be drawn universally between those who are and those who are not competent to give free consent in matters concerning their own welfare. The project concerned the development of a blood test that would measure type and level of liver damage. What was needed were data correlating blood chemicals with known liver damage. Needed therefore were blood samples and liver samples from people with liver damage. The proposal was to recruit participants at rehabilitation ("drying out") centers for alcoholics, asking the sober alcoholics there to agree to give a blood sample and a liver biopsy. They would be quite promising subjects inasmuch as most alcoholics have some degree of liver damage. At the same time, one might wonder whether it would be wise to allow another scoop to be taken from an already-damaged liver. A liver biopsy, which involves a needle being inserted into the liver and drawing out a sample, is not a negligible procedure. Adverse consequences can include death.

Let us make some assumptions about the prospective participants in the trial: They are adults, they are not diagnosed as being mentally incompetent, and they are not drunk when recruited. Moreover, let us assume that they are given realistic and credible guarantees that they will in no way be disadvantaged in their treatment at the drying-out center, or in any other way, if they decline to take part. The potential risks of the proposed procedure are thoroughly explained, and it is explained that the individuals themselves would not stand to gain from participation in the project. People often do take part in research projects for altruistic reasons. They may wish to contribute to the progress of medical science or to help future alcoholics. These are not bad reasons. Perhaps we should leave it to their free choice.

Yet we might wonder just how free their free choice is. Alcoholics tend to be people with low self-esteem. Moreover, they tend to be quite ashamed of themselves after a binge and often seek to make amends in pathetic little ways. Furthermore, can we not assume that, at least in some ways, alcoholics have a certain weakness of will? Perhaps we take advantage of that weakness when we catch them in a psychologically vulnerable situation and ask them to accept significantly high levels of risk. Still, if we tried to save people from foolishness and weakness of will, we would have to rule out quite a lot. We would have to rule out a great many forms of advertising, and not just those promoting tobacco and gambling. On top of all that, there is political sloganeering to be considered. There are professionals with a high level of expertise at exploiting people's vulnerabilities. To what extent can we protect people from their vulnerabilities? To whom dare we entrust our protection? We might take a "right wing" approach and leave it up to the absolute discretion of the individual, yet there must be limits to that. We might otherwise get a few volunteers for an experimental study of Russian roulette, using live ammunition. Just as obviously, a "left wing" approach that seeks to protect people from being carried into *any* danger is subject to the limitation in extremis that no one would be allowed to do anything. This suggests to me that as practical people making practical decisions, following abstract absolutes is not always the best course of action, if possible at all.

What sort of balance are we to arrive at concerning the alcoholics recruited for liver biopsies? At the very least, we want to give them the best protection consistent with the project proceeding. But should the project be allowed to proceed at all? Can we find a balance between allowing the alcoholics an opportunity to gratify altruistic impulses and, in contrast, inappropriately allowing them to take excessive risks? A temptation to be resisted is that of balancing the welfare of the prospective participants off against the value of the results, either as being of scientific value in their own right or as leading to improved prospects for future medical patients. Tempting as that might be, we are bound to safeguard the welfare of prospective participants as ends in themselves and not allow their welfare to be compromised for ulterior ends. To the contrary, I have heard researchers in one project or another stoutly insisting that their project, though perhaps a bit risky for participants, is really highly moral because it means that we would not have to experiment on so many other subjects in the future or, of course, because of the compensating benefits for future patients. This may perhaps have the merit of not involving future people in risky trials. However, the *Declaration of Helsinki* plainly tells us (Section 1, Point 5) the following:

In medical research on human subjects, considerations related to the well-being of the human subject should take precedence over the interests of science and society.[7]

We must put the welfare of the prospective participants first.

This we therefore must do in the case of the alcoholics. Arguably, we would be infringing on their autonomy by denying them the opportunity to act altruistically; yet, also arguably, we would be infringing on their too-weak autonomy by confronting them with a choice with which they may be ill equipped to cope. Were there some sound general principle that could be formulated for dealing with such matters, we could adopt and codify it, and that would be that. As it happens, there is no such principle. Even so, that does not leave us entirely adrift or render one decision as good as another. If we have a say in such matters, we at least can address the right question: *What course of action would best respect the well-being* (including the autonomy)

---

[7] The Declaration of Helsinki is a set of ethical principles for the medical community regarding human experimentation, first adopted by the World Medical Assembly in Helsinki, Finland, in 1964 and then amended periodically thereafter. See, for example, World Medical Organization, "Declaration of Helsinki," *British Medical Journal* 313 (1996): 1448–1449.

of the prospective participants? What course of action would best affirm their life as individual human beings? How we are to apply this approach to cases *is* a matter of cases. Whether we are making our assessments individually or collectively, it always must be a matter of finding the best fit of our principles and ideals with reality. I am not suggesting that we compromise our principles or undermine them – though we may sometimes come to refine them. What we do need to do is to work out how best to apply our principles and ideals in practice.

Free Consent and Some Continuing Problems

Astonishingly enough, there is *still* considerable pressure in particular instances to knowingly give people suboptimal treatment in the interests of this or that research project. I believe that it is only a minority, but there are some researchers who wish to validate a particular course of treatment for some condition as being superior to no treatment at all. This may take the form of trial in comparison with placebo. Typically and often, it is some pharmaceutical company that wants to get its latest product approved for clinical use that proposes and financially sponsors such a trial. However, if there is a standard treatment that is known to be of *some* value, why not test this latest Wonder Drug against that? This is an ethical matter as well as a pharmacological one. If people can be given treatment that has some proba-bility of being of benefit to them, then can it possibly be ethical to enlist them in an experiment wherein they may have little or no prospect of additional benefit but do stand to suffer adverse consequences by omission? Let me say now that I am not talking here about enormities on the scale of Tuskegee or Auckland, let alone Auschwitz. Yet there are still instances wherein people are recruited into projects that may expose them to a risk uncompensated by potential benefit. What ethical stance ought we to take in such matters? Clearly important considerations are those of informed consent and, follow-ing that, the seriousness of the potential adverse consequences. I have heard researchers defend their proposed projects as being ethical, despite possi-ble appearances – including the Declaration of Helsinki – to the contrary, because risks to participants are "outweighed" by the potential benefits to medical science. As well as having severe doubts about the morality of the justification, I have noticed a considerable reluctance on the part of the researchers to present the matter in such stark terms on their Participant Information Sheet.[8]

---

[8] My noticings in this and the following instance are based on my more than two decades of membership on the research ethics committee of a hospital heavily engaged in medical research. I understand that there would be potential legal problems were I to cite particular examples.

Before I go on to discuss further matters of minimal and reluctant disclosure, I briefly discuss another ethical issue about what the trial drug is to be trialled against. Morally sound medical practice, backed up by the Declaration of Helsinki, demands that the care of participants in a clinical trial never be compromised. This precludes trials in comparison with placebo when a treatment of known utility is available. There should be genuine uncertainty within the medical community concerning which arm of the trial has superior therapeutic merit. That is, there should be *clinical equipoise* in informed opinion about which arm is preferable. If there is no real reason to believe that a treatment is better than placebo, the trial ought not to be run.

Suppose, though, that although there is some reason for thinking that a new treatment has merit and therefore that it compares favorably with placebo, it cannot be trialled against standard treatment per se for the simple reason that there *is* no one standard treatment. Expert medical opinion might be divided among Treatments X, Y, and Z. Can a researcher ethically take part in a clinical trial comparing experimental Treatment E with Treatments X, Y, and Z if she or he does not stand in a state of clinical equipoise concerning the different arms of the trial? Perhaps she or he is convinced that Treatment X is next to useless, whereas Treatment Z is so good that Treatment E is unlikely to withstand comparison with it. Clinical trials, though, do not revolve around hunches or unverified conjecture. Good practice is based on scientific evidence. One right answer we therefore can give to this poser is that it is ethical to proceed with such a trial until informed opinion within the medical community is no longer in equipoise but recognizes that some arms of the trial are superior to others. Inferior arms ought then to be discontinued. However, another right answer is that if a researcher is persuaded that he or she has good reason, even if unverified, for believing that a particular treatment is inferior to one or more others, then the researcher may conscientiously refuse to take part in the trial arm thought to be inferior. The Declaration of Helsinki and biocentric bioethics alike call on us not to carry out research on subjects wherein the risk is not proportionate to the potential benefit for the individual subject.

There is another important point to be noted concerning informed consent and standard treatment. Ideally, the well-informed prospective participant ought to be able to freely choose between the proposed experimental treatment and whatever treatment is accepted as standard. However, the reality of the world is that prospective participants often do not have the option of receiving treatment that meets the accepted standard. Poverty is the leading cause of this, principally though not exclusively in less affluent countries. The real choice may be between experimental and, therefore, unproven treatment and treatment that is substandard or nonexistent. Accordingly, people may be recruited into taking part in a project they would reject were standard treatment available to them. About this, we may offer varying responses:

1. Poor people are benefited by being given the *chance* of effective treatment they would not otherwise receive (yet also with a chance of bad consequences).
2. Poor people are being exploited by being forced, by circumstance and by strategically offered opportunity, to take part in experiments they might otherwise reject.

Whichever response we might prefer, both responses happen to be true. However, there seems to be a serious anomaly here. In some part, we can relieve some of the worst features. We can encourage researchers to allow prospective participants to be given access to a "double-blind" trial against a standard treatment, in which neither patient nor researcher knows which treatment they are getting until the end and in which the participants have a fifty–fifty chance of getting a treatment of known value. It also would be good if participants were guaranteed treatment for possible side effects of the drug and compensation for damages (such as death). Still, though, some people may be forced by circumstance to take part in a trial they would avoid were they able. Even if implemented, such measures would only alleviate anomalies, not eliminate them.

A point of very serious importance emerges here. Moral anomalies cannot be eliminated on the basis of even the best of bioethical decision making – not so long as bioethics is conceived of as concerning only biomedical decisions made in application to individuals. But, of course, life and the need for the affirmation of life far transcend such limited boundaries. A fully effective system of bioethics would be possible only in a world that permits of one. Even if we agree, as I advocate, that *Homo sapiens* is a morally considerable entity, there must always remain anomalies so long as we are concerned only with making biomedical decisions in particular biomedical instances. An ethic of life affirmation must go beyond the bounds of such decision making toward a restructuring of that broader world of which biomedical practice is only a portion, as important as that portion is. Obviously, any such restructuring as that would go beyond the bounds of any possible book on bioethics. If somehow I could be "time-lifted" a couple of centuries into the future (which I would dearly love), I am sure that I would see not only marvelous advances in medicine but also marvelous changes in the way in which we relate to one another and the world around us. If not, then maybe the human race would be lucky to survive so long.

Returning to issues concerning disclosure of information to patient-participants, I point out another major ethical issue. As well as reluctance on the part of researchers and their sponsoring companies to disclose the unnecessary nature of certain risks, I also have noticed that there is frequently a strong reluctance to divulge any more clearly than is legally necessary what is to be done with the research data. (These are often combined in a particularly repugnant mixture.) Participant Information Sheets frequently appear designed to minimize people's awareness of possible suppression of data. In a section labeled "Confidentiality," to recall a standard expedient, we are often assured that information, medical and of other sorts, about participants will be kept confidential and not published or disclosed. Data will be stored securely, and so on and so forth. Our eyes fall to the bottom of the paragraph, where we find that we are still being assured that our personal privacy is to be respected. It is very easy, all the more so as we are now on about page four, to think "ah, yeah," and cruise on to the next section. It is likely that our awareness never settled on the statement, tucked in about two-thirds or three-fourths of the way down the "Confidentiality" paragraph, to the effect that all research data are the private property of the sponsoring drug company and will be kept private and confidential, *to be disclosed only at its own discretion.* This carries the implication that data of scientific significance may be suppressed if doing so is in the economic interests of the company.

I find this doubly repugnant morally. Biomedical research, even when commercially funded, ought always to be done in the public interest. This is particularly so when it is utilizing the facilities of a publicly funded institution. Pharmaceutical companies respond to criticism by pointing to the immense number of beneficial drugs that have resulted from research undertaken for commercial gain. There are indeed far more such drugs than there are those resulting from nonprofit research. And so long as their research (with nondisclosure of data) is done entirely privately, then *perhaps* it cannot be faulted. This is on the double proviso that the research not make use of publicly funded facilities (at least not without paying full market price) and that the researchers obtain *fully* informed consent from volunteer subjects.

This latter point is of critical importance. Many people agree to participate in medical research partly or entirely for altruistic motives, wanting to help further the progress of medical science. As a member of my research ethics committee, I started to insist that the commercial confidentiality clause be exhumed from its remote location in the fine print and stated more explicitly and in a more prominent location. This being done soon prompted a response from one of the doctors who was frequently involved with drug trials:

One of my patients has been enrolled recently in a trial that has been reviewed by the [name] Ethics Committee. I am very concerned about some aspects of the decision to give approval of your Committee to this trial. My main reason for writing is to give your Committee some feedback from a member of the medical profession who is not associated with this research. Should your Committee wish to give me some response, I would be delighted to hear it.

I have been supplied with a copy of the Patient Information. Under the heading "Open Publication of Results" the following sentence appears: "Results of Scientific or Medical Significance may be suppressed for commercial reasons, as the commercial sponsor of the project retains the rights to the data."

I find it hard to believe that this study could be regarded as ethical. Each of the human beings enrolled in this study is taking a risk. They are motivated by the belief that medical or scientific discovery is important enough to offset that risk. How could it be considered ethical to put human beings in a study in which the very medical and scientific results that justify their exposure to personal risk can be suppressed at the whim of the sponsoring drug company?

I am staggered by this. Furthermore I have shown this to three colleagues and each of them is quite shaken to see that this study received ethics approval.

I discussed the matter with the concerned physician and pointed out that what was new was *not* the reserved right of suppression of data. That had been happening for untold years. Rather, the innovation was in this being made *clearly known* to the prospective participants. For me this served as an anecdotal illustration of some major points. The reaction illustrated for me how a desire to further the progress of biomedical science is an important motivating factor for many people participating in research projects, patient-participants and doctor-participants alike. The lack of reaction on previous occasions illustrated for me how easy it is to miss the commercial confidentiality clause in its usual cryptic formulations, not only for the prospective patient-participants but even for doctors who frequently take part in such projects. Conversations with other doctor-participants in various other trials have confirmed my belief that it is not uncommon for them to be quite unaware of commercial confidentiality clauses. All in all, obfuscation of the commercial confidentiality clause seems to me to be very much contrary to the ideals of the principles of informed consent. I find it all the more reprehensible in the conviction that the obfuscation is quite intentional and quite cynically so. We still have some ways to go in addressing this problem.

There are some further ethical problems centering on large pharmaceutical companies and their power. In truth, the problems I shall be pointing to are not so much problems in distinguishing between right and wrong as problems in seeing to it that wrong is not done. A major problem concerns multicenter trials, trials that are carried out through several institutions so that larger numbers of subjects can be enrolled. Let us suppose that a research proposal is submitted to a number of ethics committees at different institutions. Ethics Committee A asks that particular changes be made. The drug company objects strenuously, noting that Ethics Committees B and C did not ask for such changes. They point out, justly, that if the project is conducted in different ways at different places, this would undermine the statistical validity of the results. With less justice, they claim that if the changes that Committee A wanted were really important, Committees B and C would have asked for them also. However, if the only changes implemented were those demanded by all (or even most) ethics committees, then this would reduce ethical review to (or toward) the lowest common moral denominator. Still, if every committee's proposed changes were to be passed around to every other committee until a consensus was arrived at, this could be an extremely tangled and prolonged process. This is indeed true – yet the concerns of Committee A might be quite valid and very important. They often have been.

In these times of economic rationalism, it is greatly and increasingly important for institutions to attract outside funding. For individual researchers, it is vital to their careers that they attract funding and publish research papers. This gives sponsoring pharmaceutical companies considerable leverage in dealing with individual researchers and with their institutional ethics committees. Bluntly put, it is a matter of doing things our way or we will give the project and its associated funding to someone else somewhere else who will do as we ask. Strictly speaking, *Argumentum ad Baculum*, that is, the "or else" argument, is a logical fallacy. However, it has considerable practical impact. On the principle that there is strength in unity, proposals have been made to centralize the review process. So far, nothing has been devised that has been accepted by all parties. One proposal has been to form one central committee to handle all multicenter trials. Yet, could that possibly do justice to whatever concerns might be raised by the various local committees? Seemingly, it would just delete them from the process. I would propose a modification of that. I advocate that research proposals for multicenter trials be distributed to the ethics committee of every institution at which it is proposed to run the trial. Meanwhile, through some rotational system, one ethics committee would be selected to serve as the final reviewing committee for the proposed trial.[9] The other committees would submit their concerns and proposed changes to that committee, which would then make a final determination of whatever changes might be required. If an institution was not content with the final result, it could withdraw from the trial if it felt strongly enough.

Another complicating factor is that some proposed trials are international in character. It might, for instance, be proposed to run a trial at institutions in Australia, New Zealand, the United States, and the United Kingdom. Ethical review in such cases would require international cooperation for which there are currently no adequate mechanisms. As countries involved become more numerous and more diverse, it becomes increasingly more difficult to regulate research trials beyond increasingly

---

9 I would also make the stipulation that the final reviewing committee be the ethics committee of one of those institutions at which it is proposed to run the trial. This might give it better input. Furthermore, though some trials are done at several sites, some are done at just two places near one another. It would seem best to just let them sort it out between them.

lower common moral denominators. Some system of international agree-
ments is clearly needed. So far, however, the need seems to be growing at a
faster rate than the means of addressing it. When worse comes to worst, if it is
worth doing for the sponsoring company, a trial can be sent to some poverty-
stricken country where it can be performed with little effective moral review
or supervision. However, as noted previously, these are more issues of seeing
to it that ethical standards are set and met than it is a discussion of what,
bioethically, the moral standards ought to be. Accordingly, let us pursue the
matter no further here, where we are more concerned with the latter, about
issues having to do with what sorts of research can be carried out.

* * * * *

There are ongoing discussions of immense practical importance about what
sorts of research ought to be allowed to be carried out, problematic factors
including outcomes and methods alike. Implicit are issues about how we
are to see to it that maximum benefit is achieved at minimal human cost
and with what sort of external oversight. In these discussions, consensus
cannot be attained easily, even less easily because practical situations are
continuously undergoing transformation. We will never find a magic wand
for dealing with it all appropriately. Biocentric conceptions, though not
offering us such an instrument, can help us think about and address the
issues.

For one thing, biocentric conceptions remind us that our consent and
even our seeming consciousness have complex depths that are not directly
accessible to our own view, let alone that of others. They also remind us
that our interests run deeper than our consciousness, consciousness being
only our surface. The consenting alcoholics remind us of that. That our
well-being interests are only contingently related to our consent and to our
consciousness we are reminded not only by the alcoholics but by the psychiatric patients – and, for that matter, children. If we are to conduct or oversee
research in an ethical manner, we must always bear in mind the whole and
complex individual with hidden depth as that specific individual occurs in
particular circumstances. Moreover, biocentric conceptions remind us that
there are human interests at stake and human injuries that could occur in
addition to the morally considerable injuries of individual humans. This is
already a matter of practical ethical importance – and certain to become
more so – in connection with genetic research. Biocentric conceptions will
not guarantee us invariably right answers, but they can lead us toward better
ones.

16

Bioethics Seen in an Eastern Light

Throughout our exploration of bioethics we have continuously had to take into account the fact that our approaches to solving bioethical issues, and therefore our conclusions, depend on our framework of assumptions and ways of thinking. We make assumptions, or presumptions, about whom and what we are as persons, about our relationships with others, and about what is good or bad for us. These are not matters in which we all have or start from just the same ideas. I have already remarked on the fact that particular cultures and societies not only offer different teachings on how life may be lived well or poorly but also provide differing environments with differing demands on how we are to live well.

I now attempt to elaborate on this and illustrate how some of the beliefs and ways of thinking originating in South and East Asia can reveal bioethical issues in a different light. I shall not attempt to give a full exposition of the Eastern system of bioethics. For one thing, there is no such thing as *the* Eastern system of bioethics any more than there is *the* Western system of bioethics. No more is there any such thing as *the* Eastern way of thinking any more than there is *the* Western way of thinking. To attempt to trace the many strands of Eastern thought as they apply to bioethical issues would be an immense and difficult undertaking, one that I lack the expertise to accomplish. My objective here is to highlight some of the major features in respect of which some leading Eastern ways of thinking often do differ from characteristically Western ones and to indicate how these tend toward differing ways of thinking about who we are with respect to those around us, about who we are within ourselves, and about the nature of our interests and the role of suffering in our lives. In doing so I will touch on a few further points about cultural differences as they touch on bioethical issues.

Our Role in Life

We have already observed that, broadly speaking, Western thinking about bioethics, as about much else, tends to be first in terms individuals, with

335

their individual identities, moral statuses, and rights, and then in terms of their relationships with other such distinct individuals. In relatively recent times, some philosophers, prominent among whom have been women, have maintained that an adequate system of ethics must take account of, perhaps focus on, interpersonal relationships. It is often maintained that this is a particularly female approach; whereas individualistic ethics has largely been a product of male thinking, women have tended to think of and to act out their lives in terms of their relationships with others. South and East Asian ways of thinking (though not feminist) also tend to support the relational view. It is widely held in Asian cultures that we have our primary identity (or a very large part of it) in terms of wider entities. First, we are members of a particular family and of that in a particular way. We are sons or daughters, husbands or wives, parents, siblings, cousins, or whatever. Beyond that, we have identity and reciprocal relationships in terms of the village or other wider identities, on out through ever wider circles. It might be said that a person has his or her identity with respect to the group – except that the term *group* suggests a collection of individuals, whereas the broader entity is thought of more as being an organic living entity. We have our identity in terms of that whole of which we are an element.

Such a point of view is particularly prominent in the Confucianist-influenced countries of East Asia, such as China, Japan, and Korea. According to Confucianism, our particular participation in five primary relationships is central to our identity, and to our reciprocal rights and obligations. These are the relationships:

Ruler–Subject
Father–Son
Husband–Wife
Older Brother–Younger Brother
Friend–Friend

Three of the five are familial relationships. The list is compiled with a male orientation, so females must make appropriate adjustments (such as older sister–younger sister). We must note that it is also a hierarchical system, with only one of the relationships being between equals.

Though hierarchical, the unequal relationships are not entirely one-sided. People have often misinterpreted Confucius' call for us to "[l]et the ruler be ruler, let the subject be subject" as a call to slavish obedience. Yet it is not meant to be that. The ruler and the subject ought each to act appropriately to the other in accordance with the proper nature of their respective roles. According to Confucianism, roles indeed do have proper natures given in the very scheme of things. For us to live well, we should have things, starting with ourselves, be and do in accordance with the proper nature of the sort of thing they are. Those in power ought to act toward those under them in accordance with the proper nature of ruler. There is more to being a good ruler than ruling. Positions of authority are positions of responsibility. Those in such positions ought to act toward those under them as they, in their turn, would wish their superiors to act toward them. We ought to act toward those serving over us as we in turn would wish those serving under us to act toward us. Thus, the Way of Heaven is followed on earth. Indeed, it is the role of the Emperor, served by all, to so serve Heaven. Thereby the benevolence of Heaven brings blessings to his subjects.

Names and reality ought to correspond with one another, so that things are as they ought to be, and are said to be what they are. This is the central idea of Confucius' famous call for the *rectification of names*. An implication of that is that if the Emperor, characteristically and habitually, does not rule wisely and well, he is not fulfilling the proper nature of emperorhood. He is therefore not truly the Emperor but merely an impostor. Accordingly, he ought to be deposed so that he who truly is the Emperor, having the nature of such, can take over the role. It is the latter who has the *Mandate of Heaven*. Implementation (and even the bare presence) of this principle has had an incalculable effect on the history of China.

More generally, every single one of us has inherent rights and obligations in accordance with our place and identity in the overall scheme of things. The political and social implications are obviously enormous, but my concern here is only with bioethics. One bioethical implication is that in matters of decision making in critical situations, the emphasis is less on the individual as an autonomous unit and more on the family as a whole and, even beyond that, on society. The physician consults with the family as a whole about the diagnosis, prognosis, and projected course of treatment. Patients may be given little say in the matter and may be told only what it is deemed appropriate for them to hear. Moreover – let the doctor be doctor – in such cultures, it is traditional for a great deal of deference to be paid to the views and authority of the learned healer. In reciprocity, the physician respects the authority and autonomy of the family as a whole.

Suppose, for instance, that active voluntary euthanasia were legal and that a patient with an appropriate condition and prognosis requested it. Should the patient's request be granted? This question was asked of members of the Japanese Association of Palliative Medicine. Of those who responded, not all would ever be willing to perform voluntary euthanasia, but of those who might do so if the patient requested and the family agreed, 56 percent would refuse the patient's request if the family objected. Only a minority would follow the wishes of the patient if the family objected. Reasons given for requiring familial consent included these, from three different respondents[1]:

---

[1] Atsushi Asai, Motoki Onishi, Shizuko K. Nagata, N. Tanida, and Y. Yamazaki, "Doctors' and Nurses' Attitudes Towards and Experiences of Voluntary Euthanasia: Survey of Members of the Japanese Association of Palliative Medicine," *Journal of Medical Ethics* 27 (2001): 324–330.

It is necessary for medical doctors to care for the bereaved family. This means that we should respect the wishes of the patient's family rather than those of the patient him/herself.

The life and death of the patient are the family's property; they do not solely belong to the patient.

I would not try to protect the patient's right to die at the cost of the right of others not to be hurt.

There is a rhetorical question here: Whose life is it, anyway? Different answers might appear to be self-evident.

With this different view of personal identity, issues of informed consent, privacy, autonomy, and rights in general have to be interpreted in terms of the wider entity. To focus only on the individual is to see things in a too-narrow light. One might also speculate that putting the moral emphasis on the wider entity might have something to do with the very liberal Japanese attitude toward abortion: If a prospective member is not welcome to the family, then that is that. Even so, the necessity is thought of as being inherently one of sorrow. It is considered appropriate to express regret to that soul and pray for it to go on to find a good birth elsewhere.

In the West, we tend to put the focus very much on the individual, with wider groupings being the arenas within which we individuals assert our lives and interests and our personal identity. The East tends to see the individual as a particular expression of the broader whole. This is to put it broadly, of course, and in terms of tendencies. I wonder: Can either polarity be entirely wrong?

We should note also that the characteristically Asian conception is that the soul long predates any particular human lifetime. It has existed many generations before, perhaps eternally. It does not come into existence at any moment of conception, or subsequently; nor can it die at any stage. Abortion cannot kill it, nor can disease, old age, or any form of euthanasia do so. The very most we might do is to help or hinder the soul on its way – and perhaps to help or to hinder our own spiritual career. Such a conviction may at least color our thinking about euthanasia.

* * * * *

In passing (and it can be no more than that here), I would observe that among different cultures there is a huge and wide variety of beliefs and practices concerning life and death, and self. From time to time, these have bioethical implications. For instance, in some cultures – those of Tibet and Japan, to mention two – it is thought that the soul lingers with the body for some while (often several days) after death. This may affect decisions about when to turn off the life-support system and when to declare a person dead, and, at least in Japan, it tends to dampen the willingness of families to allow organs to be donated. This in turn may cause severe problems for those in vital need of organ donations. It also may provoke resentment in other nations where donor organs are sought. I shall not attempt the impossible task of pursuing all such matters here, where I can only appeal for understanding, tolerance, and flexibility. Instead, I next note some Asiatic concepts of our moral fit with the universe.

Dharma and Karma

Not only have we our being in a web of personal relationships, we have our being in a meaningful world that, throughout, follows law. It is a central conviction of the principal philosophies of South and East Asia that all things and events have significance and that nothing merely happens at random. *Dharma*, the law governing all things, spans every aspect of being and is both material and moral law. It is held that, ultimately, any difference between the material and the moral is illusory. Our own being in the world is both moral and material, and all that happens to us and all that we do occur in accordance with law. One aspect of dharma is the *law of karma*. This is a law of moral causality according to which the things we do, for better or for worse, lead on to further deeds and consequences. Our karma might be thought of as the continuing impetus of all of our past doings. We reap evil in return for evil and good for good. Nor is this train of karmic causality bounded by our birth and death. We cannot escape by dying. The nature of our birth into this life is determined by our karma from our past lives, the accumulated import of all of our past doings. What we do now carries on after death into future lives. It is never interred with our bones. So we continue, life after life, until and unless we can remove ourselves from the flow of karmic consequences.

We therefore have a reason for being here, according to this conception. Our current life in this world, with all of its hazards, griefs, joys, and opportunities, is a product of our past and is appropriate to our current karmic condition. How we are born is as much determined by our initial conditions as the running of a well-functioning computer program is determined by its initial conditions. We are here in this life to live out the consequences of our past karma and to develop ourselves for a better future. Some few of us may in our current life find liberation from the toils of karma entirely but, for most of us, it is a matter of trying to improve our character and to better position ourselves in the karmic stream. The suffering we do is part of our discharging the consequences of our past, enabling us to move into a better future. Again there are possible applications to bioethical matters and our attitudes toward life, death, and suffering.

If suffering is a necessary and useful part of our development, then the relief of suffering, be it our own or another person's, must be seen in a different light. We are taught that compassion for those who suffer is important, for our own sake as well as for theirs; but, ultimately, one's healing can only be through one's own spiritual or moral development rather than by medical means. We might perhaps go on to draw the conclusion that a premature end to one's sufferings in this life would only leave one with an unresolved burden of karmic consequences to carry forward into our next life. Euthanasia would not end our sufferings but instead merely defer them – and the same might be said about the implementation of a DNR order. Indeed, seen in this light, all suffering would appear to be appropriate, if not inevitable. There would be moral virtue in refusing any pain relief, though few would wish to go consistently to that extreme.

Granted that there are far more important things in life than avoiding pain, we might still wonder what to make of all this. We might worry that this way of thinking leads to excessive passivity. For our purposes here, an important difficulty with this line of thought is that it would seemingly make it difficult to justify the conclusion, though it be stoutly proclaimed, that compassion is to be developed within one's character and put into practice, and violence is to be condemned and avoided. The annoying question remains: How can compassion be appropriate or useful? If the suffering of another person is the appropriate and inevitable consequence of his or her accumulated karma and must be resolved within that person's own life, my acting with compassion may not be appropriate, useful, or even possible. This is a problem with which Asian philosophies have grappled. One place in which it has been explored is the great Indian epic, the *Mahabharata*, particularly in that portion which is the *Bhagavad-Gita.* There it is related how before the great and bloody battle of Kurukshetra, Krishna (the incarnated god Vishnu) counsels the warrior Arjuna, who shrinks from the bloody mayhem about to take place. He tells him that those who are to die in battle have already been destined for death by their own karma. Arjuna has been called upon to be the instrument of karma, but *he* is not to be the cause of any death. Moreover, no true harm will come to any in the battle, for the true self, the soul, is not subject to material injury and is immortal:

Who believes him a slayer, and who thinks him slain,
> Both these understand not: He slays not, is not slain.
> He is not born, nor does he ever die; nor, having come to be, will he ever more come not to be.
> Unborn, eternal, everlasting, this ancient one is not slain when the body is slain.
(*Bhagavad-Gita* II: 19–20)

The significance of Arjuna's acts, or of anyone's, is the intention with which it is done and its role in our relation to God. All things should be done as a gift to God, and nothing done in the right spirit reaps bad karma. In this case, Arjuna was called upon by God to fight – in what ultimately is a spiritual rather than a moral arena.

Our True Self and Its Welfare

Nonetheless, all of these Asian philosophies do advocate compassion and (at least in principle) nonviolence. As made famous by Gandhi, this is known as *Ahimsa*. When we willfully act so as to injure others, we certainly injure *ourselves*, sowing and reaping very bad karma. However, this still does not get us to the root of the moral problem. Why, we must continue to ask, do we reap bad karma for doing acts that in no way harm those on whom they apparently impact? Indeed, these Asian philosophies unanimously proclaim that the self that incurs pain and suffering is not one's true self at all. It is an illusory self. So, it is not merely that the warriors who were to fall at Kurukshetra were to survive bodily death. *Whatever* happens to the illusory self is not harmful.

This conception of the self is one that differs widely from that which is usually presumed in the West. Most Western thought (though not all) presumes that the self centers on that which is conscious, feeling, and rational, which makes choices and has values. If that is not the whole self, it is at least presumed to be an indispensable element in it. It is in terms of that self that we characteristically pursue our well-being and seek to avoid injury. In contrast, the principal philosophies of South and East Asia – including the many forms of Hinduism, Buddhism, and Jainism – all maintain that this ego-self, all that says *I*, is a mere illusion. It is held that the true self, given various names, is not anything that can be a subject of knowledge or experience. Rather, it is the foundation that makes knowledge and experience possible. Foolishly, we mistake the illusory self – a pseudo-entity spanning the ego-self and the rest of the bodily self – for our true self, or Self, and that is the source of our many troubles. It is only the illusory self that suffers. Suffering and wrongdoing are no more than features of this world of ignorance and illusion.

Pivotal to our understanding here is the phenomenon of desire and the twofold role that it plays. Of course our desires in acting, and therefore our intentions, are central to the moral character of our acts. Willfully injuring another is clearly far worse than doing so by unforeseeable accident. Nevertheless, the role of desire in these Asian philosophies goes much deeper than that. Of foundational importance is the principle that our ignorant desires are pivotal to our incorrect identification with our illusory self and to all that follows from that. Indeed, desires are that from which illusions are spun. This conviction is very much present in Hinduism and is absolutely central to Buddhism. The Buddha proclaimed that all life is suffering. (And he meant *all*; even the finest pleasures eventually lead to suffering.[2]) He taught that suffering is due to ignorant desires and that the

---

[2] The principle that all life is suffering offers an interesting comparison with the biological truth that life is a matter of coping with an environment on which it depends (and with

way to be rid of suffering is to be rid of those desires. The Buddha then proposed a therapeutic program for achieving that end (a program that has been interpreted by the many schools of Buddhism in many different ways). As we will recall, one cannot escape suffering by dying. It is our desires and their consequences that lead us on in a continuing chain of suffering. Our suffering is ended only with the ending of our desires. Now, any sensible person, Buddhist or otherwise, would have to agree that a great deal of our troubles are due to inappropriate desires, whether or not we agree that *all* desires are ignorant and inappropriate. Moreover, we must accept that the injuries we willfully do to others are due to our catering to the demands of our ego-self. Were we to cease to be subject to those desires, we would cease to willfully injure others. If the Buddha was right, it also would follow that with the extinction of our desires, and therefore of our karma, we ourselves would cease to suffer. By any account, the extinction of our selfish desires would improve our moral character.

Yet one may feel rather skeptical about the idea that suffering is only a matter of the illusory self and not really real. We may wonder if that leaves any room at all for morality. How can it be said that my selfish desires lead me to injure others if nothing that I can do to their ego-self – which is all I can have any effect upon – is truly an injury? We might also wonder how we are to decide what to do, even with the best and most compassionate of intentions, if nothing we can do injures another's true self, and nothing benefits it either. What would be the point of giving pain relief to an ill person in great pain if pain is no injury and pain relief is no benefit? If the person in pain is terminally ill and requests euthanasia, should we just shrug our shoulders in the belief that it does not matter at all, one way or another? Yet if it does matter what we do, why does it, and how are we to determine what we ought or ought not to do? To questions such as these, the East no more than the West answers in a single voice.

One answer is that killing is very bad karma, much worse than that from other forms of ill doing. For our own sake, we ought to refuse to take part in any such thing. I am reminded here of a Hare Krishna I once knew who frequently advocated a vegetarian diet, nonviolence, and a number of other virtues, for avoiding bad karma and accumulating good karma, much as others might advocate some clever investment strategy for getting a better percentage return on one's investment. His expressed concern was always for one's personal benefit in acting in such a way. Though I never told him so, I often thought his karmic balance might do better were he motivated more for the welfare of animals and other people and less for his own karmic advantage. I wonder also about Westerners who shrink from euthanasia

which it interpenetrates) yet with which it is perpetually at least somewhat out of balance. Too much imbalance is illness, and much too much is death, yet a total lack of imbalance is an absence of life.

(or other things) on the grounds that God might not like it, or that it would detract from their moral purity, rather than on grounds having to do with the well-being of the one whose welfare is truly at issue. To be sure, if people have faith that an omniscient God knows and reveals to us that active euthanasia is always bad for the person undergoing it – though for some reason DNR orders may not be – or if they have faith that euthanasia injures those dying by forcing them to carry on an unresolved karmic burden, then I cannot quarrel with their conclusion that euthanasia must never be done. They believe that it injures rather than benefits the one dying and would therefore not be euthanasia, not being a good death. However, if one does believe that the suffering is greatly and uselessly injurious to the sufferer, I do feel that there is a moral inadequacy in allowing a narrow regard for self-interest to stop one from performing what one realizes would be an effective act of immense compassion.

East or West, there is more to true compassion than self-interest, karmic or otherwise. East and West, it is agreed that there *is* such a thing as compassion. To be sure, if (contrary to fact, I think) there were any people who truly believed that, in spite of appearances, nothing that happens ever benefits or injures another (or themselves), then I could not refute them. (No doubt, it would be a mere ad hominem argument to point out that these people would have no interest in bioethics or any other form of ethics and so need not concern us here. Indeed, how could they take an interest in anything?) Neither could I refute someone who believed that the world came into existence from nothing a mere two minutes ago – complete with memories, historical records, tombstones, and all the rest of it. Asian philosophies all hold that it does make an important difference how we treat others, however they may account for its doing so. Part of the problem in accounting for it to Westerners, so Asians often suggest, is that we Westerners tend to think too much in *either–or* terms. Perhaps our doing so oversimplifies a deeper reality. Consider the simile, presented in the Indian literature, of a man who sees a rope by twilight and mistakenly believes it to be a serpent. Clearly he was mistaken. Yet the serpent was not entirely unreal, either, unlike some pink elephant he might have hallucinated. He saw something quite real, the rope, though he mis-saw it as something it was not. His belief that he saw a serpent, though not properly true, was not entirely false. The serpent, though certainly not real, was not entirely unreal.

According to this conception, we live our lives in a world of things and events taking shadowy form part way between reality and utter non-being. The world of our awareness is to the world as it truly is as the serpent is to the rope and as the illusory self is to our true Self. All that we believe and think lies between absolute truth, which cannot be captured by the relativities of thought and word, and absolute falsity, which is nothing at all. Our self, our beliefs, and our experienced world are reality misperceived.[3] So too, everything we do that affects others, and therefore everything within the scope of ethics, lies with us within this realm of intermediate truth and being. Accordingly, any effect I might have on another is not really on the illusory self but on that being of which the illusory self is a misperception. The other's fear of suffering or desire for relief from pain may be a product of ignorance, as what the person really needs is a deeper healing of the soul. So do we all. In the meantime, while we are living this world of illusion, suffering and the need for ethical conduct coexist on the same level of being. The need for compassion and morality will disappear only when suffering disappears. While we are here in this intermediate world, our compassion for others and relief of their suffering may well help them along the way in finding their deeper healing. It also might help us in finding our own deeper healing, as my Hare Krishna friend pointed out.

* * * * *

Imagined Scene

There is a sickroom somewhere in a region of Asia wherein traditional culture is followed. A person is dying what is not an easy death. Summoned by the next of kin, three holy sages have come to attend. In the dimness we cannot distinguish their sect or their nationality. They perform rites, say prayers, and read appropriate advice for the good of the soon-to-be-departed soul. Perhaps even now the soul can find its enlightenment and freedom from suffering but, in all likelihood, it will go on to yet another life. The advice given is intended to guide the soul on its way, though the dying body is evidently beyond anything but pain. Yet what happens after death is of the greatest importance, greater than that of any bodily suffering. I shall try to relate, as best I can, what occurred.

During the long night, a family member, whose love could by no means be doubted, indicates an intention to administer a powerful herbal infusion that will banish pain and speed death.

"My child," says one of the sages, "your compassion commends you, but let not your own ignorant cravings cloud your judgment. To kill is very evil karma. Do not fall into temptation and sin."

"Then be the evil karma upon my head. I would willingly bear the consequences if that would relieve this suffering."

"Our suffering, that of each of us, is the necessary consequence of our past karma. Would you have that karma and suffering carried on into the life to come? Let this loved one go forward without this burden!"

---

[3] That there are levels of being and truth was a doctrine expounded by the great Hindu thinker, Shankara (c. 700–c. 750), systematizer of the Advaita Vedanta school of thought. Prior to that, the idea first was developed by the no less great Buddhist thinker Nagarjuna (c. 150–c. 250), founder of the Madhyamica (Middle Path) school of Buddhism.

[Because of the darkness, I cannot see which one is speaking. Nor can I be confident that I have found the best idiomatic English transcription of what they say.]

"Yet sometimes it is our karma to encounter the suffering of others so that we may relieve our own evil karma by relieving their suffering. So long as we persist in ignorance, so long as there is good and evil karma, suffering is bad. Ought the starving not to be fed nor the ill or the injured tended? Are they to be turned away with the revelation that they are being spurned for their own good?"

"Until we have found our Enlightenment, there can be no end of suffering. Nor can we find our Enlightenment until we have fully understood that the suffering of each is the suffering of all, and of all that of each."

"Thus have I heard. By having compassion for all and by accepting all suffering for our own, so may we liberate ourselves from the illusion wherein we suffer."

"So long, therefore, as we are ignorant and suffer, we must follow the path of overcoming our ignorance. Is it not part of that path to alleviate suffering? By lightening the suffering of the one dying before us, easing this one to a gentler death, it seems to me that we do well in lessening the amount of suffering in this world of illusion."

"Nay, think not so. As you have said, this is a world of illusion. In this world, all suffering and all consequences, supposedly good or supposedly bad, are illusory. Acts are not to be judged morally by their consequences. Nor are suffering and ignorance amounts that can be made more or less by adding or taking away. All that matters is . . . "

At this point I could not catch the exact words, though I tried very hard to do so. My tiredness and the incense were against me. It seemed as if the speaker was saying that what truly matters is our spiritual condition – and I am not sure whether the term *our* was meant in the singular or the plural – when the act is done. The true nature of our acts lies in our compassion and our right endeavor. Ultimately, any consequences, if there can be said to be consequences of an act, are in terms of our spiritual condition. Here it seemed that the problematic pronoun included the one to be acted on.

"But what are we to *do?*," cried a distressed relative, "What is the right answer?"

"Dear one, it is not a matter of their being some right answer. We must search within . . . "

Here, to my shame, I lost my concentration, and soon lost my consciousness. All I can tell you is that when I awoke in the morning, the relative and the three holy sages were gone. The one who had been dying was now, at least so far as this world is concerned, dead.

A Dash of Daoism: Being True to Oneself

There is an element in Asian thought that rejects rigidities of definitions, distinctions, and rules, especially when they are conceived of as occurring in a world of sharp dichotomies. This element is particularly prominent in the Daoist philosophy, originating in China. Daoism is now well known for serving as a source of criticism of Western thought. For centuries, it served to criticize the rigidities it found in Chinese thought, particularly in Confucianism. We live in a fluid world, proclaims Daoism, wherein the only permanence is change. Nevertheless, it is not random change. We live in a world of cyclic change wherein things are always reverting toward what they were before – yet they are never exactly the same. Every year, for instance, the seasons return, yet no two springs are ever quite the same. Within these cycles, no trend is everlasting. Certainly, no thing is everlasting. Nor is any boundary or feature rigid or absolute. Nor is any one way of doing things always the best way. Instead, we do better to think of the world as being an ongoing interplay of forces, continually changing their balance. In that world, we must find our way.

As I mentioned in Chapter 8, the term *Dao* literally means *Way*.[4] Daoists are those who aspire to follow the way. Which way? It is not some way *to* truth or reality. Reality *is* the way, an ever-changing, ongoing happening. We are part of that happening, and our lives go well or poorly according to how well we blend in with it. The wise person is one who reads the way in which things are moving and then goes carefully with the flow. If wise, one never goes too far toward an extreme because things will eventually and inevitably start to flow in some contrary direction. Like Kenny Roger's old gambler, we have to know when to hold them and know when to fold them. This requires an acquired skill, not a rulebook.

Traditionally, the Chinese have thought of the interacting forces of the world in terms of *yang* and *yin*, contrasting but complementary forces at work in all things and in all events. When we Westerners think in terms of dualities, we often tend to think of them in terms of firm dichotomous distinctions. We also often tend to think hierarchically, with one or the other of each pair being thought of as primary and as somehow better than the other: mind and matter, objective and subjective, rational and emotional, theory and practice, and any number of other pairs. In the classical conception, yang and yin are thought of not as opposing dualities but rather as polarities within unity, with interpenetration and interdependence. Nor is one better than the other; the polarities are equally real, equally necessary, equally important, and equally valuable.

The principal ideas of Daoism center on maintaining harmony and balance in this precarious world and on acting in accordance with the flow of events and in accordance with the nature of things. Centrally, we must be

---

[4] I am using the Pinyin system of transliteration rather than the older Wade-Giles system. *Dao* and *De* were *Tao* and *Te* in the older system. The legendary Daoists Laozi and Zhuangzi were previously known in the West as Lao Tzu and Chuang Tzu. Each has a book taking his name, that of *Laozi*, or *Lao Tzu*, also known as the *Daodejing* or *Tao Te Ching*.

true to our own nature, acting in accordance with what we are. This has tended to put Daoists at odds with formal rules and society. They held that nothing, and therefore no rule, is or could be absolute. Accordingly, they were always averse to giving or accepting concrete rules. In considerable part, they were in reaction against the state-sanctioned Confucianism of olden days, which seemed to have rules for nearly everything. Rigid rules, the Daoists held, tend to deform and injure those who must live by them. They tell a fable of man who wanted to turn ducks into cranes, the latter being a very auspicious and revered bird. When he tried to stretch a duck into a crane, he found he had created only a mutilated duck. No good as a crane, it was no longer any good even as a duck. Formal rules tend to do that to us. We must take care not to allow such rules, or those who would enforce them, to misshape or mutilate us, and never ought we to do that to another. For such reasons, Daoists often felt that a genuine life could not be lived unless one withdrew from society with its artificialities, distortions, and constraints. Instead of rules and conventions, what we need is to respect ourselves and our world and to develop the skill of understanding and going with the flow.

Daoism very much lends itself to storytelling, so I shall take the liberty of going right on to another one. Zhuangzi tells of a sage who was walking one day in the country with his disciples. Near a raging mountain torrent, they saw an old man who, to their astonishment, leapt into the cascade. The sage sent his disciples along the stream bank to effect a rescue (or, more likely, recover the body). To their astonishment, they found the old man at the foot of a cataract, quite unharmed. How, they asked, could he possibly survive? The old man replied that it was easy; all he did was to go down with the descending currents and up with the ascending currents. The Daoist point was that had he resisted the water, he would have been overpowered. However, had he just surrendered to the water like a piece of wood, he would have been destroyed by it. Rather, he maneuvered in the currents, using their natural movements to get him through safely. This is an expression of the Daoist principle of *wu wei*, doing by not doing. This is quite different from doing nothing. It is doing just that little bit in just the right way to go with the flow, but going in a way that is advantageous. This is a skill for which there can be no firm rules. It is a bit like riding a bicycle: Instructions and how-to-do-it rules are useful when one is learning, but when one has learned, then one leaves all that behind and just does it.

Our concern is only with the bioethical implications of Daoism, not with its possible implications in terms of medical practice. In any case, the latter topic has been canvassed widely, if not always well, so I will venture only a few words about it. In brief, Daoism calls on us to take a holistic approach to medicine, to be concerned with not just a particular medical condition but with the patient's entire life. Indeed, we are to take into account not only the patient's whole body but also the person's role and way of living in his or her wider world. The key is to restore, or preferably to maintain, the harmonies and balances natural to that life. This all sounds utterly wonderful, of course, but it gives us very little guidance about what to do in actual practice. For their part, Daoists would shrug off any such criticism. They are not concerned to provide concrete guidance, much less concrete rules. Their concern is to develop an appropriate attitude and approach toward dealing with concrete matters.

Whether, or in which ways, the traditional Chinese approach to healing is valid is not for me to venture an opinion. Certainly, Western medicine can no longer dismiss it, as once it did, as mere unscientific folklore. Indeed, folklore in general is achieving a better reputation than once it had. Certainly some elements of the Chinese tradition, such as acupuncture, have forced their way into respectability. The traditional Chinese pharmacopeia, like other traditional pharmacopeias, has shown mixed results when subjected to careful scientific trials and evaluation. Some pharmaceuticals therein have clear merit and some do not. Furthermore, as everywhere around the world, superstition, quackery, and mumbo jumbo have sprung up on the shadowy fringes of the healing arts. Not only as an environmentalist but as an ordinarily humane person, I am disgusted by the use of such materials as rhinoceros horn, bear bile, and tiger parts, as called for by traditional Chinese medicine – uses that have no scientific validity and that are a perversion of the true nature-friendly spirit of Daoism. One also reads of wealthy Chinese in the past who have drastically shortened their lives by attempting to prolong them through imbibing Daoist elixirs heavy on such ingredients as compounds of mercury. Whatever its marvelous metaphorical or metaphysical properties might be, mercury is factually quite toxic. My concern in mentioning these things is not to pour scorn on Daoism but instead only to pour scorn on low-grade perversions of it. Instead of pseudo-facts of occult origin, what true Daoism offers is an attitude for living.

The fundamental Daoist ideal is that of living a life of harmony and balance in tune with the ebb and flow of nature and, as I would interpret Daoism, of being life affirming. I would suggest that these ideas have some merit in application to bioethical and other ethical issues. Daoists, as we recall, were leery of any rigidities, not least that of rules. Moral rules, like rules for riding a bicycle, may be useful to start with, but once we get the hang of it, they are best left behind. As explained by Laozi (Lao Tzu), here is the problem:

After Dao was lost . . . then came human kindness
   After human kindness was lost, then came morality;
   After morality was lost, then came ritual.
   Now ritual is the mere husk of loyalty and promise-keeping
   And is indeed the first step towards brawling. (*Laozi*, 38)

To say the least, I am somewhat more favorably inclined toward moral principles than were the rule-detesting Daoists. The standard rules must be the *first* place where we look for guidance, a point that might be overlooked by Daoists, but I must certainly agree that we cannot repose our trust in rules as the ultimate authority. At best, rules only describe what is morally right, doing so only with imperfect accuracy. By no means do they constitute morality. Rules can still be a great help, but for true morality, one must have a sense of what morality is about and of what makes moral rules moral. No moral rule can be *the* one and only criterion for what is the right thing to do. When we are faced with moral choices, therefore, we must sometimes go beyond the rulebook and seek for the way that best harmonizes and balances the conflicting interests. Yet sometimes there must be losers as well as winners, so we just have to do the best we can. However, this is not a simple utilitarianism. That would be to follow just another too-rigid rule. For my part, I would interpret Daoism as lending itself to a system of virtue ethics of affirming life and its quality in its wholeness and depth. Starting with our own life, we protect and enhance the flow, quality, and integrity of life.

Some Gleanings

One could not possibly adopt all of these differing Asian philosophies, and I am not advocating that one should wholly adopt any of them. Nonetheless, I certainly hope to do more than just suggest that we look with tolerance and understanding on those who do accept them. We ought to, obviously, but beyond that I suggest that we might do well to adopt or adapt some of their important ideas. For one thing, as should be very clear by now, I would enthusiastically concur with the Asiatic conception that our self is far more than that superficial self that is conscious, feeling, and rational, that makes choices and has values. We are more than that limited self, the focus of so much Western thinking, and we are more than such a self joined together with a biological life-support system. We are a whole living system. I would not write the limited self off as being mere illusion, but if we imagine that it is our identity, we have a self-conception that is both distorted and too limited. Our roots go much deeper into reality. Our whole self must be taken into account. So too, our good is a matter of our full self and not just its surface. There may perhaps be more of value in our conscious and worldly life than Asian monks are inclined to admit, but there is certainly more to life than what fills our consciousness.

I enthusiastically concur with the Asiatic conception that our self is far more than that which is conscious, feeling, and rational, which makes choices and has values. Whether or not that superficial self is a *mis*perception, it is indeed a too-limited perception. We are more than that limited self, the focus of so much Western thinking, and we are more than that self with a biological life-support system added on. Moreover, it is quite true that our life is inherently mingled with further and morally important life. Like nearly all Westerners, and perhaps like most Easterners, I reject the idea that I am *merely* an organ of my family, or of my ethnic group or the state, or of anything else. Yet no life is ever complete and independent in itself. That is a biological fact, and it is a moral truth that can be ignored only at the cost of severely distorted moral vision. Somehow, we must find our way morally with our life in our world. It is not just that we ought to respect other living beings – as others. If we go no further than that, it is still too much a matter of *them* and *us*. Rather, our lives, our good, and our moral identity mingle with that of life around us.

I believe that we also can get some useful advice from the Daoists as we try to live well in the midst of life. I do *not* think that we ought to tear up all rulebooks, shun so-called civilization, and retreat to a mountain cave. (Well, okay, *most* of the time I do not think that.) We are social beings, even if sometimes we do not like it. Rules and conventions have vital roles, and they should be arrived at carefully and regarded respectfully. They are necessary tools. Nonetheless, they are *tools*. Daoism reminds us that we ought never to lose sight of what the rules are supposed to be about. I think the Daoists have another good point when they advise us that we live in a dynamic world of constant change, yet a world of recurrence. Always there is similarity, and always there is difference, each ever in the other. In such a world, no one set way of thinking or acting can always be right. Life is like that.

17

Toward a Wider View

As life and health cannot be contained within strict and narrow limits, neither can the *ethics* of life and health be so contained. Precise rules, however carefully formulated and useful, are not enough. Moreover, which is the next point I want to develop, a narrow application of ethics to humans only does violence to ethics; it undermines the very ground by reason of which we humans do have our moral significance. Neither the *bio* aspect nor the *ethics* aspect of bioethics can stop at narrow boundaries or human boundaries, except arbitrarily. Back at the beginning, I somewhat arbitrarily undertook to center my discussion on *human* bioethics, and I cannot claim to have fully covered that topic. No one could cover it all. Still, to restrict our discussions to human bioethics, and to that only, implies a distortion. We humans are not the sole inhabitants of the moral universe. For one thing, there are animals, and these are widely used in biomedical research. For another, as I hope to show, there is more to it than just humans and animals. Moreover, a consideration of the *reasons* why nonhumans have moral significance sheds light on why humans do and vice versa. This is true either if we restrict our attention to individuals or if we recognize wider entities, such as the human race as a whole, as having moral significance. It is also arbitrary to restrict our discussion to specifically biomedical applications. Life and health, even if we are considering only human life and health, go far beyond biomedical boundaries, however broadly construed. These are not matters that can be thoroughly canvassed here; Nor shall I attempt to do so. However, I do offer a discussion of some of the wider issues in order to both better center our discussion of human bioethics and at least sketch some of the onward possibilities.

On the Moral Status of Animals

These days, it is widely, though not universally, held that at least some animals do have some level of moral significance, though there is no consensus concerning why this might be so or concerning what (if any) limitations this might impose on human freedom of action. Reference to the cruelty of pulling the wings off flies has become a cliché – but why should one not do this? I suspect that for most of us, it not primarily a matter of respect for the feelings of flies, who probably lack any such thing, but rather of disgust at the motives of those who would do such a deed. One assumes they have sadistic motives, even if their cruel aims are vitiated by a lack of sensation or consciousness in their intended victim. We also might feel disgust at those who are unkind to cats, dogs, or horses. In these latter cases, a respect for the very real feelings of the animal presumably would be a factor in addition to our disgust at cruelty or callousness per se. We might ponder whether rats, rabbits, or battery chickens are or ought to be on a similar moral footing. Here I would pose the question of whether any nonhumans are *entitled* to our moral consideration.

There is a point of view that holds that there is no point in even asking who or what is entitled to our moral consideration. It maintains that morality is a system we humans have developed for getting along with one another, for protecting our interests and feelings. By inclination and by teaching, and because that is what makes the system work, we come to care about other people and to respect their interests. We are kind to cats and dogs because we care about them too. They are honorary members of our human community, on a lower level, and people feel bad if they are ill used. As for rats and other outsiders, we ought not to be arbitrarily cruel to them but, otherwise, tough luck. We might wonder, though, whether this conception of morality is really sustainable. Moral systems do serve human interests, beyond doubt, and may have evolved on that basis. Yet this explanation seems unsatisfactory as it stands. We might just as well posit that morality is an institution of our nation, or of our linguistic, racial, or other affinity group. To be sure, we ought not to be arbitrarily cruel to slaves or aliens, as we usually grant them a secondary level of moral concern, but they no more than dogs can have entitlements beyond what they are given. As with apartheid South Africa and other recent and contemporary societies, we can criticize their moral scheme on the basis of our own – but are there any grounds on which we can declare any "moral" scheme, satisfactory to its participants, to be morally better or worse than another? A variation on the theme is the theory that morality is a matter of a reciprocal scheme of rights and obligations for the benefit of those who participate in the scheme. (So why should I keep up my end of the bargain if I could advantageously get away with not doing so? It would be begging the question to reply that I ought to because bargain keeping is part of the scheme.) Because animals cannot reciprocate, setting aside a few special cases (such as working dogs), animals therefore have no moral entitlements. A principal implausibility of the scheme is that there are many humans who cannot reciprocate. Those who are too young or too old, or who are otherwise too feeble of body or understanding, may be not be able to reciprocate a benefit or make reprisals for an injury. Any who are deprived of power, such as slaves, would be unable to reciprocate.

One obvious response is that whatsoever their race, religion, language, mental or physical condition, or whatever else, the disadvantaged people are nonetheless *people*. However, that response begs a question or two. If racism is inherently wrong, why is not *speciesism* morally wrong also? If slaves are entitled to be emancipated and recognized as having full moral equality because they are *people*, then we might equally well conclude that animals are entitled to have their interests given full moral consideration because they can feel. Peter Singer is the one whose name is most widely associated with such a view. He advocates a *Principle of Equal Consideration of Interests*:

The principle of equal consideration of interests acts like a pair of scales, weighing interests impartially. True scales favour the side where interest is stronger or where several interests combine to outweigh a smaller number of similar interests; but they take no account of whose interests they are weighing.[1]

In this view, pain, for instance, is pain, and equal pain is to count equally, whether a human, a pig, or a rat experiences it. Singer has been widely and sometimes, I believe, maliciously misinterpreted as maintaining such alarming tenets as the belief that pigs and persons have the same moral weight. Singer quite recognizes that we humans, with our wider conceptions of our self and our world, now and future, and our deeper social relationships, have more interests to flourish or to suffer. In and of itself, however, everything else being equal, pain in a pig is exactly morally equivalent to exactly the same amount of pain in a person.

We partisan humans might wonder what would be the likely consequences of accepting the conclusion, and we might wonder whether there is any way to avoid such a conclusion. I shall first consider possible ways of avoiding the conclusion, and then I go on to consider implications of accepting it. To avoid the conclusion, we would have to locate some morally important feature that follows the species boundary. One excuse sometimes given is that we humans are morally preeminent because of our higher intelligence. That gratifies our vanity, but it also has the implication that highly intelligent people have a higher moral status than the less well endowed. Sharp con men would be entitled to separate gullible fools from their money, and Nobel laureates would be entitled to exploit the rest of us. Perhaps too we could utilize the severely intellectually disabled for injurious medical experiments now performed on animals. After all, we could learn more

---

[1] Peter Singer, *Practical Ethics* (New York: Cambridge University Press, 1979), p. 19.

from their human bodies. Without proceeding further, let us drop the IQ rationale as being morally implausible.[2]

Another half-baked excuse for our claimed moral preeminence is that we have won it by our victory in the evolutionary battle. Again, that gratifies our egos – until we stop to reflect that evolution advances no value beyond that of the ability to replicate genes into succeeding generations – if that can be said to be a value at all. At one time, the apparent trend in evolution favored well-made shells. The trilobites were evidently evolution's selected offspring. Later, the trend was toward large size and related virtues. Dinosaurs were successful for a long while. Only relatively recently has there been a trend toward things we humans prize, such as intelligence, linguistic ability, and opposable thumbs. In evolutionary terms, our reign has been brief, and already we are showing considerable signs of self-destruction. Perhaps the next evolutionary trend will favor beings resistant to pollution and radiation, with the descendants of cockroaches or sewer rats being the ultimate victors – until whatever comes after that. But this heavy satire is really beside the point. In reality, the evolutionary justification is really a thinly disguised proclamation that might makes right. That is not an ethic but the denial of ethics.

One last excuse that I will canvass here is one of the oldest in the Western world. This is that we humans, being created in the image of God, are unique in having souls (or spirit). As spiritual beings are all that really matter, and as we humans are the only spiritual beings in the material world, we humans are the only ones who count morally here beneath heaven. This view is very much controversial – and has received heavy fire from modern theologians – but this is not the place to pursue those controversies. Here I would just point out some of the important questions that are being begged. For one thing, not all religions have denied that animals have souls. That they do have souls is a view widely spread in non-Westernized parts of the world, and with some influence in the West as well. It is a mostly Western prejudice that equates soul with mind, and it is a mostly Western prejudice that denies that animals have minds in any significant sense. Perhaps all sentient (or merely living) beings have souls, or perhaps there is no such thing as soul

---

[2] Obviously, more can and has been written on the topic of the moral status of animals. The IQ argument and various others have been given far more detailed attention elsewhere. Here I offer only a brief overview as a more thorough discussion would detract from present priorities. For those who would pursue the matter further, I recommend the definitive classic of the animal-welfare movement, Peter Singer, *Animal Liberation: A New Ethics for our Treatment of Animals* (New York: New York Review/Random House, 1975. Many subsequent editions). Tom Regan, *The Case for Animal Rights* (Berkeley: University of California Press, 2004; originally published 1983); Lawrence E. Johnson, *A Morally Deep World: An Essay on Moral Significance and Environmental Ethics* (New York: Cambridge University Press, 1991); and – for a sharply contrasting view – R. G. Frey, *Interests and Rights: The Case Against Animals* (Oxford: Clarendon Press, 1980).

at all, but it seems arrogant as well as arbitrary to claim that we are unique in that regard.

Moreover, we might well ask why sentient beings without souls, if there are any, are to be counted as morally nothing. An alert and intelligent chimpanzee may be superior intellectually, socially, and in other ways to many humans. There are some submarginal humans to whom the chimp would be superior in just about every way. Perhaps the chimp merits our moral concern as much as or more than the unfortunate human – who nonetheless certainly does merit our concern. For reasons having to do with prudence and slippery slopes, we have to be particularly careful about how we treat humans but, perhaps morally, we ought to be careful about how we treat other beings as well. As for souls – well, it is reported of the medieval Cardinal Bellarmine that he allowed vermin to dine on him unmolested, making the compassionate observation that "We shall have heaven to reward us for our sufferings but these poor creatures have nothing but the enjoyment of this present life."[3] I do not care to follow his example, and I doubt whether lice can suffer to any appreciable extent, but I do take his point that the sufferings of a sentient being ought not to be morally disregarded because the being lacked a soul. Perhaps Bellarmine was right in thinking that such a being would merit all the more consideration.

Animals and Bioethics

If animals are to be recognized as being worthy of moral consideration, how ought we to act concerning them? The possible implications are immense, ranging from diet to biomedical research, from rodeos to cosmetics. These are matters of considerable and often heated controversy. That there are such controversies is itself a sign of considerable progress as at one time animals were generally regarded as amounting to little more than resources for human utilization. Though there is still no consensus on how to treat animals, our laws and institutions are coming to demand that the welfare of animals be given some form of protection. Even if we cannot quantify the moral cost of using animals, the mere realization that there is a moral cost can motivate us to find ways to reduce or even eliminate the cost.

A relatively recent illustration is provided by the infamous LD-50 (Lethal Dose, 50%) Test. Once widely used, its use is now almost unheard of – in large part thanks to its having received wide and unfavorable publicity. This test involved the administration of a test substance to a population of animals in order to determine which dose kills 50 percent of the test animals after a specified test duration. (The surviving 50 percent would

---

[3] For this citation, I owe thanks, via Peter Singer, to W. E. H. Lecky's *History of European Morals: From Augustus to Charlemagne*, 2 vols. (Whitefish, MT: Kessinger, 2003; originally published 1869), 2:172n. Lecky in turn cites (Bayle, *Dict. Philos.*, art. Bellarmine).

usually be at least a bit ill as a result of the experience.) The fact is that there is a lethal dose of *anything*, even distilled water. Any animal or any person would succumb to having enough water rammed down its throat, even if it took enough fill a small swimming pool.[4] Obviously, that would tell us little about the toxicity of distilled water. The toxicity of far smaller amounts of some more problematic substance might be suggestive, but as a technical tool for clinical pharmacology, the test was virtually useless. The LD-50 figure gave minimal information about why a substance causes the deaths that it does. In any case, the LD-50 toxicity of a substance varies widely not only between species but also within a single species. However, it was something that was traditionally done. Researchers expected to do it and were expected to do so by administering institutions and by readers of research reports who would query its omission. So, it continued under its own pointless momentum – until it became the focus of ethical outrage. Only then did it stop. Not surprisingly, other (and more effective) tests have been deployed for finding how toxic a substance is and why.

As well there was the Draize Test, also a deserved casualty of increased ethical awareness. That test had at least some technical value, though at a horrible moral cost. To test how irritating something was to sensitive tissue, the substance – perhaps a new detergent or a new cosmetic – was applied to the eyes of rabbits. Rabbits were used because their eyes lack tear ducts, so they are unable to wash irritants away. The test animals were restrained so that they could not rub their eyes with their paws. As one would expect, in some instances the effects on the rabbits were quite gruesome: cataracts, ulcers, even cancer – not to mention the extreme pain. In the face of understandably unfavorable publicity, and increasing opposition from consumers reluctant to buy Draize-tested products, alternative means of assessing irritants have been found. These may be as simple as testing irritants on cultures of bacteria or tissues. Furthermore, if anyone really needs to be told that some new bleach is not a good thing to put in one's eyes, there is already enough known about various chemicals and their effects to warrant such a conclusion.

The mere realization that there is a moral cost to using sentient beings in such ways can motivate us to find ways to reduce the cost. Guidelines and ethics committees can help us to minimize the adverse impact on animals. Of particular use is the "Three Rs" approach: reduce the number of animals involved; replace animals with nonanimals, where possible; and refine the techniques so as to cause the minimal suffering. Substitutes have been

---

[4] A woman once died as a result of trying to live on exclusively a "water diet" in an attempt to flush supposed toxins out of her system. Indeed, over a period of weeks, she washed out her vital nutrients, to a fatal extent. (She was a member of the high-IQ society, Mensa.) A more likely cause of death from having vast amounts of water forced down one's throat would be rupture of the stomach.

found not only for Draize and LD-50 testing but also for numerous other procedures involving animal suffering. These may be as simple as making a video recording of a dissection, so that the dissection need not be repeated for each class of students. Substances suspected of causing cancer can be tested on bacterial cultures (the Ames Test) or assessed in ways other than application to animals – and so it goes.

These and other successes have been cited in calls for the *total* abolition of experimentation on animals, or at least such experimentation as causes them suffering. Instead, we are told, we ought to rely exclusively on experiments that do not use animals and on computer simulations. Unfortunately, this is not one of those times when we can sidestep moral issues without penalty. The hard fact is that sometimes we do have to make hard moral choices, ones that cannot be avoided without incurring moral costs on one hand or the other. There are some biomedical research projects that do yield valuable research – valuable in terms of its application to the relief of human suffering – and do cause suffering to animals and for which we have no adequate substitute. However many instances we might be able to point to wherein we can find scientifically adequate substitutes, sometimes we cannot find any. If, for instance, we need to know the effect of a particular drug on a nervous system – not just nerve cells, but a nervous system – then we need to try it on an actual nervous system. Applying it to tissue cultures cannot tell us enough; nor can a computer simulation. A computer can work out the implications of our known data, but it cannot tell us what is not already implicit in our data. We need – or, at least, we find it very valuable – to ascertain what actually does happen. To be sure, an experiment on nonhumans will not be absolutely definitive in application to humans. Nevertheless, it will fill in many of the gaps and make it easier to proceed with humans and thereby find means of relieving human suffering.

On what moral basis ought we to consider such cases, in the awareness that animals must in some way be brought into consideration? With humans, we require informed consent for risky procedures, and the risk must not be disproportionate to any potential benefit for the participant. Humans who cannot give informed consent are used only in experiments that pose only the most minimal of risks, unless a guardian, recognized as acting in the best interests of the subject, agrees that the potential benefit *for the patient* outweighs the potential risk. Obviously, animals, unlike most humans, cannot give informed consent. As it happens, we use animals in biomedical research with far fewer restraints than we use humans. Ought this to be the case? Those who uphold a deontological system of ethics, which we will recall is a system of ethics centered on rights and duties, and who also agree that animals are within the moral sphere, may well answer in the negative, holding that animals are morally to be considered as ends in themselves.

Tom Regan is one who draws such a conclusion, denying our right to use animals for research purposes that are likely to be injurious to them.[5] To put it another way, he maintains that animals have a right not to be subjected to such treatment and that we have a duty to respect their rights. If a being is well enough developed to have sentience and self-awareness – to be a subject of a life, as Regan puts it, then it must be treated as an end in itself. His view is very similar to that of Kant, except that Regan does not demand that a being be capable of rational moral agency for it to be worthy of our moral consideration. He recognizes all sentient beings that are subjects of a life, as well as rational humans, as being ends in themselves. Thus, for Regan, a sentient human neonate just as much as a rational adult is directly a member of what Kant called the *Kingdom of Ends*. Just as we humans, infant or adult, have a right not to be subjected to injurious research without our consent, whatever the potential benefits to medical science, so too do animals have that right. Human infants and animals cannot give informed consent to the waiver of their rights.

In contrast, those who maintain a consistent system of utilitarian ethics, and who further agree that the interests of animals are of moral concern, logically also must agree that animals can, under appropriate circumstances, be used in medical research – *if* this is what brings about the greatest balance of utility. This is so even if the research causes severe suffering to the animal. Peter Singer is the most well-known advocate of such a point of view. In this view, we must act so as to bring about the greatest probable balance of good results over bad results, even when doing so is hard on some of those whose interests are at stake. Singer became notorious not because he wanted to entirely ban experimentation on animals – he never did – but because he argued that equal interests ought to be weighed *equally* regardless of the species membership of the being who has the interests. If a project is not one we would be willing to perform on humans, then we ought not to perform it on animals when the same or higher levels of interests are at stake. Conversely, if we are justifiably willing to perform it on animals, then we ought to be willing to perform it on a human when no greater interests are at stake. Perhaps it might be preferable to perform it on an unwanted and grossly mentally defective child. Indeed, if it were an anencephalic child, who could therefore feel nothing at all, a chimpanzee or a mouse or any being that could feel pain would have a higher moral status. Such a conclusion might well be distasteful to us. Distasteful also, and for stronger reason, would be the alternative, that we perform it on an intelligent and sensitive primate. Injury to *any* sentient being ought to be distasteful to us. Mere species membership is irrelevant to the moral issues.

[5] Tom Regan, *The Case for Animal Rights* (see footnote 2, this chapter).

The issues concerning the way in which animals have moral significance, and to what degree, and concerning the practical applications, can become quite complex. I can offer no definitive formula for determining to just what extent animals can be used in biomedical research to further human interests. I cannot offer even a definitive formula for determining to just what extent *humans* can be used in biomedical research to further human interests. The reader will have long since noticed that I am apprehensive of supposedly definitive formulae and prefer not to attempt to offer them. The point I want to stress here is the importance of the realization that sentient beings truly and appropriately are part of the moral universe. This is not to diminish the moral significance of us humans. Rather, it enhances it. We do not have our moral significance just because of cheap self-interest and self-presumption. Nor need we rely on some bogus story about IQ or evolution. The reason why, humans or animals, we count morally is simple, straightforward, and valid: We are morally significant and are entitled to moral consideration from moral agents because it matters what happens to us. We can be harmed or benefited. It is that simple. If we are validly to affirm human life, we must, in due proportion, affirm animal life as well. This obviously carries us beyond *human* bioethics and, therefore, the stated scope of this book, but the fact remains that the web of moral issue in bioethics has to do with animals as well as humans. Somehow we must all be taken into consideration. A biocentric system of ethics, grounding ethics in life, demands that we do so.

Health and the Living World

Not only do the implications of a biocentric system of ethics extend well beyond any concern for our own material and social needs, they extend beyond a concern for sentient animals, important as such concern is. The appropriate range of our caring extends beyond the human community, and beyond even the bounds of sentience, to the living community, our environment. Let us take a closer look at the term *environment*. The fundamental concept implicit here concerns that which surrounds us, which environs us. The term has the advantage of keeping us in contact with the idea that what is going on out there is going on in our world. What happens with Amazonian rainforests or polar icecaps is not just something happening an irrelevant distance away. At whatever distance, it is happening in our world, in *our* environment.

Though it has the virtue of locating us, to a point, within the surrounding world on which we are dependent, this conception of *environment* has some serious drawbacks. A disadvantage with the term is that it suggests a profoundly misleading picture, as if it were a matter of us in here and other things, living and nonliving, out there.

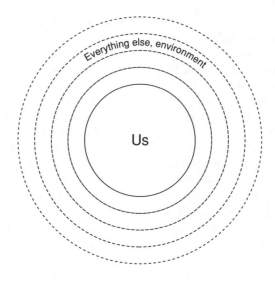

Figure 2.

It misleadingly suggests that there is a sharp distinction between us and the rest of the world. A distinction can be drawn, certainly, but not a sharp one, and certainly not an impermeable one. It is somewhat like the distinction between the planet Jupiter, which has no particular surface, and the rest of the universe. To be sure, there is a distinction, though it is a permeable one, with what Jupiter is and does interpenetrating with its surroundings. For our part, we living systems interpenetrate even more essentially and extensively with our surroundings. A rough distinction may be made that is useful to a very functional degree, but we must never presume that there is some insuperable gap between us and our surroundings.

Figure 2 is also misleading because it implicitly suggests that the whole world revolves around us. This is not true either morally or materially. At one time, it was assumed that both of those things were true. In this connection, it is worth nothing that the diagram could just as well be used to depict the medieval conception of the geocentric Heavens, with the sun and everything else revolving around the earth with its human inhabitants. Galileo got in big trouble with the authorities because he held that the earth revolved around the sun. This was not so much because his belief was in apparent conflict with certain passages in Scripture concerning the sun – those could have been interpreted away – but because the sun-centered theory evidently conflicted with the belief that *we* were the center and purpose of God's creation. Material fact eventually prevailed, but the moral conception lingered. We still tend to think of ourselves as being the center of the moral universe, with other beings having moral significance only insofar as they approximate the human or revolve around it. The aforementioned diagram, as well as suggesting a view of ourselves as being in *here*, with everything else being out *there*, also suggests a value ordering, with everything else standing in wait to attend our needs. As we had to rethink our place in the scheme of things materially, so I believe we need to rethink our place morally. However dear we might be to God (or to whatever else the Ultimate might happen to be), it seems clear enough that we are not the center of creation, much less its sole point and purpose. To my mind, this is demonstrated both by the fact that animals *can* suffer and by the existence of billions of galaxies, each with its billions of stars (a fair proportion of which, we are learning, have planets and, therefore, possibly life), all but a minute fraction unseen by the unaided human eye. Although the heavens may declare the glory of God, they also declare that there is more on God's mind than just us.

What more might God have in mind? Or, to put it in less flamboyant terms, what else might merit our moral concern? Here on our own planet, we live in a world that is biologically deep. It is replete with life. Not only are there humans and other sentient beings, there also are countless other living entities from the lowliest organism to species, ecosystems, and the biosphere itself. Some of those things are obviously of practical value to us as many of them contribute vitally to our welfare. Moreover, as we have already noted, the life processes we are and the life processes of our environment overlap or coincide in innumerable instances. Going beyond self-interest, though, my conviction is that we live in a world that is *morally deep* as well. I hold that life on all levels and in all degrees ought to be affirmed. We ought to give moral respect to all interests of all living entities – that is to say, to all interests – in proportion to the interests. Life as a whole, and in all lesser instances, is to be accorded due respect. This is not to say that all life and all interests ought always to be inviolate. To follow such an absurd suggestion would be to deny life altogether, not to affirm it. The tiger would not be affirming life by starving to death, nor would I by refusing ever to wash my hands, thereby refraining from destroying multimillions of microbes. What is incumbent on us who are capable of moral agency is to respect (and, as appropriate, protect) the fabric of life in its integrity. To use a simile I have used elsewhere, I would observe that a pebble or a grain of sand has very little weight, very little indeed compared to the lofty mountain. However, were the grain of sand to have absolutely *no* weight at all, then neither would the greatest of mountains have any weight. Such a thing could happen only if, per impossible, gravity were no more. For the mountain to have its weight, the grain of sand and all things else must have whatever weight they have. A laboratory mouse or a field mouse does not have the moral weight of a person, but for us truly to have the weight that we do, mice must have the weight that they do. A living tree may have no feeling but it still has some level of interests and therefore some moral significance. It might be cut down for some good purpose, but all else being exactly equal, it is better left unfelled. The species of which it is a member and the ecosystem in which it stands are all the more of moral importance, and the biosphere has the greatest importance of all. The extinction of a species diminishes us all. It diminishes life as a whole and, in some degree, it diminishes us individually. Unlike physical weight, moral weight cannot be determined with numerical precision, but we blind ourselves to the world around us, and to our own worth, and to the nature of the choices that confront us, if we fail to recognize that it is there. This is as true in the hospital as it is in the rainforest.[6]

Beyond Bioethics

Life and, in consequence, moral issues concerning life are of unending complexity, take innumerable forms, and go beyond any narrow or rigid boundaries. Neither life nor bioethics can be captured in detail by one central description nor adequately coped with by means of one fundamental formula. Life is an immense interweaving of living systems with their diverse interests. For us human beings, there are any number of ways in which things can go right or wrong for us. For that matter, there is often a multiplicity of ways in which things that do go wrong for us can return to (or toward) rightness. As we have noted along the way, there can be no one central description of what health is, how it can be maintained, what can go wrong with it, or how it can be restored. Yet, clearly, though it is a matter of degree, there are such things as good and bad health. This is not a bit less true for our frustration at the indeterminacy. Just how we are to go about affirming life, be it our own or that of others (not that these matters can entirely be separated), is likewise, and for similar reasons, a practical difficulty that (to have a good life) we must work our way through as best we can, even in the irreparable absence of a definitive protocol for how we are to proceed. It is a matter that goes beyond developing the right sort of principles, which can never be good enough, to developing the right sort of attitudes. That this is so is not due to the in-principle inscrutability of ethics but to the in-fact deep complexity of life. Bioethics and medical science are alike a voyage of discovery.

---

[6] That things can matter to never-sentient living beings, including plants and ecosystems, and therefore be of moral significance is something for which I have already argued at considerable length in my *A Morally Deep World* (see footnote 2, this chapter) and elsewhere. As our focus here is on human bioethics rather than on environmental philosophy, I see no reason to repeat here what I have said in detail there. A component of my argument concerning nonhumans flows from the fact that we humans have interests in matters that *never* impinge on our consciousness yet still matter morally. I there adapt an interesting thought experiment from Robert Nozick, *Anarchy, State, and Utopia* (Oxford: Blackwell, 2001; originally published 1974). See the section "Mental States" in the chapter "A Matter of Interest" in my *Morally Deep World*. In that same work, see the section "Do Species Have Interests?" in the chapter "Holism."

There is another reason similarly rooted in life why bioethics cannot be precisely bounded and codified. Our health is a matter of our *whole* life and not just the part of it that comes in contact with medical science. More than medical care is needed. Our medical needs are only part of our health needs and, for that matter, our physical health (even if we take physical health to encompass our psychiatric health) is only part of our overall health. Adequate *health* care obviously includes adequate medical care but goes well beyond it. Maintenance of safe and healthy living conditions is required, and likewise required are proactive measures to maintain good health and prevent bad health. Ultimately, our health needs broadly construed and our overall well-being needs are identical. Even the portion of our well-being needs that come in contact with medical science is highly influenced by our surroundings. After all (and before all), we are fundamentally thermodynamically open systems. A truly healthy life can take place only within an adequately sustaining environment. Moreover, as living systems, we have to be open to and in effective interaction with our surroundings. Although particular medical problems might be treated, needed also are surroundings that permit and support a healthy life. Preventive medicine in many cases can be even more important than therapeutic medicine, but our need for supportive surroundings goes well beyond that. Adequate nutrition is an obvious requirement, and also of critical importance is an environment adequately free of noxious pollutants and unsanitary conditions. Wits have remarked – very truly – that in terms of lives saved from death caused by communicable disease, plumbers have saved far more lives than have doctors. One may say as much for refrigeration.

Yet we live not by bread alone, whatever more than nutritious and hygienic bread may be required. A life with all of one's material needs met may still not be a good one – else why do many multimillionaires commit suicide? (One might think it a shortcoming on their part that none of the contented people living pleasant but empty lives in *Brave New World* felt moved to do so.) Being a person, let alone being a well-developed person, requires more than just being a biologically healthy human. Nonetheless, to be a well-developed person, one must be so in a human way. Each of us needs a life of developing and living our capacities as a human person. Not only must we get along well with ourselves, we must live in reciprocity with other people in a way that permits us to feel self-esteem and to feel that our life has meaning and value.

For good health in the fullest sense, we require surroundings conducive to a healthy life. We require community. If we are to be life-affirming people living in a life-affirming community, we certainly need more than a morally decent level of health care conducted with moral decency. What is mostly needed is a sociopolitical structure supportive of a good life. To be sure, I do not presuppose a social determinism of some sort. People have managed to live good lives in poor surroundings, even managing to find strength from adversity that would overwhelm nearly anyone else. Others have lived very poor lives in the midst of great advantages. For that matter, some people have lived long and well without medical care and many have died having it. Yet, going with the odds, good medical services and good sociopolitical surroundings contribute to a healthy well-lived life. For one thing among many, societies we live in can be conducive to poor mental health as well as to poor physical health, incubating fears, anxieties, repression, and neuroses. Other ways of structuring society can be improvements. Bigotry and discrimination based on race, sect, gender, language, or any of the many other ways we have of pitting *us* against *them* can be very repressive and hurtful, even when our particular *us* gets to dominate. An attitude of life affirmation on our part requires that individuals be treated with dignity and respect. Even the most utterly vile of people require to be treated with some minimal level of respect – if only because failing to do so would be to detract from ourselves. And even the best of us cannot flourish in the withering absence of a decent regard from others.

People cannot be compelled to live a good life, even if we know what is good for them, and it likely would be an infringement on their autonomy to try to compel them. What a good – that is, life-affirming – sociopolitical system should do is give people access to a fair opportunity to live a good life. Inherent in that must be the opportunity to develop one's highest and fullest potential. *How* we are to structure our sociopolitical system is more than I know in anything like detail, nor is it anything that possibly could be explained in one book, nor is it something I am called on to explain in a book on bioethics. Here I can only sketch some of the major points.

Of critical importance is education, and this must be more than just a process of milling people into particularly shaped pegs to fit particularly shaped holes prepared by extraneous forces. Proper education would help people with their personal development and help them find a useful and fulfilling place in the world. This would include meaningful, fulfilling, and adequately safe employment permitting a decent standard of living. For a decent standard of living, we need good food, adequate housing and clothing, adequate health and medical care, and we need to learn the life skills to cope. But certainly, we do *not* need all the things that clever advertising can persuade us to desire. The Buddha was quite right in warning us that great suffering results from ignorant desires. It is all too easy to want too much or to want the wrong things. In a healthy society, this would be widely understood, and the attainment of those things we actually do need would be facilitated.

To continue what only can be a sketch of our surrounding needs as healthy living beings, we should note that as well as a sociopolitical environment that is healthy for us, sustaining and not undermining our health, we also need an extrahuman environment, living and nonliving, that does likewise. This is for more than one reason. Certainly, a well-functioning society can do much to create or maintain a materially healthy environment for us. Evident headings are public hygiene, disease eradication (such as the successful campaign against smallpox), and the maximal alleviation of health-threatening pollution. How life affirming is a society that permits serious pollution – let alone climate change – because "it is good for the economy"? Again, we have a well-being need, beyond any economic need, for a healthy and morally decent relationship with a healthily living extrahuman world. We need a healthy personal relationship with that world.

The great naturalist and preservationist John Muir (founder of the Sierra Club) once made this remark:

When we try to pick out anything by itself, we find it hitched to everything else in the Universe.[7]

Our knowledge that this is true deepens all the time. It is strongly and strikingly true in the living world. Our relationship with the living world, and therefore our moral relationship with it, is complex and deep, from our conscious surface to the deepest aspects of our being, from the level of the species or the biosphere as a whole down through degrees to the most vanishingly trivial instance of protolife. We cannot pick out bioethics without finding its concerns in some way hitched to all the other issues facing our lives in this wide world.

As individuals, our life is best and healthiest for us when we live as well-integrated organic wholes. To live healthily, we must strive to attain – to the best degree we can attain – a life that is coherent and richly diverse, living in harmonious balance with our own selves and with the world around us. Our concern always must be to affirm life, our own and that around us, affirming it in terms of that which is most true to it. Toward such ends, bioethics is only a part of our interconnected concerns. Yet, it is a central and vital part of our concerns.

---

7 John Muir, *My First Summer in the Sierra* (New York: Penguin Books, 1997; originally published 1911).

Bibliography

Ainsworth, Claire. "The Stranger Within," *New Scientist* 180 (2421) (2003): 34.

Aristotle, *The Basic Works of Aristotle*, ed. Richard McKeon (New York: Random House, 1921).

    Nichomachean Ethics, ed. J. A. K. Thompson (New York and London: Penguin Classics, 1976).

Asai, Atushi, et al. "Euthanasia and the Family: An Analysis of Japanese Doctors' Reactions to Demands for Voluntary Euthanasia," *Monash Bioethics Review* 20 (2001): 21–37.

Atsushi Asai, Motoki Onishi, Shizuko K. Nagata, N. Tanida, and Y. Yamazaki. "Doctors' and Nurses' Attitudes Towards and Experiences of Voluntary Euthanasia: Survey of Members of the Japanese Association of Palliative Medicine," *Journal of Medical Ethics* 27 (2001): 324–330.

Augustine, *City of God*, many editions.

Barker, Pat. *Regeneration* (London: Penguin, 1991).

    The Eye in the Door (London: Penguin, 1993).

    The Ghost Road (London: Penguin, 1995).

Beauchamp, Thomas L. and James F. Childress. *Principles of Biomedical Ethics* (New York: Oxford University Press, 1979, with many subsequent editions).

Bentham, Jeremy. *Introduction to the Principles of Morals and Legislation*, 1823, many editions.

Blass, Thomas. *The Man Who Shocked the World: The Life and Legacy of Stanley Milgram* (New York: Basic Books, 2004).

Brandt, Richard. *A Theory of the Good and the Right*, revised edition (Amherst, NY: Prometheus Books, 1998).

Broderick, Robert C., ed. *Catholic Encyclopedia* (Nashville, TN: Thomas Nelson, 1990; available online at http://www.newadvent.org/cathen/14153a.htm).

Burke, Edmund. *Reflections on the Revolution in France* (New York: Oxford, 2009; first published 1790).

Cartwright, Silvia. *The Report of the Committee of Inquiry into Allegations Concerning the Treatment of Cervical Cancer at National Women's Hospital and into Other Related Matters* (Auckland: Government Printing Office, August 5, 1988).

Coney, Sandra. *The Unfortunate Experiment: The Full Story behind the Inquiry into Cervical Treatment* (Auckland: Penguin Books New Zealand and Camberwell, Victoria: Penguin Books Australia, 1988).

Confucius (K'ung Fu Tse). *The Analects of Confucius*, trans., Arthur Waley (London: George Allen & Unwin, Ltd., 1938).

Coser, Lewis A. *Masters of Sociological Thought: Ideas in Historical and Social Context* (New York: Harcourt Brace Jovanovich, 1977), pp. 99–101.

Cusack, Odean and Elaine Smith, *Pets and the Elderly: The Therapeutic Bond* (Kirkwood, NY: Haworth, 1984).

Dawkins, Richard. *The Selfish Gene* (Oxford: Oxford University Press, 1989; originally published 1976).

Dennett, Daniel C. *Darwin's Dangerous Idea: Evolution and the Meanings of Life* (New York: Simon and Schuster, 1995).

Descartes, René. *Meditations on First Philosophy* and *Rules for the Direction of the Mind*, in *Philosophical Works of Descartes*, trans. Elizabeth Haldane and G. R. T. Ross (Cambridge: Cambridge University Press, 1911). My citations are to the Dover edition (New York: Dover, 1955).

Dickens, Charles. *Hard Times*, many editions.

Epicurus, *Letter to Menoeceus*, trans. Robert Drew Hicks, available at ebooks@Adelaide, 2007.

Frazer, Sir James George. *The Golden Bough: A Study in Magic and Religion* (New Delhi: Cosmo Publications, 2005; originally published 1900).

Frey, R. G. *Interests and Rights: The Case Against Animals* (Oxford: Clarendon Press, 1980).

Frost, Robert. "Mending Wall," *North of Boston* (London: David Nutt, 1914).

Frost, Robert. *A Further Range* (New York: Henry Holt, 1936).

Fung, Yu-Lan. *A Short History of Chinese Philosophy* (New York: Macmillan, 1948).

Ghiselin, M. T. "A Radical Solution to the Species Problem," *Systematic Zoology* 23 (1974): 536–544.

  The Economy of Nature and the Evolution of Sex (Berkeley, University of California Press, 1974).

Gibbon, Edward. *The History of the Decline and Fall of the Roman Empire*, 1776, and many subsequent editions.

Gould, Stephen Jay. "The Origin and Function of 'Bizarre' Structures," *Evolution* 4 (1974): 191–220.

Graham, Bernie. *Creature Comfort: Animals That Heal* (New York: Prometheus Books, 2000).

Gray, Fred D. *The Tuskegee Syphilis Study: The Real Story and Beyond* (Montgomery, AL: New South Books, 2002).

Hacking, Ian. *The Taming of Chance* (New York: Cambridge University Press, 1990).

  The Emergence of Probability: A Philosophical Study of Early Ideas about Probability (Cambridge: Cambridge University Press, 1990).

Hare, R. M. *Essays on Bioethics* (New York: Oxford University Press, 1996).

Hippocrates, *Hippocratic writings*, edited with an introduction by G. E. R. Lloyd; translated by J. Chadwick and W. N. Mann, et al., Harmondsworth and New York: Penguin, 1978.

Ho, Mae-Wan. *The Rainbow and the Worm: The Physics of Organisms*, 2nd. ed. (Singapore: World Scientific Publishing Company, 1998).

Hofstadter, Richard. *Social Darwinism in American Thought (1860–1915)* (Philadelphia: University of Pennsylvania Press, 1944; reprinted 1992 [Boston: Beacon Press].

Hölldobler, Bert and E. O. Wilson, *The Ants* (Cambridge, MA: Harvard University Press, 1990).

Hull, David. "Are Species Really Individuals?," *Systematic Zoology* 25 (1976): 174–191.

"A Matter of Individuality," *Philosophy of Science* 45 (1978): 335–360.

"Kitts & Kitts & Caplan on Species," *Philosophy of Science* 48 (1981): 141–152.

Hume, David, *A Treatise of Human Nature*, 1751, many editions.

Huxley, Aldous. *Brave New World* (New York: HarperCollins, 1998; originally published 1932 by Harper & Brothers).

Ishiguro, Kazuo. *Never Let Me Go* (New York: Knopf, 2005).

Johnson, Lawrence E. "Profiles in Princeliness: Hal and Arjuna," *Soundings* 58 (1980): 94–111.

"Humanity, Holism, and Environmental Ethics," *Environmental Ethics* 5 (1983): 335–343.

"On the Self: The Chandogya," *Darshana International* 99 (1987): 69–83.

A Morally Deep World: An Essay on Moral Significance and Environmental Ethics (New York: Cambridge University Press, 1991).

"From the Chariot: The *Phaedrus* and the *Katha*," *Darshana International* 126 (1992): 42–57.

Focusing on Truth (New York and London: Routledge, 1992).

"Species: On Their Nature and Moral Standing," *Journal of Natural History* 29 (1995): 843–849.

"A Biocentric Approach to Issues of Life and Death," *Monash Bioethics Review* 21 (2000): 30–45.

"Euthanasia, Double Effect, and Proportionality," *Monash Bioethics Review* 22 (2001): 30–45.

"Future Generations and Contemporary Ethic," *Environmental Values*, 12 (2003): 471–487.

Jones, James H. *Bad Blood: The Tuskegee Syphilis Experiment* (New York: The Free Press, 1981 and 1993).

Kant Immanuel. *Groundwork of the Metaphysics of Morals* (Cambridge: Cambridge University Press, 1997). The AK number refers to the pagination of the standard German edition. First published 1785.

Kauffman, Stuart. *At Home in the Universe: The Search for the Laws of Self-Organization and Complexity* (Oxford: Oxford University Press, 1995).

Kuhn, Thomas. *The Structure of Scientific Revolutions* (Chicago: University of Chicago Press, 3rd. ed., 1996; first published 1962).

Kuhse, Helga and Peter Singer. *Should the Baby Live? The Problem of Handicapped Infants* (New York: Oxford University Press, 1985).

Lawrence, T. E. *Seven Pillars of Wisdom: A Triumph* (Hertfordshire: Wordsworth, 1997; originally published 1926).

Leavitt, Judith Walzer. *Typhoid Mary: Captive to the Public's Health* (Boston: Beacon Press, 1996).

Lecky, W. E. H. *History of European Morals: From Augustus to Charlemagne*, vol. 2 (New York: Braziller, 1953).

Lecky W. E. H. *History of European Morals: From Augustus to Charlemagne*, 2 vols. (Whitefish, MT: Kessinger, 2003; originally published 1869), 2:172n. Lecky in turn cites (Bayle, *Dict. Philos.*, art. Bellarmine).

Lillard, Lee A. and Constantijn W. A. Panis. "Marital Status and Mortality: The Role of Health," *Demography* 33 (3) (1996): 313–327.

Lucretius. *De Rerum Natura*, many editions.

Marcus Aurelius. *Meditations*, many editions.

Margulis, Lynn and Dorion Sagan. *What Is Life?* (New York: Simon and Schuster, 1995).

Maturana, Humberto R. and Francisco J. Varela. *Autopoiesis and Cognition: The Realization of the Living* (Boston: Boston Studies in the Philosophy of Science, D. Reidel, Vol. 42, 1980).

Midgley, Mary. *Animals and Why They Matter: A Journey around the Species Barrier* (Harmondsworth: Penguin Books, 1983).

Midgley, Mary. *Heart and Mind: The Varieties of Moral Experience* (London: Harvester Press, 1981).

Milgram, Stanley. "Behavioral Study of Obedience," *Journal of Abnormal and Social Psychology* (1963) 67: 371–378.

Mill, John Stuart. *Autobiography*, many editions; first published 1873.
Utilitarianism, many editions; first published 1863.

Millay, Edna St. Vincent. "Eight Sonnets," in *American Poetry: A Miscellany*, ed. Louis Untermeyer (New York: Harcourt Brace, 1922).

Molière (Poquelin, Jean-Baptiste). *The Imaginary Invalid (Le Malade Imaginaire)*, 1763, many editions.

Muir, John. *My First Summer in the Sierra* (New York: Penguin Books, 1997; originally published 1911 by Cambridge: Riverside Press).

Murphy, Michael P. and Luke A. J. O'Neill., eds. *What Is Life? The Next Fifty Years: Speculations of the Future of Biology* (New York: Cambridge University Press, 1997).

New York Times Magazine, December 15, 2002, Section 6, p. 116.

Noddings, Nel. *Caring: A Feminine Approach to Ethics and Moral Education* (Berkeley: University of California Press, 1984).

Nozick, Robert. *Anarchy, State, and Utopia* (Oxford: Blackwell, 2001; originally published by New York: Basic Books, 1974).

Olds, James. "Pleasure Centers in the Brain," *Scientific American* (1956).

Orians, Gordon H., "Diversity, Maturity, and Stability in Natural Ecosystems," in *Unifying Concepts in Ecology*, ed. W. H. van Dobben and R. H. Lowe McConnell (The Hague: Dr. W. Junk B. V. Publishers, 1975).

Parfit, Derek. "Rights, Interests, and Possible People" in *Moral Problems in Medicine*, ed. Samuel Gorovitz, et al. (Englewood Cliffs, New Jersey: Prentice-Hall, 1976: 369).
"Future Generations: Future Problems." *Philosophy and Public Affairs* 11 (1982) 113–172.
"Personal Identity and Rationality," *Synthese* 53 (1982): 227–241.
Reasons and Persons (Oxford: Oxford University Press, 1984).
"Lewis, Perry, and What Matters," in *The Identities of Persons*, ed. Amelie Oksenbergs Rorty (Berkeley: University of California Press, 1976).

Plato, *Euthyphro*, many editions.
Phaedo, trans. R. Hackforth (London: Cambridge University Press, 1952).

Phaedrus, trans. R. Hackforth (London: Cambridge University Press, 1952).

The Republic, many editions.

Prigogine, Ilya and Isobelle Stengers. *Order Out of Chaos: Man's New Dialogue with Nature* (Bantam Books, 1984).

Rachels, James. "Do Animals Have a Right to Liberty?," in Regan and Singer, 1971.

Rawls, John. *A Theory of Justice* (Cambridge, MA: Harvard University Press, 1971).

Regan, Tom. *The Case for Animal Rights* (Berkeley: University of California Press, 1983, 1999, first published).

Regan, Tom and Peter Singer. *Animal Rights and Human Obligations* (Englewood Cliffs, NJ: Prentice-Hall, 1976): 205–223.

Reich, Warren T., Editor in Chief. *Encyclopedia of Bioethics* (New York: Simon and Schuster Macmillan, 1995).

Rolston, Holmes, III. *Conserving Natural Value* (New York: Columbia University Press, 1994).

Ross, David. *Aristotle* (London: University Paperbacks, Methuen, 1964; first published 1923).

Rousseau, *The Social Contract*, many editions.

Sacks, Oliver. *The Man Who Mistook His Wife for a Hat* (New York: Simon & Schuster, 1970).

Sadler, T. W. *Langman's Medical Embryology*, ninth edition (Philadelphia: Lippencott Williams and Wilkins, 2004).

Sagan, Dorion and Lynn Margulis. "The Gaian Perspective of Ecology," *The Ecologist* 13 (1983): 160–167.

Sartre, Jean-Paul. *L'existentialisme est une humanisme*, translated as *Existentialism Is a Humanism*, Carol Macomber (New Haven CT: Yale University Press, 2007) from 1996. French edition.

L'Etre et le neant (Paris, 1943). English translation by Hazel E. Barnes as *Being and Nothingness: A Phenomenological Essay on Ontology* (New York: Washington Square Press, 1992).

Sayre, Kenneth. *Cybernetics and the Philosophy of Mind* (London: Routeledge & Kegan Paul, 1976).

Schrödinger, Erwin. *What Is Life? The Physical Aspect of the Living Cell* (New York: Cambridge University Press, 1944).

Schweitzer, Albert. *Civilization and Ethics, Part II of The Philosophy of Civilization*. Translated by John Naish (London: Adam and Charles Black, 1923).

Singer, Peter. *Animal Liberation: A New Ethics for our Treatment of Animals*, New York: New York Review/Random House, 1975. Many subsequent editions.

Practical Ethics (New York: Cambridge University Press, 1979, and subsequent editions).

Spencer, Herbert. "A Theory of Population, Deduced from the General Law of Animal Fertility," *Westminster Review* 57 (1852): 468–501.

Stone, Jim. "Advance Directives, Autonomy and Unintended Death," *Monash Bioethics Review* 15 (1996): 16–33.

Thomson, Judith Jarvis. "A Defense of Abortion," *Philosophy & Public Affairs* 1 (1971): 47–66.

Thomas, Stephen B. and Quinn, Sandra Crouse. "The Tuskegee Syphilis Study, 1932–1972: Implications for HIV Education and AIDS Risk Education Programs in the Black Community," *American Journal of Public Health* (1991) 81: 1393–1394.

Warnock, Mary, et al. *Report of the Committee of Enquiry into Human Fertilisation and Embryology*, presented to the U.K. Parliament, 1984.

Wechkin, Stanley, Jules H. Masserman, and William Terris, Jr. "Shock to Conspecific as an Aversive *Stimulus*," *Psychnomic Science* 1 (1964): 47–48.

Weindling, Paul. "The Origins of Informed Consent: The International Scientific Commission on Medical War Crimes, and the Nuremberg Code," *Bulletin of the History of Medicine* (2001) 75: 37–71.

Wilson, E. O. *Biophilia: The Human Bond with Other Species* (Cambridge, MA: Harvard University Press, 1984).

Wollstonecraft, Mary. *A Vindication of the Rights of Women*, many editions; first published London: Joseph Johnson, 1792.

Supreme Court of New Jersey, USA: Matter of Quinlan 70 N.J. 10, 355A.2d. 647 (N.J. 1976).

McFall v. Shimp, 10 Pa. D. & C.3d 90, Court of Common Pleas of Pennsylvania [USA], Allegheny County, July 26, 1978.

CODES (Widely found on the Internet.)

World Health Organization, *Declaration of Alma-Ata*, 1978.

World Medical Association, *Declaration of Helsinki*, 1964 plus eight revisions, latest 2000.

Nuremberg Code, 1947. See Weindling, Paul. (2001).

Anonymous and Traditional

Katha Upanishad, many editions.

Bhagavad-Gita, trans. Franklin Edgerton (Cambridge, MA: Harvard University Press, 1972).

Biblical quotations are taken from the King James Bible.

Laozi (also *Lao Tzu, Daodejing* or *Tao Te Ching*).

Zhuangzi (also Chuang Tzu).

Vedas.

Index

abortion, i, v, 1, 8, 9, 38, 49, 65, 83, 94, 96, 97, 98, 105, 106, 107, 108, 109, 110, 114, 115, 116, 195, 206, 223, 238, 239, 240, 241, 242, 243, 244, 246, 247, 248, 249, 254, 255, 256, 257, 259, 260, 261, 262, 264, 281, 282, 283, 285, 309, 312, 316, 338

abortion pill. See RU-486

active and passive, distinction, 180, 196, 198, 199, 200, 211, 212

act-utilitarianism, 53, 54

advance directive/s, 186, 209, 221

advice, good and bad, 177

Ahimsa, 341

Ames Test, 357

amour de soi, 167

amour-propre, 167

animal/s, 7, 8, 16, 18, 20, 22, 23, 24, 26, 31, 32, 47, 48, 59, 87, 122, 135, 151, 154, 172, 173, 175, 193, 195, 196, 201, 207, 233, 240, 244, 249, 251, 265, 275, 280, 294, 295, 309, 342, 351, 352, 353, 354, 355, 356, 357, 358, 359, 361

Antarctica, 134, 152

apotemnophilia (amputation fetish), 79

Arendt, Hannah, 321

Argos pheasant, 267

Aristotelean virtues listed, 171

Aristotle, 4, 22, 23, 24, 25, 26, 27, 34, 36, 64, 122, 139, 144, 148, 167, 168, 169, 170, 171, 172, 173, 175, 178, 245, 265

Asia/n thought, 19, 228, 335, 336, 339, 341, 344

Atman, 152

atomism, 33

Auckland, New Zealand, National Women's Hospital, 322, 323, 325, 328

Augustine, 19

autocatalysis, autocatalytic, 125, 126

autocatalytic, autocatalysis, 125

autopoiesis, 133

a.v.e. active voluntary euthanasia. See euthanasia, active; euthanasia, voluntary

Barker, Pat, 164, 210

beauty as good, 81

Beethoven, Ludwig van, 69

Bellarmine, Cardinal Roberto, 355

Belmont Report, 323

Bentham, Jeremy, 40, 41, 153

Bhagavad-Gita. See Mahabharata

biocentric approach, characterized, 8

biocentric conceptions, 2, 7, 9, 10, 35, 36, 38, 148, 167, 192, 195, 221, 238, 260, 334

bioethics, 1

biophilia, 152, 176

Brahman, 152

brain-death. See death

Brave New World, 68, 69, 161, 291, 292, 313, 363

Buddha, Gautama, 20, 153, 341, 342, 364

Buddhism, Buddhists, 19, 20, 341, 342, 344

Burke, Edmund, 117

caring, 61, 62, 63, 182, 202, 259, 284, 359

categorical imperatives, 45

cellular cloning, 307, 308, 311

chimera/s, 249, 317